Contributions to Economics

Abdullahi Dahir Ahmed • Sardar M.N. Islam

Financial Liberalization in Developing Countries

Issues, Time Series Analyses and Policy Implications

Physica-Verlag
A Springer Company

Dr. Abdullahi Dahir Ahmed
Professor Sardar M.N. Islam
Centre for Strategic Economic Studies CSES
Victoria University
Level 13, 300 Flinders Street
Melbourne 3000
Australia
abdullahi.ahmed@vu.edu.au
sardar.islam@vu.edu.au

ISSN 1431-1933
ISBN 978-3-7908-2807-8 e-ISBN 978-3-7908-2168-0
DOI: 10.1007/978-3-7908-2168-0
Springer Heidelberg Dordrecht London New York

Cover design: WMXDesign GmbH, Heidelberg

Printed on acid-free paper

Physica-Verlag is a brand of Springer-Verlag Berlin Heidelberg
Springer-Verlag is part of Springer Science+Business Media (www.springer.com)

Acknowledgements

The authors would like to thank the following journal and its publisher for giving permission in this book for publishing previously published materials from the following article: Ahmed, A. (2006), 'The impact of financial liberalization policies: The case of Botswana', Journal of African Development (formerly Journal of African Finance and Economic Development), Spring, Volume 8, No.1, pp.13–38, Publisher; African Finance and Economics Association and New York University.

Chapter 7 of this book is based on materials from Islam, S.M.N. and Clarke, M. (2004), *Economic Growth and Social Welfare*, North Holland Publishing, Amsterdam and Chapter 8 of Hansanti, S., Islam, S.M.N. and Sheehan, P. (2008), *International Finance in an Emerging Market: Issues, Welfare Analyses and Policy Implications*, Springer, Heidelberg. The authors thank these publishers (North Holland Publishing and Springer) to give permission to prepare this chapter on the basis of the materials published by them. It is a revised version of an earlier *paper presented at the Australian Association for Professional and Applied Ethics Annual Conference*, Victoria University, Melbourne, 2–4 October, 2003.

Foreword

The recent global financial crisis has made financial liberalization a topic of great academic and practical interest. This book makes new contributions to the topic by combining fact-finding, empirical analysis, and theory to examine the relationship between financial liberalization and economic growth.

Among its contributions, the book provides detailed country assessments on the effects of financial liberalization, including its striking impact on the banking sector. Although an important goal of financial deregulation has been to help financial institutions better perform their role in intermediating resources, the book models how deregulation may fail to achieve that goal in countries with underdeveloped financial markets and institutions. For that purpose, the book draws on actual experience in Kenya, Malawi, Botswana, and Thailand.

This book should constitute important reading for students of financial economics, researchers and general academics, financial practitioners, policymakers, and teachers of economics.

North Carolina, USA
December 2008

Steven L. Schwarcz
Stanley A. Star Professor of Law & Business,
Duke University Founding Director,
Duke Global Capital Markets Center
Durham

Abstract and Preface

The latest global financial and economic crisis of 2008 shows the need to re-examine the desirability of financial liberalization and the basis for the view that financial deregulation by itself cannot be considered as a substitute for better economic management.

The literature on financial liberalization has identified various mechanisms through which removing controls on interest rates may impact economic growth. In particular, the mainstream literature suggests that financial liberalization improves the efficiency of resource allocation and boosts savings, which ultimately stimulates economic growth. However, the actual experience of the effect of financial liberalization has been uncertain. In Africa, in particular, and partly in Asia, financial sector reforms appear to have created controversy. The objective of this book is to examine the effects of financial liberalization, using a case study approach on a sample of three Sub-Saharan African countries (Kenya, Malawi and Botswana) and an Asian country – Thailand – in which reforms were implemented. As noted earlier by a number of researchers, limitations in the number of observations and lack of credibility in the available data have made direct econometric analysis either undesirable or ruled out as an alternative at this stage. In contrast, the case study approach enables a comprehensive and thorough examination of the available facts to arrive at a more realistic conclusion about the level and the direction of progress. Furthermore, some supportive empirical investigation is also undertaken to assess the McKinnon-Shaw proposition that financial liberalization boosts growth.

It is shown that market imperfections and market non-existence in the banking system can explain to a significant degree the observed behaviour of the financial variables after liberalization. The model implies that, given the oligopolistic structure of the commercial banking sector, the spread will go up neither than down as expected, if there is no further entry of new firms, or even with entry, if a threshold level was not achieved. It is observed that under general conditions in developing countries some financial repression can be beneficial to the economy, as argued by Stiglitz. Indeed, the actual experience of the four countries is quite consistent with the model predictions. In Kenya and Malawi, where the concentration ratio is high, the intermediation spread is much wider. In these two countries, where the corruption problem is endemic, institutional deficiencies are serious, and sound regulatory systems are lacking, running costs borne by banking institutions are significantly higher and effectively increase their fixed costs. The resulting uncompetitive market structure (together with some other factors) reduces the overall benefits of financial liberalization. Thus, future policies should aim to reduce legal and institutional deficiencies to encourage 'potential entry' and enhance operational efficiency in the banking industry to create a successful environment for financial liberalization.

Moreover, having observed that Botswana was able to develop a competitive financial market after reforms, while there has been limited financial integration in Kenya and Malawi, initial analysis indicates a positive change in private agents' savings behaviour in response to liberalization reforms in Botswana. Therefore, we conducted a further empirical investigation using a cointegration approach. Our preliminary results show that private savings rate is positively related to real deposit rate. Other investigations also indicate a positive and significant link between the financial liberation index, private savings, and per capita output in Botswana. The cost benefit analysis exercise for Thailand shows that costs of financial liberalization may be higher than their benefits in a developing country, given the country's socio-economic conditions and institutional set up and development.

In addition to contributing a different dimension to the debate on financial liberalization while providing some new evidence, this book has made an important contribution, due to its overall approach, in the following areas:

- Case studies of African countries which have not been included in the existing literature. This is for the purpose of identifying what has actually been done as opposed to what should be done and diagnose the routes through which reform-led changes are expected to influence real economic activities. This integrated approach also helps understand the links between policies pursued and the realized outcome of the financial market reforms.
- Comparative analysis of Asian and African countries in regard to implementation, progress, government policies, and outcomes relating to financial liberalization is also provided.
- Very sophisticated econometric and time-series analyses of financial liberalization issues have been undertaken in this book. These rigorous econometric and time-series analyses of the impact of market reforms have not been done in the existing literature.

This book should be useful to students, academics, practitioners, and policy makers in the areas of finance, banking, economics and development management. It can be used as a reference and/or an additional textbook on empirical finance for graduate students at Masters and Doctoral levels.

Like any other major goal, the completion of this book would never have been possible without the support of a number of individuals. Firstly, our deepest appreciation goes to Professor Catherine De Fontenay and Professor Sisira Jayasuriya for their intellectual and enthusiastic support. We are grateful to Professor Peter Dixon and Professor Peter Sheehan for their help, encouragement and incisive comments at various stages of our project. The authors are grateful to Dr. Hayat Khan for sharing many of the ideas and valuable feedback. Many thanks go to Margarita Kumnick and Dr. Andrew Van-Hulten for their constant editorial assistance in preparing and putting many pieces together. Finally, this book could never have been completed without the continuous support of our family members; my heartfelt thanks go to my wife Hafida and other family members: Hamida Yare, Abdi Omar Nalow and Zein Abass for their endless love, encouragement and understanding during these years.

Melbourne, Australia
March 2009

Abdullahi Dahir Ahmed
Sardar M.N. Islam

Reviews

Review 1
This book discusses a key issue in international and development finance which is financial liberalization. While taking various case studies of emerging economies and time series econometric estimation procedures, the book examines the effect of the decade-long market reforms and financial liberalization.

By
Associate Professor Rose N. Lai, Ph.D.
Executive Editor, International Real Estate Review,
& Associate Professor of Finance,
Department of Finance and Business Economics
University of Macau
Macau

Review 2
The book makes an original contribution to the international finance and financial economics literature by presenting a model that highlights how in an imperfectly competitive financial market structure, financial liberalization may fail to achieve some of its intended outcomes. Moreover, the net benefit of financial liberalization is assessed using a new cost-benefit analyses approach to evaluate the social welfare implication years of public policy changes. It is an essential reading.

By
Prof. Bruno S. Sergi
Professor of International Economics,
University of Messina
Italy

Contents

Chapter 1
Introduction

1.1 Contemporary Issues in Finance

The financial system, both domestic and international, is undergoing rapid, complex and fundamental transformation. A very important transformation, which is enormously controversial as well, is financial liberalization. The process has created uncertainties and confusion amongst policy makers and raised important issues that need to be better understood and resolved. Some of these issues are summarised below as an introduction to the debate about financial liberalization.

International financial integration, financial globalization, financial capital market regulation, financial crisis and international financial contagion, and the issues of financial liberalization/financial repression are some of the important contemporary topics in the field of international finance and development economics. Issues more specific to financial liberalization debate are financial repression, capital control, risk management, moral hazard, asymmetric information, financial instability and systemic risk and dysfunctionalities in the financial system (Hansanti, Islam and Sheehan, 2008; Stiglitz, 1994).

The present global financial and economic crisis in 2008 shows the need for re-examination of the desirability of financial liberalization as the deregulation and liberalization of financial systems have been posited as the main causes of the financial turbulence and collapses in 2008. This book provides some important new insights into the desirability of financial liberalization in developing group of countries (DGCs). In doing so, it contributes to research for providing further insights and finding solutions to one of the most pressing policy questions facing developing countries today, and current national and global economic management.

1.1.1 Financial Repression

Financial repression has been one of the contentious issues in contemporary finance – global and local. There are various ways and mechanisms that the government can

A.D. Ahmed and S.M.N. Islam, *Financial Liberalization in Developing Countries*, Contributions to Economics,
DOI: 10.1007/978-3-7908-2168-0_1, © Springer Physica-Verlag Berlin Heidelberg 2010

intervene in the normal workings of the financial market. Financial repression policies include, but are not limited to, subsidizing loans for specific sectors, heavily regulating the banking sector, and controlling interest rates. Berthelemy and Varoudekis (1996a) define all such policies and regulations which prevent financial intermediaries from operating in accordance with there full technological potential as forms of financial repressions. Financial repression is generally equated with controls on interest rates and, in a strict sense, controls which result in negative real interest rates on deposits (Kitchen, 1986). In most developing countries these practices were common, and imposed by governments, resulting, often argued by some economists, an actual interest rate which is different from equilibrium rate of interest that would prevail in a competitive financial system. From the mid-1980s, policy recommendations from many economic think tanks as well as from world financial bodies such as World Bank and IMF were in favor of policies of financial liberation. However, it has been argued by economists (Kose, Prasad and Terrones, 2003; Prasad et al., 2004; Kose et al., 2006) such financial liberalization can lead to serious financial crisis and collapse.

1.1.2 Financial Liberalization

In the late 1980s many developing countries including Asian and Sub-Saharan African countries adopted structural adjustment programs (World Bank, 1994; Cavoli et al., 2003) to revive their ailing economies. It is argued that the major goals of these adjustment programs were to pursue broad economic liberalization measures to enhance resource mobilization, increase productivity, and eliminate operational deficiencies that had retarded the process of economic development (Aryeetey et al., 1996). In a more general sense, this was a move to a more liberal economic system.

A central part of this process of economic liberalization was reform of the financial sector (also commonly referred to as financial liberalization). For the financial sector to play a greater role, particularly in the areas of increasing national savings and ensuring that capital was more efficiently allocated, it was suggested that price controls and directed credit programs be ended and that competition in the financial system be encouraged. Specific measures taken included the deregulation of interest rates, removal of controls on credit allocation, easing of entry into the financial markets by new (non-traditional) types of financial institutions and even more generally, changing the legal and supervisory structures of the financial industry (Fry, 1995).

1.1.3 Financial Crisis and Financial Contagion

The term financial crisis and financial contagion are closely related. Financial contagion is a process of spreading financial crisis, which generally results in a sharp contraction in incomes and standards-of-living, outside the original country in crisis (Claessens and Forbes, 2001, p. 10). In the past two decades, a number of financial contagions, as a result of different financial crises, have been experienced in many emerging markets. These crises have certainly produced deep and devastating economic effects that can be compared to a disease transmission by direct or indirect contact that can spread quickly across many regions.

Recent examples of international financial contagion include the 1982 debt crisis of Chile, the 1994 Mexican crisis, and the 1997–1998 East Asian crisis, which spread to a sample of twenty other countries. It has been argued that not only were most of the crises severely contagious but have triggered fundamental changes to market sentiment and serious macroeconomic restructuring such as debt maturity, exchange rate flexibility, and capital controls (Claessens and Forbes, 2001, p. 105). A number of factors may have promoted these crises including weak economic institutions, poor policy making and bad macroeconomic management.

Because of the intensity and difficulty in understanding international financial crisis-led contagion, understanding the factors causing these crises and how they occur has remained a challenge. This has also raised a considerable debate in the wake of international financial liberalization and globalization about the cause of financial crises and how they occur. From the large number of studies analysing the causes of crisis, it has been argued that most of the post-war financial crises occurred because of changes in investor psychology or mainly due to mismatch between fiscal and monetary policies pursued (Bordo and Schwartz, 1996). Similarly, Hansanti, Islam and Sheehan (2008) observe that different factors may trigger financial crisis. This include speculative attacks on the currency, which are then driven by the incompatibility of a pegged exchange rate and expansionary domestic financial policy (Krugman, 1979; Flood and Garber, 1984a). Complementing this, other studies elaborate that financial crisis is not only necessarily the attributable to the fundamentals and pegged exchange rate regimes, but can also initiate from a self-fulfilling speculative attacks (Flood and Garber, 1984b; Obstfeld, 1986). With few market imperfections (as is the case in most of emerging economies), this then generates adverse shocks in one asset market which is then further associated with asset sales in other unrelated markets. Similarly, others have also noted that numerous empirical papers find that macroeconomic weaknesses are an important cause of contagion as they make a country vulnerable to a local or international crisis (Claessens and Forbes, 2001, p. 15).

1.1.4 International Capital Mobility/Capital Control

Another notable controversy in international finance has been the issue of international capital mobility and capital control. In the last three decades or so, enabling and promoting the free flow international financial and capital have been the common objectives for many countries in the emerging economies. Capital openness or international capital mobility can be defined as the capacity of capital to cross borders free from government regulation (Andres, 1994). To operationalize and position themselves as attractive destination to international flows, such as foreign direct investment and other private flows (including portfolio investment), countries have adopted business-friendly environments by rapidly opening their capital accounts and through changing their domestic economic policies in the recent years. Other countries have also been liberalizing their controls on financial system (giving more autonomy to the relevant management bodies), exchange market transactions (foreign exchange markets) and the capital movements gradually. In this regard, well-functioning capital/equity market, attractive exchange arrangements and unrestrictive capital and exchange regimes have been part of a comprehensive rethinking about accessing global markets for capital to reducing reliance on foreign aid (Aryeetay and Senbet, 2004, p. 21).

The free flow of capital has a number of advantages for a host nation. Firstly, in addition to bringing new capital investment, its greatest benefit is related to its ability to facilitate technology transfer, encourage innovations and stimulate export growth. Secondly, capital mobility also enhances liquidity and maturity transformation (ability to exit on short notice) and encourage the design and use of alternative (or rather new) instruments which facilitate diversification and risk sharing (Aryeetay and Senbet, 2004, p. 23).

However, even though perfect capital mobility is the appropriate framework at least theoretically (and as a result the trend has been a marked increase in flexibility of exchange rates since 1970s),[1] this has also brought along the risk of higher volatility of exchange rates, inflation, macroeconomic instability and balance of payment problems. Consequently, a turbulent wave of exchange rate volatility (hikes) has increased financial and currency crises in the last three decades. In recent years, the risk associated with this has been amplified by financial liberalization and the realignment of the domestic financial system towards a more open global financial and trading system.

Chaisvasawatsuk and Chaisvasawatsuk (2006), Limskul (2000), and Brooks and Queisser (1999) elaborate on whether financial liberalization, exchange rate volatility and crisis are linked when they argue that financial crisis in East Asia reflects a mismatch between the liberalization of external economic relations and the slow pace of adjustment of domestic institutions (see also Hansanti, Islam and Sheehan, 2008, p. 11). Further, Corsetti et al. (1998, 1999) argue that capital openness, weak financial institutions, poor corporate and public governance and policy mistakes (including bad exchange management) heighten the risks associated with financial liberalization in their analysis of the 1997–1998 Asian crisis. For this reason, it is not surprising that, despite numerous benefits related to promoting inflow of global capital, many countries continue to have some restrictions on the free movement of capital in and out of their countries, while others, such as Malaysia, were able to

[1] It could be said that exchange rate regime is not necessarily directly linked to capital mobility, although it is much harder to fix rates with high mobility.

manage better the recent East Asian currency crisis by adopting some form of capital control (Hansanti, Islam and Sheehan, 2008, p. 23).

1.2 Financial Liberalization: Opposing Views

There are two broad groups about the possible benefits of this reform process aimed at financial liberalization: (a) the Goldsmith- McKinnon-Shaw school and (b) Keynes-Tobin-Stiglitz (also called the Structuralist and Neostructuralists School). Using various economic models, each provides background, rationale and intellectual justification for financial liberalization *vis a vis* financial repression. Each of these groups also nominate various monetary and financial policies in which if pursued would promote economic growth and ensure financial stability.

From the earlier works of Goldsmith (1969), McKinnon (1973) and Shaw (1973) to recent studies, the benefits of financial liberalization have been emphasized. All these authors have pointed out that by providing higher incentives to save and allocating funds to the most productive and profitable project, financial liberalization improves productivity in the economy as a whole. Put simply, by increasing saving and enhancing the allocation of capital, financial liberalization stimulates long-run economic development. While there seems to be a general consensus on the importance and the vital contribution of a financial system to the economy, some initial studies have shown that reforms towards a more liberal economy have worked differently in Asia, Africa and Latin America (Pill and Pradhan, 1997 and Barajas et al., 2000).

From a theoretical perspective, financial liberalization is said to benefit developing countries in a number of ways. Levine (1996) and Claessens and Glaessner (1998) observe that liberalizing financial markets may generate significant gains through foreign entry which increases competition and so lowers the cost of finance for domestic users, who gain easier access to cheaper funds from external sources.

Additionally, Sauve (1999) elaborates that there are at least three main reasons as to why developing countries could benefit from financial liberalization. First, the opening up of financial markets provides more opportunities for foreign investors to invest, leading to a spillover into savings and investment, which contributes to higher growth and development in the long run. Second, financial globalization potentially brings large benefits related to foreign firm penetration such as better technique for credit analysis, reduced risk of domestic financial instability (which in turn enhance economic growth rate and reduce poverty), and improved quality of financial and management services which can enhance productivity and efficiency. Third, liberalization can promote innovation and modernization of the domestic financial system through transfer of capital, technologies (new foreign innovation) and skilled labour (foreign expatriates), which results in improved services that lead to better quality investments.

This view is opposed by the Keynesian-Tobin-Stiglitz school of thought (Fry, 1995). This group (called *neostructuralists*) has brought forward a number of economic rationales to justify some sort of financial repression (such as low interest rate policies, lower inflation and directed and/or selective credit policies). Through various models (such as the Keynesian liquidity trap and Tobin's portfolio allocation models), they argue that without careful management, liberal attitudes to finance and financial market may disrupt economic activity quite seriously (Fry, 1995, p. 18). Stiglitz (1994) has also argued that, since credit markets are prone to market failures, government intervention in the area of prudential regulation and supervision is justified, particularly due to the *de facto* role of government as an insurer of the financial system (Fry, 1995, p. 131).

1.2.1 Approaches to Financial Liberalization

There are two main approaches in the process financial liberalization, domestic and international (also sometimes referred to as external financial liberalization). There is broad agreement among proponents of financial liberalization that the liberalization process should be gradual (also called the sequencing strategy) starting with domestic liberalization which includes deregulation/removal of controls over deposit and lending rates, reducing reserve requirements, reducing entry barriers to financial services industry, pursing a program to stabilize the price level and generally decrease the state's involvement in the activity of financial intermediaries. This is then followed by trade liberalization before moving up to external capital account liberalization and changes in the institutional framework of fiscal and monetary policies. There are various and different forms of external and capital account liberalization implemented by different countries. In general, removal of capital control encompasses measures that will allow domestic firms to access foreign external financing while also enabling foreign residents to hold domestic assets (Ghosh, 2005). In another dimension, external financial liberalization involves the removal of restriction on domestic residents wishing to purchase assets abroad, and in a broader sense, it also includes the introduction of measures to enhance currency convertibility and access to foreign currency assets.

However, this move towards domestic and external liberalization may have various negative effects which sometimes are claimed to outweigh its positive effects. Given high levels of financial and banking fragility in developing economies, financial liberalization exercise may render economies more unstable and vulnerable to external shocks. From the literature (Kaminsky and Schmukler, 2001; Kaminsky and Schmukler, 2002; Detragiache and Demirguc-Kunt, 1998), first, domestic financial liberalization may increase risk-taking activities. As bank interest rate ceilings are lifted and entry barriers to financial activities reduced, leading to greater market penetration of foreign banks and significant decreases in monopoly powers (while commercial banks are allowed to venture every segment of credit market previously forbidden), financial institutions will be tempted to finance riskier projects in return for a higher promised return. However, given adverse external economy-wide shocks, commercial banks may become more vulnerable

(Detragiache and Demirguc-Kunt, 1998) and this may have adverse effects on growth. Second, information asymmetries (as a result of market distortions) may lower allocative efficiency, leading to reduced economic activity. This coupled with poor financial regulation and supervision could encourage capital flight and trigger waves of financial crisis. Third, in pre-liberalization era where financial systems are tightly controlled, there is little development in terms of expertise in risk management strategies, credit analysis techniques (since funds are largely directed by government agencies), and engagement in foreign exchange transactions. With a more competitive commercial banking environment post-liberalization, various institutions may not have the ability to better assess and price new risks or undertake alternative diversification strategies, thereby increasing likelihood of a banking crisis.

1.2.2 Financial Liberalization and Country Experience in Africa and Asia

Although there is no consensus on the precise benefits of financial globalization and liberalization, there are claims that they do have net long-run benefits (Sikorsi, 1996). In addition, international financial integration and the rapid financial liberalization of developing Asian countries observed in the last decade did appear to bring substantial benefits, as is indicated primarily by the surge in the volume of international flows to Asia during much of the 1990s (Sheehan, 1998a, 1998b; Siksamat, 1998). Specifically, Sheehan (1998b) observes that private capital flows to Asian countries rose more than fivefold between 1993 and 1996. Given their low level of physical capital stock in pre-liberalization era, Asian countries such as Thailand, Indonesia, Malaysia and South Korea experienced high economic growth in post-reforms as a result of increased capital inflows (through global relocation of capital), exports diversification and foreign investments (Siamwalla, 2000). It has been observed that the value of exports increased rapidly during 1993–1995. For instance, Malaysian exports grew at an average of 18%, with 12% for South Korea and Indonesia, and 16% for Thailand (Gab, 2000). Furthermore, Park (1998) found that real income of Asian countries also rose significantly at the rate of 8.4, 6, 5.7 and 6.2% in Indonesia, Thailand, Malaysia and South Korea, respectively, during the period of 1985–1995. This impressive economic performance supported by sustained economic growth and poverty reduction pattern led the World Bank and other Bretton Wood institutions to regard these countries as "economic miracles" and declare them the fastest growing in the world (World Bank, 1993b).

A similar pattern has also been revealed in Africa and Latin America (Reinhart and Tokatlidis, 2003; Aizenman, 2005). The existence of two opposing school of thought about the beneficial effect of financial liberalization and the experiences of financial crises at different times in different countries provide serious academic and practical justifications for understanding an empirical study to investigate the actual consequences of financial liberalization in developing countries.

Two possible candidates for such an empirical investigation can be (a) some sub-Saharan African countries and (b) an Asian country, Thailand, for the reasons discussed below.

To integrate their economies with the rest of the world, stimulate domestic capital formation, improve efficiency and productivity and allow adoption of new foreign technologies, Nyawata and Bird (2003) suggest that the African countries in general embarked on programmes of financial liberalization which constituted the following elements:

- Freeing up interest rates;
- Relaxing entry and exit conditions (for new entrants) into the banking sector to promote the inflow of international capital;
- Allowing the privatization of state-owned banks;
- Redrafting financial and central bank statutes;
- Liberalizing trade and exchange regimes;
- Adopting indirect instruments of monetary policy;
- Improving regulatory practices and enhancing legal institutions;
- Eliminating indirect and quantitative controls.

Following this, while the range of financial instruments increased in some countries, financial depth (measured by the ratio of broad money to GDP) increased from 42.2%, 29.6%, 27.1% to 79.9%, 87.4% and 31.1% in Mauritius, Seychelles and Botswana respectively between 1980–1985 and 1999. Similarly, commercial bank credit to the private sector (percentage of GDP) has increased from 22.1, 14.6% and 14.1% to 57.5%, 15.1% and 15.2% in Mauritius, Seychelles and Botswana respectively in the same period (Nyawata and Bird, 2003).

It has also been reported that the financial and trade liberalization program led to a gradual reduction of tariffs and tariff dispersion. Mouna and Reza (2002) provide evidence that while tariff dispersion ranged between 0 to 400% prior to the reform, in post-reforms the maximum customs tariff declined from 60% in 1984 to 45% in 1986 and to 40% in 1992 in Morocco. The number of tariff bands was limited to nine in 1992 in most countries of the Middle East and North Africa. In Morocco, Tunisia and Algeria, the maximum tariff rate, except for a few agricultural products with tariffs up to 230%, is today as low as 35%. Thus, it seems that the effect of the reforms has made these North African countries more open, and as a result, their share of the trade sector in GDP has increased from 53% in the 1980–1984 period to 64% in 1999, and from 83% to 86%, respectively in Morocco and Tunisia. This increased evidence of trade diversification and export growth may have been due the fact that productive resources are reallocated away from less efficient activities towards activities where they are used with comparatively greater efficiency.

These facts led Phongpaichit and Baker (1998a) and others to conclude that the improvements in some of the Asian and African economies derived partly from the benefits of liberalising their financial and trade systems. Unfortunately, the miracle of the Asian economic tigers did not last and ended when a crisis surprisingly erupted in Thailand and soon spread to strike the neighbouring countries of South Korea, Malaysia and Indonesia. Therefore, a case study of Thailand for another possible empirical investigation of financial liberalization has been chosen in this book as it was the first country to trigger the Asian financial crisis (Hansanti, Islam and Sheehan, 2008).

For the African countries, the decade-and-half long liberalization reforms did not seem to instigate the sustained growth pattern expected in these Sub-Saharan African (SSA) economies. With this in mind, this book evaluates in detail the success of the financial liberalization programs in Sub-Saharan Africa using a case study approach and a sample of three countries (Kenya, Malawi and Botswana). Why are Kenya, Malawi, and Botswana taken to be the focus of this research? These countries got their independence almost in the same period. Immediately after independence, the countries adopted similar development plans where priorities were set to target growth with equity, to raise incomes and the standard of living, and in order to achieve sustainable growth rates. In terms of its structure, Botswana has managed to achieve a stable economy, with well functioning market institutions, while its growth achievements heavily relied on diamond and other mineral resource revenues. On the other hand, Kenya and Malawi have had substantially varied growth performance, with a respectably impressive level of GDP growth up to the 1980s and more modest achievement in 1990s. In both countries, economic performances were mainly driven by agricultural sectors.

Over the years, the three countries have also seen different market and economic transformations. Malawi has a small manufacturing sector, and an agricultural sector that is dualistic, involving both large scale estate farming and many smallholder agriculturists. Kenya has a reasonably larger manufacturing sector and a more commercially oriented agricultural farming. Botswana is a mono-economy that is heavily dependent on minerals although there have been some efforts to reverse this structural bias (to achieve a more balanced growth contributions) in the recent years (Maipose and Matsheka, 2002).

Notwithstanding these differences, the three countries have a number of inherent similarities which supports our argument for selecting them to form our sample. These include initial conditions, where all the three countries had a very close estimated real gross domestic product at independence. Secondly, there are also similarities in terms of resource endowments. Although not diamond-based, Kenya and Malawi are endowed with substantial natural wealth similar to Botswana. These include good agricultural land and viable cash crop farming (see Chapter 2). Thirdly, the three countries have similar national political institutions; they remain reasonably democratic (without military intervention since independence) and have adopted a policy of gradual nationalization to assist local involvement in the mainstream economy. Nevertheless, it should also be noted that there are some dangers of structural differences which may give the impression that there exists little justification for the countries to serve in a common sample in a study such as this. While admitting this, we propose that these differences are not strong enough to jeopardize policy lessons derived on the effect of financial sector reforms.

A few other factors have motivated our choice of these countries. First, these countries have implemented liberalization measures and started their reforms at almost the same time. These governments have also adopted other common policies where the propensities of government interventions have been substantially reduced while regulatory practices have been significantly improved. On these grounds, they will provide us with a range of experiences of financial liberalization to evaluate the extent to which specific outcomes are related to special policies pursued. Second, for a cross-country study, the sample will also provide geographical representation (Eastern, Central and Southern).[2] Third, the selected countries have good documentation of their financial systems and policies. Such availability of consistent and continuous sets of records is particularly important when trying to identify the timing of a major move towards a more liberal financial and macroeconomic environment.[3]

To address and manage the above issues, financial liberalization has been advocated and practised widely as a panacea for financial stability, economic development and efficiency as will be outlined next in Sects. 1.3–1.5.

1.2.3 Benefits of Financial Liberalization: An Empirical Issue

The above analyses show that there are strong arguments in support and against of financial liberalization. Therefore, it is not possible to resolve the question of desirability on a theoretical basis. We may, however, resort to historical and empirical analysis, on a pragmatic basis, to find the evidence and facts about financial liberalization experience (to reveal whether the process has created benefits or costs to the developing countries). A cost-benefit analyses, based on historical experience data and pragmatism, is necessary to determine the relative benefits of financial liberalization.

The book, therefore, evaluates important issues in financial liberalization debate while also looking at other possible but rarely mentioned net welfare gains of this process by applying a numerical cost-benefit analysis.

---

[2]However, as noted by Nissanke and Aryeetey (1998), this sample excludes West Africa where most of the countries are Francophone members and have close financial and monetary policies with France and between themselves.

[3]Additionally, while these countries can provide sufficient data for our analysis, the derived policy implications are generalisable since they represent markets that have different degrees of development.

1.3 The Objectives of this Book

In the view of the above controversies about the impact of financial liberalization, the objective of this research is to assess the impact of the economic liberalization policies undertaken and to examine whether the recent financial sector reforms have enhanced the process of long-term economic progress in Sub-Saharan African countries and in a typical developing country in Asia (where the recent financial crisis started) – Thailand. In achieving this, the study reviews the financial liberalization (repression) hypothesis and also gives a survey of works, both theoretical and empirical, to identify the expected channels of transmission towards improved economic outcomes and growth prospects. From this systematic evaluation of the theoretical validity and associated transmission mechanisms, country-specific assessments are provided. Building on these results, further theoretical and empirical analyses are provided to explain why liberalization measures have led to the observed outcome rather than the desired one. In doing this, the study has a number of specific objectives:

1. While providing a comprehensive examination of the financial system and the related macroeconomic environment, it aims to evaluate the impact of reforms with regard to allocative efficiency, resource mobilization and social welfare. There has been some extensive empirical testing of the effects of financial deregulation and liberalization on the volume of saving, the quantity and efficiency of investment and the short-run and long-run impact on economic growth (Fry, 1995, pp. 156–179). However, the empirical investigation in this book will give new insights since (1) tests on these countries have not been done, (2) sufficient data points are only now becoming available, and (3) these investigations are conducted in a more rigorous and robust manner.
2. To review the literature on financial sector reform and that of international finance. This will focus on financial liberalization and the difficulties of recent financial sector and institutional reforms in Sub-Saharan Africa.
3. To undertake detailed case studies of individual countries which could address a number important questions: what policy measures were implemented as part of the financial liberalization reforms? What are the effects/outcomes of such policy re-orientations? Did these reforms facilitate financial deepening, development of monetary policies, and enhance savings mobilization and financial intermediation?
4. To determine a precise measure of the impact of financial liberalization, this study will undertake a quantitative cost-benefit analysis of financial liberalization in terms of net social welfare implication of such reforms in a typical Asian developing country: Thailand.
5. From the outcome of the case studies and the supporting theoretical assessments, it will identify the key causes of failure following the reforms.
6. Based on these results and assessments, this study also intends to highlight some pragmatic policy framework and institutional changes needed to reduce impediments that limit effective financial development in these countries. This will

serve as a guideline for future policies required to create a successful environment for financial liberalization.

7. Finally, to provide a systematic analysis of the reforms, elaborating on the general outcome, challenges confronting the financial system, and broader market institutional conditions that can help improve the functioning of aggregate financial market in Africa and other developing countries.

Importantly, in this attempt to develop a better understanding of the effect of financial reforms, this book takes a case study approach. Some previous studies such as Naude (1995), Lensink et al. (1998) and Olomola (1994) have used empirical econometric analysis applying data from the region to assess the impacts of financial reform programs. However, due to a lack of credible data and a limited set of observations, such an approach may not provide robust results and adequate examinations. Specifically, gaps in the available data may require such studies to resort to inappropriate proxies of important macroeconomic indicators, thus failing to capture some vital relationships. Additionally, since financial liberalization in developing countries began in the late 1970s and was only implemented in Africa in the early 1990s, the new data set on indicators of financial liberalization and related macroeconomic variables that may be able to explain differences in the post-liberalization period may as yet be unavailable.

1.4 Methodology

In exploring the impact of a more open finance and financial system on economic development, the book uses a number of approaches: (1) integrated interdisciplinary analysis, (2) financial time series methods and (3) cost-benefit analysis. Following a review of financial development in various countries - with the view of dissecting the underpinning reforms measures - a simple framework of imperfectly competitive banking industry is used to examine the behaviour of the interest rate spread. Issues such as the allocative efficiency of financial intermediation, effective competition, loans and deposit equilibrium are modelled. Additionally, an important feature of the book is that, despite looking at the outcomes financial reforms in a developing country context, it focuses on specific issues and dilemmas confronting African countries. In this regards, we have undertaken a careful institutional analysis of what is distinctive about the African case. The book looks at the links between financial institutions, regulatory authorities and other political national institutions; something that may not have been captured in existing time series tests. Moreover, time series financial econometrics and cost-benefit analysis are used in this book to evaluate impact of financial liberalization in the selected African and Asian countries.

1.4.1 Time Series Financial Econometrics

In the last decade and half, the uses of time series and financial econometric techniques have been increasing. There has been rapid growth in techniques of analysing high frequency financial data (daily, weekly, monthly, etc.). Numerous advances have also been made recently in (1) the methods of analysing financial time series with time varying volatility and multivariate time series models; (2) methods of determining stationarity and cointegration between two or more non-stationary macroeconomic and financial time series; (3) new econometric tools for model estimation and inference; (4) other ways of studying the extent to which series can be analysed and forecasted more precisely.

Within the context of these developments in financial econometrics, time series techniques for model estimation and the determination of long term relationships such vector autoregressive (VAR), the Johansen maximum likelihood (ML) cointegration procedure and vector error correction (VECM) are applied in this study to analyse the effects of financial liberalization and stabilization policies. These approaches allow us to examine both long-run equilibrium relationships and short-run dynamics in relation to equilibrium. In determining the number of cointegration relationships, we implement the Johansen and Juselius cointegration tests.

1.4.2 Cost Benefit Analysis

Cost-benefit analysis is a technique that evaluates the desirability of an economic activity (such as financial liberalization and globalisation) in terms of net benefits (net present value) and the optimal social welfare criterion. A cost-benefit analysis can be developed by using normative social choice perspectives (Islam and Mak, 2006). In this book, the estimation of the costs and benefits of financial liberalization are made on the basis of operational normative social choice theory (see also Hansanti, Islam and Sheehan, 2007).

1.5 Contribution of this Book

This research will contribute to the existing body of economic literature in general, and financial reforms in particular, in a number of ways. Firstly, by investigating the effect of financial liberalization on economic development, the study will analyse whether the numerous economic liberalization policies have stimulated the pace of economic growth in Sub-Saharan Africa. In accordance with economic theory, practical experience from Asian countries showed that financial reforms have enhanced the pace of resource mobilization and promoted the entry of new financial instruments and institutions in their financial systems (Sikorski, 1996 and Pill and

Pradhan, 1997). In contrast, a recent study on the effect of liberalization and reform changes in Sub-Saharan Africa remarked that these measures had limited developmental effects (Nissanke and Aryeetey, 1998). Accordingly, this research aims to contribute to this discussion by providing additional evidence in this area. Moreover, in conducting this investigation, a different sample of countries from the region is used and when the results are contrary to expectations, attempts are made to identify the underlying causes.

Secondly, although a number of studies have commented on the existence of a high degree of monopoly power in much of the African commercial banking industry, which has led to persistently wide interest rate spreads (Mlachila and Chirwa, 2002; Chirwa, 2001; and Nissanke and Aryeetey, 1998), none have adequately modelled the problem of lack of entry of potential financial institutions. This study seeks to fill this gap in the literature by looking at some of the factors that act as a barrier to entry for these prospective banking institutions. This will not only highlight the factors discouraging a competitive market and the subsequent observed behaviour of financial variables, but will also explore mechanisms to encourage competitive entry. It is expected that, by allowing new institutions to enter, the financial liberalization process will increase competitive pressures and hence lead to a better allocation of available resources.

Thirdly, by taking a case study approach, the methodology itself is useful in terms of enabling thorough examination in which more conclusive evidence is gathered. Furthermore, any inference made about specific directional or causal relationships can easily be verified or supported by anecdotal empirical evidence and/or further empirical research when data limitations improve. The majority of the previous literatures on the interrelationship between financial liberalization and economic growth have used empirical methodologies. Thus, pooled data from a diverse group of countries have been utilized. Such studies include, among others, Galindo et al. (2002), Kaminsky and Schmukler (2002), Bekaert et al. (2001), Galindo et al. (2001) and Kaminsky and Schmukler (2001), who have all used a sample of countries from Asia, Latin America, Europe and the OECD countries. Unfortunately, these countries have quite dissimilar economic foundations in many aspects. Similarly, it has also been argued that the widespread use of pooled data models or cross-sectional empirical econometric methodologies to infer a financial liberalization-economic growth relationship may only indicate an average relationship which may not hold true in any specific country (Nyawata and Bird, 2003). Equally, another question that arises is what these results imply for particular countries. If, for example, it is concluded from these results that liberalizing the interest rate has an influence on savings and hence investment, will this conclusion be equally applicable to all countries? To remedy this problem, the current approach is advantageous in the sense that country-specific factors are taken into account while also giving some empirical evidence where possible.

Lastly, of no less importance is that our study will constitute additional research work on the regional economy of Sub-Saharan Africa. It is a recognized fact that research on the impact of financial reforms in less developing economies is far from giving a conclusive, uni-directional link. However, by focusing on a regional economy with common features, a better understanding, whether through analytical or empirical examination, can be achieved. Importantly, this region also houses the world's slowest growing economies and therefore by analyzing financial liberalization and economic development such a study will be important for formulating policy recommendations that account for regional-specific characteristics.

In addition, a numerical cost benefit analysis of financial liberalization of Thailand is an innovative approach (to the study of the effect of financial liberalization) since both the benefits and costs of structural liberalization need to be analyzed in making any conclusions about the impact of financial liberalization on growth, efficiency, resource utilization, financial stability and finally social welfare.

A question that has not fully been answered by the existing financial reforms literature in developing economies and current analytical dialogue, and which remains vividly in the minds of many researchers and financial practitioner is "whether financial liberalization is desirable given all the uncertainties post-liberalization?" Based on our evidence, financial liberalization in developing countries may have high costs and create short-run crises, and especially in the process of seeking to navigate the transition. However, financial liberalization may be desirable from the point of view of creating and increasing healthy financial market competition; reducing monopoly powers particularly in the commercial banking sector; and most importantly raising efficiency of investment.

Although there exists a large literature on financial liberalization; this book, therefore, makes contribution to the following areas: (a) it conducts country case studies to provide an in-depth information about country positions. This helps understand various country-specific (heterogeneous) financial characteristics that can impact outcomes of financial liberalization in a third world context. (b) It goes beyond the existing literature on financial market reforms by applying a model of imperfect competition to examine the commercial banking behaviour and issues of market efficiency, to further evaluate the general performance of the financial market in some of the developing countries. (c) It looks further beyond the existing literature by conducting cost-benefit analyses, a new concept in the subject area, which provides a qualitative and numerical exercise of cost benefit analysis of financial liberalization in a typical developing country. Thus, evaluating the net benefits (costs) of financial and market reforms in terms of social welfare and other economic gains. This concept and methodology applied here is new in this subject area.

1.6 The Structure of the Book

In working towards this contribution, the book is organized as follows. Chapter 2 proceeds to give an economic background of the countries of our sample. It presents the economic foundation and structures of these countries dating from independence to the recent period where the gradual transformations of economic systems were largely implemented. It also points out the main features of their financial systems and highlights the evolution of some of the important institutions that dominate economic affairs. To be able to predict the outcome of future changes on understanding of this institutional set-up before, during and post-reforms, is vital.

Chapter 3 presents a review of the relevant literature, both theoretical and empirical, that discusses the role of financial liberalization in the process of economic development. These works will form the basis of our arguments for and against the adoption of liberalization measures. In particular, this chapter reviews some of the theoretical explanations put forward to identify the mechanisms through which reforms are expected to influence economic growth in either direction. To observe the validity of these theoretical claims, results from various empirical investigations, both from Africa and abroad, are discussed. While outlining these investigations, this chapter also explains how these studies may be relevant to the current task.

Chapter 4 begins by revisiting the theoretical underpinning of the financial liberalization (repression) hypothesis to diagnose the routes through which reform-led changes are expected to influence real economic activities. Having identified this, the chapter presents assessments of the actual performance of the sample economies while emphasizing the important aspects that are critical to the subject matter of this research. Therefore, the movements and behaviours of key financial variables are noted. Chapter 5 expands on the main findings of Chapter 4 and gives an analysis of the observed imperfect banking competition in the sample countries, despite changes in the banking legislation to moderate new admissions. Applying a Cournot strategy to determine oligopolistic solutions, the behaviour of the spread and the level of loan and deposits is derived. This section also looks at the absence of "meaningful entry" of commercial banking institutions and hypothesizes that higher fixed costs deter new entrants. Anecdotal evidence to substantiate this claim is also provided.

In Chapter 6, empirical examination is undertaken to assess the potential impact(s) of macroeconomic reforms on saving rates. Firstly, saving trends are depicted for the three countries of interest. After observing that savings behaviour in Botswana has shown a significant shift, data from this country is used to investigate the reforms-savings relationship using a vector-error correction cointegration approach.

Chapter 7 provides a quantitative numerical exercise of cost benefit analysis of financial liberalization in a typical Asian developing country, Thailand, to consider the benefits and costs of financial liberalization in terms of social welfare in evaluating the benefits and effects of financial liberalization.

Chapter 8 concludes this book by summing up the key findings and drawing out some implications for policies, institutions and financial reforms.

Chapter 2
Background, Structure and Financial Reforms

"It has been said that figures rule the world; maybe. I am quite sure that it is figures which show whether it is being ruled well or badly".

(Goethe 1749–1832)

2.1 Introduction

Owing to persistent slowdown in economic growth and failure to achieve significant improvement in the standard of living, the period of early 1980s witnessed, almost worldwide, radical initiatives aimed at safeguarding and intensifying national economic performance in a more competitive world in many developing countries. A number of new programs were aimed at stimulating productivity and improving the economic environment in a national, regional and international context (Himbara, 1994). For African countries, despite this integration of the economic environment of the world and recognition of the need for new social, economic and political strategies, the Sub-Saharan African economic direction remained unaltered. Surprisingly, as noted by Himbara, the region remained engrossed in a crisis that consisted of every conceivable malaise. In total even 'where population were not threatened by starvation, disease, or war, dissipation of the economic infrastructure amidst astonishingly widespread corruption became the norm' (p. 2). Due to these reasons and under such circumstances African countries became increasingly marginalized in the 1980s and early 1990s. Clearly by the mid 1980s symptoms of malaise were evident everywhere. The returns on investment projects were relatively much lower in Africa than in other regions and more than a quarter of the existing projects failed to generate a positive rate of return (World Bank, 1994). This resulted in a drastic reduction in the region's share of international trade and foreign direct investment. In effect, Sub-Saharan African countries (SSA) had the least growth compared to other developing regions (and more so as compared to East Asian Economies) (World Bank). Clearly it was time for Sub-Saharan African countries to begin to adjust and improve their policies to restore economic growth

A.D. Ahmed and S.M.N. Islam, *Financial Liberalization in Developing Countries*, Contributions to Economics,
DOI: 10.1007/978-3-7908-2168-0_2,

along with other developing countries including Thailand. Beginning with late 1980s many governments of the region undertook major policy reform programs and restructured their economies to varying extents. Thus this was the beginning of the era of the 'structural adjustment program' with the objective of establishing a market-friendly set of incentives that can encourage the accumulation of capital and more efficient allocation of resources.[1] As part of the structural adjustment program, financial systems (markets) were restructured in most of the countries, with a major emphasis on liberalization measures and reduction or removal of controls and state interventions.

The impacts of these reform measures seem to have had little positive effect in this region so far (Nissanke & Aryeetey, 1998). In particular, despite efforts to improve the macroeconomic environment and strengthen the public and private sectors, savings rates in Sub-Saharan African countries remained low while GDP growth rates show minimal improvement (see Table 2.1). Various studies have attempted to explain Africa's poor performance before and after reforms, mostly employing different quantitative tools to analyse econometrically the factors behind the economic stagnation and decline of the region. This includes some of the recent work such as Oyejide (2000), Hoeffler (1999), and Ghura and Hajimichael (1996). These studies generally conclude that poor policies and some hostile external factors account for the major part of the low economic growth in Africa. However, due to inherent limitations in the use of statistical data for African economies, the quantitative analysis cannot be considered to exhaust the possibilities in explaining African growth. There are a number of reasons as to why econometric analysis does not fully explain Africa's low growth. Firstly, the statistical data used for econometric analysis is either inconsistent or highly subject to errors in measuring the variables (Nyawata & Bird, 2003; Aryeetey & Udry, 2000). Secondly, the easily accessible policy indicators fail to capture the intricacies of policy intervention. It is a clear fact that states in Africa play an active part in setting prices, nationalizing banks, controlling allocation of funds, creating public monopolies for agricultural export, restricting the activities of the private sector through directly or indirectly regulating them, and creating many state enterprises for various economic and non-economic reasons. None of these interventions or their impact is easily quantifiable since the required data are unavailable or unreliable. Lastly, in the 1970s and 1980s there was a widespread deterioration in governance. As states tried to meet the aspirations for quick developments which were promised during independence, the role of the state expanded rapidly, influencing each and every economic activity. More often political interest preceded a country's developmental targets. To such an extent, the government becomes an object of political annexation rather a target of policy. Precisely Jackson (1977) sums this up, by referring to government in Africa as 'neither wholly public nor wholly private' but rather 'para-public'. Realistically then, the cost associated with poor governance extends beyond what

[1] These were some of the objectives of the adjustment program according to the World Bank, which could have been different from the point of view individual countries.

Table 2.1 Assessing the impact of structural adjustment program for African countries

Country	GDP growth rate		Gross Dom. savings		Private savings rate		Public savings rate		Investment (% GDP)	
	1981–1986	87–97	1981–1986	87–97	1981–1986	87–97	1981–1986	87–92	1981–1986	87–97
Botswana[a]	5.9	6.7	26.1	38.8	−1.1	16.0	26.8	29.6	31.6	23.6
Burkina Faso[a]	3.9	3.7	−4.3	6.9	−3.2	3.3	−1.1	0.5	20.0	22.5
Burundi[b]	4.2	−0.3	3.1	−1.3	1.7	−2.0	1.4	1.5	16.4	14.1
Cameroon	5.7	−1.6	29.1	19.3	18.5	19.9	10.6	0.3	24.8	17.2
Cote d'Ivore	0.0	2.2	21.3	15.6	18.1	22.4	3.2	−9.8	17.9	11.0
Gabon	−0.7	3.3	49.2	39.1	33.1	34.2	16.0	−1.0	37.2	25.6
Gambia[a]	3.2	3.1	6.2	6.3	7.6	8.4	−1.4	1.0	19.0	19.8
Ghana[a]	2.7	4.5	5.6	7.7	7.3	2.2	−1.7	2.6	6.3	18.0
Kenya[b]	3.6	3.2	20.7	15.3	20.8	16.4	−0.1	−1.1	23.1	18.1
Madagascar[b]	1.0	1.5	1.9	4.7	1.7	3.2	0.2	1.5	9.1	11.8
Malawi[b]	3.2	3.7	13.3	5.8	16.0	11.0	−2.7	−0.3	17.6	19.2
Mali[b]	2.6	3.3	−2.9	6.3	−0.6	4.2	−2.3	0.8	17.2	22.4
Niger[b]	−3.0	1.5	5.1	4.4	5.4	9.0	−0.3	−2.7	12.9	10.1
Nigeria[a]	−0.1	4.0	14.4	24.1	10.8	25.6	3.6	−1.2	16.5	18.4
Senegal[b]	3.1	2.7	−0.4	8.5	2.9	7.5	−3.3	−0.1	11.2	14.9
Sierra Leone	−0.5	−1.8	7.4	2.6	16.3	21.1	−8.9	−8.0	13.9	8.9
Tanzania[a]	2.6	3.1	9.7	1.5	13.9	2.9	−4.2	−1.6	18.3	22.6
Zimbabwe[a]	1.6	3.7	17.9	17.3	21.6	19.3	−3.7	−2.5	19.6	18.9

[a]Indicates that the country showed large improvement in macroeconomic indicators

[b]Indicates that the country showed little improvement in macroeconomic indicators, while the rest showed some sign of deterioration. Gross domestic, private, public saving rates and investment share are all in percentage of GDP.

Source: World Development Indicators (various issues) and Nissanke and Aryeetey (1998).

is usually captured in policy variables. In this regard, this study intends to assess the impact of the recent financial liberalization in many Sub-Saharan African and Asian countries using a case study approach on a sample of three countries from the region (Kenya, Malawi, and Botswana) and Thailand in Asia in which reforms were implemented.

2.2 The Case of Kenya

Kenya was a British colony and protectorate from as early as 1890 and gained its independence in 1963. Immediately after independence, the country inherited an economic system and infrastructure that made it possible to formulate and administer development plans and other important policies. During the early years of independence, the government had a number of development programs aimed to increase productivity through developing agricultural sectors, and training the people to assume a greater role in the economy. The *Swynnerton plan* for land reform was fully implemented.[2] This was to ensure that land development occurred and at the same time progressive farmers emerged, who would be able to obtain credit by mortgaging their property rights (Azam & Daubree, 1997). In addition, the *Development Program 1963–1967* outlined priority areas which were to receive a large share of government expenditure. This program included improving education and infrastructure, extending government administration, and training manpower. These sectors were viewed to provide a quick return in a shorter period of time (IBRD, 1963). Through these policies and considering projections from development programs, it can be said that the Kenyan government started from a situation of great advantage in what has been done prior and immediately after, often cited as equal to the best in Africa. The pay-off from these bold steps was immediately observed. In the first 15 years of post independence saw the Kenyan economy grow at an average annual rate of 6.7%, believed to be one of the highest in Africa during this period.

Post-1963 Economic Performance: Table 2.2 shows actual and predicted per worker economic growth decomposition, where an upward surge in the growth rate in the 1964–1980 period is observable. It is clear that the growth in the early years was higher than predicted by the outside academics. There was a substantial improvement in the growth of physical capital as well as the education per worker until the early 1980s. It is necessary then, to look at some of the events that took place during this period, which led to such an improvement. Specifically, if we look at the investment trend (see Table 2.3), the ratio of investment to GDP improved reasonably, reaching an average of 16% for the period of 1960–1964, and further improved to 18.3% in the 1965–1969 period. Following independence, the uncertainties

[2]This was a plan to intensify the development of the agricultural sector by transforming the economy of the land and extending individual and cooperative ownership. For specific details refer to IBRD (1963).

Table 2.2 Decomposition of Kenya's economic growth (percentage)

Period	Growth in real GDP per worker	Predicted growth in real GDP per worker	Growth in physical capital per worker	Growth in education per worker
1960–1964	0.38	0.31	−2.60	0.03
1965–1969	3.67	1.37	1.05	1.15
1970–1974	4.85	2.46	1.39	1.51
1975–1979	1.62	2.21	0.46	1.14
1980–1984	−0.76	1.45	1.30	0.87
1985–1989	1.99	1.18	−1.90	0.73
1990–1994	−1.83	0.92	−2.60	0.43

Source: Mwega and Ndungu (2002).

Table 2.3 Investment and education indicators

Period	Initial real GDP per capita 1985 prices	Initial average years of education attained population >=15 years	Ratio of investment to GDP at current international prices
1960–1964	659	1.5	16.1
1965–1969	614	1.7	18.3
1970–1974	586	2.2	19.3
1975–1979	837	2.2	15.1
1980–1984	911	3.4	13.7
1985–1989	794	3.4	11.9
1990–1997	911	3.7	7.2

Source: Hoeffler (1999) and *Penn World Tables*, Mark 6.1.

of the transition period diminished and the government began to increase its own development spending while private investment quickly recovered (Mwega & Ndungu, 2002). Investment in human capital development increased as the government enabled schools to expand into rural areas and enrolment rates improved substantially. This raised the average years of schooling for those of at least 15 years of age in the population to 1.7 in 1969 from 1.5 in 1965. Owing to this, Azam and Dubree (1997) report that up until the boom in tropical beverages in the late 1970s, the Kenyan economic growth was driven by accumulation of human capital whereas the physical capital lagged behind.

The trend in gross domestic investment was upward till 1980 in Kenya, while the general downturn experienced afterwards was less immediately drastic. One reason that could explain this is that the country was moderately indebted during this period, and hence was able to allocate enough of its national income to domestic investment (Himbara, 1994). The government also pursued strategies that emphasized economic development over equity and built upon the institutions and policies inherited from the colonial era. Such policies included emphasis on private sector growth, and expanding production of the two principal crops – coffee and tea – for which the country enjoyed a comparative advantage in the world market and which could be grown by small farmers. Further, this attitude also helped increase the receptivity of foreign private investment (Barkan, 1994). In pursuit of this expansionary phase, the government expenditure increased rapidly during the mid 1960s and early 1970s (Table 2.4).[3] A number of reasons necessitated this, first, there was a pressure on the government after independence to expand facilities and harness production from various regions across the country. Second, such expenditure was necessary for the government to consolidate ethnic harmony among diverse tribes in Kenya, and consequently a significant portion of the budgetary expenditure went to rural development and settlement, and administrative expansion. Despite this, there was macroeconomic stability, as inflation generally remained low. The monetary policy was very conservative and the rate of expansion in money supply was low. This was because the public sector was also pre-empting an increased share of total resources to finance its activities (Mwega & Ndungu, 2002). Understandably, Kenya did have a competitive edge over many countries around the region even as the country attained its independence. Having the largest port in East Africa and a railway system that connected a large part of the country, it was well placed to become a manufacturing and service hub for East and Central Africa. The East African Co-operation treaty[4] which was signed in 1967 enabled expansion of free trade within the Eastern African community and Kenya became a large supplier of manufactured goods and petroleum products within East Africa (Azam & Daubree, 1997). In this regard, the country was already fairly industrialized with significant manufacturing exports in the mid 1960s and it was already a step ahead of a number of today's African economic giants as noted by Himbara. By 1965, Kenya earned US$14 million from manufacturing exports compared to US$1 million for the combined total earned by Mauritius and Botswana in the same year (World Bank, 1989).

2.2.1 The Structure of the Financial System

Kenya had an operative financial system as early as 1910 following the British occupation and the construction of the Kenya-Uganda railway. As at 1956, Kenya had 3 large foreign banks which dominated the sector for quite a long period: National and Grindlays Bank, the Standard Bank of South Africa, and the Bank of India, while a number of others were founded a few years later.[5] At independence, the country shared a monetary institute with Tanzania and Uganda, and therefore had a developed financial sector by African standards. Various problems with the

[3]With long collection lags and fixed level of expenditures, the money value of taxes deteriorated with prices raising, resulting widening deficit in real terms. On the other hand, foreign loans and aid disbursement declined from 8.15% in 1972 to 4.2% of GDP in 1996 (Mwega & Ndungu, 2002).

[4]This free trade agreement was signed by Kenya, Tanzania and Uganda in 1967, but the East African community had a custom union as early as 1937 (Hazelwood, 1979).

[5]NSE (2001) gives a historical background of the financial system in Kenya, including dates of establishment of numerous today's famous banks.

Table 2.4 Real economic growth rates in various sectors (*annual percentage rate*)

Sector	1960–1964	1965–1969	1970–1974	1975–1979	1980–1984	1985–1989	1990–1994	1995–1999
GDP growth	3.86	7.2	8.9	5.4	2.8	5.7	1.6	2.7
Government	12.0	14.9	17.1	18.4	18.5	18.1	16.7	16.1
Population	3.1	3.3	3.5	3.7	3.7	3.3	2.8	2.5
Agriculture (%GDP)	39.4	35.6	34.1	37.1	33.3	31.9	29.5	27.6
Manufacturing (%GDP)	9.7	11.4	12.1	11.8	12.2	11.7	11.2	10.8
Inflation	1.5	2.1	7.8	14.1	13.6	9.9	28.0	6.0

Source: World Bank, *World Tables* (several editions).

Table 2.5 Important events that had significant economic influence in Kenya

Date	Event
1977	Collapse of East African community
1976–1979	Terms of trade improvement (coffee boom)
1979	Oil price shock
1983–1984	Severe drought across the country
1991	Oil price shock following Gulf war
1991	Financial liberalization following structural adjustment program
1991–1993	Aid suspension
1992	Ethnic clashes (first multiparty elections)
1997–1998	Changes in weather condition (El-Nino rains)
1997–2000	Further aid embargo
1999	Extended drought (power supply shortage in many parts of the country)

Source: Authors' compilation from various publications.

East African Currency Board and the need for each country to pursue different economic and political policies prompted the establishment of the Central Bank of Kenya in 1966 (see Table 2.5 for other related reasons). From then on, Kenya had an independent monetary policy. Through the Central Bank Act, the Central Bank had supervisory powers over commercial banks and financial institutions. Up until 1991, the Central Bank used four main instruments for conducting its monetary policies (Central Bank, 2000). The minimum liquid asset ratio was first imposed on commercial banks at 12.5% of their deposit liabilities and later (in 1974) extended to cover other deposit taking financial institutions (NBFIs).[6] The Central Bank also required commercial banks to maintain a cash balance calculated as a percentage of their deposit liabilities.[7]

The objective of this was to reduce banks' free cash reserve and enhance their capacity to give loans. Another instrument that was most consistently used was the quantitative credit guidelines for the growth of bank credit. These guidelines were meant to influence the directions of credit and encourage lending to sectors of high priority.[8] Finally, the Central Bank also used interest rate structure to direct credit growth and to promote savings. The bank pursued a low interest rate policy during the first 20 years of independence in order to encourage investment and protect small borrowers (Central Bank, 2000).

During this period both the inflation rate and the spread between lending and deposit rates were low (see Fig. 2.1) while the real interest rate remained negative or insignificantly positive. Conventionally, such a low interest rate did not encourage savings, however, it did enable the government to finance its expenditure cheaply (Mwega & Ndungu, 2002). Initially there was a statutory limit to the

[6]The minimum liquid asset ratio for NBFIs was set at 10%.

[7]In particular this was used from late 1971 onwards.

[8]For example the banks were required to extend 17% of their deposit liabilities as credit to agriculture.

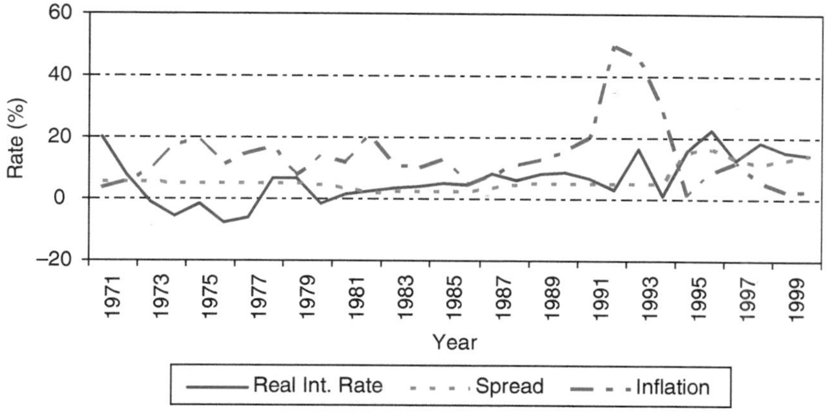

Fig. 2.1 Inflation and interest rate movements
Source: World Bank, *World Tables* and *World Development Indicators*, various issues.

Table 2.6 Government deficit financing (5 years averages)

Indicator	1969–1973	1974–1978	1978–1983	1984–1988
Public saving (%GDP)	1.5	2.3	0.7	−2.0
Budget deficit (%GDP)	−4.9	−7.1	−9.4	−5.0
Bank loans (%GDP)	0.7	1.6	1.5	1.7
Share of private sector (in total domestic credit)	82.0	71.0	65.0	58.0

Note: Bank loans do not include borrowing by public enterprises. Public saving is current account balance/GDP and budget deficit is the overall expenditures in excess of revenues including external grants as a percentage of GDP.
Source: Azam and Dubree (1997).

amount of credit the Central Bank could extend to the government, but that provision was scrapped in 1972, enabling the Central Bank to put ceiling on lending by commercial banks, in particular to the private sector and to impose directives regarding the allocation of credit (Azam & Daubree, 1997). As can be seen from Table 2.6, the government did not keep fiscal discipline, especially from 1970. The budget deficit was 4.9% in 1963–1973, rising to 7.1% and 9.4% in 1974–1978 and 1979–1983 periods respectively. Eventually the government turned to monetary financing of these deficits. In assessing the budget deficit and public savings, we observe that public saving was quite low, quite reasonably indicating that the deficit was mainly due to public investment. Additionally, it can be observed that the share of the private sector gradually decreased as lending to the state and public sector increased, due to budget deficits.

Undoubtedly this is an obvious case of crowding out of the private sector. In this regard, and as noted in Figure 2.1, there are clear signs of financial repression as substantiated by a systematically negative real interest rate from 1972 to 1982. The nominal interest rate also shows clear signs of rigidity as the spread appears to be constant throughout the period. On average the real interest rate was marginally low, obviously showing excess demand for credit, leading to the rationing of credit by the banking system. Consequently, this gave the government some level of discretionary power over the allocation of investment, power that it did not fail to use to channel funds to the public sector or financing the deficit (Killick & Mwega, 1990). Nevertheless, even though the low interest rate structure did not encourage savings, capital accumulation was enabled since it was indirectly subsidized, resulting in a capital intensive import substitution industrialization strategy.

As noted by Mwega and Ndungu (2002), this was going to affect the economy in three major directions. Firstly, with cheap availability of capital, firms invested in significant capacities assuming that future demand for their goods would not constrain production. Additionally, given the rising rate of population growth in this period and labour abundance in the country, such a trend did not help the labour market, resulting in a production sector that is capital intensive in labour abundant state. Lastly, given the umbrella protection and political patronage, the heavy investment capacities led to low capacity utilization given the size of the market. This led to underutilization in various sub-sectors, raising average overhead cost. Under such a production system, product prices increased further and further damaging profitability. Accordingly, the economic system could not be efficient and the production level was far from optimal. Admittedly, though the GDP growth was still positive, undoubtedly this was going to have a negative impact on the economic performance in the long-run.

In parallel with the above policies, the banking industry expanded rapidly during the 1968–1980 period. This was part of the government policy of nationalizing institutions and allowing greater local participation. In 1968 the government established National Bank of Kenya (NBK) and 3 years later it acquired 60% of the National and Grindlays Bank, renaming it Kenya Commercia Bank (KCB). Both these banks increased their branches across the country and soon KCB was the largest bank in terms of deposits, having 49 braches out of 161 bank branches in the country (Azam & Daubree, 1997). In line with the *Development Plan 1964–1970*, the government had two objectives in doing this. Firstly, it wanted to promote vigorously the African people's participation in every sphere of the national economy, hence giving them greater access to credit, while loosening the domination of the banking structure by a few powerful banks (Grosh, 1990). Secondly, by increasing the government share in the banking sector, it would facilitate expansion of credit to priority sectors and redistribute activity towards less favoured regions. As the government invested heavily in the financial sector, Kenya's financial sector grew steadily in the 1980s as indicated by the growth of the share of the financial sector in GDP from 9.8% in 1974 to 12.4% in 1980.[9] Subsequently the deposits at the public owned banks and other non-bank financial institutions increased significantly, reaching 37.5% of all deposits of the Kenyan financial sector.

---

[9]Refer to Mwega and Ndungu (2002) for further discussion on this and for the breakdown of contributions by other important sectors.

However, due to financial repression policies, the nationalized banks were subject to various forms of government pressure that frequently threatened their efficiency (Azam & Daubree, 1997). Such banks were required to extend their services to areas that were disadvantaged, where returns were low. Additionally they were subjected to pressure from specific political groups who channelled funds into projects with returns below par in the name of priority areas. Further, the nationalized banks were quite often called in to help drowned public and parastatal enterprises in different sectors by injecting funds using doubtful justification. Indeed, with time, the financial sector led by national banks grew weaker and weaker. As noted by Mwega and Ndungu (2002), such banks were extensively used to fund state enterprises which were often unable to service their loans due to poor management, ineffective statutory power to raise funds independently and vulnerability to political patronage and abuse. Due to such practices, it is reasonable that the size of non-performing loans increased in this period. By late 1980, it was estimated that bad loans made up at least 15% of the loan books of both NBK and KCB (Grosh, 1990).

2.2.2 Agricultural Sector and Other Policies Framework

Since the British rule, Kenya's rate of economic growth and improvement in the standard of living has depended primarily on development in the agricultural sector. As early as 1950 tea and coffee alone contributed more than 30% of the total export (IBRD, 1963) and in 1961 the two crops contributed 42% of the total value of export. In the early years of independence, economic policies were geared towards expanding agricultural production to increase the prospect for world trade in commodities the country had competitive advantage to produce. Following *Sessional Paper No.1,*[10] a substantial amount of previously European owned land was transferred to local farmers and large resources were devoted to land registration and development (Bigsten & Ndungu, 1991). To increase productivity, high yielding crops were introduced and smallholder farmers were encouraged to increase the share of high value crops. Thus the agricultural sector contribution remained significant even after independence. In 1963, the share of agricultural production in GDP was 38% and on average this share was 35% for the period of 1961–1970 (see Table 2.4). Although in an expansionary phase, the government had overall budget discipline as fiscal and monetary policies were on the whole cautious (Bigsten & Ndungu). In effect agricultural productivity improved in between 1967 and 1969, but the agricultural policies were founded on the principle of equitable income distribution, employment and self efficiency (Mwega & Ndungu, 2002). To achieve this, the state was the sole decision maker, controlling prices and marketing channels of almost all major crops. These policies weakened the agricultural

[10]A detailed description of the content of this plan can be found in Kenya (1965).

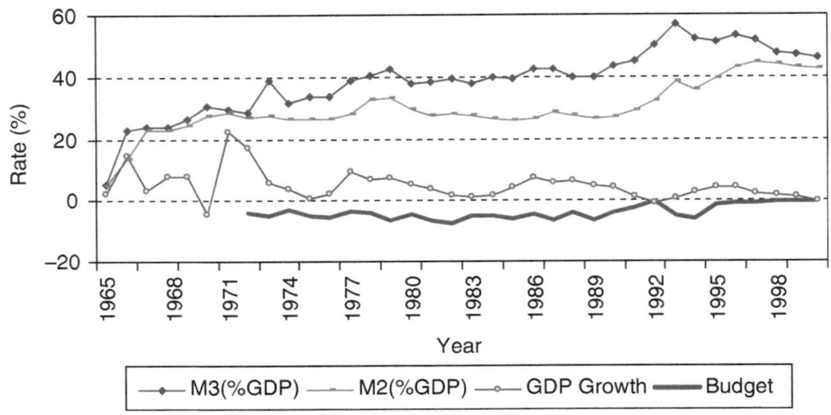

Fig. 2.2 Performance analysis in Kenya
Source: World Bank, World Tables and International Financial Statistics (IFS).

sector as it was not allowed to fully integrate with other sectors and the product market, while there was little incentive left for farmers to apply extra effort. In 1971, Kenya experienced its first balance of payment problems resulting from unfavourable terms of trade coupled with its expansionary budget (Fig. 2.2). This crisis was further worsened by the 1973 oil shock which caused a 30% increase in all other import prices (Bigsten & Ndungu, 1991).

Following this, a number of restrictive budgetary policies were introduced: (1) Import controls were increased, and specific quantitative restrictions were implemented. Import licensing became more restrictive as the government introduced highly protective policies for domestic producers, empowering them to authorize the imports of certain goods through a 'No Objection certificate'. Additionally the government set up a sales tax system which was biased against importers since local producers could do away with their dues benefiting them even further. (2) Domestic credit was restricted. Through the central bank the commercial banks and NBFIs were instructed to reduce their lending, resulting in a reduction in domestic credit to an annual average rate of 12.2% during 1971–1972 compared with 30.2% in 1970 (see also Table 2.6).[11] (3) In response to built-in price increase expectation, the government further tightened price controls. Consequently, in 1971–1972 inflation slowed down to an annual average of 4% compared with 7% in the previous year (Fig. 2.1).

With such huge policy intervention during this period, the Kenyan economy was once again on the whole closed after it had appeared relatively open for less than 5 years. Domestic competition and competitiveness reduced and shifted incentives

[11]See also the behaviour of M2 (% of GDP) and M3 (% of GDP) during this period in Figure 2.2.

against export production (Mwega & Ndungu, 2002). The relatively smaller and weaker[12] manufacturing sector accrued all the incentives at the expense of important sectors such as agriculture and services which undoubtedly contributed most to the economic growth. While various policies were introduced during 1967–1971, the exchange rate was minimally used as an instrument of monetary policy. The Central Bank pursued a fixed exchange rate system between 1966 and 1982. Up to 1974, the Kenya shilling was pegged to the US dollar, but after a number of devaluations the peg was changed to Special Drawing Rights (SDR) (Ndungu, 1999). In an effort to arrest the deteriorating balance of payment (see Fig. 2.2), government borrowing from the banking system was reduced in fiscal years 1973 and 1974 while interest rates for both lending and deposits were raised for the first time (Fig. 2.1). But inflation accelerated again in 1975 to an average of 15.5% while the GDP growth was down to 2.8%, leading the way for investment and imports to fall drastically (see Fig. 2.3). In the wake of slowed economic growth, the government realised something was wrong. Through *Sessional Paper No.4 of 1975* a further strategy of coping with the crisis was spelled out. The Kenya shilling was devalued by 14% while an export subsidy of 10% was instituted, both aimed at improving the level of exports.

Subsequently while a tight credit stance was to be maintained, the government considered it necessary to channel more credit to agriculture in view of its significant contribution to the overall national economy. In this context the commercial banks were required to increase their loans to the agricultural sector from 14% in 1974 to 17% of their deposits in the following year. This is also reflected in the

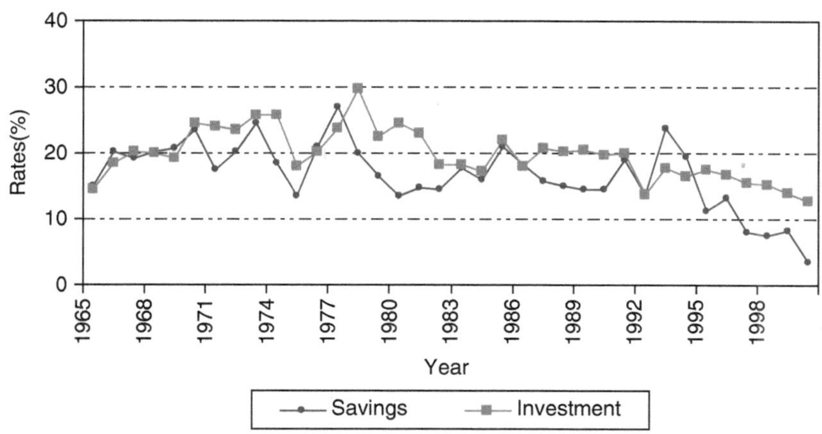

Fig. 2.3 Savings-investment analysis in Kenya
Source: African Development Indicators (various issues).

[12]Refer to my previous analysis for various reasons for inefficiencies in the manufacturing sector.

movement of both money supply (M2 and M3 in Fig. 2.2) and inflation (Fig. 2.1).[13] Bigsten and Ndungu (1991) argue that following a temporary trade shock (the coffee boom of 1976–1979)[14] the above mentioned economic restructuring was neglected. Due to a temporary external shock, the price Kenya received for its coffee exports significantly increased between 1975 and 1977. Initially the boom directly constituted a 38% improvement in the barter terms of trade, but it further instigated a substantial improvement in the Kenya tea prices and other export items, taking the total terms of trade improvement to 54% (Bevan, Collier, & Gunning, 1999). As the prices of both coffee and tea increased and exports improved, a large part of the gains was to be passed on to the producers, while after a certain period the government revenue and public expenditure both increased remarkably. This income gain redirected the private sector interest in the agricultural sector and the growth in the industrial sector also improved to 14% in 1977. Effectively then, the average real GDP growth for the 3 years of the windfall was 6.8% (Azam & Daubree, 1997). The improvement in income during this period also resulted in changes in savings and investment rates (see Fig. 2.3). Enhancement in the income of peasant coffee and tea farmers triggered significant increases in their savings. It is estimated that in the first year of the windfall, the farmers saved about 45% of their windfall income in bank deposits (Bevan et al., 1999).[15] Following the windfall, the relative size of the government budget increased dramatically beginning with 1977, causing rapid expansion in government spending (Table 2.7). In this regard, over the years what really mattered for the progress of the economy was not only why did government spending increase but where did such expenditure fall

Table 2.7 Fiscal aggregates over 1976–1983 following the coffee boom

Year	Total revenue	Total expenditure	Consumption	Gross fixed Capital formation	Surplus/deficit
1976	4.2	9.5	8.1	1.5	−5.3
1977	36.6	28.9	22.7	6.1	7.7
1978	38.4	48.5	41.7	7.4	0.0
1979	76.8	84.1	63.7	20.2	−7.3
1980	86.7	94.9	67.5	27.4	−8.2
1981	72.9	84.7	85.5	9.3	−21.8
1982	57.6	69.4	77.5	−8.1	−11.8
1983	52.7	49.2	58.2	−9.1	3.4

Note: All figures are in million of Kenya shillings.
Source: Bevan, Collier and Gunning (1999).

[13]For close comparison of money supply, domestic credit and interest rate movement in this period refer to Ndungu (1999).

[14]The boom did not actually result from coffee alone; in fact the price of most of the tropical beverages improved in one way or the other, but since coffee accounted for more than 70% of the terms of trade improvement, Bevan, Collier, and Gunning (1999) as well as other researchers termed this as the coffee boom.

[15]This trend is also revealed in Figure 2.3 where dramatic upward swings in savings and later investment rates are especially distinguishable.

to. The data indicate that the bulk of the increase in the spending was in form of consumption, though initially there was some level of success in raising the development component of the budget relative to the recurrent component.[16]

The gross capital formation did not improve much consistently and was reduced to a very small share of the GDP at the end of the period. Beginning with 1976, rapid increase in government revenue is observable. Bevan et al. (1999) observe that the increase resulted from indirect taxation and foreign borrowing. Both sales taxes and import duties were raised for the purpose of financing the expenditure increase resulting from the boom. However due to a large drought in 1979 and the second oil price hike, the government increased its level of foreign borrowings. In the period of 1978–1981, 15% of the budget was financed by external loans and grants following a fiscal deficit of 1.9% of GDP. Such action did not favour future economic improvement because the policy makers chose to increase future debt-servicing rather than immediately crowding out private domestic capital formation (Bevan et al., 1999). In sum, the evidence from various sources suggests that the government did not create the required regulatory framework to maximize the benefit of the temporary trade shock. The existing financial and monetary policy did not encourage private savings. The unanticipated gain by the private sector induced an investment boom leading to a rise in the demand for non-tradable goods. Therefore the private windfall saving was channelled to the construction industry, causing a surge in imports of consumer durables and a general increase in the price level due to a temporary expansion in disposable income. Inflation accelerated from year to year, reaching the peak in 1982, while the overall budget deficit continued to widen, hitting 10% of the GDP in 1980. This proved hard to reverse largely because the growth rate of the population was quite high, bypassing GDP growth for the first time in 1980. Similarly, the public sector workforce had increased during the boom (Bigsten & Ndungu, 1991). The large fiscal deficit of late 1980s made it extremely difficult for the government to contain its spending, necessitating a new credit negotiation with the IMF. This expensive foreign borrowing to sustain economic growth in the 1980s meant a rise in the debt-service ratio to over 30% at the end of the 1980s from 5% in the mid 1970s.

2.2.3 Liberalization and the Era of Structural Adjustments

For the large part of the late 1970s and early 1980s the government was faced with serious imbalances, increased external debt and a rapidly rising rate of population growth. These factors were eroding the basis for economic growth, and hence they paved the way for structural adjustment programs (SAPs). SAPs actually began in Kenya in the mid 1980s but because of shortcomings in the implementation, it was not until the early 1990s that some serious reform measures were implemented. The

[16] A breakdown of the fiscal pattern and analysis of transmission mechanism from private to public has been given by Bevan, Collier, and Gunning (1999, pp. 75–79).

objectives of SAPs in Kenya included initiating: macroeconomic policies that would promote stability, agricultural reforms that would help farmers improve productivity and trade policies that would boost exports and liberalize imports (World Bank, 1994). To a large extent these policies were intended to help markets and market development in Kenya through encouraging competition while minimizing the unnecessary government regulation and involvement. In the long-run this will encourage the accumulation of capital and enhance the efficiency of allocation of resources which are needed to move on to a faster economic growth path and reduction in the level of poverty. To enhance the competitiveness of the Kenyan product in the global market, a number of reform measures were taken. Of these the three most significant were trade liberalization, exchange rate adjustment and financial sector reforms.

As part of the structural adjustment program, prominent features of these stabilization measures included financial liberalization which involved the abolishment of directed credit mechanisms, removal of ceilings on interest rates and importantly, the pursuit of price stabilization through appropriate macro-policies. Meanwhile, there had also been other broad measures of the trade and exchange rate reforms. Improving terms of trade and increasing the level of export has ever been the goal of the Kenyan government, but many of the past policies hampered this target either directly or indirectly. Trade liberalization, both internal and external, received greater attention in various phases of the reform program (Mwega & Ndungu, 2002). Major steps that were taken to accomplish this included abolishing quantitative restriction (quotas), reducing tariff levels and introducing a more flexible exchange rate regime. Import barriers were also significantly reduced through lifting import controls. This enabled many domestic manufacturers, both in private and parastatals, to get access to imported inputs and to cheaper external credit to finance the required capital goods at a more reasonable exchange rate. Mwega and Ndungu report that between 1980 and 1985 alone, the share of items that could be imported without any attached restrictions increased from 24% to 48% of total value of imported items. In 1987–1988 the import licensing system underwent significant improvement while a wave of tariff reductions, which were instigated by World Bank as part of the adjustment program for the industrial sector, took place. Consequently, between 1987 and 1991, the number of goods subject to quotas reduced from 40.3% to 22.1% of the total. This drastic improvement in access to imported goods boosted the manufacturing sector, where quotas covered virtually 100% in 1986, 79% in 1988, 45% in 1990 and 28% in 1991 (Azam & Daubree, 1997). By the end of 1991 imports requiring licensing were largely restricted on health, security and environment reasons only (Mwega & Ndungu). Kenya generally pursued a fixed exchange rate policy for the period prior to 1982. The fixed exchange rate regime was replaced in 1983 by a more flexible regime. A crawling peg system was first introduced, where discrete devaluations were undertaken to account for inflation and external payment conditions. Following structural adjustment and financial reforms, further liberalization of the foreign exchange market was undertaken in 1993. The Foreign Exchange Bearer Certificate (Forex-Cs) was introduced by the Central Bank to curb capital flight and attract foreign exchange outside the domestic banking system. A floating exchange rate system was adopted to enable reflection of external imbalances in the money market and supply constraint in the economy. Despite this, it immediately turned out that the exchange rate was no longer stable, imposing risks on importers, exporters and those with future contracts (Ndungu, 1999).[17] This led to a significant uncertainty in the market and prices instability, producing a spiral of inflation (see Fig. 2.1).

2.3 The Case of Malawi

Malawi was a British protectorate from 1891 until it gained independence in 1964. Up until shortly before independence, the country had no established economic infrastructure as the level of technological adoption was low, domestic manufacturing was relatively insignificant and means of transportation and communication generally inadequate (Pryor, 1990). In addition to this underdeveloped economic condition, the country is geographically disadvantaged as Malawi is land locked, small and with few rough roads linking it to its neighbours. Given these conditions, Malawi had little chance for economic success following independence. Since the colonial government had relatively few economic policies to develop an economic platform, the new nation had to create plans for economic development and construction of an economic infrastructure. The new government concluded that the country's economic future lay in the export-oriented agricultural sector, and hence provided strong support for the agricultural development path (Channock, 1972). But the country started from such a low level of productivity that the long-term target of achieving an acceptable level of economic development seemed unattainable (Pryor, 1990). Further, the short-term problems were as many as the long-term ones. The government revenue resources were so limited that it could only cover about half of its expenditure,[18] the requirements for investment were rising while domestic savings were clearly quite low (see Fig. 2.4).

Post-Independent Economic Performance: Malawi's GDP growth rates in real terms improved considerably from 1960 until the late 1970s when it started slowing down markedly. Specifically the surge in the real GDP growth was exceptionally significant from 1960 to 1974 (refer to Table 2.8 and Table 2.12). The real GDP grew at an average rate of 5.8% during first 5 years following independence (Pryor, 1990). During the subsequent half a decade, the economy even grew at an impressive rate registering an average annual growth rate above 7% (see Table 2.8). For the period of 1976–1980 the annual average growth rate was 5.1%, only subsequently moderately slowing down before hitting rock bottom in the late 1990s. However, looking at the state of the economy following independence,

---

[17]For example, in 1993 alone the Kenya Shilling was devalued three times losing about 70% of its value.

[18]This point is further elaborated by both Pryor (1990) and Channock (1972).

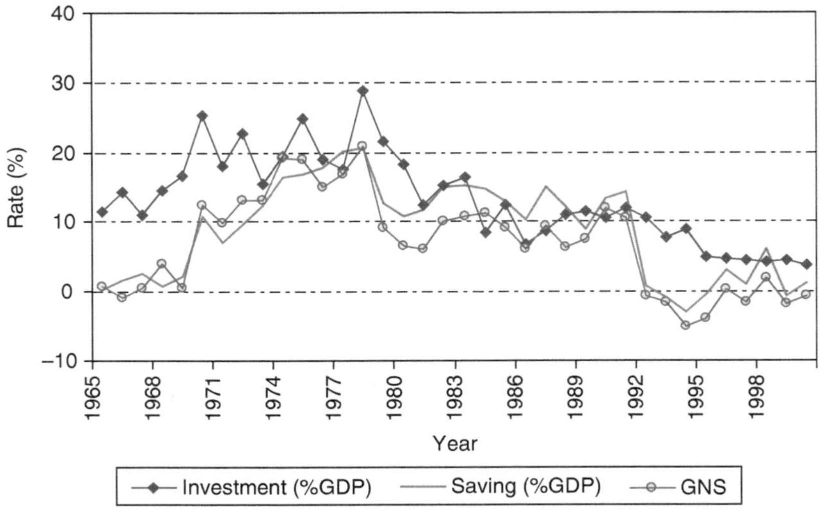

Fig. 2.4 Investment-savings analysis in Malawi
Note: GNS stands for gross national savings.
Source: World Bank, African Development Indicators.

such progress was not visible, and hence, the quick economic growth seemed spectacular. Chipeta and Mkandawire (2002) remark that a considerable level of structural transformation had also occurred during the period of 1964–1979. The share of agriculture in GDP declined on average from 46.1% in 1965–1970 to almost 41% in 1981–1985 while the share of manufacturing in GDP increased from 4.5%[19] to 14% in the same period. Similarly, the share of industry as a whole to GDP increased from 15.7% to 21.2% respectively (refer to Table 2.11) due to an increase in import-substitution manufacturing. This indicates that despite Malawi placing agricultural development on top of the list priority sectors, other important sectors including manufacturing and industry as a whole also experienced satisfactory progress during the same period. Moreover, even though there was a reduction in the contribution of agriculture to the GDP, the locus of agricultural production also changed. Estate production significantly increased from 7% of the total agricultural value added in 1964 to 20% in 1979 (Pryor, 1990).

The above economic growth trend was only possible with the strategic and tactical economic policies undertaken by the government. In the period of 1964–1979 three major development plans were successfully implemented.[20] These development plans stressed the highest priority areas intended to increase productivity,

[19]This figure is according to Chipeta and Mkandawire (2002) though it is not provided in Table 2.11.

[20]This includes the long-term development plan of 1965–1969, Gwedo No. 2 plan and DevPol I (Malawi, 1971).

Table 2.8 General macroeconomic indicators of Malawi (*percentage*)

Indicator	1971–1975	1976–1980	1981–1985	1986–1990	1991–1995	1996–2000
Growth rate of real GDP	7.6	5.1	2.2	2.3	3.5	4.0
Growth rate of GDP p/c	4.4	1.5	−1.1	−0.9	1.9	1.7
Current account deficit of BOP/GDP	10.6	15.6	9.3	5.3	20.5	30.4
Budget deficit including grants (% GDP)	1.6	8.9	8.8	5.7	4.2	6.2
Budget deficit excluding grants (% GDP)	2.5	12.1	9.3	7.8	13.5	19.8
Inflation	9.5	9.5	12.9	18.9	31.9	31.8

Source: World Bank, African Development Indicators.

Table 2.9 Total capital flows to Malawi

Period	LTD (US$M)	Debt service (% of Exports)	Debt service (% of GNP)	FDI (%GDP)	Aid (% GNP)
1971–1975	210.4	n.a	2.5	1.4	8.4
1976–1980	403.7	15.1	3.9	0.5	9.6
1981–1985	711.6	34.4	9.0	0.1	11.8
1986–1990	1189.9	36.4	8.9	0.0	27.4
1991–1995	1,760.2	23.6	6.3	0.5	30.8
1996–2000	2,331.1	13.2	3.9	2.5	22.4

Note: LTD is the Long-Term Debt and FDI is the Foreign Direct Investment net inflows.
Source: World Bank, Global Development Finance.

allocated incentives for private investment and to some extent enhanced foreign trade. These plans constituted an integrated program intended to achieve specific aims (essential for economic progress) (Pryor, 1990). To achieve the objective of the abovementioned strategic plans, the government was able to mobilize the necessary funds, both externally and internally, by raising the level of savings (see the savings trend in Fig. 2.4). At independence, the gross domestic savings were 4% of the GDP while the gross national savings were almost insignificant. Chipeta and Mkandawire (1992) observe that together the gross domestic savings and gross national savings financed only 8% of total investment between 1967 and 1969. But from 1969 savings started catching up with investment. Both public and private sector savings increased rapidly, causing the gross domestic savings to increase to 14.9% in 1979 from 1% in 1965 (World Bank, 1985), financing almost 50% of the total investment. Further, because of the steps taken by the government to revive the private sector as well as expand income, internal sources of funds grew and foreign investment increased, while aid to GNP recorded 8.4% on average for the period of 1971-1975 (see Table 2.9).

As funds were mobilized from both domestic and foreign sources, investment as a share of GDP rose steadily from 8.9% in 1964 to 29.1% in 1974. The five year average of 1971–1975 stood at 23.8% from 16.4% for the period of 1964–1969 (see Fig. 2.4). Pryor (1990) has looked at the effectiveness of such high investment levels in Malawi. Using incremental capital ratio (ICOR) as a measure of investment effectiveness,[21] he reports ICOR of 3.7 for the period 1964–1979, climbing to 9.9 in 1979–1986. This rate of ICOR was much lower than that of many African countries, indicating high investment effectiveness. Due to the suitable environment (socially and politically) that had been created by the government in the post-independence, the per capita GDP, investment and savings were able to increase remarkably. In particular, the political stability and visionary leadership enhanced the chances of mobilizing funds and providing strategic policies for economic take-off (Table 2.10).

[21]Note that the lower the measure of ICOR the higher the effectiveness, other things being equal.

Table 2.10 Major events that had significant economic influence in Malawi

Year	Event
1964	The country received its independence from British rule.
1971–1975	The country introduced new currency (Malawian Kwacha) to replace the Pound. In 1975 the Malawian Kwacha was pegged to Special Drawing Rights (SDR) of the IMF.
1979	Oil price shock and civil war in Mozambique.
1979	Terms of trade deterioration set in, eventually leading to financial difficulties in various sectors.
1981	Crop prices were adjusted to encourage production by smallholders to boost exports.
1982–1984	Series of devaluations of Kwacha to achieve balance of payments equilibrium. The Kwacha was later pegged to weighted basket of strong currencies.
1988	As part of structural adjustment program, import controls are relaxed and scope of export licensing reduced.
1989	Review of legal framework for financial sector leading into a new and revised legislation.
1990–1992	Interest rates are liberalized, credit controls eliminated and financial markets opened up to allow competition.
1994	Malawian Kwacha is floated for the first time.
1995	Stock market is established to integrate the financial system.
1995–1996	Public sector 'downsizing' begins as privatization is introduced.
1996	Introduction of Export Processing Zone (EPZ).

Source: Reserve Bank of Malawi, Financial and Economic Review (various issues), Chipeta and Mkandawire (2002) and UNDP (1999).

Chipeta and Mkandawire (2002) have attempted to decompose the economic growth in Malawi for the period of 1960–1997. They observe that physical capital per worker contributed more to the growth of real GDP per worker than education and total factor productivity. They note that for the period of 1960–1979, where GDP per capita had been high and increasing, the physical capital per worker had remained high. This is not a surprise as the investment rate was gradually increasing, while uncertainties over the political future of the country were over and with a peaceful transition, the government was able to lure foreign funds, either through grants or loans (see Table 2.9).

Beginning in 1979, the GDP per capita started falling as the upward trend in savings and investment reversed (Fig. 2.4).[22] The investment share of the GDP fell from 30.2% in 1979 to 12.3% in 1986 while the gross domestic savings fell from 14.9% to 10.1% in the same period. Consequently the growth of real GDP per capita and physical capital per worker both subsequently declined. This led to a large resource gap where an amount equivalent to K30 million in real terms (at constant 1978 prices) were needed each year to meet the country's total investment requirement

[22]This was due to a combination of inconsistent government policy choices and repressive financial operations.

(Malawi, 1986). The economic slowdown of this period set in a widening budget deficit and triggered an upward pressure on inflation (see Table 2.8). As a result, the share of gross fixed capital started to decline while public investment fell on average from 16.3% and 14.4% in 1976–1980 to 10.8% and 9% in 1981–1985 respectively. For the first time, the government's long-term development policies appeared to have lost focus and the economy was generally forced to continue to rely heavily on external sources of finance (Chipeta & Mkandawire, 2002).

2.3.1 Structure of the Financial System

Having a sound financial system has been shown to be necessary for performing critical market functions, such as payment facilitation, savings mobilization, risk diversification, resource allocation and trade integration. An increasing body of literature demonstrates that financial sector development is very closely linked to economic development (see for example, World Bank (1994), King and Levine (1993), Fry (1988) and Goldsmith (1969)). Although Malawi was a British protectorate from 1891, the country did not inherit either a well functioning financial system or a good economic infrastructure at independence. This was partly because the colonial government found no mineral resources and extensive agricultural development (which the country was suitable for) was discouraged due to high transportation costs and lack of sea outlet (Pryor, 1990). Because of these factors, the colonial government had little control over the economy and did not take bold steps to build integrated economic institutions. Up to 1964 Malawi had no central bank although even during the colonial period some foreign interests owned several commercial banks (Chipeta & Mkandawire, 1992). In the post-independence era, as the country moved to realize its own economic philosophy and development ideology the Reserve Bank of Malawi (RBM) was founded. This was necessary to regulate the market as well as ensure the proper functioning of various economic units. The RBM officially started its operation in June 1965 taking over Malawi's share of the assets and liabilities of the Bank of Rhodesia and Nyasaland (Chipeta & Mkandawire).[23] As financial systems in Sub-Saharan African countries have traditionally been characterized by, interest rates were controlled in Malawi, and credits were directed while prices were heavily regulated, particularly for the period of 1964–1979. These severe market interventions which lead to limited competition and groom inefficiencies are behavioural traits of financial institutions under a financially repressive regime (Gibson & Tsakalotos, 1994). Chipeta and Mkandawire (2002) observe that central bank policies in Malawi, specially in the 1960s and 1970s encouraged financial repression, characterized by direct controls of bank credit, interest rates, and free entry into the financial markets. The RBM was passive rather than active in encouraging new entrants in the financial and banking sector. The main function of the bank remained as the regulatory body of the

[23]This was an administrative federation to which Malawi belonged from 1954 to 1964.

banking sector and a major lender of the government but it played no major role in non-banking private sector. The banking sector has not been competitive as such, as the players were ever few. From independence, there were two banks (Barclays and Standard) which merged in 1971 to form the National Bank of Malawi (NBM). In 1970 a new commercial bank was established, named the Commercial Bank of Malawi (CBM).

It is surprising that up to the 1980s when the Malawian economy was growing remarkably, these two banks were the only commercial banks competing with few other Non-Bank Financial Institutions (NBFIs). Together for the period of 1964–1979 there were eight financial institutions including six NBFIs, of which only three were newly established (Chipeta & Mkandawire, 2002). Malawi experienced a high degree of financial repression from independence until the early 1980s, with administered interest rates, a credit ceiling, a segmented capital market and high intermediation costs. Apparently until July 1987 the RBM set the prime lending rates, allowing the central government borrow large amounts cheaply. Accordingly, for most of the 1970s and early 1980s the real interest rates were either very low or negative (refer to Table 2.14). Despite setting the prime lending rate, the central bank did not enforce any specific mechanism to mobilize savings beyond its regulative responsibility over the commercial banks (Cromwell, 1992). Commercial banks and other financial institutions determined by themselves what facilities to offer to the public as they created savings deposit instruments deemed profitable (Chirwa, 2001). Due to the passive role by the RBM there were no incentives for entrance by new financial institutions into the financial market as the old institutions consolidated their monopoly power. To some extent, this must have limited the resource mobilization since the Central Bank might have assisted in increasing the level of savings mobilization by playing a more active role in institutional development in the financial sector (Bhatt, 1986).

Despite the lack of competition in the banking sector, the commercial banks provided a large range of deposit instruments and a wider network of savings infrastructure which enabled steady increase of savings, particularly in the private sector. Chipeta and Mkandawire (1992) recognize that the major source of savings in Malawi has been the private sector, which accounted for more than 80% of total during 1972–1984. Interest rates data show that generally up until the end of the 1970s the real bank rates were positive (though quite low) as inflation remained minimal. This environment was favourable for private savings. With regard to this Pryor (1990) reports that for a large part of the 1970s, the time and savings accounts paid 2.5% above the banks' rate, providing depositors with a real positive return at very little risk since the government guaranteed the major banks. By 1983, the GDP growth was clearly slowing down, registering an average growth of 1.5% for the period of 1979–1984. Cromwell (1992) gives three major reasons for this downturn which ultimately triggered the decline in economic development. External factors have had a major influence on this as to begin with, the 1990 terms of trade were barely 59% of the 1970 level due to the relative fall in the world market prices of Malawian exports (mainly agricultural products). Specifically, the substantial reduction in the world prices of tea and tobacco was a major concern (refer to

Table 2.11 Selective economic indicators of Malawi (*annual average*)

Year	Agriculture (% GDP)	Manufacturing (% GDP)	Industry (% GDP)	Services (% GDP)	Export (% GDP)	Import (% GDP)	TOT
1965–1970	46.1	n.a	15.7	38.2	27.3	44.7	120.8
1971–1975	42.0	13.1	17.5	40.5	26.3	39.2	122.7
1976–1980	43.9	13.0	21.0	35.0	26.3	38.9	120.5
1981–1985	41.6	14.0	21.2	37.1	24.3	29.0	105.9
1986–1990	47.0	17.0	25.4	27.6	22.9	30.7	100.3
1991–1995	37.4	17.7	24.8	37.8	24.4	42.6	90.4
1996–2000	37.7	13.9	18.4	44.0	26.2	37.1	90.3

Note: Terms of Trade (TOT) is calculated taking 1987 = 100. Industry includes manufacturing, mining and construction sub-sectors of the economy. Whole GDP is composed of agriculture, industry and services while manufacturing is given since it is the leading sector in industry.

Table 2.11). Exports grew by only 0.6% a year from 1979 through 1985 compared to 5.8%, the average annual growth rate of 1964–1979 (Pryor). Further, the world oil price shock of the 1970s and the escalation of civil war in Mozambique led to an increase in the cost of imports as well as transportation cost.[24] Second, although the government's economic policy at post-independence was relatively clear, some of its plans were not spelled our explicitly (Pryor).[25] Inevitably, this gave rise to economic mismanagement as the government deficit continued to widen, averaging 10% of GDP in the 1970s. The central government had to sustain its budget through heavy borrowings, from both external and internal sources, consequently crowding out the private sector which largely contributed to economic growth and provided the largest share of the total savings (UNDP, 1999).

Third, Malawi's development plan was biased towards the agricultural sector as the government placed its highest priorities on it, ruling out the promotion of highly capital intensive manufacturing and industry sectors (Pryor, 1988).[26] This heavily concentrated strategy had a disastrous impact when Malawi's terms of trade deteriorated due to a shock in international world prices. This triggered serious structural problems as many agricultural estates that were highly geared were forced into bankruptcy. These economic complications led to a balance of payment crisis, debt rescheduling and necessitated frequent but partial restructuring of the economy in the early 1980s (Pryor, 1990). In an attempt to achieve balance of payment equilibrium, the government almost doubled its tariff rate in 1980 while quantitative restriction of inputs increased, a move that signalled government reversal on its former liberal trade policy (Chipeta & Mkandawire, 2002). These

[24]List of important events that had largely influenced economic performance in Malawi are given in Table 2.10.

[25]For example DevPol II and various trade policies were either differently implemented or ambiguously projected.

[26]Despite these agricultural oriented plans, the contribution of the manufacturing sector to the GDP in particular was significant during the 1970s (see Table 2.11).

Table 2.12 Annual average growth rates of various sectors (*percentage*)

Year	GDP	GDP p/c	Export	Import	Agriculture	Manufacturing
1965–1970	7.7	4.5	13.9	20.4	20.5	n.a
1971–1975	7.6	4.4	5.8	4.6	6.6	20.4
1976–1980	4.9	1.5	8.5	1.8	4.3	16.7
1981–1985	2.2	−1.0	2.7	−1.9	6.4	2.4
1986–1990	2.3	−0.9	1.9	3.2	1.3	3.6
1991–1995	3.5	1.9	1.5	−2.7	8.0	2.1
1996–2000	4.0	1.7	4.4	1.4	10.5	1.1

Source: World Bank, World Development Indicators.

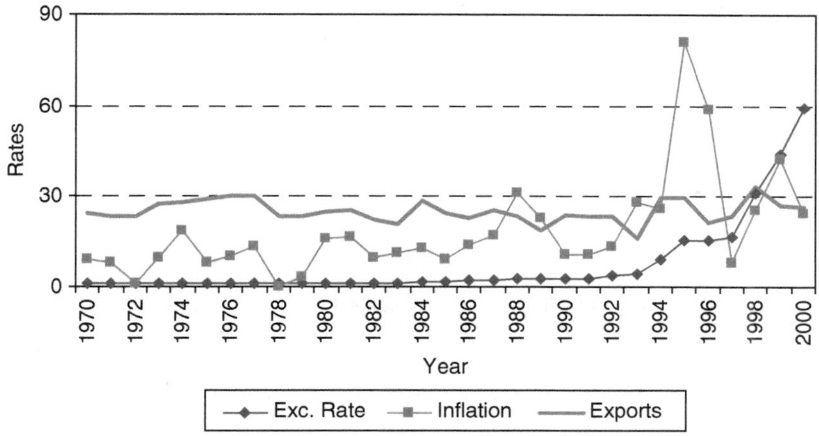

Fig. 2.5 Trends in selected macroeconomic indicators
Note: Exc. Rate is the official exchange rate, Inflation is CPI (Annual percentage) and Export is a percentage of GDP.
Source: IMF, International Financial Statistics (IFS).

measures somehow managed to discourage imports however, resulting in marginal growth in net exports (Table 2.12). Examination of the economic trend of Malawi from independence to 1979 shows that the country encouraged trade openness and, hence, export growth was sustained, contributing significantly to the GDP (see Table 2.11 and Table 2.12).

On the other hand, the country pursued a managed exchange rate system with the objectives of attaining real income growth, maintaining a viable balance of payment position and stable domestic prices (Malawi, 2000). Subsequently the Malawian Kwacha appeared undervalued for a large part of the 1970s as inflation remained under control (refer to Fig. 2.5). The growth in money supply remained moderate, closely matching the GDP growth (Pryor, 1990). Over time, as terms of trade worsened and the balance of payment problem was seriously exacerbated, the growth rate in money supply (M1) increased at an average annual rate of 27%,

Table 2.13 Measures of financial deepening in Malawi

Year	Deposit/GDP	M2 (%GDP)	M3 (%GDP)	DCP	TLCB
1971–1975	16.2	20.0	24.6	12.0	18.5
1976–1980	17.4	19.5	24.7	17.6	31.3
1981–1985	18.5	20.0	24.0	17.0	41.0
1986–1990	17.7	19.9	24.2	10.9	27.7
1991–1995	15.9	18.7	24.5	13.3	24.4
1996–2000	16.0	13.9	17.4	6.2	9.3

Note: DCP is the ratio of domestic credit to the private sector while TLCB is the total lending by the commercial banks.
Source: World Development Indicators and International Financial Statistics (IFS).

Table 2.14 Trends in various forms of interest rates in Malawi

Period	Lending rates	Deposit rates	T. bills	RIR (Bank)	RIR (T. bills)	RIR (Deposits)
1971–1975	8.5	4.4	5.6	−2.0	−3.3	−4.8
1976–1980	11.0	6.4	6.9	−1.3	−2.5	2.6
1981–1985	14.3	9.9	10.6	−2.5	−2.2	−2.7
1986–1990	18.7	11.6	13.7	−6.0	−4.4	−6.2
1991–1995	29.9	21.2	21.3	−5.0	−5.5	−6.7
1996–2000	43.6	24.4	24.6	10.2	−0.2	−6.0

Note: RIR is real interest rate in banks lending, deposit and treasury bills.
Source: World Development Indicators and International Financial Statistics (IFS).

inflicting an upward trend in inflation (refer to Fig. 2.5). To finance the deficit, the state increased its borrowing from the banking sector, receiving a large share of domestic credit (Table 2.13). This, together with the adverse external shock of 1979–1982, further depressed private income, which led to a fall in domestic savings (Chipeta & Mkandawire, 1992).

2.3.2 *Agricultural Sector and Other Policies Framework*

Since independence, agriculture has remained the largest economic sector in Malawi by serving as the major source of income and provision of employment. A typically small landlocked country with rich soil, agricultural production was suitable and further enhanced by abundance of labour force.[27] In both the 1970s and 1980s exports were largely agricultural oriented, accounting for more than 95% of raw and manufactured exports. Likewise in this regard it was estimated that 80–85%

[27]With difficulties in the capacity to create wage employment and uncertainties in wage policies, elasticity of employment in industrial sector was weak compared to the agricultural sector.

of the total population were employed in this sector during the same period (Cromwell, 1992). In the first two decades post-independence, the government's development policy initially centred on the agricultural sector. Land allocation, credit extension, and wage and other general government policies favoured agricultural development relative to other economic units (Pryor, 1990). Through government involvement, the agricultural sector was sub-divided into large scale commercial estate firms and smallholding farmers, most of them privately growing diverse crops in small and customary held lands as opposed to leasehold or freehold lands in the estate sector. These distinctions were particularly visible in tobacco, tea and sugar plantations (Chipeta & Mkandawire, 2002). Estate farmers enjoyed multiple privileges including cheap access to domestic credit, better infrastructure, reliable market information and competitive prices. Due to this, the agricultural sector enjoyed a higher annual average growth rate of 20.5% in the 1965–1970 period (see Table 2.12), causing estate sector's contribution to export to increase by 13% per annum over the period of 1973–1983 (Chipeta & Mkandawire). In this respect, agriculture played a leading role in the growth of the country's GDP and exports as it accounted for 46.1% and 42% of the GDP in 1965–1970 and 1971–1975 respectively, enabling real GDP growth of 7.7% and 7.6% in the same periods (see Table 2.11). The sector's role was further boosted by the temporary positive trade shock Malawi experienced, despite it being short lived (1977–1979)[28] before severe deteriorations terms of trade. Improvement in prices of tea (57% increase) which accounted for over one-fifth of Malawi's export, and a rise in tobacco prices (estimated to be 18.8%) which accounted for over 50% of the total export, led to a 19% total increase in terms of trade (Harrigan, 1999). The above trade improvement had an obvious impact on the disposable income level, government expenditure and tax policies. Since initially the windfall income accrued to the private sector, the government implemented revenue collection measures intended to raise government revenue (Harrigan). Likewise, because of the expansion in income base and the low level of inflation, the demand for industrial product increased (World Bank, 1988). Thus, the estate agricultural production expanded further and the industrial base broadened, facilitating import-substitution manufacturing enterprises to a considerable extent (Chipeta & Mkandawire, 2002).[29] As noted by Cromwell (1992), although the shock was temporary the public expenditure sky-rocketed, continuously exceeding the total revenue before finally resulting in a consistent overall deficit increase from 7.7% of GDP in 1976 to 10.1% in 1979 to a further 15.5% in 1980 (see also Table 2.8).[30]

Drastic deceleration of GDP growth set in around 1980, when the average annual growth rate of GDP fell from 4.9% to 2.2% in the periods of 1976–1980 and 1981–1985

[28]Refer to Harrigan (1999) for an examination of Malawi's temporary positive trade shock.

[29]Both Table 2.11 and Table 2.12 give the trend in contribution and average annual growth of the manufacturing sector, indicating that the sector's contribution to GDP was improving up to 1991–1995 although the average annual growth rates were only particularly high in 1971–1975 and 1976–1980.

[30]An extensive coverage of the fiscal pattern of 1970 to 1983 is also given by Harrigan (1999).

respectively (see Table 2.11) while the current account deficit increased sharply on average from 10.6% in 1971–1975 to 15.6% in 1976–1980. This dramatic downturn in growth was caused by many factors, of both an internal and external nature. Ballooning public parastatals, poor weather conditions, bad public management, deteriorating terms of trade, civil war in Mozambique and increased transport and utility cost are among the many factors that are believed to have contributed to such poor performance (Chipeta, 1993). Following this, the country embarked upon a number of stabilization measures aimed to restore macroeconomic stability and economic growth. Since the agricultural sector was the leading economic sector, the principal objectives of structural adjustment programmes focused on correcting the price determination policy and improving fiscal and monetary mechanisms (Chipeta). Three consecutive structural adjustment loans were made with the specific purpose of expanding the role of the private sector, by removing pricing and marketing constraints on smallholder agriculture and gradually increasing efficiency of land use and productivity, and enhancing the income of smallholder farmers (Cromwell, 1992). The above early reforms were implemented to rationalize domestic agricultural prices, liberalize marketing strategies – which were predominantly given to the Agricultural Development and Marketing Corporation (ADMARC) – and remove agricultural subsidies while granting smallholding farmers the choice to grow what was desirable to them (UNDP, 1999). The impact of the above reforms on the general economy was positive, though not significant. The real growth rate slightly improved on average from 2.2% to 2.3% from 1981–1985 to 1986–1990 respectively (Table 2.12). In the same period, the contribution of the agricultural sector to the GDP improved from 41.6% to 47%. This improvement had seemingly been enabled by the availability of imported inputs and more discretion by smallholder farmers to grow profitable product such as burley tobacco and other cash crops (Chipeta). However, UNDP (1999) notes that the growth of the smallholder sub-sector after reforms was hampered by higher and continually rising input costs. On the other hand, other macroeconomic instability (such as higher inflation, frequent devaluations and inadequate credit facilities) coupled with unfavourable internal terms of trade have cancelled out the effectiveness of the above corrective measures (see Fig. 2.5). Meanwhile, the structural reforms brought with them new public and quasi-public institutions such as the National Rural Development Programme and the Agricultural Sector Adjustment Credit, which was created in the late 1980s to improve the general standard of living in the rural areas and to help in expansion of smallholder farming while ADMARC was restructured (Cromwell). This did not bring about much improvement in the smallholder sub-sector since other market imperfections such as lack of market information and limited capabilities for marketing channels prevailed (Chipeta & Mkandawire, 2002). With the introduction of financial liberalization and improvement in the level of competition, the share of the agricultural sector's contribution to the GDP has been decreasing on average, from 47% in 1985–1990 to 37.7% in 1996–2000, while total exports have also seen downward moving trends (see Table 2.11 and Fig. 2.5).

During the reform period and even after financial sector liberalization, exports marginally improved; hence, it is observable from Table 2.11 that the economic liberalization overall did not feed to a remarkable expansion in trade. Both agriculture and exports were subsequently troubled by a series of currency depreciations which directly induced higher inflation (Fig. 2.5). In support this of argument, Chipeta and Mkandawire (2002) report a one-to-one relationship between elasticity of domestic inflation and currency devaluation. Since the post-independence policies were agriculture biased, the manufacturing sector was not considered for long-term transformation and contribution to the economy. Although the Malawi government did not have deliberate policies to expand the manufacturing sector, the general economic development of the 1960s and 1970s was favourable to this sector (Pryor, 1990). Initially, as savings improved and public investment expanded due to improvement in GDP in the early decades, venture into manufacturing was facilitated by the availability of capital as well as improvement in the level of infrastructure, indirect tax incentive and enhancement in the local demand (Chipeta & Mkandawire). But due to heavy price regulation and lack of qualified human resource, the sector could not flourish. As prices could not adjust upward, while input cost increased frequently due to a diminishing transport network and communication system, further burdened by frequent changing of government regulation, profitability in the sector was a major concern (Pryor). During the reform period, the contribution of the manufacturing sector slightly improved from 13% on average in 1976–1980 to 17% in 1986–1990 (see Table 2.11). As the budget deficit widened in the 1980s and external sources of funds drastically reduced (refer to Table 2.9), government borrowing crowded out the private sector's credit expansion. Partly this also limited the growth of the manufacturing industry in Malawi in post-structural reforms. But gradually with implementation of the reforms programme, prices were decontrolled and until recently, petrol and motor vehicle spare parts were the only major items covered by the price regulation scheme (UNDP, 1999). In the recent years and especially after 1990, the share of the manufacturing sector to GDP decreased from 17% on average in 1986–1990 to 13.9% in 1996–2000, which is barely different from the sector's contribution in the early 1970s.

Despite reforms in various dimensions, the gradual transformation of the manufacturing sector to the mainstream economy has not been possible, although the level of competition has improved. This scenario has been created by a number of factors. First, internal factors which include poor state of utilities and high transport cost have killed the growth of the sector. It is reported that Malawi has one of the highest internal transportation costs in Africa, estimated to account for almost 47% of imports as at 1997 (Chipeta & Mkandawire, 2002).[31] Second, an overvalued exchange rate in the 1970s and 1980s made it difficult to export and compete with foreign firm. Then, the unstable exchange regime in the 1990s, which directly induced high inflation during the structural adjustment programme, has

[31]Likewise Kayanula and Quartey (2000) estimate that cost, insurance and freight (CIF) margins increased from an average of 15% in early 1970s to about 40% during 1980s.

also not helped manufacturing. Thus, although devaluation may have increased the volume of exports in the short-term, in the long-run this jeopardizes the whole economy as it does not promote diversification.

Financial Reforms and Structural Adjustments: As discussed above, until the late 1990s Malawi's financial sector was generally repressed and inefficient (see Table 2.14). Although the government did not directly or fully own all assets in the banking sector, the ownership in the banking industry was highly concentrated (Chirwa, 2001). Other visible characteristics of financial repression included controlled interest rates, a ceiling on commercial banks credit expansion and relatively subsidized and directed fund flows (Chipeta & Mkadawire, 2002; UNDP, 1999; Cromwell, 1992; Pryor, 1990). As part of the World Bank and IMF recovery program proposed to most of the SSA countries, Malawi embarked on economy-wide structural reforms from the mid-1980s, which included reorganization of the country's financial system.

Financial reforms in Malawi took off in 1987 where lending interest rates were initially liberalized and subsequently deposit rates were also deregulated in 1988, while formally the government was geared towards abolishing the credit ceiling and rationing (Chirwa, 2001). The objectives of taking these determined steps in the financial sector were to facilitate competitiveness, enhance financial services offered and enable institutions to increase and introduce new financial products (UNDP, 1999). To accommodate the new changes and enlist ways to deal with any post-era ambiguities, new financial legislation was introduced.[32] These new legal frameworks significantly empowered the RBM and gave it the mandate to supervise, regulate and monitor effective running of the financial system. It was also given the powers to introduce indirect monetary instruments and amend entry regulations of new banks and other financial institutions into the financial system (Mlachila & Chirwa, 2002). Prior to the recent financial reform progress, there was modest development of the financial sector in Malawi. For many decades after independence, the formal financial system was dominated by RBM and two other large commercial banks (Nissanke & Aryeetey, 1998). The government heavily directed resource flows while the central bank had no direct role in promoting savings and investment beyond setting the level of interest rates (Chipeta & Mkandawire, 1992). As given in Table 2.15 and also discussed by Mlachila and Chirwa (2002) and Gelbard and Leite (1999), as at 1987 all the six indicators of financial development were ranked either minimally developed or underdeveloped. Overall, in 1987 the level of financial development in Malawi was generally underdeveloped. Subsequently, we can also asses the transformation of the financial system over a decade which coincided with the era of structural reforms that had begun in 1987. In total, there has been an improvement in all the indicators of financial development over the period. Among all other indices, market structure and competitiveness of the financial system were ranked highest in both 1997 and

[32] In this aspect the government amended the Reserve Bank Act 1965 and the Bank Act 1965 and enacted the Reserve Bank Act 1989 and the Bank Act 1989.

Table 2.15 Financial market transformation in Malawi

Indicator	Quartile 1987 index	Quartile 1997 index	Improvement (%)
Financial liberalization	20	43	115
Financial product	6	56	833
Financial openness	31	45	45
Monetary policy instruments	0	43	n.a
Market structure	56	62	11
Institutional environment	29	43	48
Overall	24 (Underdeveloped)	47 (Minimally Developed)	96

Source: Gelbard and Leite (1999).

1987, while over the period, indices of financial liberalization and financial products have seen the highest improvement, both recording more than 100% improvement. Similarly financial openness, institutional environment and monetary policy instrument indices have also seen remarkable changes over the decade. However, even though the financial sector in Malawi has seen 96% improvement in the overall index, it still largely remains minimally developed and far from being fully competitive and at par with the rest of the world.

2.4 The Case of Botswana

The post-independence period's economic performance of Botswana has shown it to be one of the fastest growing economies in the world, surprisingly when the economic stagnation and deterioration was widespread in the African continent. Extensive literature on the economic development of Botswana points out that the State of Botswana is a unique African institution, and the economic progress achieved within the short period of three decades has been described as 'impressive', 'exceptional', 'unusual', and 'a miracle' (see for example, Samatar (1999), Leith (1997), and Harvey (1992)). For the past two and half decades the country's growth has been one of the fastest in the world. More or less, during 1960–1990 Botswana was the fastest growing country in the world, with an average annual increase in GDP of 13.9% from 1965 to 1980 and 11.3% from 1980 to 1990 (Good, 1992). Overall, the average real GDP growth has been almost 10% for the period of 1960–2000, while real GDP per capita growth was above 7%. These rates are well above the average for Sub-Saharan Africa. Being a member of the African continent that has been characterized by economic mismanagement, complex economic and political instability and continuous ethnic conflict and tension, Botswana managed to achieve political stability and sustained economic development. In this perspective, the country has earned the reputation of having some of the most effective institutions and technocrats, the most efficient public sector management and sound and liberal democratic political system in Africa and indeed among developing countries in general (Sharma & Mhlauli, 1994). Botswana achieved its independence in 1966 and was geographically disadvantaged in the sense that the country is landlocked and predominantly tropical.[33] Additionally, it was classified as one of the poorest countries in the world and has since been transformed into one of the richest economies in Africa and is now grouped by the World Bank and the United Nations as an upper middle income country (Hope, 1997). When the country attained its independence, the GDP per capita stood at US$236 and, like many other less developed countries, was heavily dependent on foreign aid for all its recurrent and development spending. Since then, the economy has been moving positively and the average annual growth of the GDP per capita has been 5.6%, 11.2% and 6.4% for the decades of 1961–1970, 1971–1980 and 1981-1990 respectively. Similarly the share of investment to GDP has been increasing from 4.3% in 1960 to nearly 20% on average for the period of 1981-1990, recording the highest level of above 24% in the 1971–1980 period. This trend was necessary as the country had no infrastructure worthy of mention, no real telecommunication or power supply network and only had unreliable water and electricity supply when it achieved full independence. These all required urgent attention from the new independent state (Harland-Thunberg, 1978).

At independence, the economy was heavily dependent primarily on subsistence agriculture and the cattle industry, as the agricultural sector contributed 40.6% of the GDP in 1960 and 31.8% in 1965. The industry sector contributed only 13.6% and 19.7% respectively in the same periods (see Table 2.16). The country had a number of acute problems in the years after independence: a highly unskilled labour force,[34] shallow financial base, and hostile and racist neighbours (Samatar, 1999). This required an aggressive development plan capable of promoting economic development and at the same time reducing the political, institutional and economic problems. Samatar discusses that the government used a dual strategy to overcome

Table 2.16 Annual growth rate of various sectors *(annual percentage)*

Sector	1961–1970	1971–1980	1981–1990	1991–2000
GDP growth	8.7	15.2	10.1	4.8
GDP per capita	5.6	11.2	6.4	2.4
Agriculture	5.1	8.3	3.2	1.4
Manufacturing	1.1	19.7	9.7	4.4
Industry	10.8	17.4	10.7	2.8
Inflation	2.8	10.8	10.6	10.5
Population	4.0	4.0	3.0	2.5

Source: World Bank, World Development Indicators.

[33] It is estimated that only about 4% of all the land can easily be cultivated while the rest is either desert or barely suitable for grazing land (Acemoglu, Johnson & Robinson, 2001).

[34] Acemoglu, Johnson and Robinson (2001) remark that at independence there were only 22 Batswanans who were university graduates and 100 others from secondary school.

these problems. First, it kept very close ties with its former colonial power and other donors for financial support to run its annual budget and establish effective public administration. It further decided to remain within the Southern African Custom Union (SACU)[35] and renegotiate for a new formula of revenue distribution which enabled the country to receive a stream flows of revenue which were needed to implement various developmental plans. Second, it moved to retain any expatriate former protectorate officers willing to stay, while approving an immediate program of establishing institutional capacity to train Batswanans in significant numbers. This strategy not only enabled a smooth transition but allowed the government to have the necessary human resources for high level policy making and professional services, and effective implementation of the government plans. Effectively during the first decade of independence, growth in the GDP relied heavily on donors' aid which to a large extent financed whole of the development budget and almost half of the recurrent expenditure (Maipose & Matsheka, 2002). Two other events later boosted the pace of economic growth. Most importantly, the government's continued effort to exploit the country's natural resources paid off with the successful discovery and exploitation of a number of mineral resources, notably nickel, copper and later diamonds in the early 1970s. Secondly, the end of the drought and the modernization of the livestock industry which eventually resulted in Botswana gaining access to the EEC for beef export at prices above the world market was particularly a big boost for the agricultural sector and the economy as a whole (Maipose & Matsheka). In post-independence eight National Development Plans (NDP) were formulated and implemented. The eighth NDP (1997–2002) was launched in 1998. Each of these development plans were aimed to achieve four overall national development objectives of rapid economic growth, social justice, economic independence and sustained development.[36] In pursuing these objectives, Botswana needed to keep close ties with the outside world for budget financing before self sufficiency and afterwards for marketing its natural resources. Hence the country kept a very open economy, with both exports and imports accounting for a substantial ratio of the GDP (above 50%) and as the expansion of the diamond industry increased the export earnings, these ratios grew even higher during the period of 1981–1991 (refer to Table 2.19).

Looking at the savings and investment trends, it is obvious that savings were lower than investment before the mineral exploitation in late 1970s (Ahmed, 2006).[37,38] During this period, the foreign savings contributed significantly to the capital stock. Hence for the period of 1966–1989, the economic growth was to a considerable degree dependent on funds from abroad (Maipose & Matsheka, 2002). The productions of copper, nickel and diamond for export has increased the

[35]This union was founded in 1910 and Botswana has been a member since then.

[36]For further discussion on the specifics of these national development plans see Maipose and Matsheka (2002).

[37]This section is heavily based on facts, issues and analyses provided in Ahmed (2006)

[38]The analysis of savings and investment trends is depicted in Figure 2.6.

government revenue tremendously by virtue of its large shareholding and royalty payments. Due to this, the government revenue increased from US$540 million in 1985 to US$1.6 billion in 1994 (Hope, 1997). This large windfall for the state, particularly from diamonds, was managed effectively unlike in other African countries such as Nigeria, Angola, Zaire and Sierra Leone where abundance of such natural resources appeared to be a curse rather than a blessing. The increase in the government revenue in parallel with diamonds' income resulted in complementary avenues of employment creation and rural development, as the expenditure on infrastructure, education, health services and other social aspects increased proportionately.[39] Likewise the structure of institutions in Botswana limited domestic political instability and conflict over control of resources, something quite common in other Sub-Saharan African countries. Obviously, good institutions are not nature-given but something that evolves over time, and hence a plausible question that many have asked is how Botswana did acquire these institutions from the beginning. Unfortunately, a comprehensive answer to this question can only be given by looking at political and historical trends in the country even prior to the colonial era, something which is beyond the scope of this study. But generally there are two important factors that enabled the establishment of relatively 'good institutions' in Botswana. First, the existence of a strong tribal institution, particularly tribal chiefs, has encouraged broad participation in political and economic affairs (Acemoglu, Johnson, & Robinson, 2001). Moreover the *Tswana* customs of *kgotla* (town meeting) induced a strong tradition of participation and broad consultation at all levels of public life from village to central government (Maipose & Matsheka). Additionally, although there is a significant amount of ethnical diversity, the highly accommodating culture of Tswana (the largest tribe) coupled with the small size of the country configured a population that is largely homogenous. Second, the class of leadership during post-independence, particularly Khama and Masire,[40] set high ethical standards. This led to the establishment and continuity of a strong, independent, and accountable political elite and a civil service which remained committed to economic development within the framework of a largely democratic, liberal and competitive system.[41]

The rapid progress attained by Botswana has also brought about the sectoral transformation during the last three and half decades. The share of the industrial sector contribution to the GDP grew from 13.6% in 1960 to 54.6% in 1990. The sharp increase is largely due to the increasing level of mining activities in the period. The manufacturing sector's relative share remained almost unchanged as it accounted for 6% in 1960, 4.9% in 1990 and 5.3% in 1997 (Table 2.17). Maipose and Matsheka (2002) attribute the sluggishness in the growth of this sector to the small size of the domestic market, lack of skilled labour, free trade with SACU and

[39] A fairly detailed analysis on this can be found in Sharma and Mhlauli (1994).

[40] These are the first and second presidents of the country.

[41] Samatar (1999) devotes a whole chapter for the purpose of discussing the class of leadership in Botswana.

Table 2.17 Components of the GDP, 1966-2000 *(percentage share)*

Year	Agriculture	Manufacturing	Mining	Industry
1966	39.0	8.0	0.0	17.3
1975	25.4	6.9	12.5	32.5
1977	21.3	5.8	15.2	34.6
1979	13.1	3.7	31.2	44.0
1982	8.9	6.7	32.0	43.9
1985	5.5	5.2	47.2	56.1
1987	7.2	5.1	45.5	57.2
1989	4.8	5.0	51.2	61.1
1991	4.4	5.0	37.7	53.2
1993	4.4	4.6	35.7	47.8
2000	4.2	6.0	33.7	44.3

Source: World Bank, World Tables and Bank of Botswana annual reports.

high utility cost especially of electricity and water rates. On the other hand the contribution of the agricultural sector to the GDP has been declining over time. The share of the agricultural sector has shrunk from 40.6% in 1960 to 4.6% in 1990 while mining looks to have moved in the opposite direction in a similar magnitude (Table 2.17). Despite having some signs of mono-economy where diamond revenue constitutes more than 50% of the total government revenue, Botswana looks to have avoided 'Dutch disease' by investing a large share of these resources in physical and social infrastructure and other non-mining productive areas of the economy. Through its prudent management system, the government managed to channel surpluses away from the recurrent budget to be used in other areas prioritized to be beneficial for the country. Like other small open economies, the Botswana economy is exposed to a variety of external shocks which can have an immediate impact on its local economic affairs. The government revenue is highly dependent on mineral rent which is directly related to the foreign sector (Hope, 1997). Additionally foreign reserve earnings and customs revenue are highly externally influenced while the agricultural sector, especially the beef industry, is also directly affected by fluctuations in the world prices and environmental changes (Maipose & Matsheka). While subjected to all the above income vulnerability, Botswana has kept inflation relatively low and even recently it has been on a declining trend. The average annual rate of inflation was 10.8% in 1995 compared to 11.4% in 1990 and 12.7% in 1993.[42] Seemingly, by instituting a policy making process that develops the budget and monitors program implementation, Botswana was able to continuously keep a budget surplus and enforce a fiscal discipline which remained free from any serious political influence. On this point Maipose and Matsheka remark that the economic progress of Botswana was based on institutional quality and highlight four significant interrelated institutional factors. First, the institutionalization of a stable and largely less corrupt and more democratic system of government

[42]This depicted trend in the inflation seems to be very closely linked to the rates in South Africa, reflecting declining prices in both countries as discussed by Hope (1997).

that set exemplary leadership has helped to create public accountability, responsibility and transparency. Second, the establishment of national development planning and its integration with the annual budget process have avoided the many planning and budgetary conflicts that are common in other developing countries. Third, realistic and strategic state intervention in financing development plans and distributing wealth fairly has loosened physical and manpower constraints for successful economic transformation. Lastly, prudent macroeconomic management ensured economic and political stability while successfully avoiding ad hoc economic problems.

2.4.1 Structural Developments of the Financial System

At independence in 1966, Botswana was one of the poorest African countries, heavily dependent on foreign aid and colonial grants.[43] The country did not only have any independent financial structure but also infrastructure and communication system to support and promote economic development. From 1895, Botswana used various South African currencies as legal tender and did not regard it necessary to establish its own currency and monetary system until a decade after independence. Up to 1976, Botswana had been a member of the Rand Monetary Area (RMA) where all the monetary, foreign exchange policies and other economic policy instruments were directly determined by South African authorities.[44] Interest rates, foreign exchange rates and even exchange controls were all regulated by South Africa, without required consultation with the small member countries (Harvey, 1997). This gave Botswana little room for the necessary monetary and macroeconomic reforms during this period (Dahl, 1981). Additionally, because of the absence of a national central bank, almost all operating financial institutions were foreign subsidiaries with their headquarters in South Africa.

Despite lacking the flexibility necessary for conducting its own economic affairs and policy options to combat various internal and external shocks, Botswana continued to be part of the Rand Monetary Area for two major reasons. Firstly, the newly independent government of Botswana was indebted and relied heavily on grants for its expenditure due to its limited resources. For this reason, it was necessary to stay in the RMA to increase government income earned from custom's revenue. Under the South African Customs Union Agreement, withdrawing from the union would have drastically reduced the share of revenue due to Botswana. Secondly, having a serious shortage of skilled and educated labour, Botswana did not have the capacity to effectively run such an institution (Samatar, 1999).

[43]See Table 2.18 and further discussions later.

[44]With Botswana, the other two countries who used Rand currency issued by South Africa were Lesotho and Swaziland.

Moreover, hiring expatriates and professional services from abroad was clearly not an affordable alternative at that point. The country also could not afford the cost of creating new financial institutions for this purpose, as there were other important national projects such as infrastructure establishment and educational enhancement that the country needed urgently (Harvey, 1985). Instead, the government renegotiated the Customs Union Agreement in 1969 and signed a new formula where Botswana's share of customs union revenue was proportionately linked to growth in imports.[45] In this respect, despite achieving political independence, the Botswana government did not rush for economic independence for justifiable reasons. However other attempts were made to enable a liberal economic environment for the sake of attracting foreign investment as well as maintaining an open economy (Maipose & Matsheka, 2002). Commercial banks were free to allocate credit while individuals and institutions were able to freely invest their liquid funds in the Johannesburg money market (Harvey). Thus, the government's role was not to control but rather to 'assist the private sector in every way' in pursuance of the attainment of social and economic development goals (Harvey, 1996).[46]

Botswana's economy grew rapidly in the early 1970s due to expansion in mineral and other agricultural industry (cattle ranching). As a result the GDP (at constant 1974 prices) rose by 13% a year in the 10 years to 1977–1978 (Makgetla, 1982). Investment in infrastructure and other economic areas also increased significantly during this period (see Table 2.18 (a)). Increase in the mining activities (the share of mining as a percentage of GDP increased from 0% to 12% in 1975) and subsequent expansion in trade (exports) enabled the government to balance the recurrent budget expenditure by 1973 without grants-in-aid from the British government (Harvey and Lewis, 1990, p. 189).[47] As observable from Table 2.18 (b), the building up of foreign reserves together with a consistent increase in the government's share of the revenue transformed Botswana's finances. To an extent, this was a necessary condition for building an independent financial system. In 1976 Botswana took the alternative of setting up its own monetary institution to manage and direct its financial macroeconomic policies and hence withdrew from RMA. After the creation of the Bank of Botswana, which started operating in January 1976, a national currency 'Pula' was introduced (Dahl, 1981).

Looking at the banking sector, Botswana only had two foreign owned commercial banks in operation since independence: Standard and Barclays. Following the adoption of independent financial regulation, these two commercial banks were required to incorporate locally, even though the government maintained its former policy of non-interference in the affairs of these institutions. Unlike other African countries, there have been no changes in the ownership and control of these commercial banks despite their increasing dominance in the financial sector. To

[45]For an extended discussion of the renegotiation of the new Customs Union Agreement, see Harvey and Lewis (1990, pp. 189–192).

[46]This was outlined in the Transitional Plan for Social and Economic Development, 1966.

[47]See also Table 2.19.

Table 2.18 GDP per capita, investment, aid and foreign exchange reserves

(a) GDP per capita, investment and aid

Indicator	1966	1961–1970	1970	1971–1980	1980	1981–1990	1991–2000
GDP per capita	236	284	413	1062	1984	3,430	5,909
Investment (ratio of GDP)	12.5	11.1	23.6	24.1	20.7	18.4	16.0
Aid (ratio of GDI)	30.9	19.2	14.1	12.5	9.7	7.6	2.1

(b) Debt and foreign exchange reserves

Year	Foreign exchange (US$)	Import cover (No. Months)	Long-term debts (US$)
1976	75	4	169.1
1979	267	6	123.4
1983	396	7	230.1
1987	2,013	24	545.5
1991	3,719	24	613.2
1995	4,696	23	693.2
1999	6,240	29	454.7
2000	6,658	34	397.6

Note: The GDP per capita is at constant 1996 US$.
Source: Bank of Botswana Annual Reports, *Penn World Table* and Harvey and Lewis (1990).

instil business confidence and maintain an open economic system, the authorities opted for the use of indirect policy instruments rather than a direct market intervention policy widely used in other parts of Africa at that time, despite there being some concern and political pressure (Harvey & Lewis, 1990).[48] However, the creation of the Bank of Botswana and the introduction of the local currency 'Pula' decreased the power of the local banks to dictate interest rates and transfer funds abroad (Makgetla, 1982). Partly due to this, growth in credit by the commercial banks decreased from 46% in 1976 to 5% in 1979. On the other hand, to encourage foreign capital inflows and make more credit available to local borrowers, selective exchange controls (controls on capital account) with South Africa were introduced. In this regard, while residents were obliged to sell their portfolios in Rand, large corporations were also required to hold their liquid balances in Pula bank deposits (Harvey, 1996) under the new requirements.[49] These amendments and a continuous increase in mineral exports led to a steady increase in foreign exchange reserves from US$75 million in 1976 to US$267 million in 1979 (see also Table 2.19), while the government had on deposit at the Bank of Botswana between 30% and 50% of a year's current revenue for the period (Harvey, 1985).

However, it became obvious that the changes in the financial environment did not lead to a growth in the bank's lending activities. This was observable from the fact that commercial banks were making minimal advances to developmental sectors, such as manufacturing and other industrial activities, at a time when their liquid assets were more than the amount required for precautionary purposes (Makgetla, 1982). For this reason, the government claimed that there was a lack of long-term and project financing while domestic savings grew faster but were not utilized to accelerate economic development. Although the commercial banking sector argued that this was due to the lack of parallel long-term deposits, some evidence appear to supports the government's claim: (1) FDI inflows continued despite a significant

Table 2.19 Balances in various sectors (*as a percentage of GDP*)

Indicator	1971–1975	1976–1980	1981–1985	1986–1990	1991–1995	1996–2000
Budget balance	−7	−1	7	14	7	8
Current revenue	23	25	38	49	45	44
Expenditure	25	29	31	32	36	35
Exports	36	44	55	64	49	40
Imports	49	49	49	43	39	35
FDI	−2	7	4	3	−1	1

Note: Budget balances include grants while FDI means foreign direct investment.
Source: World Bank, World Development Indicators.

[48]Of specific concern was the behaviour of the commercial banks where, despite taking deposits from Botswana, they invested more than 50% of their funds outside the country when these funds were seriously needed to finance many development projects in the country.

[49]Additionally, to discourage large capital expatriation, foreign companies were not allowed to borrow more than they brought into the country.

build up in the country's reserves in the late 1970s and 1980s (see Table 2.19). Since FDI comes with technical, management and necessary market links, foreigners must have observed that there were good investment projects, which local investors did not take up. (2) Because commercial banks' excess liquidity build up increased from 32% in 1976 to nearly 60% in 1981 (Harvey, 1996), it appeared these institutions were not taking the initiatives to expand their investment horizons.

Concerned with the size of the long-term lending by the commercial banking sector, the government tried to remedy the situation by giving a number of incentives to compel the investment of resources in productive activities. The margin between prime lending rate and the return on additional liquid assets was allowed to increase from 3.5% to 6.5% points between 1975 and 1979, with the aim of giving more incentive to lending (Harvey, 1996). Additionally, Botswana's interest rates were lowered in the hope that more businesses would be established in the country, since interest rate differentials were significant, and lending terms made easier (see Fig. 2.6). Further, to increase long-term deposits available to the banks (since they claimed it was not possible to make project lending out of short-term deposits) the government also deposited some of its surpluses for a long term, while enabling the commercial banks to take cattle as security against loans (Harvey, 1985). However, these incentives were ineffective. As noted by Harvey and Lewis (1990), there are two reasons as to why these measures did not work. First, commercial banks were making enormous profits from their existing business (short term loans and foreign exchange transactions). Therefore, there was little need for banks to take the considerable effort to invest their resources into new and unconventional projects. Second, these commercial banks did not have the staff with the necessary experience and skills to evaluate and nominate long-term projects. With the higher risk of undertaking new investment initiatives, banks were reluctant to pursue business lines in which they were neither supported for nor technically equipped to adopt.

The problem of over-liquidity became even more serious in 1978 when the Bank of Botswana had to act as the deposit taker of last resort (Harvey & Lewis, 1990, p. 223). Primarily, this was created by the mining and government sectors which had large savings deposits but little need for any loans, while in the other sectors of the economy, there were few investment projects matching the requirements for the commercial banks. With these problems, there was an increasingly need for a new set of financial institutions, to identify and support a new range of borrowers. A number of financial parastatals came into existence for this purpose. The National Development Bank (NDB) and the Botswana Development Corporation (BDC) were formed with the main aim of extending credit to parastatals and other productive agencies as a mechanism to handle extra liquidity (Makgetla, 1982). Furthermore, these institutions were also meant to ease the availability and provision of finance on terms better adapted to local circumstances. With these changes and the gradual institutional and financial market development, including the establishment of the Botswana Stock Market (BSM), the financial system in Botswana overall improved from being minimally developed in 1987 (with an index of 49 compared to 33 for SSA average) to somewhat developed in 1997

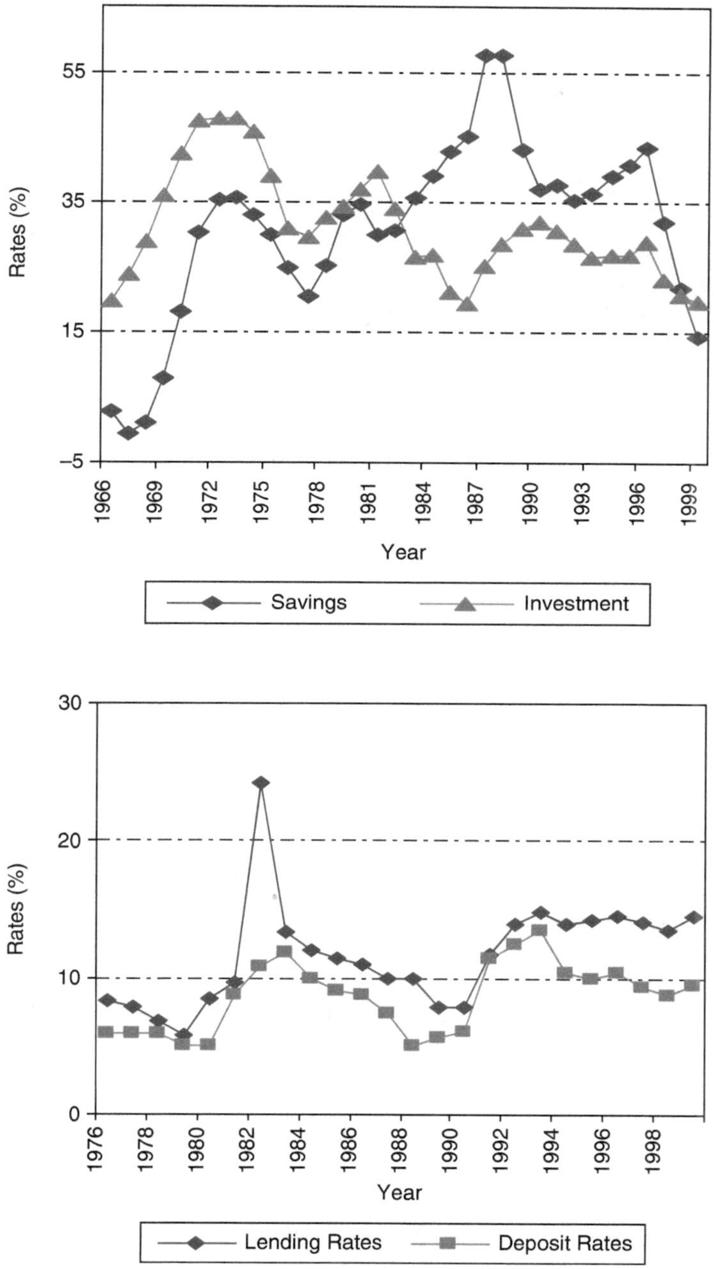

Fig. 2.6 Interest rate, savings and investment trends in Botswana
Source: IMF, International Financial Statistics, IFS (various issues).

Table 2.20 Financial development index in Botswana

Indicator	1987 Level	Index	1997 Level	Index
Market structure	Largely developed	76	Largely developed	92
Financial product	Underdeveloped	17	Somewhat developed	51
Financial liberalization	Repressed	20	Somewhat liberalized	65
Institutional environment	Somewhat supportive	71	Somewhat supportive	71
Financial openness	Somewhat open	54	Minimally open	46
Monetary policy	Minimally developed	29	Somewhat developed	71
Overall development	Minimally developed	49	Somewhat developed	62
Highest – Overall development	Largely developed	77	Largely developed	87
SSA – Overall development	Minimally developed	33	Somewhat developed	56

Source: Gelbard and Leite (1999).

(with an index of 62 compared to 56 for SSA average). Botswana's financial system index scores above the SSA in both 1987 and 1997 although the level of improvement is marginal, just 27% over the decade (see Table 2.20). In support of this process, there was an increase in the accumulation of financial assets and liabilities in the economic system, reflecting growth in the monetarization process (see the trend and behaviour of M2 and M3 in Figure 2.9).

2.4.2 Supplementing Role of Foreign Aid in Botswana: The Two-Gap Model

In a small open economy, such as is the case in most of developing countries, there are generally two major constraints; lower level of savings which ultimately limits investment and foreign exchange constraint which also limits the ability of importing skill intensive capital goods. Imports, particularly of capital goods and machineries play an important role in international transfer technology and enhance local technological innovation. This has formally been discussed by Williamson (1983) as two-gap model (referring to saving and foreign exchange constraints). Taking the case of a developing economy where two goods are produced, capital intensive good K_c is always imported while labour intensive good K_l is exported.

Let us denote α and β as fixed input coefficients per unit of both labour and capital intensive goods and assuming full employment,[50] then:

$$S = (\alpha + \beta)\Delta Y \tag{2.1}$$

where S is the savings necessary to finance change in output and ΔY is change in output. Further in an open economy imports affect level of savings and hence:

[50] Here we are considering savings necessary to finance both goods K_c and K_l.

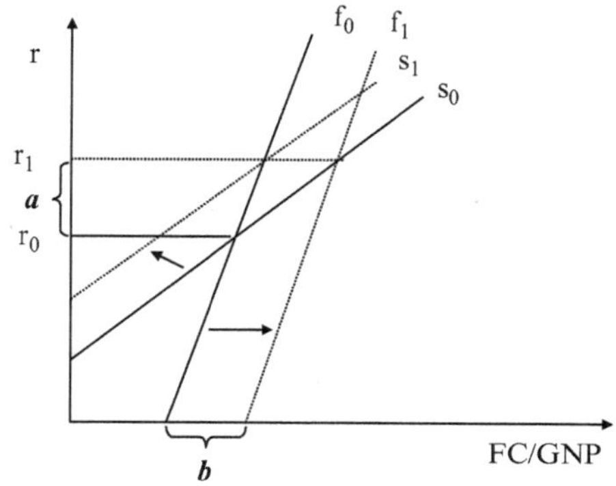

Fig. 2.7 Savings and Foreign exchange constraint

$$S_d = s(1 - m)Y \tag{2.2}$$

where S_d is the total domestic savings. When domestic savings can be supplemented by foreign savings (either through aid or private capital inflows) to finance growth in output then:

$$\Delta Y = \left\{ \frac{s(1 - m) + \eta}{\alpha + \beta} \right\} Y \tag{2.3}$$

Here η denotes the portion of foreign capital inflows. Deriving growth equation from the above we get:

$$r = \Delta Y / Y = \frac{s(1 - m) + \eta}{c} \tag{2.4}$$

where r is the growth in the national income and c is the incremental capital output ratio $(\alpha + \beta)$. The above growth equation indicates that growth is positively related to rate of savings and foreign capital inflow while it is negatively related to the incremental capital output ratio. Figure 2.7 shows diagrammatical representation of the two-gap model.

Growth in the national income is shown in the y-axis denoted by r. S_0 shows savings constraint which increases with an increase in marginal propensity to save out of domestic income, s, and decreases with the marginal propensity to import. Foreign capital-GNP ratio is shown on x-axis denoted by FC while line f_0 shows foreign exchange constraint, determined negatively by export-GNP ratio and positively by marginal propensity to import.

As also noted by Frimpong-Ansah and Ingham (1992) and indicated by the diagram, the national growth rate can either be raised by an increase in the domestic savings rate or an increase in foreign capital inflow (i.e. either by change a or b). Typically Botswana's rapid economic growth highly depended on foreign capital (aid and private inflows). Aid constituted almost 31% of gross domestic investment

Fig. 2.8 Aid decline as savings rate increases in Botswana

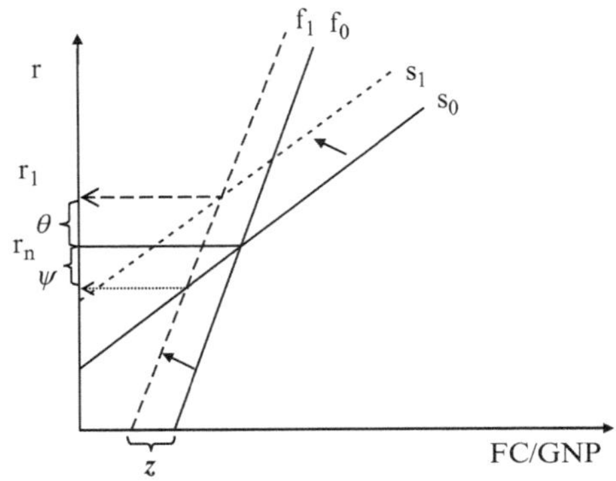

in 1966 and reached an average of 17.2% for the period 1961–1970 (see Table 2.18) while foreign direct investment has been improving though marginally (Table 2.19). On the other hand, domestic savings as a percentage of GDP was negative in the early years after independence improving continuously to reach its peak in 1990s with an average of 42% between 1986 and 1990 (refer to Table 2.19 and Fig. 2.6). In parallel the country's debt increased from US$169.1 million 1976 to US$545.5 million in 1987 while foreign exchange reserves continued to rise from US$75 million to US$2013 million in the same period (Table 2.18).[51]

Initially, Botswana relied almost entirely on aid to finance its budget and hence attracted grants from an increasing number of donors through efficient management of aid-finance projects (Harvey & Lewis, 1990). Indeed Botswana has had the highest per capita aid in sub-Saharan Africa and foreign capital in the form of grants which continued to flow even after the country attained middle-income status (Maipose & Matsheka, 2002). In Figure 2.8 we denote Botswana's move from aid-dependent to self-sustained growth path.

The country initially depended on foreign capital inflows to supplement domestic savings. Botswana effectively managed its aid resources and was able to sustain the economic growth with decreasing dependence on aid. In Figure 2.8, national income growth increases from r_0 to r_1 as a result of increases in savings rate. Hence savings constraint line shifts from s_0 to s_1 whereas foreign constraint line shifts from f_0 to f_1. This demonstrate that decline in aid is exactly compensated for by an increase in domestic saving equivalent toψ. The portion θ represents the net additional growth after fully compensating for reduction in aid-foreign capital inflows, which further stimulate more savings.

Typically as income grew, domestic savings increased continuously, whereas the marginal rate of savings was higher than the marginal rate of investment, the savings gap declined overtime. Similarly the foreign exchange gap became gradually less restrictive as exports increased faster than the increase in imports.

---

[51]Good (1992) notes that external debt stood at US$14miilion in 1970.

2.4.3 Trends and Policies in Agriculture and other Sectors

Botswana is situated in the centre of the Southern African Plateau and is totally landlocked. It is not an ideal country for arable farming as the soil is of poor fertility and the rainfall is low (Jones, 1981). Prior to independence, and even up to the late 1960s, Botswana depended heavily on agriculture (see Table 2.17). The sector contributed about one-third of the GDP although since 1970s its importance has been diminishing. According to the 1964 census, almost 90% of the economically active population was engaged in agriculture and as at 1971 the rate was as high as 86% (Harvey & Lewis, 1990). In 1966, agriculture contributed about 39% of the GDP. Effectively, cattle raising remained the major agricultural activity, accounting for about 80% of the marketed agricultural output in 1966 (Harland-Thunberg, 1978). As crop agriculture has never been a major source of income in rural Botswana, important government policies have been biased towards the livestock sector which was a major export earning source before mineral exploitation. Immediately after independence the government took direct action to improve the management of the national herd to improve its quality and value as an economic resource. A livestock diseases control program was launched where steps were taken to enhance animal health, and a Tribal Grazing Land programme was implemented to provide adequate grazing space (Harvey & Lewis). The impact of this was immediately realized as Botswana gained access to the European Economic Community (EEC) for beef export at prices above the world market. The cattle population increased by 8% during the years 1970–1975 as a result of these encouraging policies. Hence, from 1966 to 1977, the net sales of the Botswana Meat Commission (BMC) which had exclusive export rights of beef and cattle increased from P7 million to P42 million (Hubbard, 1981). In recent years, the contribution of the agricultural sector to the GDP has been reducing. As noted in Table 2.17, the share of the sector in GDP has shrunk from 39% in 1966 to 4.2% in 2000, compared with the mining sector that rose from zero to almost 34% in the same period. But this does not mean that the sector is no longer important. The magnitude of public investment has been quite high although increase in agricultural productivity and output has been low. The government's planned development spending in various NDP plans[52] for the agricultural sector has been large relative to revenue from the sector in the post-independence period. The government generously supported the industry with revenue from diamond exports, as it has stepped in on many occasions to pay BMC's tax liabilities when the institution had not performed well (Samatar, 1999). In the recent past, the government has shown commitment to economic diversification including ways to improve agricultural contributions as this has been the main focus of NDP8 (1997–2001). Ultimately, the state intends to achieve structural transformation where large revenue from the diamond sector can be used to boost the growth of non-mineral sectors to reduce the

[52]Harvey and Lewis (1990) give a breakdown of planned development spending on agriculture. This spending has been significantly increasing from NDP2 (1970–1974) to NDP5 (1980–1984).

degree of dependency on the vulnerable mining sector only for growth (BoB, 2000) In spite of various initiatives to spur growth in the sector, such as the restructuring of the Botswana Agricultural Marketing Board and easing of financial assistance, the sector's contribution continues to fall. Such a progressive decline in agriculture in the 1980s and 1990s has to a great extent been caused by natural phenomena such as unfavourable weather conditions and persistent drought combined with a number of structural problems (BoB).

Like many other African countries in the region, Botswana had minimal industrial development at the time of independence, as indicated in Table 2.17. The contribution of the industrial sector in 1966 was 17%. A large part of this was due to the cattle industry, led by the BMC which exported meat after minimal processing including tinning and freezing. This accounted for a large proportion of manufacturing activities estimated to be more than one-third (Makgetla, 1982). Other forms of manufacturing or production were almost entirely non-existent as the country lacked adequate power supply, infrastructure and communication facilities. Meanwhile, the share of the mining sector rose from almost zero to nearly 34%, reaching its peak of 51% in 1989. The opening and exploration of three diamond mines[53] (Orapa, Letlhakane and Jwaneng) in the 1980s and copper-nickel mines at Selebi-Phikwe in the 1970s provided much of the stimulus to growth in other sectors such as government and infrastructure. Hence the Botswanan economy expanded rapidly from a moderate average GDP growth rate of 8.7% in 1961–1970 to 15.2% in 1971–1980. In the same period the average annual growth rate in the industry increased from 10.8% to a record of 17.4% in a decade. These changes had an impact on the rest of the economy. Total fixed capital formation, exports and government revenue increased significantly, and resulted in two investment booms in 1969–1974 and 1977–1981 (Fig. 2.6).[54] These booms were led by heavy investment in the mining sector as both Letlhakane and Jwaneng mines were underway. Despite Botswana's rapid rate of economic growth and high level of foreign reserves, the structure of the manufacturing sector did not change. The share of the manufacturing sector has remained almost constant, contributing 6% of the GDP in 2000 compared to 8% in 1966. Due to this, the new economic development strategy issued by the government in NDP8 (1997–2002) stresses the importance of transforming mineral endowment into an endowment of physical and human capital (Maipose & Matsheka, 2002). In this regard, the government initiated a number of Financial Assistance Programs (FAPs) to encourage labour intensive operations and to provide capital grants to small-to-medium sized industries while extending subsidies to infant industries (Harvey & Lewis, 1990). There are a number of reasons why the growth of the manufacturing sector has been modest. First, Botswana still remains a member of SACU where South Africa plays a dominant

[53]Note that the Orapa mine was opened in 1971 and expanded in 1978, the Letlhakane mine was opened in 1976 and the Jwaneng mine was opened in 1976 and expanded in 1983 (Hill & Knight, 1999).

[54]Harvey and Lewis (1990) analyse the impact of these two booms on the whole economy and on the mining and non-mining sectors.

role. Although Botswana receives a good share of the customs union revenue, such membership is detrimental to the rate of industrialization as citizens and businesses have complete access to inexpensive and indirectly subsidized South African products (Maipose & Matsheka). Hence young and small local industries will find it hard to compete with such well-established foreign industries. Second, even though capital is generally available in Botswana, other constraints such as the shortage of skilled labour – particularly in technological, professional and managerial positions – still exist. Likewise the cost of production is high, as water and electricity rates are higher relative to Zimbabwe and South Africa (Harvey & Lewis). This partially explains why the manufacturing sector has not provided the expected impetus to the economy and, therefore, under such circumstances, the ability of producers to export and significantly compete with imports from internationally competitive firms is hindered without some level of protection. In the immediate years after independence, the country was dependent on foreign support for all its development expenditure and more than half of its recurrent expenditure. Savings had been negative or marginally low (see Fig. 2.6). Domestic savings as a share of GDP was negative in the mid 1960s, low in the late 1960s before reaching 17% in 1970. During this period, the ratio of investment to GDP had been increasing. This difference was largely financed by capital from abroad. Aid as a percentage of GDP stood at 31% in 1966 and, on average, recorded more than 19% between 1961 and 1970 (refer to Table 2.18). Similarly, foreign direct investment (as a percentage of GDP) was increasing and remained positive on average until the late 1990s (see Table 2.19). Between 1966 and 1970 investment ratios were high in Botswana recording 30% on average, while in the next half decade they reached the peak of 45%. These high levels of investment were necessary due to the expansion in infrastructure and exploration in copper/nickel and diamonds which were underway during the period.

Because of expansion in mining exports and a rise in imports, public revenue almost quadrupled in 1976–1980 (Oden, 1981). Between 1971 and 1975, the savings ratio improved to almost 33%. Hence, the rapidly increasing revenue enabled the government to finance its entire current budget and a substantial share of the capital budget with locally generated funds.[55] The discovery of mineral resources further enhanced the country's image in attracting foreign capital. As its source of revenue expanded, the government saved an increasing share of its income. In the period 1971–1975, public savings was 15% compared to 6% in the private sector. It is not surprising that the real development expenditure in 1967–1987 grew at an average annual real rate of 12.6%, and, in spite of this, the revenue growth was consistently more than the growth in expenditure (Hill & Knight, 1999). The continuous increase in exports over imports enhanced foreign exchange accumulation and the growth of government cash balances at the central bank. Resultantly, the savings pace increased more than investment over time and finally outmatched investment levels in 1986 (Fig. 2.6), and until recently, saving rates in Botswana

[55] A detailed statistical breakdown for the period of 1976–1980 is given by Oden (1981).

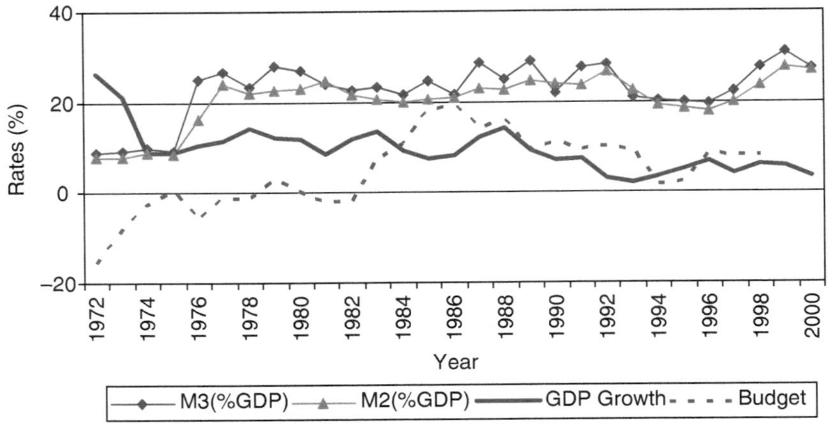

Fig. 2.9 Performance analysis in Botswana
Source: African Development Indicators and International Financial Statistics (IFS)

remained higher than investments. Ultimately, domestic savings financed almost all of the government finance capital formation for the first time in 1984 while foreign capital inflow still remained positive. With constant increases in mineral exports, Botswana's balance of payment has also transformed. Overall, the country had a balance of payment surplus by 1980, and, except for the 3 years of the diamond depression period (1980–1982), where Botswana's terms of trade fell significantly due to a rapid rise in import prices and a significant fall in diamond exports, the balance of payments was mainly surplus (Fig. 2.9).[56] As the positive diamond shock gradually improved the balance of payments position, exports also increased rapidly. This gradually resulted in an appreciation in the exchange rate (the famous Dutch disease effect) which, in turn, would have harmed the non-booming tradable sector (Hill & Knight). The government realized this effect and intervened in time, introducing necessary policies to prevent the contraction of non-boom tradables through controlling real appreciation in the exchange rate. Furthermore, real appreciation would have reduced export diversification by making manufacturing exports unprofitable. More than this, however, it would have decreased the import-substitution process in both manufacturing and agricultural sectors by making imports cheaper relative to domestic production (Harvey & Lewis, 1990). Likewise, both the recurrent and development expenditure grew faster over the period of 1966–1987, and hence, such excessive spending by the government would have caused rising trends in costs in Botswana compared to its major trading partners. This is reflected in inflation which had been consistently increasing in the same period.

To moderate the abovementioned effects, the government used an exchange rate policy. The main objectives of the exchange rate policy in Botswana were to

[56]For a complete discussion of the nature, causes and impact of the diamond boom and shock in Botswana, see Hill and Knight (1999).

achieve international competitiveness in pricing and to manage inflation, particularly by avoiding imported inflation from main trading partners as much as possible through import prices (Harvey & Lewis, 1990). Oden (1981) observed that, on average, more than 70% of significant increases in inflation during the period of 1976–1981 were imported, especially from South Africa. This was not untypical as the Botswana economy remained extremely open which is reflected by, among other things, high imports of goods and services which, on average, corresponded to close to 50% of the GDP in 1976–1980 (as given in Table 2.19). To curb inflation, the Pula was revalued upwards consistently by 5% in 1977, 1979 and 1980.[57] These revaluations were expected to have a favourable effect also on income distribution. This is because, in Botswana, poor people have a higher import propensity (more than 70%) relative to the rich (almost 40%) since the poor spend largely on imported basic foodstuffs, whereas the rich spend significant amounts on locally produced products and services (Hill & Knight, 1999). It was also estimated that reductions in inflation would feed back into lower wage increases, and hence, the net effect of exchange rate and income policy would not be, in total, to make the country uncompetitive (Harvey & Lewis).

From the 1970s, government revenue was transformed from being heavily dependent on beef and customs revenue to being almost entirely dependent on mineral income. Before 1976, the revenue growth was led equally by customs revenue and mineral revenue. In contrast, after the 1976 mineral revenues accounted for more than 60% of government revenue, and as at 1986 they reached 72%, whereas tax and customs revenues accounted for only 16% (Hill & Knight, 1999). Thus, when the demand for higher quality gems fell sharply in 1980–1982 – due to a serious recession in the diamond market especially in industrialized countries – Botswana was hit hard. With the opening and expansion of the Orapa mine in 1979 diamond production increased rapidly. But the country was not able to sell, and effectively from August 1981 onwards, diamond exports stopped (Hill & Knight).[58] As depicted in Fig. 2.9, this caused a serious balance of payments problem. In 1982, the government implemented a package of measures aimed to adjust the economy to the fall in the diamond revenue which included 10% devaluation in the Pula (Harvey, 1985). Other measures which were indeed undertaken included a wage freeze, restrictions in credit and increases in interest rates. Although these measures worked to control the shock, the Pula was again devalued by 15% in 1985 in order to avoid a loss of international competitiveness, and to correct an upward drift of the Pula against the Rand (Harvey). The policy objectives of the exchange rate in recent years remained to maintain a stable environment for the export sector as the government geared towards achieving economic diversification. Unlike previous instances where the main concerns were either curbing inflation or

[57]While most of the African countries had a fixed exchange rate during the 1970s and 1980s, Botswana adopted flexible exchange regimes earlier and more frequently relative to other SSA. Probably this positioned the country more competitively and helped it face booms and slumps.

[58]Formally this only continued for 3 months before exports returned to their normal level.

widening income distribution, the recent trend has been leaning towards promoting economic diversification by enhancing non-traditional manufacturing in both production and exports.[59] Hence the Bank of Botswana has focused on maintaining stable and competitive real effective exchange rates for the Pula.

2.5 The Thai Financial System

Financial sector reforms in Thailand started back in 1987 to achieve and sustain high rates of economic growth. Thus from late 1980s to mid 1990s Thai economy has witnessed various forms of market liberalization and globalization, resulting a more open and an integrated financial system. This market reforms and relaxation led to massive investment in Thailand's stock market and inflow of foreign capital and investment into the domestic economy. Thailand's financial system and stock market is made up of eight major financial institutions, performing different and specialized financial roles. This includes commercial banks; specialized banks; development finance corporations; the stock exchange; finance, securities, and credit companies; saving cooperatives; insurance companies; and other mortgage institutions (Islam & Wanapalachaikul, 2005, p. 13). Although commercial banks account for 71% of the financial assets, other specialized financial institutions (such as Government Saving Bank, the Industrial Finance Corporation of Thailand, the Bank for Agriculture and Agricultural Cooperatives) also play a major role in financial mobilization (Warr & Nidhiprabha, 1996) and, together with a well-developed foreign exchange market, aid domestic banking business and investment (Ho, 1991).

Similar to the African countries we have discussed above, reforms priorities in Thailand mainly included a comprehensive financial deregulation to enhance foreign trade, promote greater financial intermediation, encourage financial deepening and improve productivity of investment. Thus interest rate deregulation and relaxation of exchange rate and capital controls was the core of Thailand's reform policies and financial liberalization programme. Supported by a further improvement of supervision and examination of financial institutions, these changes have led to the development of better financial instruments, services and the payments system (Islam & Wanapalachaikul, 2005, p. 17). The country achieved a high private investment growth, became a leading destination for international foreign capital and recorded rapid and sustained economic growth during this period, although the financial system became vulnerable to shocks and unstable as evidenced in the fact that the Asian financial crisis in 1999 (Hansanti, Islam & Sheehan, 2008) started in Thailand.

[59]The recent exchange rate objectives are as stated in the Bank of Botswana Annual Report 2000.

2.6 Conclusion

This chapter aimed to give background and status of the four countries of our sample before and during the era of the structural adjustment program. It turns out that the success of economic stabilization and liberalization aimed at improving efficiency and increasing investment and productivity depends on underlying economic foundations as well as commitments of the individual country. Kenya and Malawi have taken similar development strategies where even though reforms were market-oriented, government expenditure and fiscal indiscipline have often limited private sector activities. These countries had pervasive economic intervention and imposed controls which skewed resource allocation and discouraged financial and institutional development. This, to a large extent, must have negated the traditional economic role played by the private sector and hence limited the effective contribution to the economic development. These high level interventions discouraged savings mobilization. Contrastingly, markets in Botswana faced modest intervention in the pre-stabilization period. In most cases those interventions were intended to foster financial intermediation (to induce allocational efficiency) and encourage the general level of lending in the economy.

In all the four countries, financial liberalization was undertaken to integrate the financial system and strengthen the regulatory framework. Accordingly, reforms encouraged financial sector development and enhanced private agents' involvement in all the three countries. However, governments financing requirements and increased macroeconomic uncertainties have reportedly rendered the contribution of such market-based economic transformation to be at best negligible in emerging economies especially in Kenya and Malawi.

Given the mixed experience of financial reform in African and Asian (Thailand) countries, it is essential to evaluate the specific and quantitative impact of financial liberalization in terms of allocative efficiency, savings, financial intermediation and risk-sharing, fiscal condition and social welfare in these countries. Further, it is important to assess the monetary and non-monetary gains to the society and to consider and capture all direct and indirect benefits and costs in an attempt to sum all the impact for financial liberalization and globalization in each period before using appropriate technique (cost-benefit analysis model) to calculate its net social welfare impact.

Chapter 3
Literature Review

"To the man who only has a hammer in the toolkit, every problem looks like a nail"
Maslow (1908–1970)

3.1 Introduction

The role of finance in the economic development is not something of a recent discovery and the literature on the importance of the financial system for economic growth is voluminous. Bagehot (1873), Schumpeter (1911), Robinson (1952) and Gurley and Shaw (1955), among others, have written on the subject of the relationship between financial development and economic development. Bagehot (1873) notes that the financial system played a critical role in igniting industrialization in England by mobilizing capital effectively and efficiently. Schumpeter (1911) asserts that there is a positive influence by the development of the financial sector on the level and rate of growth of a country's per capita income. This led to the belief by many development economists that the financial system has considerable importance for economic growth. Specifically, there seems to be a strong belief that lack of a developed financial system impedes economic development, and therefore policy makers should enact policies that encourage and strengthen the existence of a proper financial system. Some have taken a more neutral position and argue that like any other factors that serve as an ingredient for economic development, the development of the financial sector is not a necessary condition but can only fairly be ranked *pari passu* with other numerous inputs (Newlyn & Avramides, 1977). At the extreme other end, some have argued that the financial system has a minor role to play in the development of the general economy and merely enables the players in the private sector to 'make' and 'lose' money. This view, which is termed as the 'casino hypothesis'[1] of the financial system would simply mean that policy makers might easily ignore the need for strengthening such an institution.

[1]Kitchen (1986) termed 'casino hypothesis' the views of a group that do not consider the financial sector as an important contributor to the general economic development.

A.D. Ahmed and S.M.N. Islam, *Financial Liberalization in Developing Countries*, Contributions to Economics,
DOI: 10.1007/978-3-7908-2168-0_3, © Springer Physica-Verlag Berlin Heidelberg 2010

But why is the development of the financial system important? By answering this question the link between financial and economic development will become clear to us. Attempts to answer this question have resulted in a range of literature on the subject. Indeed among others, Gurley and Shaw (1967), Goldsmith (1969), McKinnon (1973) and Shaw (1973) represent some of the more comprehensive efforts to cover this subject. Leading the others, Goldsmith (1969) tested the relationship between the financial system and economic development. Using representative data from a mixture of 35 developed and developing countries for the period of 1860–1963, his finding indicated that the presence of a financial institution enables the surplus unit (an economic unit that has more income than it spends) to save in financial assets as well as the deficit unit (an economic unit that has spending greater than its level of income) to invest in excess of their level of savings. Choosing the financial interrelations ratio (FIR)[2] to characterize the level of a country's financial development, he finds that developed countries had a higher FIR than the less-developed countries. This suggested that there was a rough close correlation between a country's financial development and its level of economic development.

One can then further ask, if financial development and the level of economic development are correlated, what exact role do financial markets play? If financial systems enhance the level of interaction between savers and investors, then, it should somehow, directly or indirectly, influence the rate of economic growth. Goldsmith (1969) states that in the absence of a financial superstructure, the attainment of a required capital investment greater than a firm's individual savings will be impossible and the presence of a financial markets allow firms to operate at the minimum cost level (including cost of funds) while increasing the marginal productivity of capital. The development of financial institutions and instruments facilitates investors who have projects that require a considerable amount of capital expenditure to be financed by savings from elsewhere. It becomes quite clear that if an economy is financially under-developed, the transfer of funds (savings) from one individual to another will be minimal, and hence the only investment possible will have to come out of personal savings. In such a scenario, resources may not be utilized properly as many agents who want to invest in rewarding projects might not do so, while others who have the ability to save will have no incentive to do so. Indeed then, in this manner the development of financial institutions, instruments, and markets will provide increased opportunities for both borrowers and lenders. With the creation of specialized capital and security markets, best investors and investments will be recognized and rewarded, and funds are channelled to the most efficient projects, resulting in higher returns. In addition Kitchen (1986) recognizes that financial institutions perform other vital roles. First, the role of maturity transformation; the creation of financial institutions permits savers to save in short-term assets and maintain their liquidity plans while investors will be able to

[2] Goldsmith (1969) calculated FIR by taking the value of all financial instruments outstanding divided by the value of national wealth.

acquire long-term funds. It is through this intermediation that each group will be able to meet its specific requirement simultaneously. Second, financial institutions play the role of risk transfer. In lending and borrowing both savers and investors have some level of risk. Savers do not posses the skill or the legal 'muscle' necessary to protect their loans, hence the need for a financial intermediary, in whom savers have confidence. Finally, financial institutions will then provide funds to many savers and thereby diversify risk. It is such a capacity that the presence of financial institutions affects the level of economic activity. By performing the above functions, the existence of a financial system substantially increases the mobilization of savings and the level of investment which, at least in a theoretical sense, affects the rate of economic development. In this context Goldsmith (1969) appeared to have a resolved position when he remarked:-

> The theoretical discussion of the effect of financial superstructure on economic development may then be concluded, with some but not a decisive loss of accuracy into one statement; the financial superstructure, in the form of both primary and secondary securities accelerates economic growth and improves economic performance to the extent that it facilitates the migration of funds to the best user (p. 400).

3.2 Financial Development and Economic Development

Based on the theoretical foundations we have stated above, various studies have considered the importance of financial development on economic growth. A significant number of theoretical works have incorporated financial factors in growth models to analyse more formally the interactions between financial institutions and economic development. Rajan and Zingales (1998) examined whether financial development facilitates economic growth by analysing the impact of financial development on the cost of external finance to firms. Their study shed light on channels through which financial development spurs development. Their evidence suggests that financial development has a substantial supportive influence on the rate of economic growth by decreasing the cost of external finance of financially dependent firms. They postulated that financial development (which was proxied by the level of credit and the size of the stock market) may predict economic growth simply because financial markets anticipate future growth, stock markets capitalize 'the present value' of growth opportunities, while the crucial role of financial institution is to evaluate and lend more to specific sectors with growth potential. Similar results were also reported by some previous studies. In particular, Greenwood and Jovanovic (1990) developed a model to test the extent to which financial intermediation[3] and economic growth are endogenously determined. They concluded that financial intermediaries can invest more productively than individuals

[3]Financial intermediation is the process where financial institutions act as a middle agent to transfer funds from savers to potential borrowers while providing both these groups of investors the opportunity to earn a return (Kitchen, 1986, p. 12).

since institutions have stronger abilities to identify investment opportunities. Therefore financial intermediation promotes growth, since it allows a higher rate of return to be earned on capital. From the contentious conclusion of Goldsmith (1969) which documented a financial and economic development relationship, development economists have rigorously considered the channels through which the emergence of financial markets and institutions affect economic development.[4] Levine (1997) notes that a significant number of empirical analyses from different studies including firm level, industry level, individual country studies and cross-country comparisons indicate that there exists a strong positive link between the functioning of a financial system and long-run economic growth. From the results of his investigation, he concludes that:-

> I believe that we will not have a sufficient understanding of long-run growth until we understand the evolution and functioning of financial systems. This conclusion about financial development and long-run growth has an important corollary: although financial panics and recessions are critical issues, the finance-growth link goes beyond the relationship between finance and short-term fluctuations (p. 721).

Emphasizing the role of the financial system, Levine (1997) looked at what necessitated the emergence of financial markets and institutions. Importantly, the need for fund mobilization, cost of acquiring information, and risk management led to this evolution. Hence, the major roles of a financial system remained facilitating trade and risk management, allocation of resources, mobilization of savings, enabling the exchange of goods and services, and providing public information. Considering this, the more developed and efficient a financial system is, the better it can direct resources, foster efficient investment and support long-run development. In line with this view, Berthelemy and Varoudakis (1996b) observed that insufficient financial development has often created a poverty trap, through limiting the capacity of savings and its allocation, and hence has become a severe obstacle to economic growth even when a country has other necessary conditions for sustained economic development, such as political and economic stability, educational attainment and trade openness. Berthelemy and Varoudakis (1996a) summarised the importance of a financial system for economic development when they indicated that there are three major functions played by a strong financial system: (1) it ensures the working of an efficient system of payment, (2) it facilitates the mobilization of savings and (3) it improves the allocation of savings to investment.

Further, De Gregorio and Guidotti (1995) examined the relationship between long-run growth and financial development (where they took ratio of bank to private sector and GDP as a proxy for financial development). Their findings indicate that there is a positive correlation between financial development and growth in a large cross-country sample. However, their results were not conclusive and the impact varied across countries and over time. Particularly, their results showed a negative and significant effect of credit on growth in a panel data for Latin America. This finding constituted some of the first evidence of

[4] For detailed analysis and discussion of diversified views on this refer to Levine (1997).

cases where there exists a negative and robust relationship between financial intermediation and economic growth. The basis of the result is supported by the experience of unregulated financial liberalization in, and high expectation of government bailout of, Latin American countries between 1970s and 1980s. Thus their evidence predicts that the move from financial repression to financial liberalization requires a stable and appropriate regulatory framework to avoid any backlash. De Gregorio and Guidotti (1995) also further looked at the channel of transmission. Their analysis suggests that except for high income countries, the effect of financial development on the volume of investment is relatively small and hence the main channel from financial development to growth seems to have come from increased efficiency of investment rather than its level. Table 3.1 below gives various mechanisms through which financial sector development enhances economic progress.

In a somewhat similar study, Rousseau (2002) examined how well the available historical time series supports the role of financial factors in real sector activity in four economies that were generally considered as 'financial revolutionist' over the past 400 years. An analysis using data from the Dutch republic (1600–1794), England (1700–1850), the United States (1790–1850) and Japan (1880–1913) indicates that the emergence of financial institutions, instruments and markets played an important role in promoting trade, commerce and industrialization. Precisely the above literature has shown that the link between financial and economic development exists, though the direction of causality is not conclusive.

Table 3.1 Financial development and economic growth: evidence from some previous studies

Mechanism to influence growth	Study	Data
Improving efficiency of investment	De Gregorio and Guidotti (1995)	1950–1985
Similar results in:	Becivenga and Smith (1991)	
	Greenwood and Javanovic (1990)	
Liquidity risk management	Levine (1991)	–
Similar results in:	Bencivenga and Smith (1991), Levine (1992)	
Technological specialization	Saint-Paul (1992)	–
Turnover* and law enforcement	Demirguc-Kunt and Maksimovic (1996)	1980–1991
Similar results in:	King and Levine (1993)	
	Levine and Zervos (1998)	
Market liquidity (stock market and banks)	Levine and Zervos (1998)	1976–1993
Similar results in:	Levine (1991), Bencivenga et al. (1995)	
	Rousseau and Wachtel (2000)	
Reducing the cost of external finance	Rajan and Zingales (1998)	1980–1990

Note: *This refers to general stock market turnover while – indicates the study was theoretical.

3.3 Financial Liberalization

From the seminal papers of Goldsmith (1969), Shaw (1973), and Mckinnon (1973), there has been a clear criticism against financial repression and a call for financial liberalization of financial markets. In the decades of the 1970s through the 1980s, it was a common feature that a significant number of developing countries were characterized by the phenomenon of 'financial repression'. There are various ways and mechanisms that the government can intervene in the normal market working conditions. Financial repression policies include, but are not limited to, subsidizing loans for specific sectors, heavily regulating the banking sector, and putting a ceiling on interest rates. Berthelemy and Varoudekis (1996a) define all such policies and regulations which prevent financial intermediation from operating in accordance with their technological full potential as forms of financial repression. Financial repression is generally equated with controls on interest rates and, in a strict sense, controls which result in negative real interest rates on deposits (Kitchen, 1986). In most developing countries these practices are common, and are imposed by governments resulting in a distorted actual interest rate from the equilibrium rate of interest that would prevail in a competitive financial system. In a broad sense, financial repression also includes other government restrictions which do not encourage the proper existence of and development in financial institutions and instruments, resulting in weak, uncompetitive and fragmented financial markets.[5] With regard to this, many researchers and authors in economics have attempted to demonstrate the problems related to financial repression.

Berthelemy and Varoudekis (1996a) highlight the cost of financial repression as: Putting a ceiling on the rate of interest that the banks pay on deposits limits the size of funds intermediated, causing a reduction in deposits and a lower level of credit supply, which in turn results in unnecessary and artificial increase in the cost of borrowing. Furthermore, with little savings available, this causes a reduction in the capacity of the banking system to create credit and therefore affects the size of the banking sector. Thus the shrinking of financial markets and its intermediation role could negatively influence the rate of economic development. Likewise Kitchen (1986) hinted at the weakness of financial repression when he said:

> It should be noted that a repressed interest rate system impinges on the current assets of enterprises, as well as on the investment in fixed assets. If credit is scarce or rationed, then a firm's capacity utilization may be restricted, because it cannot obtain credit to finance its working capital... liberalization of interest rates, leading to greater availability of short-term credit, may have the effect of increasing the utilization of existing capital stock (p. 82).

Here we review a few of those early theoretical works which gave the groundwork for modelling a financially repressive developing economy. In a simple two-sector model which assumes a traditional sector with a lower rate of return on capital (r_1)

[5]For analysis of other forms of government regulations that are common features of financial repression refer to Berthelemy and Varoudekis (1996a, p. 39).

and a modern sector with a higher return on capital (r_2), Galbis (1977) demonstrates the inefficiencies caused by a repressive financial regime and the associated lower investment and output levels. In an environment where output (Y) is competitively produced he specifies that:

$$Y = Y_1 + Y_2 = r_1K_1 + w_1L_1 + r_2K_2 + w_2L_2 \tag{3.1}$$

where r and w are respective returns for factors of input capital and labour employed. With the assumption that total capital is constant, capital in the second sector (K_2) can only be raised by proportionately decreasing that of sector 1 (K_1). However since return on capital in the second sector is higher, this increases the aggregate output (Y). To consider the savings-investment decisions in each sector, Galbis (1977) postulates that:

$$I_1 = H_1(r_1, d - \pi^*)Y_1 \tag{3.2}$$

where $\partial I_1/\partial r_1 > 0$, $\partial I_1/\partial(d - \pi^*) < 0$ and $d - \pi^*$ is the real rate of interest on deposits (where π^* is expected rate of inflation). Sector 1 is self-financing and therefore its investment decisions are only influenced by the rate of return on capital and real return on bank deposits. Given this, the savings (S) of the sector are then composed of investment in physical capital and other financial deposits with the banking system. Thus:

$$S_1 = I_1 + \frac{d}{dt}(M_1/P) \tag{3.3}$$

where (M_1/ P) represents real deposit balances of the banking system. On the other hand, sector 2 has an alternative source of funds since it can borrow to finance investment needed that is in excess of its own savings from banks. Therefore:

$$I_2^S = S_2 + \frac{d}{dt}(M_1/P) = \frac{d}{dt}(M_2/P)^S \tag{3.4}$$

The above equation represents the supply of investible resources for the modern sector (sector 2). Clearly, this is the sum of its own savings and the accumulated bank deposits from sector one. Moreover, the investment decision of sector 2 is not only affected by the rate of return on capital (r_2) but also by the real loan rate.

$$I_2^D = H_2(r_2, l - \pi^*)Y_2 \tag{3.5}$$

where $\partial I_2/\partial r_2 > 0$ and $\partial I_2/\partial(l - \pi^*) < 0$ while $l - \pi^*$ is the real lending rate (where l is nominal lending rate). Given that money supply in equation (3.4) is fixed at a pre-judged level and real lending is set by authorities at a rate (say $(l - \pi^*)_{\text{set}}$) that is below the market equilibrium and assuming a simple incremental money demand in the second sector, we get:

$$\frac{d}{dt}(M_2/P)^D_{set} = \beta I^D_2 = \beta H_2\big(r_2, (l - \pi^*)_{set}\big)Y_2 \tag{3.6}$$

where β represents the fraction of credit demand for investment purposes. A number of relationships can be outlined from the Galbis (1977) model. First, a decrease in the real deposit rate would directly reduce the volume of bank deposits which will be made available for credits. This negatively influences both investment in sector 2 and overall output level (Y). Second, when $d - \pi^*$ is lower, investment in sector 1 (I_1) increases, thereby increasing the proportion of inefficient investment inducing the economy to suffer from lower rate of growth and loss of income, since $r_2 > r_1$. Third, because demand and supply of investible resources are in disequilibria while interest rates are fixed (since demand for credit is not reduced through response in l while deposits are not allowed to increase through d), this leads to higher inflation further reducing real rates of interest on the financial assets (Sikorski, 1996, p. 78). Ultimately to correct such economic inefficiencies and imbalances, a policy of liberalized financial environment will be required.

A few years later Mathieson (1980) also analyzed the dynamics of stabilization and financial reform programs. Following Kapur (1976) and assuming an economy with an unlimited supply of labour, as typically characterized by a developing country, he specified an output (Y) and capital (K) relationship such that:

$$Y = \sigma K \tag{3.7}$$

where σ is output/capital ratio. Capital constitutes both fixed and working, and a fixed proportion θ of all capital is financed by bank loans. Thus the real demand for loan is given as:

$$\frac{L}{P} = \theta K \tag{3.8}$$

where P is the general price level. Mathieson then gives the firms' capital accumulation behaviour and defines their savings by:

$$\mathring{K} = s(r_K - l + \pi^*)Y \tag{3.9}$$

Clearly the rate of capital accumulation is a function of the return on capital, r_k, and real loan rate of interest. This equation also gives the demand for new loans. On the other hand, the supply of bank loans is not only determined by demand but also the rate of the reserve requirement (k). Thus:

$$\frac{L}{P} = (1 - k)\frac{D}{P} \tag{3.10}$$

Additionally the demand is identified as a positive function of real income and the real deposit rate:

$$\frac{D}{P} = f(d - \pi^*)Y \tag{3.11}$$

With a little manipulation and applying (3.9) the rate of economic growth y $(\dot{Y}/Y)$ is derived as:

$$\gamma = s(r_K - l + \pi^*)\sigma \tag{3.12}$$

Observably γ is positively influenced by the real return on capital, output/capital ratio and expected rate of inflation and negatively with the nominal lending rate. Finally in the steady state with zero cost of banking while utilizing (3.8) and (3.10) an equilibrium deposit rate is given as:

$$d = f(d - \pi^*) = \frac{\theta}{(1-k)\sigma} \tag{3.13}$$

This rate is positively related to the proportion of funds channelled by the financial system and reserve ratio, and negatively related to the output/capital ratio.

Moreover, in the steady state and with the assumption of zero banking cost and non-interest earning reserves:

$$d = (1-k)l \tag{3.14}$$

From (3.14) and as pointed out by Fry (1982) a number of relationships can be depicted. First, since l and d are positively related, if l alone is fixed by the authorities and the banking system is competitive, the deposit rate will still be related to this loan rate through $l = (d/1-k)$. Second, if l is fixed below its competitive market equilibrium, d will also be sub-optimal leading to a lower level of capital investment (K) through L/P. However with a lower rate of lending, savings will be higher through (3.9) inflicting a disequilibrium market scenario. Thus in this process, a loan rate ceiling could be evaded and market equilibrium restored through reducing reserve requirements and/or inflation rate, or by paying interest on reserve balances.

Extending this and the analysis of the effect of financial conditions by McKinnon-Shaw, Fry (1982) showed the interdependency between savings, investment and economic growth which can be enhanced by innovative financial markets. Beginning his modelling by specifying a national savings function he proceeds:

$$\frac{S_n}{Y} = f\left[\gamma^+, \frac{S_f}{Y}, d - \pi^*, r^*, \left(\frac{S_n}{Y}\right)_{t-1}\right] \tag{3.15}$$

$$\frac{\partial s_n/Y}{\partial \gamma^+} > 0, \frac{\partial s_n/Y}{\partial s_f/Y} < 0, \frac{\partial s_n/Y}{\partial d - \pi^*} > 0, \frac{\partial s_n/Y}{\partial r^*} > 0, \frac{\partial s_n/Y}{\partial (s_n/Y)_{t-1}} > 0$$

where s_n/Y is national savings, s_f/Y is the foreign savings rate, $\gamma^+$is the long-run or the normal growth rate, r^* is the expected real return on investment when self-financed and other terms are as defined previously. With this savings rate specification, he also outlines investment (I/Y) to depend on r^* and the real effective lending rate, $l - \pi^*$, where:

$$\frac{I}{Y} = \left(s_n/Y + s_f/Y\right) \tag{3.16}$$

In this set-up, with a binding deposit rate ceiling (as required under repressive financial policies) and a non-price banking competition (which does not influence real demand for money), the feedback process of investment through the interest rate to savings made available is eliminated. Here, the lending rate, l, simply plays the role of merely equating investment to some predetermined savings rate. Related to these savings and investment rates is also the long-run (normal) growth rate. This is determined by the previous year's investment level and the efficiency associated with that investment. Linking efficiency to output/capital ratio, σ', Fry (1982) elaborates that this is determined by the real rate of deposit:

$$\sigma' = f\left[(d - \pi^*)_{t-1}\right] \text{ where } \frac{\partial \sigma'}{\partial (d - \pi^*)_{t-1}} > 0 \text{ and } \sigma' = \gamma_t^+/(\mathrm{I}/\mathrm{Y})_{t-1} \tag{3.17}$$

Therefore by combining these relationships, the long-run (normal) growth rate is:

$$\gamma^+ = \frac{f\left[\left(\gamma^+, \frac{s_f}{Y}, d - \pi^*, r^*, \left(\frac{s_n}{Y}\right)_{t-1}\right) + \left(\frac{s_f}{Y}\right)_{t-1}\right]}{1/f\left[(d - \pi^*)_{t-1}\right]} \tag{3.18}$$

where in the steady state of equilibrium actual growth is equal to the normal growth rate. Further, using a standard form of real money demand function, the inflation rate is derived as:

$$\pi = \mu - n - b\gamma^* - a\Delta(d - \pi^*)$$

In this equation μ is the rate of monetary expansion, n is the rate of population growth and γ^* is the rate of change in per capita real performance income. For the case of most developing counties, it is anticipated that b>1. Consequently, an increase in the deposit rate towards its market equilibrium will raise γ and reduce inflation at the same time. Thus Fry shows that, through these repressive financial mechanisms, the economy will suffer a reduction in the rate of economic growth.

Considering the financial-economic development nexus together with recognition of the cost of financial repression raised awareness of the need for financial liberalization. Policy recommendations from economic think tanks as well as from world financial bodies such as the World Bank and the IMF were policies of financial liberalization. Hence, most developing countries embraced the idea, while Bretton Wood organizations designed a loan package meant to ease the borrowing constraints for such countries. A significant number of studies looked at the impact of financial liberalization programs from various directions. Jaramillo, Schiantarelli, and Weiss (1992) looked at micro-evidence to trace the credit trend after liberalization. Using data from Ecuadorian firms for the period of the 1980s, they find an increase in the flow of credit to technologically more efficient firms after liberalization. This evidence shows more efficient allocation of resources after adjustment. Similarly, Galindo, Micco, and Ordonez (2001) examined whether financial liberalization improves the allocation of investment in developing countries. Their objective was to assess whether such a program succeeds in directing resources towards those uses which result in higher marginal returns. Using firm level panel data from 12 developing countries, they find that in the majority of cases, financial reforms have led to an increase in the efficiency with which investment funds are allocated. Two indices of efficiency in allocation of investment are calculated using sales per unit of capital and operating profits per unit of capital. Applying different groups of countries, they find general evidence that the efficiency index is positive and significant following introduction of liberalization measures. Therefore, their results are very supportive of the idea that financial liberalization leads to an improvement in resource allocation. Loayza, Schmidt-Hebbel and Servén (2000) empirically tested the effect of policy variables on saving rates. This study examined the effectiveness of policies such as fiscal, financial linearization, and consumer and housing lending in raising the level of saving. In what they believe to be the largest cross-country time series macroeconomic data set on savings assembled to date, covering a 30 year period and from a combination of industrialized and developing countries, they find: (1) the effects of financial liberalization are largely detrimental to private savings while greater financial depth and a higher real interest rate do not raise the level of saving.[6] (2) The private saving rate rises with the level and growth of real per capita income. Hence policies that spur development indirectly raise the private saving rate. (3) A change in fiscal policy such as an increase in public saving is an efficient mechanism to raise national saving. (4) An increase in macroeconomic uncertainty (inflation taken as a proxy measure) induces people to save more, confirming the precautionary motive for saving. These findings are quite interesting, particularly with respect to financial liberalization and financial development variables. Both high interest rates and larger private domestic credit flows exert a negative effect on the private saving rate. This evidence is contrary to Mckinnon and Shaw's hypothesis.

[6]The author defines saving as Gross National Disposable Income (GNDI) less consumption expenditure, both measured at current prices.

Over the last 25–30 years many developing countries have made important national policy decisions to liberalize. There has been a claim that adopting financial liberalization will enable countries to benefit from the frontier of financial technology which the large volume of endogenous growth literature has shown will lead to increased growth (see among others Saint Paul (1992); Bencivenga and Smith (1991); Greenwood and Javanovic (1990)). Bekaert, Harvey and Lundblad (2001) investigated whether financial liberalization spurs growth. Using four different data samples from 95 countries and the panel data technique, they find that financial liberalization leads to a 1% increase in annual real per capita GDP growth over a 5 year period. The results predict that liberalization contributes 4.1% of total growth over 3 years, 5.7% over 5 years and 8.2% over 10 years. In general this shows that 70% of liberalization's effect on growth takes place in the 5 years following the liberalization. On the channel of transmission through which financial liberalization affects growth, Bekaert et al. observe that (1) liberalization is associated with higher significant investment to GDP ratio, (2) financial liberalization lowers the cost of capital through reducing the capital market imperfection, enhancing external flow of funds, (3) liberalization improves the efficiency of capital allocation and hence influences the rate of economic development. All together, they predict a positive relationship between financial liberalization and growth, and conclude that it contributes approximately 40% of the total growth increment.

The numerous studies that prophesize financial liberalization claim that it derives various advantages which directly or indirectly contribute to economic development. It is argued that liberalization improves the functioning of the financial system, facilitates cross-country diversification, channels world saving into their most productive uses beyond boundaries, increases the availability of funds and encourages transparency and accountability (Obstfeld (1998), Mishkin (2001), and Stulz (1999)). Considering these issues, Kaminsky and Schmukler (2002) investigated the short-term and long-term effects of financial liberalization on capital markets, paying particular attention to any possible time-varying effect using a database from 28 countries[7] for the period of 1973–1999. Kaminsky and Schmukler (2002) focused on booms and busts in stock market prices. The result indicated that financial liberalization is followed by more pronounced boom-bust cycles in the short-run. Importantly the result also showed that liberalization has been a smooth process in most developed markets while it has been characterized by interruptions in emerging markets, notably cases of capital controls, government intervention and some degree of restriction. The study also looks at the problems associated with liberalization. In most developing countries at pre-liberalization, the level of inefficient allocation is high or at least significant and domestic markets are protected from outside pressure. At liberalization, competition increases and banks' profit lowers.[8] Considering the countries' pre-liberalization poor evaluation and screening

[7] The sample countries though were regionally fully representative; they were taken from Asia, Latin America, Europe and G-7.

[8] This is also associated with decline in bank franchise value after financial liberalization. Demirguc-Kunt and Detragiache (1998) gives further analysis on this.

procedure in the domestic market, post-liberalization the share of good loans may decrease, as interest rates rise, leading to further moral hazard problems. Hence there will be a need for institutional reforms at some stage of liberalization, whether before or after. Kaminsky and Schmukler (2002) consider this argument further and observe that institutional reform does not predate liberalization but rather in most cases reforms are implemented within a few years after the opening of the financial market. In such an environment, liberalization may unveil a new problem that could lead to some form of financial crises.

Many studies indicated that financial development enhances the efficiency in the allocation of resources, while having a stronger financial system reduces the liquidity risk and enables the management of risk by both saver and investors.[9] Therefore, ideally financial intermediaries exist to channel savings into long-term assets that are more productive than into short-term assets and directly enhance the growth process. Allen and Ndikumana (1998) investigated the role of financial intermediation in stimulating economic growth for the members of the Southern African Development Community (SADC). Using the panel data technique and a data set from SADC countries, they test the hypothesis that financial intermediation has a positive impact on economic growth. Their result shows that financial development[10] (proxied by credit to the private sector, volume of credit provided by banks and liquid liability of financial system (M3)) is positively and significantly related to economic growth.

Although the link between financial liberalization and financial development has been documented in part through empirical evidence, suggesting that financial liberalization can increase the rate of future economic growth, others have pointed out some possible drawbacks in this process. An important critique of the movement towards financial liberalization is its negative effect on savings accumulation, particularly from the household sector. Borrowing constraints pre-reforms and prudence by households to shield themselves against unexpected shocks (such as uncertainty about future income) generate precautionary savings. However, as financial reforms ease borrowing constraints, this may encourage households to accumulate less saving before major purchase and hence stimulate consumption rather than savings (Japelli and Pagano, 1989). Liberalization of financial markets, together with other reforms, can lead to higher economic growth through contributing to the efficiency with which financial markets transform financial resources into savings, and thus reducing financial constraints of firms and boosting overall investment. However, this may not necessarily be the case in Sub-Saharan Africa since firstly, even though future income prospects may have improved with liberalization, advanced market developments such as personal credit cards and increased credit ceiling is still absent. Secondly, behaviour- inducing factors such as previous shocks may still require households to maintain a 'desired precautionary' savings. This may not result a permanent reduction in aggregate propensity to save in these

[9]Levine (1997) and Becivenga and Smith (1991) both give detailed analysis of this topic.

[10]'Financial development' and 'financial intermediation' are used interchangeably.

economies. When financial liberalization relaxes consumer credit constraint, lower savings ratio is expected and thereby lower rate of capital accumulation (Campbell and Mankiw, 1991). Demirguc-Kunt and Detragiache (1998) have contributed to this debate by considering the negative aspect of financial liberalization and examining its link with financial fragility. Applying a multivariate logit model and data from 53 developed and developing countries during 1980–1995, they analyse the relationship between banking crises and financial liberalization. The findings establish that banking crisis is more likely to occur in a liberalized financial system. They notice that financial fragility is influenced by multiple factors including bad macroeconomic policies and vulnerability to balance of payment crisis, something which is a common characteristic of many developing economies. However, even when such factors are accounted for, financial liberalization shows a negative effect on the stability of the banking sector. Demirguc-Kunt and Detragiache (1998) further analyse the impact of liberalization on financial fragility in the presence of a stronger institutional environment. The evidence shows that a better institutional environment tends to weaken the effect of financial liberalization on the probability of a banking crisis. It is evident then that financial liberalization does have a negative aspect and supporting this finding with previous experience,[11] benefits should be weighed against the cost of increased fragility. Thus the view taken by Stiglitz (1994) and Capiro and Summers (1993) among others, that some degree of financial regulation/repression is preferable than ineffective liberalization looks to have some basis. The remarks given by Demirguc-Kunt and Detragiache (1998) illustrate this clearly:-

> Financial liberalization should be approached cautiously where the institutions necessary to ensure law and contract enforcement and effective prudential regulation and supervision are not fully developed even if macroeconomic stabilization has been achieved (p. 3).

Despite the effectiveness of financial liberalization as a tool to inspire long term economic development, some authors have attempted to justify the use of financial repression policies. Among those who have given a strong argument on this issue is Stiglitz (1994), famously known for the 'Stiglitz controversy'. Stiglitz argues that because of the fact that financial markets are subject to failure, to some extent, certain forms of government intervention will not only make markets function better, but will also improve the performance of the economy. Considering the possibilities of market failures and imperfections, he points out that (some level of) financial repression is an alternative. *First*, without intervention financial institutions may not allocate funds to those projects for which the social returns are the highest. *Second*, with financial repression firms' equity is increased because of the lower cost of capital. Hence firms are more likely to engage in projects with higher expected returns. *Third*, financial repression can be used with other incentive schemes to reward specific sectors that contribute more to economic growth such as manufacturing, export oriented and high technology industries to give them more

---

[11] Such experience includes Chilean as well as the recent East Asian crisis.

access to capital. Stiglitz (1994) remarks that raising the interest rate can lead to adverse selection and hence a 'moderate' level of financial repression (without a negative real interest rate) can improve risk attributes of investment projects undertaken in the whole economy. Despite the above, the last decade has seen a number of authors covering the theoretical and empirical grounds for financial liberalization and the majority of them explicitly criticized financial repression policies. On the other hand, studies have also shown instances where the Mckinnon-Shaw hypothesis (believed to be the cornerstone of financial liberalization) breaks down. In particular cases where financial markets are characterized by imperfect information, imperfect competition, or where they are categorically segmented,[12] market liberalization may have a lesser impact than expected (Arestis and Demetriades (1999), van Wijnebergen (1983) and Stiglitz (1994)). To further contribute to this argument, Demetriades and Luintel (2001) recently examined the impact of financial restraint on financial deepening in South Korea. The authors point out that South Korea experienced extensive government intervention in allocation of resources as well as control over lending and deposit rates from as early as the 1960s, and only in the mid 1990s did the government relax all interest rate controls. Hence their study attempts to establish the effect of such financial restraint on economic development. Their empirical evidence shows a positive and significant relationship between financial restraint and financial development, while the impact of the real interest rate on financial development is positive, but not statistically significant.[13] Their finding sheds light on two important issues for developing countries. Firstly, financial repression to some extent could be beneficial but only if it contributes to the efficiency of allocation of funds. The fact that markets in most developing countries are fragile necessitates this, specifically when such intervention is guided by policies that facilitate channelling of resources to priority sectors. Secondly, the success and failure of financial liberalization or financial repression depends on policy targets of the government and the intention upon which such policies are based. For success of either, there is a need for an effective legal system, uncorrupted civil servants and the existence of appropriate institutions.

3.3.1 Financial Liberalization in Sub-Saharan Africa

Post independence Africa experienced continuous economic decline, an increased level of poverty and an increasingly heavy external debt burden accompanied by a lower rate of savings. Many African and Asian governments have realized that there was a need for policy change and as a result resorted to the structural adjustment program proposed by the IMF and the World Bank (Hope, 1999).

[12] An example of this is where financial markets can be classified into official and curb markets (informal market). This is not uncommon in most developing countries.

[13] The study uses a data set covering the period of 1956–1994.

Similar to many developing countries, most countries pursued these policies to mobilize resources, both from domestic and external sources, to stimulate and sustain economic development (see Naude (1995)). But this attempt to inspire change requires development in the financial sector. By reducing transaction costs and information asymmetries, development in the financial sector encourages financial savings and investment. A number of papers have looked at the state of finance in Sub-Saharan Africa (SSA). Gelbard and Leite (1999) developed a set of indices for measuring financial development in SSA. Surveying 38 SSA countries, they attempted to document the progress achieved in restructuring financial systems over the decade(s). Their assessment of a financial system considered six major areas, including: the market structure and competitiveness of the system; the availability of financial products; the degree of financial liberalization; the degree of integration with foreign financial markets; and the degree of sophistication of instruments of financial policy. Based on this, six indices are constructed to represent each of these areas[14]: market structure; financial products; financial liberalization; institutional environment; financial openness and monetary policy instruments, while each of these indices were measured on a 0–100 scale.[15] The result indicates that significant financial development took place in the 1987–1997 period. The number of countries with largely developed or somewhat developed financial systems increased from two countries in 1987 to 27 in 1997. In particular, the findings indicate that most countries had taken steps to liberalize their financial system, while only one country (Nigeria) still showed real lending rates that were negative in real terms. Interestingly, the institutional environment index (which measures the presence of supporting institutional features) showed great improvement, with 23 countries classified as largely or somewhat supportive.

Pill and Pradhan (1997) undertook a comparative study on financial liberalization in Africa and Asia. Looking at the experience of liberalization in both continents they give an analysis as to why the outcomes differed. Using a financial deepening[16] indicator (ratio of broad money to national income) the study shows that liberalization seems to have been much more successful in Asia than in Africa. They elaborate that for financial reforms to succeed there are 3 necessary prerequisites: (1) macroeconomic stability is essential for successful liberalization. Macroeconomic imbalances such as balance of payment and fiscal deficit should be brought to a manageable level and inflation lowered. They observed that in Asian countries where the above conditions were not adhered to (the Philippines and Sri-Lanka for example) reforms were not successful. Most African countries which attempted to liberalize did so in an environment with excessive levels of inflation

---

[14]To allow comparison over time, these indices were constructed for 1987 and 1997 only.

[15]The following formula was used to calculate the index:
$d_{ij} = [(k_{ij} - \min_{i=1...n} k_{ij})/(\max_{i=1....n} k_{ij} - \min_{i=1...n} k_{ij})] \times 100$ where k is value of attributes and d is the measurement within a 0–100 scale of each attribute.

[16]This is mostly defined as the increase in the volume of financial capital stock to be intermediated by the financial sector or the increase in the degree of financial intermediation (mostly associated with more efficient use of capital).

(some having triple digit, for example Zambia) and large fiscal deficits. (2) A 'well behaved' financial system is required along with macroeconomic stability. Sound banking practices are important and practices such as credit rationing, government intervention and directed allocation should be abolished. They state that banks in many African countries are largely public owned and hence are still accessible to the government, while those privatized depend on subsidies for survival because of the large stock of non-performing loans inherited from the directed lending program. Thus for successful liberalization, there is a need for restructuring banks to remove bad debts, privatizing public owned banks and creating a conducive environment to promote competition in the banking sector. Pill and Pradhan (1997) observe that several Asian countries who implemented such structural reforms had greater success in liberalizing their economies. (3) Since financial liberalization is implemented within a general framework of complex interrelated institutions, the need to strengthen institutional functioning in the financial system before liberalization is high. Specifically, the legal, accounting, supervisory and management infrastructure should be strong. It is indicated that such institutions are underdeveloped, highly fragile or non-existent in Africa. Therefore, this analysis shows that the general environment for financial liberalization was far less favourable in Africa than in Asia.

Naude (1995) also looks at the appropriateness of financial liberalization in Africa. Taking a case study of five SSA countries,[17] he observes both the level and the volatility of interest rate increases following financial liberalization while the spread between the deposits and lending rates also increased over time. Referring to Southern cone countries[18] where a similar trend was observed, he remarks that experience shows these as symptoms of inappropriate bank management. In the aftermath of liberalization, competition increases and to attract deposits banks increase deposit rates to a very high level. This may increase adverse selection problems and banks might make high risk loans, while poor screening methods could enable ineffective firms in the market to borrow to cover their temporary losses. In the end, this creates a large share of non-performing loans in the banking system. Naude (1995) identifies three common features between the experience of Southern cone and African countries: - the preference of banks for granting short-term loans, the increase in banking crises and financial restructuring accompanying financial liberalization, and late recognition by authorities of existing financial distress. He critically points out that financial liberalization creates a significant interest rate risk and hence African banks' role will become one of service brokerage rather than enhance credit creation. In another study, Lensink, Hermes and Murinde (1998) examined the effect of financial liberalization on capital flight in African economies. Importantly, it estimates the effect of various measures of

---

[17] The countries taken for this study included Gambia, Kenya, Ghana, Zimbabwe and Nigeria.

[18] The Southern cone countries refer to Argentina (1997–1980), Chile (1975–1981) and Uruguay (1977–1982) where the period in bracket shows the period such high interest rates were experienced.

financial liberalization on capital flight, to establish whether the previous trend of scarce domestic funds flowing abroad in the presence of negative real interest rates, will be reversed by reforms. Applying a portfolio model and data set from nine SSA countries[19] they find a negative and significant relationship between capital flight and increase in the domestic deposit rate. The study further augments the portfolio model with sub-models for the banking, external, and government sectors to render it suitable for conduction of a simulation experiment. Three different measures of financial liberalization were taken: - interest rate deregulation, decrease in reserve requirement and a change in exchange rate policy. The evidence shows that capital flight is reduced by all the three measures taken, however the effect is very small. In general, they conclude that that although capital flight can be decreased by the introduction of financial liberalization, other types of reforms are necessary to prevent scarce domestic funds from flowing abroad.

The evidence from the literature on SSA and other developing countries we have seen so far appears to provide some support to the hypothesis that financial liberalization contributes positively to economic development. However some point out that it has some destabilizing consequences (Naude (1995), Demirguc-Kunt and Detragiaches (1998), and Kaminsky and Schmukler (2002)). Arestis and Demetriades (1999) attempt to explain these differences and argue that financial liberalization in theory is based on assumptions which are quite difficult to be met in reality. They state that the assumptions made in financial liberalization hypothesis are perfect information, perfect competition and institution-free analysis which in practice are unlikely especially in developing countries. Markets face imperfect competition since information is mostly never equally distributed even in the developed world. This creates the problem of moral hazard and adverse selection which Stiglitz (1994) has discussed in detail. Arestis and Demetriades (1999) indeed recognize that at post-liberalization, interest rate increases which further exacerbate the information related problems threaten the stability of the banking sector. Secondly, Arestis and Demetriades (1999) state that markets are never perfectly competitive and with banks in developing countries' oligopolistic characteristics, financial liberalization will led to increased spreads between lending and deposit rates without necessarily an increase in the share of financial capital. Thirdly, because financial markets do not exist in a vacuum, Arestis and Demetriades (1999) suggest proper development of necessary institutions. Importantly they note that the literature should incorporate the role of banking supervision and quality of regulation. Finally, they argued that in theory we should develop models that take into account institutional weakness and information relation problems, while the impact of a strong institutional framework such as a low level of corruption, well functioning legal system and effective bankruptcy laws and procedures should also be considered.

---

[19]This included Ghana, Kenya, Malawi, Rwanda, Nigeria, Cote d'Ivore, Madagascar, Sierra Leone and Mauritius.

3.3.2 *The Thai Case*

In a period where the global economy is struggling, the best panacea is increased trade and investment. This was the dynamism behind Thai financial liberalization. Following an unstable global macroeconomic environment in Asia, Latin American and Africa in 1970s and 1980s, many countries in East Asia decided to implement a comprehensive market reform programme to enhance stability, efficiency, flexibility and more importantly regional competitiveness. It was also in line with the advice of international bodied such as World and IMF to pursue market liberalization in order to gain greater financial intermediation, promote financial deepening and improve productivity of investment (Tseng and Corker, 1991). For these reasons, Thai government implemented comprehensive structural and financial reforms in early 1990s, to integrate with the world economy and open up the industrial, agricultural and financial markets.

Domestically, financial liberalization was also influenced by internal and external needs. Hansanti et al. (2008, p. 35) elaborate that internal factors such as export-led growth policy and the need for a sound fiscal policy condition (see Table 3.2) necessitated financial market globalization. From 1985, a greater government policy concentrated around promoting export-led economic growth (Warr and Nidhiprabha, 1996) and in early 1990s Thai economy was also increasingly becoming industrialized (Ratanakomut, 1999). Externally, the opening of the neighbouring economies and a general trend towards globalization of financial systems strengthened the momentum to bring a change towards a liberal market-oriented approach that will increase export activity and enhance the growth of the required investment finance (Hansanti et al., 2008).

The implementation of Thailand's financial liberalization was mainly in two phases. First, deregulation of interest rate which started in from 1991 was the initial phase (Limskul, 2000; Hansanti et al., 2008). Prior to this, Thai financial system faced various form of interest rate ceiling and dismantling interest rate control was

Table 3.2 Thailand's fiscal balance and International reserves

Year	Fiscal cash balance (% of GDP)	International reserves (Months of imports)
1987	−1.4	4.7
1988	1.9	4.3
1989	3.2	5.0
1990	4.7	5.3
1991	4.9	5.8
1992	3.1	6.3
1993	2.2	6.8
1994	1.8	6.8
1995	1.0	6.3
1996	2.2	6.5

Note: Cash balance is the difference between import and export. International reserves include forward rate.
Source: Adopted from Hansanti et al. (2008).

Table 3.3 Financial institutions in Thailand ranked by asset, 1997

Financial Institution	Assets*
Commercial Banks	7,279,365
Finance and Securities Companies	1,616,948
Government Housing	310,195
Government Savings Bank	280,933
Saving Cooperatives	276,230
Bank for Agriculture and Agricultural	236,432
Industrial Finance Corp. of Thailand	217,499
Life Insurance Companies	173,243
Mutual Fund	102,462
Credit Foncier Companies	74,161
Export – Import Bank of Thailand	61,377
Agricultural Cooperatives	38,790
Securities Companies	32,423
Pawnshops	16,900
Small Industry Finance Corporation	1,765
Small Industry Credit Guarantee Corporation	580

Note: *Unit: Million bath.
Source: Adopted from Islam and Watanapalachaikul (2005).

seen as an important package to facilitate long-term deposits and mobilize savings. From 1993, the second stage of financial reform was implemented. This included establishing of new banking facilities (to serve and enhance international intermediation), authorizing Export-Import bank (to offer short-term and long-term credit and strengthen Thai's business competitive edge), and expanding off-shore banking business (BOT 1998; Hansanti, Islam and Sheehan, 2008). As a result Bangkok International Banking Facilities (BIBFs), Export-Import Bank of Thailand were born and host of other commercial banks were licensed (BOT, 1996).

Prior to these reforms, commercial banking sector in Thailand was characterised by a high degree of concentration and with 16 families dominating their ownership. Similar to other developing economies, distinct features of monopolistic/oligopolistic features were visible in the commercial banking (Islam and Watanapalachaikul, 2005). Further, more than three-quarter of all short-term and long-term deposits were handled by these commercial banks, allowing them to dominate other financial institutions and determine financial instrument and services offered (see also Table 3.3).

Following the full implementation structural and financial reforms and relaxation of entry-exit restrictions, new local and foreign banks were attracted, and by 1996 more than seven new banks were licensed while 22 others granted permission to offer new banking facilities (BOT, 1996, 1998; Hansanti et al., 2007). As a result range of short-term and long-tern financial instruments become available, domestic and international capital inflows were enhanced and the country became a regional trade competitor and financial centre.

3.4 Conclusion

As indicated by this survey of important literature on financial developments and financial liberalization in particular, it has been suggested that financial markets ensure better mobilization of the available savings by facilitating the aggregation of the economies' financial resources. On the other hand, it has been indicated that in a fragile financial environment, liberalizing the financial sector may not be a panacea and a cautious approach is required to avoid serious negative drawbacks. In this aspect, Fig. 3.1 provides a summary of various mechanisms of how financial sector liberalization may be linked with economic growth. In general, the issues highlighted in this chapter have focused on tracing the relationship between financial and real economic development. In this attempt the objective was rather to provide a rich insight into the interactions and the resulting effect of financial market

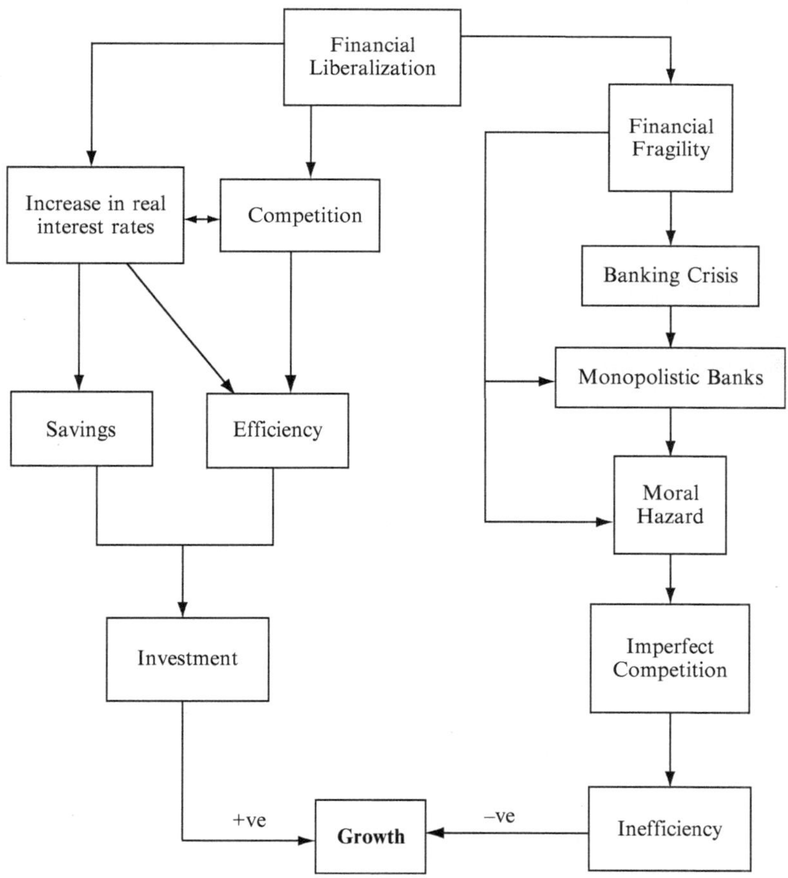

Fig. 3.1 The link between financial liberalization and economic growth

enhancement and improvement in productivity. Having provided the above general survey, there is a fairly strong theoretical argument in support of movement towards an environment of a financially liberalized market rather than a repressed one. In essence and for the purpose of complementing this further, the next chapter will specifically also look at the theoretical underpinning of the financial repression (liberalization) hypothesis, before evaluating routes through which these liberalization-led changes are expected to influence real economic growth using evidence from the countries of our sample.

Chapter 4
The Theory of Financial Liberalization and its Economic Impact: An Assessment

"Nations control their own economic destiny".
(Summers & Lawrence, 1992)

4.1 Financial Liberalization

4.1.1 A Brief Theoretical Assessment

Led by the seminal papers of McKinnon (1973) and Shaw (1973), a significant number of studies have pointed out that financial liberalization can exert a positive effect on growth rates as interest rate levels rise towards their competitive market equilibrium, while resources are efficiently allocated. Accordingly, eliminating controls on interest rates and allowing them to increase could stimulate a higher level of savings. Moreover, with the assumption of a strong response of savings to the rate of interest, higher interest rates are expected to increase financial intermediation (the level of financial asset channelled by the financial system).[1] Strictly under these strong assumptions, it is likely that financial liberalization produces higher savings which ultimately fosters economic development through changes in quality (by allowing efficient allocation of resources) and quantity of investment (Reinhart & Tokatlidis, 2003).

From the past and recent theoretical work, we could briefly outline the route via which liberalization is expected to show its impact on important growth-related variables (refer to Table 4.1). Right from the early work of McKinnon (1973) and Shaw (1973), a primary premise behind the call for financial liberalization has been that an increase in real interest rates (particularly the real rate of deposit) will increase the level of savings which will in turn increase the supply of credit, hoping

[1] We have also defined financial intermediation earlier.

A.D. Ahmed and S.M.N. Islam, *Financial Liberalization in Developing Countries*, Contributions to Economics,
DOI: 10.1007/978-3-7908-2168-0_4, © Springer Physica-Verlag Berlin Heidelberg 2010

Table 4.1 Expected impact on financial liberalization on key economic variables

Route	Sign	Impact
Real deposit rate	Increase	• Increase in volume of savings
		• Increase in supply of credit
		• Composition change in lending: improved performance of investment
		• Decrease in the curb market rate
Real lending rate	Increase	• Increase in productive investment
Competitive level (No. of firms)	Increase	• Decrease in intermediation spread

that this will eventually lead to a higher rate of growth (Fry, 1995; Kitchen, 1986, p. 82). Initially, under a financially repressive system, a major instrument through which the government controls the financial market is the ceiling on the lending rate (even though in many instances reserve requirements and foreign exchange controls are also frequently used) where it assumes the pricing and allocative functions of the financial market, and as a result, influence the investment and intermediation process.[2] Within the financial repression framework, the lending rate is kept artificially low to both encourage investments in general and further to enable the use of other incentives to direct credit to preferred sectors (Kitchen, 1986, p. 83). In the presence of such a ceiling on the interest rate, the economic system is distorted in a number of ways: (1) funds are not allocated to the most productive and profitable projects. Due to the repressed lower lending rate, the pool of borrowers includes firms with low-yielding projects that will not otherwise get credit allocations under a more competitive market-clearing mechanism (Fry, 1997). Moreover, credit allocation based on non-market determinations (such as government direction and connections) which enables elastic supply of credit to low-yielding highly favoured investments crowds out the undertaking of profitable but unfavoured investments. Likewise, to maximize incentives received, banking activities may be directed towards rent-seeking, influencing connections and corruption dealings instead of putting emphasis on risk-reduction measures and acquiring of banking and loan appraisal skills.[3] These multi-dimensional inefficiencies in allocation and market perception lead to sub-optimal quality of investment and lower production in the long-run, (2) it is also highly likely that at such a low rate of deposits, the supply of funds will be much lower than usual given that there is little incentive to save. In this regard, the level of savings may be below the social optimum as agents are tempted to substitute current consumption against the future or save in real assets

[2]However, in other literature this is termed as ceiling on interest rates since deposit rates are also indirectly controlled in the process.

[3]It is also likely that controls by their nature create favourable conditions for corruption and other unscrupulous economic dealings by all economic agents (Mauro (1997) and Sikorski (1996, p. 65)).

rather than time deposits (Fry, 1997). Consistently, with resources not fully mobilized and savings at sub-optimal level, relatively few loans can be made, (3) the economy can only accommodate a few banks. Thus, typically this becomes the case of too little resource base and too small funds to be handled by the financial system. Under these considerations, liberalization of financial structure is expected to trigger a host of different mechanisms through which savings, investment and efficiency are all influenced (refer to Table 4.1). We shall briefly discuss some of the areas where we expect to observe some changes as a result of adopting policies of financial liberalization which will improve productivity and hence accelerate economic growth.

(a) *Increase in propensity to save and more savings available to investors.* A policy of liberalization will result in an increase in deposit rates (in real terms) to their competitive market-clearing levels. Here, an obvious assumption is that interest rates are held below their competitive level under a repressed financial system, a phenomenon common in developing countries for the purpose of achieving adequate flow of bank credits to priority sectors. This effect lowers both savings and investment and causes a high disparity between the lending and borrowing rates which may also induce a lower volume of business (Kitchen, 1986, p. 83). However, as opposed to this, financial liberalization is expected to correct these non-market disparities through allowing market determination of all institutional interest rates and stabilizing inflation. The combined impact of these changes will result an increase in real interest rates. Consequently, by providing higher incentives for savings, liberalization leads to a higher interaction among economic agents where both savings and investment levels are now improved. By opening up the financial sector and allowing competition among the players, the market mechanism works better in predicting these interest rates. In response, potential depositors will switch to the new alternative of saving in time deposits rather than investing in real low-yielding long-term assets. Ultimately, the financial deepening[4] process is also enhanced as part of the general benefit derived from financial liberalization in a broad sense (Gibson & Tsakalotos, 1994). The change to liberalization is expected to lead to financial deepening as a result of increase in the volume of funds handled by the financial institutions in aggregate. Besides, an increase in the number and varieties of financial institutions also increases the array of financial instruments available, and promotes the designing of new financial instruments. This stimulates the use of more financial instruments of savings by investors relative to non-financial instruments while reducing liquidity risk and eventually increasing the flow of funds into activities of higher productivity. Specifically, it is not uncommon in most developing countries that a substantial amount of savings are held in non-monetary assets such as livestock, houses, land, gold, or even hoarding in the

[4]Financial deepening is defined as the process of accumulating financial assets within the economy at a pace faster than that of accumulating non-financial assets (Shaw, 1973, p. vii).

form of foreign currencies kept under the pillow. Thus, this will lead to agents reconsidering their investment portfolios, since savings in financial assets (which may be more flexible in terms of liquidity) are now equally or more rewarding (Aziakpono & Babatope-Obasa, 2003), while making more funds are available to other productive investment within the economy.

(b) *Allocative efficiency and improved performance of investment.* Under a repressed financial system, a number of mechanisms ensure enough credit flows to 'perceived-necessary' projects earmarked to receive higher proportions of loans from both public and private sources.[5] Such measures include quantitative credit guidelines, concessional rates of interest to specific sectors, stipulated liquidity and cash reserve ratios, and even from time to time special credit directives. Indirectly, under such a system, market mechanisms will also favour direction of credit to priority areas. When interest rates are repressed, banks cannot properly match the expected return and the assumed risk. With a liberal market environment banks match return to risk by adjusting the lending rate depending on the likelihood of default. However, under a repressed financial system they will not be able to match perceived risk characteristics by a higher lending rate to compensate for the possibility of non-payment (Sikorski, 1996, p. 140). Furthermore, due to high demand for credit given the lower interest rate, effective classification of borrowers is a major constraint. Lastly in response to this, since all projects have a similar return horizon (as maximum lending rate is fixed), to maximize their revenue banks' lending policies will be based on minimum risk criteria. Notably, it has been usual that banks automatically give maximum priority to either lending to government or projects guaranteed by the government under a priority policy scheme (Kitchen, 1986, p. 82). Both these arrangements have none or minimal risk of default. Despite this, credit distribution under these mechanisms may cause a breakdown in the channelling of funds to various necessary economic sectors, leading to their collapse. For instance, allocations to the service sector may substantially reduce relative to trade for the mere reason of correcting deteriorating balance of payment in the short-run by the government. Additionally indeed, to maximize the amount of deposits channelled under this guaranteed income alternative, banks may engage in active lobbying to attain a higher stake in such allocation or qualify for other related subsidies. However, in sum, such mechanisms do not constitute an efficient allocation or an optimal use of resources.

In contrast, financial liberalization involves eliminating all the above non-market mechanisms, paving the way to only market systems of pricing and allocating funds. Financial reforms also enhance the efficiency of investment through effective use of available resources, which will ultimately improve the

[5] Since interest rates are repressed, banks have a surplus of investors asking for funds. Hence credits have to be directed.

level of productivity. To illustrate this while following De Gregorio and Guidotti (1995), let us take a simple production function where output depends only on the level of capital stock:

$$Y_t = f(K_t) \tag{4.1}$$

where Y_t represents the level of output and K_t is the capital stock. Differentiating the equation above with respect to time and taking g to represent the growth of output:

$$g = y_t/Y_t = k_t/y_t f'(K) \tag{4.2}$$

In the above equation $y_t = \partial Y/\partial t$ and $y_t = \partial K/\partial t$. If we take s_t to denote the savings, i.e. the ratio of change in capital over time to output and γ_t to represent the marginal productivity of capital, then:

$$g_t = s_t \gamma_t \tag{4.3}$$

Elaborating on this, De Gregorio and Guidotti (1995) point out that financial development has a dual effect on economic growth. On the one hand, the development of the financial market may enhance the efficiency of capital accumulation through an increase in productivity, γ_t, while on the other hand, enhancement in financial market development can contribute to raising the savings rate. Liberalization of the financial system that promotes savings is likely to diversify liquidity risk through pooling of resources from different depositors – who will have the required flexibility and at the same time are adequately rewarded – and investing it into less liquid but highly profitable projects (De Gregorio & Guidotti, 1995). This further raises demand for savings, and thus raises deposit rates and savings. Reforms that enhance the financial system will also induce change in the quality of lending. As the real lending rate increases, the pool of unviable projects is eliminated. Thus, on the demand side, the inefficient low-yielding group of investors will be rationed out, where the remaining pool of creditors are now only those with competitive projects at the new market-clearing lending rate, therefore resulting in only the high-paying profitable projects being undertaken. Unsurprisingly then, given the same level of total savings in the economy, this channel enables the optimal use of such limited funds to be diverted into real profitable investment. Through this increase in quantity and quality of investment, financial liberalization is expected to promote growth even in cases where savings are interest inelastic (Sikorski, 1996, p. 75).

(c) *Reduction of corruption and rent-seeking activities.* The implementation of a financial liberalization policy will reduce government participation in the allocation and pricing of credit, leading to drastic reduction or even elimination of subsidies and incentives related to this function. Furthermore, because of the market-clearing interest rate level, most forms of intervention are not warranted as there are enough funds for every project that is worth investing in, at this rate. On the basis of this, the allocational-related incentives of corruption, political influence and rent-seeking are reduced since only interest rates play the allocative role of equating demand and supply for loanable funds. The distribution criteria will be based on creditworthiness (repayment abilities) and riskier projects will only receive funds at a higher rate of interest, while safer projects will be able to borrow elastically.

(d) *Level of competitiveness.* The process of liberalizing the financial sector enhances competition by inviting prospective players with economies of scale and scope to enter the market. It is the effect of financial liberalization as a result of changing the financial structure of the economic system that will warrant the entry of such firms. In post-liberalization, both volume of loans to be channelled and profitability prospects are enhanced, signalling room for more banks. As depicted by Fig. 4.1 the level of financial assets handled together with lending activities are both improved as the volume of savings and loans within the formal financial system change. More specifically from the market-response perspective, competition is expected to increase for two major reasons. First, because of the improvement in the intermediation process and the traded volume of lending that is realized, there is now enough volume for more banks to channel and allocate this large size of investment funds (indicated by ΔL). Notably, the market lending capacity improves from L_0 to L_e as a result of increasing real interest rate from i_o to i_e. It will be an automatic market response (unless there are other barriers) to observe more firms entering the market as there are enhanced incentives that warrant entry. Second, as opposed

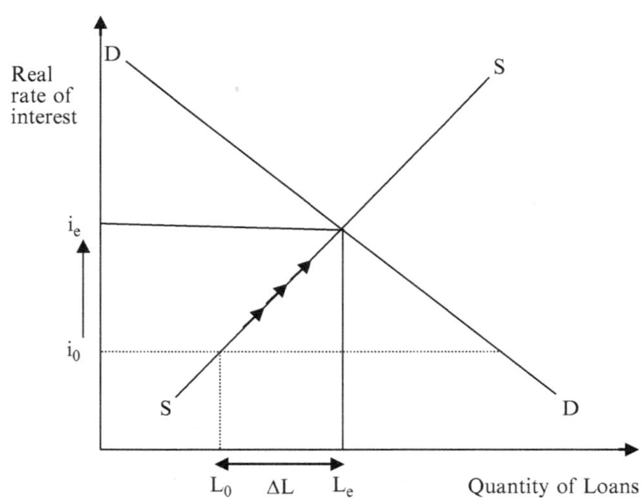

Fig. 4.1 Change in volume of loans

to when interest rates are controlled, market-clearing equilibrium interest levels enable financial institutions (especially banks) to allocate credit at higher prices reflecting its market worth. Meanwhile, this coupled with higher intermediation levels enable firms to receive an increased return, giving prospective institutions an additional incentive for entry.

On the other hand, as countries revise their legal framework for the financial sector and adopt measures to lower barriers to entry into the banking sector (through amendments in regulatory, approval and procedural red-tapes), entry of potential financial institutions is expected. An increased level of competition is expected to provide greater pricing competition for banking services. Consequently, this will induce vibrant competition and influence interest rate spread negatively. A low spread is very important because it implies that a higher interest rate in lending will be passed on to depositors. Otherwise, the savings rate may not rise much.

In support of this Kitchen (1986) points out that "if the banking sector is competitive, then the disturbance from the equilibrium position caused by differential borrowing and lending rates may be slight" (p. 83). Moreover, with the assumption that intermediation margin is an indicator of efficiency, in this process the level of financial efficiency may be significantly enhanced. Chirwa (2001) suggests that "competitive pressures that result from conditions of free entry and competitive pricing will raise the financial efficiency of intermediation by decreasing the spread between deposit and lending rates" (p. 13). From their case studies of a number of developing countries where economic reforms were implemented, Nissanke and Aryeetey (1998) argued that "it was expected that the spread would narrow as more efficient business practices were adopted in the face of increasing competition and as credit demand stabilized" (p. 200). Therefore in principle, the intermediation margin is expected to decrease in the long-run. In the short-run, the supply of credit is more inelastic (s_S) compared to the long-run case (s_L). Initially the few banks in the market can charge a higher intermediation margin (r_S) especially when they have oligopolistic market power (as demonstrated by Fig. 4.2).[6] However, with time banks will have to reshape their cost structure, streamline their profit margin, and adopt more efficient business strategies to retain their market share in the wake of stiffer competition.

(e) *Curb market rate*. In an economic system where financial markets are segmented into formal and informal (curb market) sectors, financial liberalization may lead to decline in the curb market lending rates. As more borrowers have access to the formal market, the curb market may decline. If the players in the curb market are to compete and remain active, they will have to reduce their lending rate charged to their borrowers to lower than that of the formal sector. This benefit of lower interest rates will result in a gain to the whole economy since some

[6] An obvious assumption here is that deposit rate is taken as given.

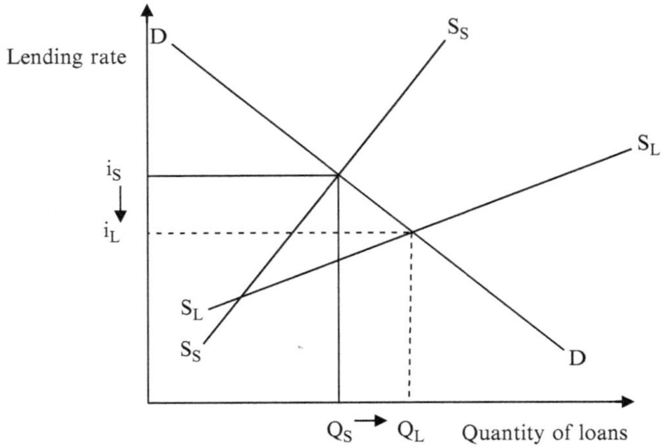

Fig. 4.2 Intermediation margin and competition

borrowers who are rationed out of the formal market will have access to credit to engage in trading activities (Chipeta, 1994). From a different perspective, in which formal and informal sectors are more complementary, it is also possible that when financial reform increases the amount of credit available, informal moneylenders may benefit through gaining access to funds from the formal sector which will in turn lead to increased availability of funds for borrowers, and possibly even lower interest rates. On the other hand, if the market segmentation is strong and there is little competition between the formal and curb market sectors, borrowers will be in a weaker position to strongly negotiate for a lower interest rate. If such borrowers are excluded from the formal sector, they will totally be relying on the curb market sector to source their credit demands. On the basis of this, money lenders may be able to charge higher lending rates, and thus, the informal sector will only be dominated by a bad credit group who will not be able to borrow from the formal sector because of their credit ratings, increasing the risk of strategic default. Ultimately, this will weaken the competitiveness of the curb market sector and its ability to complement the formal sector.

4.1.2 Observations from the Case Study

Having discussed various channels through which liberalization is expected to influence mobilization and allocation of resources from the theoretical perspective, we now compare these predictions with specific country observation from our case studies. Potentially, the following scenarios are emerging from our analysis: as highlighted by Table 4.2, real deposit rates are positive in Kenya and Botswana

Table 4.2 Theoretical predictions vs country observations

Channel	Effect	Kenya	Malawi	Botswana
Real deposit rate	(↑)	Increased (−1 to 1%)[a]	Negative (−13 to −6%)[a]	Increased (−1 to 1%)[a]
Real lending rate	(↑)	Increased (4–18%)[a]	Increased (−6 to 13%)[a]	Increased (1–6%)[a]
Competitiveness (No. of firms)	(↑)	Limited (26–50)[b]	Limited (2–12)[b]	More competitive (2–5)[b]
Spread margin	(↓)	Widened (4.3–17.9%)[a]	Widened (7.1–19.2%)[a]	Acceptable (2.2–4.8%)[a]
Financial deepening (M3 as proxy)	(↑)	Enhanced (43–46%)[a]	Not enhanced (24–17%)[a]	Enhanced (42–49%)[a]
Savings (% of GDP)	(↑)	Decreased (19.6–8.1%)[a]	Decreased (4.1–2.1%)[a]	Decreased (42–29%)[a]
Curb market rate	(↓)	Not changed	Decreased	Not available

Note: [a]Indicates that these values are averages of pre-reform (1986–1990) to post-reform (1996–2000), while [b]shows the number of firms in 1991 and 2000.
Source: Authors' calculations from respective central bank reports and other sources.

while remaining negative in Malawi for the period after the reforms. On average, the rates of deposit have improved from −1% to 1% in both Kenya and Botswana. In Malawi the real deposit rate remains negative at 6% even a decade after liberalization. While reform programs were implemented in these countries under different economic environments and backgrounds, despite the fact that they were initiated almost at the same time, the savings rate in all three countries indicated a declining trend. Savings (as a percentage of GDP) declined from 4.1% and 19.6% in 1986–1990 to 2.1% and 8.1% in 1996-2000 in Malawi and Kenya respectively. Over the same period, these figures stood at 42% and 29% in Botswana. Additionally it is policy expectation that reforms of the financial sector will lead to an improvement in the efficiency of allocation and investment. In line with this, although it is difficult to quantify efficiency, liquidity levels (as measured by M3) and private sector credits are widely used as a good proxy to infer the level of financial deepening and effective allocation. Thus, it is observed that financial depth in Malawi still remains shallow as opposed to Kenya and Botswana where the financial deepening process seems to have been enhanced by the reforms. However, with economic liberalization at its peak, only Botswana has seen an improvement in competition within the banking sector compared to Malawi and Kenya where these sectors remain highly oligopolistic and show strong dominance by few existing firms. Numerically, the number of firms has increased in all three countries, however the degree of dominance by few banks is significant in Malawi and Kenya. Consistent with this, the trend in the intermediation margin supports this argument. The spread margins widened from 7.1% and 4.3% to 19.2% and 17.9% in Malawi and Kenya respectively following liberalization programs. Of particular note is that this intermediation spread has marginally increased from 2.2% to 4.8% in the case of Botswana. Another equally important issue pertains to the movement in the interest rate of the curb market (the informal sector). Generally, the informal sector in Africa is characterized to be highly heterogenous and strongly segmented. Hence, it is not precisely possible to look at a single rate to specify the trending direction as the sector serves different borrower categories with different terms and conditions (Atieno, 2001). Despite this, from the informal sectors' perspective money lenders provide the largest loan amount while their rates are in general the most expensive (Nissanke & Aryeetey, 1998, pp. 208–210). This may be because money lenders tend to be more accessible and often have a higher likelihood of credit success and degree of flexibility compared to other segments. Following the reforms, Nissanke and Aryeetey (1998, p. 209) observe that, on average, the rate charged by money lenders declined in response to changes in financial needs and availabilities in Malawi,[7] although their rate still exceeded that of the formal financial sector. However in Kenya the money lenders' rate remains almost unchanged, estimated to be in the range of 85–95% by this group[8] compared to 95% in years before reforms (World Bank, 1984).[9]

4.2 Contrasts Between the Theory and Country Performance

4.2.1 Introduction

As we have detailed in the assessment of financial liberalization theory in the previous part, reforms towards a liberalized financial system were expected to change the characteristics, performance and composition of the financial sector as well as economy-wide structures. It is hoped that these changes will be observed through a number of policy-related variables such as interest rate structure, intermediation margin, fund distribution, degree of competition and the size of financial assets channeled. However, the comparative evidence given in Table 4.2 indicates that there has been little improvement observed either in terms of reduction in the financial intermediation margin or improvement in the functioning of the banking sector through enhancements in efficiencies or competitive levels, particularly in Kenya and Malawi. To further look at various reasons as to why impacts of financial liberalization have been limited or rather in the wrong direction, we separate our diagnosis to each country individually to figure out these specific influential factors. In our analysis, the coverage of Kenya is relatively more detailed in compared to others since our examination in this area is based on a trip to the country for field study.

---

[7]They estimate the monthly interest rate in the money lenders segment to be between 47–50% even years after reform.

[8]See "Financing the poor through micro-enterprises-lesson from Kenya" in *Indian Express*, February 8, 2000.

[9]In a survey of 44 developing countries, the average informal sector interest rate was estimated to be 95%.

4.2.2 *Economic Impact of the Recent Financial Reforms: Kenya*

4.2.2.1 Review of Financial Sector

Although the pace of financial development has not been remarkable, Kenya's financial system has been considered one of the most developed in the African standard, comprising commercial banks, non-banking financial institutions (NBFIs), mortgage market, insurance industry, micro-finance institutions and capital market (see Fig. 4.3). In this aspect, the financial system in Kenya is relatively diverse although largely dominated by the banking sector (Ndungu & Ngugi, 2000; Ngugi & Kabubo, 1998). It is evident from Table 4.3 that the number of commercial banks has more than doubled since 1984 (from 24 to 50) even though the pace of NBFIs growth was rapid in the 1980s and 1990s, and has only showed a declining trend in the last decade. In addition to NBFIs, other financial institutions include building societies, mortgage finance companies and cooperatives, and post bank savings.

In the past two and a half decades, the financial system has transformed in various dimensions. A number of legal and policy guidelines issued have brought about institutional and structural changes. In the 1980s to the late 1990s, the number of NBFIs had more than tripled, from 23 in 1981 to 52 in 1990. The growth of NBFIs and other Development Financial Institutions (DFIs) was a national policy meant to cater for long-term projects financing as commercial banks experienced financial repression measures including concessional interest rates and stipulated cash resources and liquidity ratios (Ndungu & Ngugi, 2000). However, this induced

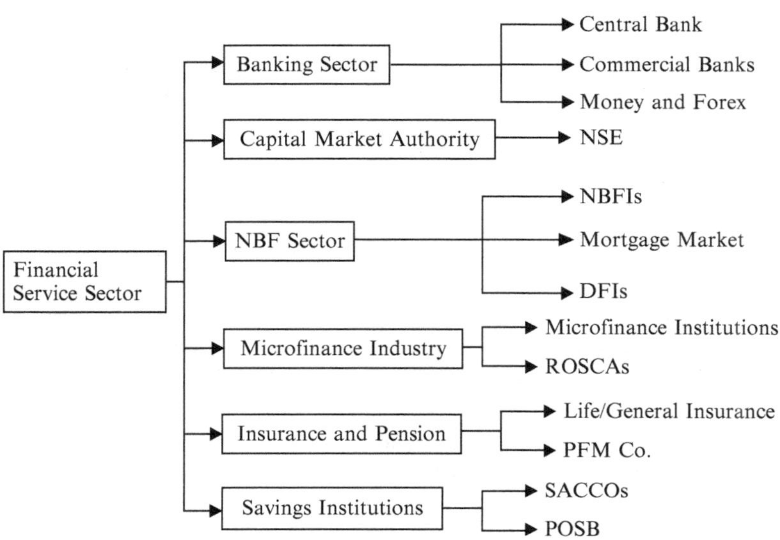

Fig. 4.3 Overview of Kenya's financial sector
Note: NSE Nairobi stock exchange; *ROSCA* rotating savings and credit association; *PFM* pension fund management; *SACCO* savings and credit co-operation societies; *POSB* post office savings bank

Table 4.3 Evolution of financial sector and other economic indicators

Period	CB	NBFIs	GDPg	M2	Loans	Deposits	LQD
1985	24	48	4.8	28.3	21.9	35	20
1986	23	52	5.6	31.7	21.8	37	20
1987	23	51	4.9	31.4	22.1	34	22
1988	24	54	5.1	29.2	21.5	35	20
1989	25	54	5.1	28.2	21.7	36	20
1990	26	52	4.3	29.7	21.2	36	20
1991	26	52	2.1	31.5	24.0	38	20
1992	28	51	0.5	37.4	25.0	36	20
1993	33	51	0.2	37.1	20.2	37	20
1994	36	48	3.0	40.6	21.8	39	25
1995	41	39	4.6	41.4	27.8	39	25
1996	48	24	2.4	45.2	30.1	41	25
1997	53	16	1.8	44.6	30.5	41	20
1998	55	13	1.4	41.2	31.9	38	20
1999	53	11	0.3	39.8	33.2	37	20
2000	50	7	1.3	38.5	33.0	36	20

Note: GDP growth rate is in constant prices.
M2, loans and deposits are all percentages of GDP while liquidity ratio (LQD) is reserve requirement as a percentage of total deposit liability.
CB stands for number of commercial banks.
NBFI is the number of non-banking financial institution while loans and deposits are only from commercial banks.
Source: Quarterly Economic Review, various issues and Ndungu and Ngugi (2000).

wider financial sector fragmentation and later raised the risk of financial crisis particularly of NBFIs due to poor management and weaknesses in the regulatory framework. Thus these difficulties together with an unstable macroeconomic environment and prolonged recession which depressed GDP growth led to the collapse of a significant number of NBFIs. Owing to this and as a result of financial liberalization measures, the Banking Act was reviewed several times from 1993 to consolidate the financial sector and further strengthen the supervision role of the Central Bank. In line with the objectives of stabilizing the financial system and intensifying the growth prospects of the private sector and the economy as a whole, fiscal and monetary policies were tightened and NBFIs were asked to convert to commercial banks or maintain a healthy bill of affairs in terms of capitalization and liquidity, to enable the integration of the financial market (Ndungu & Ngugi, 2000). Inevitably, even though most of the recent amendments affecting the financial sector have been useful in strengthening institutional infrastructure, in this sense it has intensified the growth of commercial banks given the high rate of conversion and mergers which took place, thus further increasing the domination of banks in the financial system (refer to Table 4.3).

As can be seen from Fig. 4.3 even though financial sector development in Kenya looks relatively sophisticated and fairly diversified, the past decade's reforms did not result in introduction of many new financial instruments. At the moment there are very limited services offered by the financial institutions in general. About 70% of the financial services offered by commercial banks are deposits and savings facilities, loans and advances and foreign exchange services (GoK, 2000). Therefore to improve banking activities and facilitate greater mobilization of savings within various sectors, introduction and adoption of new financial tools are needed. Indeed introduction of instruments such as negotiable certificate of deposits (NCDs), specific investment deposits, premium savings certificates or even establishment of unit trusts would provide the public with greater flexibility and realistic return for medium and short-term funds.

4.2.2.2 Commercial Banking Sector and the Impact of Market Liberalization

In Kenya, the operation of the banking system is stipulated in the Banking Act where a 'Bank' is defined as "a company which carries on banking business" and banking business includes "accepting from members of public money on deposit repayable on demand or on current account and payment on and acceptance of cheques". Accordingly, banking business is clearly distinguished from other business operations of the other financial institutions where a financial institution includes a "company other than a bank which carries out or proposes to carry out financial business". Tables 4.3 and 4.4 show significant proliferation of financial institutions in Kenya over the last two and half decades. It can be noted that although the financial sector has been diverse in terms of number of institutions (Ndungu & Ngugi, 2000), commercial banks still retain their traditionally dominant position. Table 4.4 provides analysis of deposits in commercial banks, NBFIs and Post-Banks.

Indeed, as is the case with the financial system elsewhere in most developing countries, commercial banks stand to be the largest and the most important group of financial institutions. Table 4.4 reveals this dominant role where commercial banks mobilized deposits equivalent to Kshs.24.5 billion in 1985, accounting for more than 68% of the total deposits. Ten years later the amount of deposits channelled by commercial banks reached more than Kshs.180 billion. This accounted for over 78% of the total deposits of the banking sector. On the other hand, the NBFIs in total accounted for only 29% from 1985 to 1995 while Post-Office Savings Banks accounted for barely 1.5% of total deposits. In recent years, the commercial banks' share of deposits increased to almost 92% while that of NBFIs declined to a marginal 6.5%. However, this is not surprising as it is inline with the Central Bank's policy of financial integration that to a substantial extent favoured commercial banks relative to other financial institutions. The liquidation of a significant number of NBFIs in the early 1990s has also triggered a shift of funds from such depository institutions to the more reliable commercial banks.

As in the other third world countries, even though the financial system in Kenya faced financial repression policies that encouraged inefficiencies and limited the intermediation process, there was a significant growth in commercial banks, both numerically and in terms of geographical coverage since independence. Essentially, following the commercial bank nationalization program that led to the establishment

Table 4.4 Analysis of deposits in Kenya's banking sector (share of the total)

Year	CB	Share (%)	NBFIs	Share (%)	Post-bank	Share (%)	Total
1985	24,593	68.8	10,379	29.0	668	1.9	35,740
1986	30,955	69.6	12,707	28.6	784	1.8	44,546
1987	33,602	64.3	17,675	33.8	979	1.9	52,356
1988	37,270	63.0	20,757	35.1	1,109	1.9	59,236
1989	45,039	62.8	25,485	35.5	1,240	1.7	71,864
1990	50,338	59.3	33,225	39.1	1,348	1.6	85,011
1991	62,190	62.0	36,736	36.6	1,385	1.4	100,411
1992	81,431	65.5	41,645	33.5	1,336	1.1	124,512
1993	109,897	69.2	46,593	29.3	2,328	1.5	158,918
1994	139,399	71.6	52,257	26.9	2,937	1.5	194,693
1995	180,304	78.4	46,197	20.1	3,524	1.5	230,125
1996	228,887	84.4	38,309	14.1	3,910	1.4	271,206
1997	269,511	91.2	21,667	7.3	4,274	1.5	295,552
1998	280,202	90.9	23,230	7.5	4,908	1.6	308,440
1999	291,253	91.7	20,527	6.5	5,748	1.8	317,628
2000	300,082	91.9	19,888	6.1	6,518	2.0	326,588

Note: CB stands for commercial bank. Deposits are in Kshs.million.
Source: Central Bank, *Quarterly Economic Review*, various issues.

of two major government owned banks, i.e. National Bank of Kenya (NBK) and Kenya Commercial Bank (KCB) in 1968, bank branches were expanded nationwide and particularly to rural areas. However, the nationalization program alone was not significant enough to ensure that financial services were accessible to the rural masses, as there had been no direct government policy[10] to encourage long-run expansion of banks to *under-banked* towns and cities in rural and semi-urban areas unlike other developing countries[11] where proper incentives were given to maintain geographical distribution of banking facilities (Athukorala & Sen, 2002). Accordingly, bank concentration is high in urban and metropolitan areas, and hence, examination of branch network and preference of commercial banks will reveal urban bias, typically as is the case in most of African countries (Ikhide, 1996).

Market liberalization: Kenya adopted stabilization and adjustment programs in the late 1980s when the economy entered into a period of macroeconomic instability and continuously worsening fiscal problems. The major aspects of these adjustments were in financial and fiscal dimensions. As the basic objectives of the structural reforms were to revive economic growth through effective and efficient use of

[10] The government recognized the need to expand and maintain banking facilities to rural and largely populated districts but there has been no direct and committed policy to achieve this. In his Budget Speech in 1983, the Minister for Finance announced an increment in branch licensing fees for any new openings but recommended to discount such fees by 15% for any rural opening (GoK, 1983). Thus, even though there was a need to encourage rural banking, such bold steps were either not taken or remained rare and inconsistent when taken.

[11] A good example of this is India, where to ensure wide distribution and national coverage of commercial banks, the Reserve Bank of India directly restricted branch licensing of banks in highly concentrated urban and metropolitan areas.

resources and increase their mobilization (Kabubo-Mariara & Kariti, 2002), reforms of financial management, its regulation, and planning were all necessary to achieve this. Before these structural changes, Kenya's financial sector experienced various forms of financial repression that created market distortions and depressed competition.[12] Thus, a core part of the reform program was liberalization of the financial sector that entailed deregulation of interest rates, encouraging competition through elimination and/or minimizing entry and exit controls of financial and other market institutions, abolishing unnecessary price controls, and completely discouraging forced credit allocation at concessional rates of interest. It seemed likely that such an unfettered financial set-up would encourage savings mobilization and promote financial depth and efficiency (Olomola, 1994). Table 4.5 shows the actual trend in the nominal and real interest rates together with the intermediation spreads.

Since all interest rates were almost fully deregulated in 1991, it is observable that nominal interest rates, with the exception of deposit rates, significantly improved following their liberalization. For the period after liberalization, it can be seen that real deposit rates were either negative or insignificantly positive (refer to Table 4.5). Similarly, T-bills and inter-bank rates still have some years when they appear to be negative. On the other hand, although nominal lending rates increased significantly following reforms, more importantly deposit rates increased minimally and in general recorded levels similar to or less than that of pre-liberalization while the inflation rate remained above two-digits in most of the years. Hence, in the period between 1992 and 1995 the spread between lending and deposit rates increased from almost 12 to 23% and then reduced slightly to 18% in 1999. This shows that contrary to the financial repression hypothesis, as real deposit rates recorded negative values in most years after liberalization, a widening spread between lending and deposit rates is clearly visible (refer to Fig. 4.4). Thus, this initial examination of macroeconomic trends following reforms establishes that although liberalization efforts were expected to enhance efficiency through reduction in intermediation margins, such an effect so far remains unsubstantiated at least in Kenya's context. However to establish this further, we investigate other mechanisms to analyse the impacts of reforms and deduce additional evidence. We first examine how the performance in allocation and mobilization of funds evolved after liberalization.

4.2.2.3 Allocational Behaviour After Reforms

Financial institutions have the important role of facilitating economic development through efficient allocation of limited resources to the deserving and most productive sectors of the economy. However, if there is extensive intervention in channeling

---

[12]It has been argued that such restrictive policies largely obviate the need for intermediation, and discourage financial integration (Maje, 1996).

Table 4.5 Nominal and real interest rates and intermediation margins (percentage)

Year	Nominal rates					Real rates				
	Deposit	Lending	T-bills	Inter-bank	Inflation	Deposit	Lending	T-Bills	Inter-Bank	Spread
1985	11.0	14.0	14.1	12.5	10.7	0.3	3.0	3.1	1.6	2.7
1986	11.0	14.0	11.2	12.5	5.7	5.0	7.9	5.2	6.4	2.9
1987	11.0	14.0	13.0	12.5	8.7	2.1	4.9	4	3.5	2.8
1988	10.0	15.0	15.0	16.0	12.3	−2.0	2.4	2.4	3.3	4.4
1989	12.5	15.5	14.0	16.5	13.3	−0.7	1.9	0.6	2.8	2.6
1990	13.5	19.0	15.9	19.4	15.8	−2.0	2.8	0.1	3.1	4.8
1991	14.5	29.0	16.8	19.7	19.6	−4.3	7.9	−2.0	0.1	12.2
1992	14.8	30.0	17.0	26.9	27.3	−9.8	2.1	−8.0	−0.1	11.9
1993	22.5	72.0	39.3	36.8	46.0	−16.0	18.0	−5.0	−6.0	34.0
1994	12.1	30.9	17.9	8.9	28.8	−13.0	1.6	−8.0	−15.0	14.6
1995	9.5	33.1	20.9	24.6	1.6	7.8	31.0	19.0	23.0	23.2
1996	11.2	34.6	21.5	16.0	9.0	2.0	23.0	11.0	6.4	21.0
1997	9.7	30.4	26.4	18.7	11.2	−1.3	17.0	14.0	6.7	18.3
1998	8.0	27.1	11.1	9.4	6.6	1.3	19.0	4.2	2.6	17.7
1999	6.2	25.2	20.5	13.0	5.0	1.1	19.0	15.0	7.6	17.9
2000	4.5	19.6	13.5	9.8	6.2	−1.6	13.0	6.9	3.4	14.6

Note: The spread is the difference between real and nominal interest rate while real interest rate is calculated as ((i−inf)/(1 + inf)) × 100, where i indicates the nominal rate and inf is inflation.
Source: Central Bureau of Statistics, *Economic Survey*, various issues.

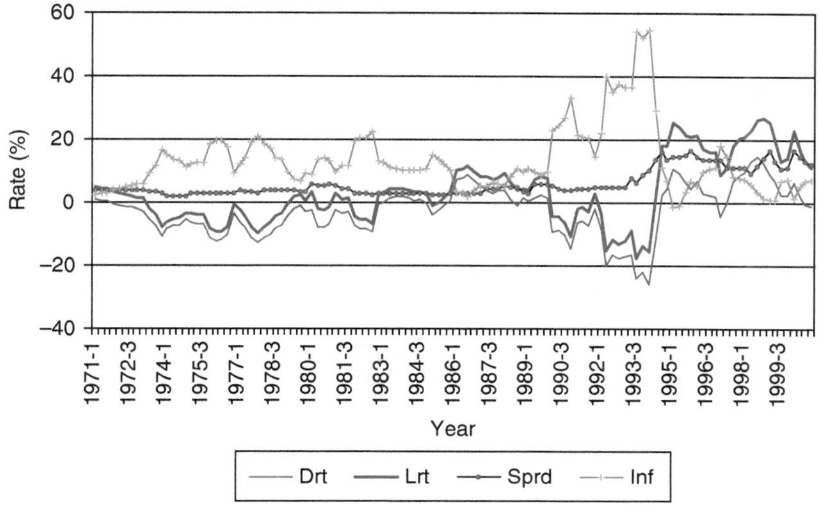

Fig. 4.4 Trend in real interest rates and intermediation spread (1971–2001 to 2000–2004)
Note: Drt deposit rate; *Lrt* lending rate; *Sprd* spread; *Inf* inflation
Source: Central Bank, *Quarterly Economic Review*, various issues.

such funds to preferred sectors (not necessarily for return based reasons), this may indirectly affect efficiency and hence growth in output. In the pre-liberalization period, the state through the Central Bank had quantitative credit guidelines in favour of priority areas perceived to stimulate growth and maintain export competitive advantage. As such, on a regular basis the state issued guidelines on how much banks should lend to these preferred sectors. For example, from 1975 till 1991 when reforms were implemented, banks were required to lend 17% of their deposit liabilities to the agricultural sector (Central Bank, 2000). Such quantitative controls and diversion of credit away from other 'could-be' deserving areas suppressed the efficiency benefits associated with it. Indeed, while fiscal imbalances increased in the 1980s, the total domestic credit reduced as these deficits were principally financed through heavy domestic borrowings from the banking sector crowding out the private sector. The private sector credit (as a percentage of GDP) was only 22% on average from 1981–1990. Indirectly, the efficiency of investment was affected as this improper allocational system favoured the channelling of resources towards capital-intensive projects in a labour abundant country due to an inappropriate interest rate or its control, making capital artificially cheaper. Besides, the presence of large government owned parastatals (estimated to have been 250 in 1990s) that effectively depended on state handouts induced the bulk of allocation to be directed towards financing budgetary needs, crowding out more effective and commercially oriented trade and service sectors. However, parastatals and the government sectors are known in Kenya to be inefficient, uneconomical and, more seriously, corrupt and mismanaged (Mwega & Ndungu, 2002). In the years following liberalization, credit rationing policies were abolished and advances to the private

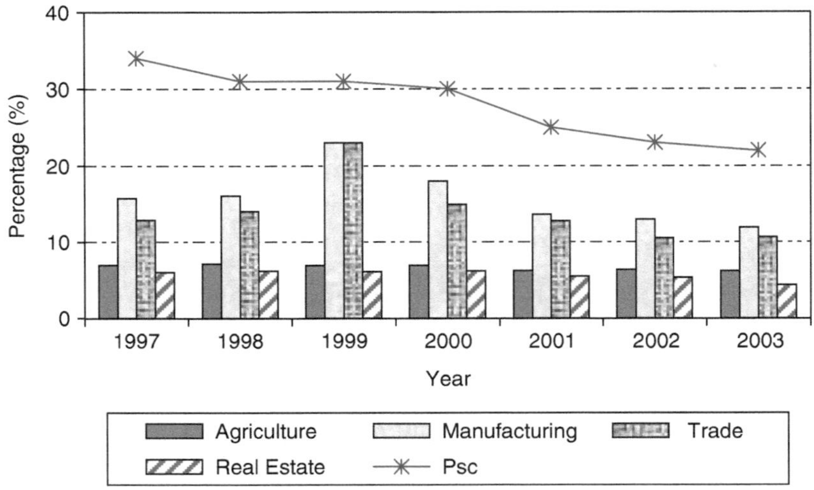

Fig. 4.5 Allocational transformations in Kenya
Note: Psc is credit to the private sector
Source: Central Bank of Kenya, *Quarterly Economic Report*, various issues.

sector increased from 19% in 1986–1990 to 29% in 1996–2000. However, through the use of indirect instruments, lending to the government sector still remains significant as the government-backed treasury bills yield higher returns, leaving the functioning of the financial sector improper in terms of its capacity to intermediate. Furthermore, this may also lead to an inappropriate interest rate since such a rate reflects the high demand of government for credit as opposed to being a by-product of the relative scarcity of capital and/or other purely financial market risks that contribute to the opportunity costs of capital. Consequently, banks have opted to invest in the less risky government stocks than the private sector, possibly reducing output and leading to misallocation of the national resources.[13]

Despite this, there has been a compositional change in private lending activities following liberalization. Manufacturing and trade receive the largest share of total advances as they account for 23% each while advances to the agricultural sector fell to only 6% as at 1999. These sectors received 13%, 10% and 17% of the private sector advances respectively in 1990, while lending to public institutions and parastatals has decreased and is only based on their creditworthiness and economic viability (Central Bank, 2000). More importantly, it is observable that reforms have led to an improvement in credit allocation to trade and manufacturing (refer to Fig. 4.5). This development is clearly related to external market liberalization that accompanied the reforms. Since 1994 trade and exchange controls have been amended and in particular that foreign exchange market has been made freer (Mwega & Ndungu, 2002). These changes in the economic environment favoured

[13]Currently banking institutions hold more than 58% of the outstanding treasury bills.

the trade and manufacturing sectors through enabling importation of high-tech machines and encouraging private sector investments. As a result it is not surprising that the prospects of attracting capital by these sectors largely improved as depicted (see Fig. 4.5). Consequently, it could be argued that liberalization has allowed banks to allocate credit more competitively to some extent and allocate it more freely depending on their creditworthiness and economic viability. This transformation in a broad sense implies that repressive financial polices in the pre-reform era may have deprived credit access to various productive economic sectors.

4.2.2.4 Analysis of Deposits and Advances

The analysis so far provides evidence that reforms towards financial liberalization did not lead to the anticipated increase in efficiency and competition in Kenya. Accordingly, the financial data indicate decline in the rate of savings. A similar trend can be observed from the deposits in the banking system (as a percentage of GDP). As can be seen from Table 4.3, the level of deposits marginally increased, from 36% in 1990 when liberalization measures were underway for full implementation to 41% in 1997, before finally showing a continuously declining trend and hitting 36% in 2000, the same level as in the pre-liberalization period. However, despite this and even though liberalization in the financial sector did not produce the anticipated results, at least so far, as deposit rates are either marginally positive or negative, there has been some improvement in savings and credit mobilization in some segments. The reform measures have led to further development in the information technologies used and improvement in customer care, particularly in the major banks. This has resulted in an increased use and adoption of new information processing and transmitting mechanisms, automated teller machines (ATMs) and even online banking.

In this regard, the few large banks (peer group 1) have experienced growth in deposits and advances level (see Table 4.6). For example, the level of deposits in KCB has more than twice doubled from Kshs.14 billion in 1991 to Kshs.43 billion in 2002. Mainly, this is because as deposits have shifted away from NBFIs and troubled smaller institutions, the largest share in this movement has been attracted to such bigger and more prudent banks. On the basis of this, the large banks have maintained their dominance in the banking sector by instilling customer confidence as they are perceived to be less vulnerable to government intervention, liquidation problems, and other market risks.[14] Moreover, the few dominant banks may have a lower base lending rate as they enjoy economies of scale and have a lower cost of funds. Given in Table 4.6 is a base lending rate of a leading bank (Barclays bank) closely mimicking the T-bill rate and consistently lower than the nominal interest rate. Thus, even as at 2002, the leading five banks control more than 60% of the total deposits as a result (see Table 4.16 for details).

---

[14]This is particularly the case in Kenya as many banks either have bad and doubtful debts or have large NPLs. With NPLs forming 38% of the total loan, this rate is one of the highest in the world (Kinyua & Musau, 2004).

Table 4.6 Activities by peer group 1 type commercial banks

Year	Base rate	T-bills	Nominal interest rate	Deposits (million)	Advances (million)
1985	n.a	14	14.0	4,772	4,270
1986	n.a	11	14.0	5,550	4,890
1987	n.a	13	14.0	6,644	5,297
1988	n.a	15	15.0	7,638	6,505
1989	13	14	15.5	10,044	7,346
1990	14	16	19.0	10,722	8,405
1991	16	17	29.0	14,018	10,609
1992	19	17	30.0	16,252	11,539
1993	23	39	72.0	24,413	15,535
1994	18	18	30.9	40,156	18,808
1995	23	21	33.1	34,897	25,313
1996	21	22	34.6	32,326	27,728
1997	26	26	30.4	37,260	35,469
1998	19	11	27.1	38,883	40,882
1999	23	21	25.2	48,539	44,963
2000	16	13	19.6	48,638	39,104
2001	15	11	19.5	44,037	32,554
2002	14	8	18.3	43,096	27,651

Note: Before 1989, most of the banks did not have specific base lending rates as each branch had to set their rate depending on the risk projected and the lending manager.
Source: Authors' compilation from various sources.

Loan evaluation procedures: As usual in most of the financial institutions, banks have standard lending procedures. Before any lending is approved, there are strict evaluation and selection mechanisms to nominate projects that are economically visible and have lower risk. Applicants are required to complete an official loan application form which contains a questionnaire on the purpose of the loan, amount, cash flow projection, source of income to service the credit, capitalization of the applicant, and the security to be offered. Looking at the lending structure, it is observable that banks, especially of peer group 1 type,[15] prefer to lend to corporate or multinational sectors relative to small and household sectors of the economy. Consequently, it is usual that loan approvals are biased towards lending to expansion-type projects of a bigger size than start-up and small size ones.[16] This has largely been influenced by the fact that the economic slowdown of the past decade and half has made it difficult for growth and stability of new projects, and hence, loans in this regard are perceived to have much higher risk. Further, banks charge a very high premium to cover such risks, further increasing the payment burden on the infant business. Despite this, with the general slowdown in business activities in

[15]Peer group classification is based on the level of total assets. A bank is rated peer group1 if it has an asset accumulation of over Kshs.5 billion.

[16]Through interviews with the relevant staff, I have been told that risks of failures and high monitoring cost have led to this.

recent years, there has been an improvement in the personal and household sector lending. As an illustrative example, the consumer lending side of Barclays Bank has increased from 4.3% of total advances in 1996 to 16% in 2002. Based on this evidence it looks as though banks are moving towards short-term consumption loans. This relief in borrowing constraints may actually hamper future savings as individuals' flexibility to borrow against future income increases and thus reducing the incentives to accumulate precautionary savings. Ultimately, this conflicts with the macroeconomic goal of increasing productivity through higher investment. Overall, although quality of banking services and accessibility may have improved in recent times, enhancement in the intermediation process that would allow financial access to small and medium scale, existing and new business sectors, particularly for long-term projects, did not occur, limiting the expected benefits of liberalization.

4.2.2.5 Explaining the Spread

As this analysis reveals that liberalization of the financial sector in Kenya has not brought about much improvement in enhancing efficiency (often proxied by the difference between lending and deposit rates), a number of explanations may be applicable for the case of Kenya. This includes the high liquidity and reserve requirement, the infant equity market, the non-financial cost structure of the banking sector, the lack of significant competition (see the next section) and perhaps the size and concentration of non-performing loans (NPLs).[17] To enable us explain the performance of liberalization and pin down the factors behind the failure to conform to the Mckinnon-Shaw hypothesis, we will look at each of these factors separately.

Liquidity reserve requirements: Even though there has been general reorientation of the economy following financial sector reforms, in an environment where banks are subject to high liquidity and reserve requirements, interest rates may be forced to remain high, as banks ultimately tend to transfer economic cost of such funds to the final customers.[18] Following structural adjustments and financial reforms, as the central bank geared up to tighten prudential regulation, the liquidity reserve requirements and cash-balance ratios in Kenya either stayed the same as the pre-liberalization era or increased as observable in the period between 1994 and 1996 (see Table 4.3). In this aspect, the liquidity ratio measured by the ratio of net liquid assets to total deposits remained as high as 20% in 1997. Liquidity reserve

[17]Ndungu and Ngugi (2000) point out that in a liberalized financial environment banks charge a higher risk premium and therefore may lend to risky projects. In a highly unstable economic environment and with little or non-existence of hedging instruments, this may increase the level of NPLs. However, for the banks to maintain their profit margin they may compensate for this by increasing their lending rates.

[18]Mostly high liquidity requirement is viewed as an implicit financial tax leading to a high interest rate.

requirements of an average industrialized country are estimated to be around 5%, and thus, a range of 20–25% must be extremely high (Chirwa, 2001), and will most likely translate to persistently high spread in the banking sector. This is because of the fact that banks will have to adjust lending rates upwards faster than deposit rates as they struggle to maintain their profitability margin and reasonably service customers' deposits.

Alternative equity market: As the equity market is at an infant stage in Kenya, business enterprises have to raise all their investment funds only through debt-financing. In this regard, financial institutions as well as the business sector absorb too much risk (Ndungu & Ngugi, 2000). Consistent with the above argument, Cho (1986) also notes that substantial equity market development is a necessary condition for effective financial liberalization and, hence, in the absence of this, material reductions in the intermediation margins will not be realized. However, as the equity market gradually matures and the necessary financial instruments become available, the share of debt-financing reduces and the risks absorbed by the banking and business sector fall, while deposit rates will gradually rise to compete for savers' funds (Ndungu & Ngugi, 2000), leading to reduction in the intermediation spread. Capital markets are formed of Stock Markets and Money Markets. In Kenya, the Nairobi Stock Exchange was formed in the late 1990s, and it continues to function, firms sell shares to raise equity capital. However, the Stock Exchange remains small. And the money market, in which interest-bearing securities such as corporate bonds and commercial papers with maturities less than a year are traded, that is likely to attract short-term or even managed medium-term investors, is almost non-existent. With the exception of government treasury bills, the money market in Kenya is very much inactive and does not even have a specific center for trading (NSE, 2001). This has left industrialists with little alternative but to turn to banks for provision of short-term loans.

Costs: The non-financial costs of the banking sector also partly explain the widening difference between lending and deposit rates. As banks have to pay for huge non-financial costs in the form of employees' wages, cost of physical capital and other general overheads at times when business enterprises are facing activity slowdown due to continuous economic recession, banks are not able to extend new credit while absorbing risks of non-payment for outstanding loans (see Table 4.7). As more businesses close down or continue to fail, this will have a multiplier effect that will continuously reduce the banks' profitability, directly widening the intermediation margin.

Observably, the poor economic environment that has led to frequent communication network failures and unreliable infra-structural support, is currently forcing the commercial banks and other financial institutions to incur large expenditure on supportive systems such as power supply, communication, security and water supplies (Kinyua & Musau, 2004). Hence, in addition to resulting limited profitability prospects, this will obviously also affect the size of the overhead costs.

From the global banking sector's profit and loss analysis, we observe that operating expenditures of the commercial banks have been on the rising turn (see Table 4.8). The operational expenditures rose by 145% from 1995 to 2000

Table 4.7 GDP growth and overtime shift in employment trend

Year	GDP growth (%)	Formal sector (%)	Informal sector (%)
1988	6.2	77.5	20.0
1989	4.7	76.2	21.3
1990	4.2	58.8	39.2
1991	1.4	56.4	41.6
1992	−0.8	53.1	44.9
1993	0.4	49.2	48.9
1994	2.6	44.8	53.8
1995	4.4	40.4	58.0
1996	2.5	37.4	61.1
1997	2.1	35.1	63.5
1998	1.6	32.7	65.9
1999	1.3	30.5	68.2
2000	−0.2	28.4	70.4

Note: Formal sector is the wage employment sector.
Source: Economic survey, various issues, and Manda (2002).

Table 4.8 Profit analysis of the global banking sector (Kshs.million)

Item/year	1995	1996	1997	1998	1999	2000	2001
Interest on advances	35,049	40,339	49,876	49,256	35,193	31,987	28,370
Interest on government securities	8,185	8,289	9,507	12,082	8,772	9,779	10,266
Other income	8,993	9,302	10,388	10,334	10,849	13,800	14,853
Interest expenses on deposits	25,091	27,848	34,709	35,405	19,149	17,617	14,347
Other expenses	7,044	7,716	9,287	10,513	12,014	10,834	11,467
Operation expenses	13,088	14,279	17,515	23,806	38,314	32,046	24,048
Profit before tax	15,346	14,885	17,425	9,261	3,496	4,748	8,939
Total income	60,569	64,728	78,936	78,985	62,163	57,959	58,801
Total expenses	45,223	49,843	61,511	69,724	58,667	62,708	49,862

Source: Central Bank of Kenya, *Bank supervision department's annual report*, various issues.

(from Kshs.13.1 billion to Kshs.32.1 billion). As a percentage of total expenses, the operating expenditures have increased from 29% in 1995 to 51% in 2000. There is no evidence to indicate that such expenses were going up due to an expansion trend in this sector.[19]

On the other hand, another important factor which may have influenced such costs is NPLs. It is likely to observe high NPLs after liberalization due to old

[19]Through my interview with staff from the three leading banks in this sector it has been revealed to us that they have been continuously closing a number of countrywide branches rather than expanding to rural areas since 1997.

[20]Further discussion on NPLs and changes in NBFIs is given in the next section.

Table 4.9 GDP growth, lending rate and non-performing loans (percentage)

Year	GDPpc growth	Lending rate	NPLs (NBFI)	NPLs (CB)
1987	2.5	14	n.a	n.a
1988	2.8	15	n.a	n.a
1989	1.4	16	n.a	n.a
1990	1.1	19	n.a	n.a
1991	−1.4	29	n.a	n.a
1992	−3.5	30	n.a	n.a
1993	−2.3	72	n.a	n.a
1994	0.0	31	28	18
1995	1.8	33	23	18
1996	1.6	35	27	27
1997	−0.4	30	40	30
1998	−0.8	27	48	31
1999	−1.1	25	47	34
2000	−2.4	20	44	38
2001	−1.0	20	46	33
2002	−0.9	19	49	37

Note: GDP per capita is at constant local currency and lending rates are nominal.
CB commercial banks.
Source: Central Bank, *Quarterly Economic Review*, various issues.

government meddling (which should have encouraged lending to bad sectors) while interest rate has gone way up post-reforms.[20] From Table 4.9 it is observable that NPLs were as high as 37% in 2002. Given the reduced economic activity and business levels, the interest on advances declined from Kshs.35.1 billion in 1995 to Kshs.28.4 billion in 2001 while total income declined from Kshs.60.6 billion in 1995 to Kshs.58.8 billion in 2001. Similarly, during the same period the sector has also seen profitability decline (profit before tax) from Kshs.15.3 billion in 1995 to Kshs.4.7 billion in 2000, marginally improving in 2001. Indeed, with declining profitability and increasing operational cost coupled with poor economic performances, many banks have opted to close down most of their unprofitable up-country branches. More so, to respond to these developments, banks have also taken other measures including adoption of new technologies – to enhance consumer relations – and reduction in full time staff, to bring down the general overhead costs (Kinyua & Musau, 2004). But ultimately, in an effort to maintain profit margin there is a higher possibility of the lending rate adjusting upwards given the same rate of deposits and the interest rate spread being an increasing function of such costs.

Government borrowings: Kenya has faced a continuous overall budget deficit since the 1980s and hence total expenditures have consistently exceeded the available revenues for the last 15 years.[21] To finance the deficit, the government

[21]See Kabubo-Mariara and Kiriti (2002) for analysis of Kenya's fiscal deficit and its financing.

has been borrowing heavily from the domestic market. Since this has increased competition for loanable funds between government and private investors, where banks are more secure in lending to the government, the lending rate has been pushing up significantly faster than the deposit rate. Under such circumstances the lending-deposit rate differentials widened as deposit rates remained almost unchanged (see Table 4.5). Furthermore, the government is not competing with banks for funds since constraints such as the minimum investment capital level, block auctioning and other administrative costs deter individual investors from competing for government securities (Ndungu & Ngugi, 2000).

In line with the above arguments and despite observing some positive aspects of liberalization-led reforms, many have already lamented that controls were needed to stop the surging interest rate spread in the financial sector. Recently, through a bill tabled in the parliament in 2000 famously knows as the "Donde Bill", it was claimed that the government must take a second look and rethink its position on interest rate liberalization (IEA, 2000). The proposed amendment challenges the government to formulate ways to discourage arbitrary increases in the nominal interest rate and instead help harmonize lending-deposit differentials to reflect their market levels. It is proposed that lending and deposit rates must be pegged and only allowed to fluctuate within specified limits. Unfortunately, if accepted, this will reverse the financial reform objectives and eliminate salient intended features of liberalization program including flexibility, discretional power and market based mechanisms of risk and return evaluations that ultimately will hamper savings mobilization and resource allocation.

4.2.2.6 Level of Competition and Market Structure: Another Explanation of Spread

In Kenya, two major statutes, i.e. the Banking Act and the Central Bank of Kenya Act generally guide the regulations of the banking sector. In addition to this, there are a number of other statutes which include Building Societies Act, Cooperative Societies Act, Capital Market Act and Companies Act which all provide further supportive regulatory and supervisory guidelines. Thus, the entry, exit, renewals and relocation requirements of banking activities are all stipulated in the Banking Act. As prescribed in subsection 5 of the Banking Act, both foreign and local new entrants are required to get prior approval from the Minister for Finance. Upon studying the background of the company, which includes among other things, the historical and the financial conditions of the institution, characteristics of its management team, professional and moral suitability of its management, and adequacy of its capital structure, the minister may grant permission to carry out banking business or extend further a branch network. In this regard, the act is fairly restrictive in terms of entry and further extension of banking business in Kenya. According to the Banking Act provisions, there are no differences in terms of considerations between branch extension of a locally owned already existing bank and a foreign owned local bank. However the law does not allow for a foreign branch extension until such a branch is locally incorporated.

An examination of the relevant indicators in Kenya reveals that the market structure of the banking sector looks to be a more or less monopolistic or oligopolistic type, where few major banks (peer group 1) possess high market share (see Table 4.16).[22] Entry of new firms in this sector is expected to improve efficiency and increase access to banking facilities by reducing the monopoly power of the dominant banks and bringing down banking transaction costs. Despite this, the entry of new banks, particularly of big foreign banks with large economies of scale is not forthcoming. Rather, the increase in the number of commercial banks that the country has experienced for the past two decades (refer to Table 4.3) is reflected in the mushrooming of small banks of which mostly are locally owned. This did not translate into an increase in the level of competition as the newly established institutions are still at infant stage and control an insignificant volume of business. As is evident from Table 4.16, the existing structure of the banking sector is such that five out of 46 banks control 61%, 62% and 60% of the market share in terms of total assets, loan advances and total deposits respectively in 2002. Ten years ago (1992) the corresponding figures were 71%, 75%, 73%, clearly indicating little sign of improvement following the economic liberalization. As such, and on this evidence, it is apparent that the banking sector in Kenya faces a highly concentrated market structure, typically characterized as either an oligopolistic or monopolistic type.[23]

Effectively, as initially indicated by Seck and El Nil (1993) and recently tested by Chirwa (2001), it has been pointed out that financial liberalization may not lead to a reduction in intermediation margin if interest rate liberalization, freedom of entry and exit, and decrease in liquidity and other reserve requirements in the banking sector are not accompanied by an increase in competition. Similarly, the market structure, conduct and performance (S-C-P) hypothesis predicts that "high interest rate spread may persist if financial sector reforms do not significantly alter the structure within which banks operate" (Mlachila & Chirwa, 2002). In Kenya, the banking sector has seen little change, as the small and medium sized banks that are mainly new entrants and form the majority only in terms of number are not able to compete favourably with the few big and old ones in terms of capital and provision of a full range of products and services.[24] Hence, it can be argued that the financial structure basically remained the same since the 1980s and as such, this lack of an effective competitive environment and incomplete restructuring has led to inefficiencies that in real terms translate to wide spreads between lending and deposit rates.

[22]Note that Table 4.16 is given in the Appendix.

[23]Death of NBFIs and implicit barriers to entry also explain lack of competition. Discussion on entry barriers is given in Chapter 5 while the transformation of the NBFIs is outlined in the next sub-section.

[24]Some indicative evidence on this was given earlier.

4.2.2.7 Transformation in NBFI Sector and NPLs

As the economy was small in the immediate years after independence there was little need for many commercial banks or additional Non-Banking Financial Institutions (NBFIs) in Kenya. Therefore, there were few NBFIs, which were not very active in the financial sector. The quick proliferation of NBFIs started in the early 1980s for two major reasons. First, as the coffee boom was realized in 1976–1979 and a large part of this windfall was passed on to households, raising their income significantly, many Kenyan entrepreneurs opted to venture into the banking business and established a number of NBFIs benefiting from lenient entry. In addition to this, the new-comers' interest in this venture was supported by the fact that commercial banks concentrated on short-term working capital financing. Second, in a move to finance various state projects and channel funds into priority sectors the government also established a number of Development Financial Institutions (DFIs) with the objectives of providing long-term capital (Mwega & Ndungu, 2002). Although NBFIs were part of the depository institutions, entries into this sector were made much easier with lower minimum capital requirements while having much wider investment portfolio choices at a higher interest rate relative to commercial banks (Central Bank, 2000).[25] However, as part of the repression policies the government fixed the minimum savings (depository) rate as well as the maximum lending rate in both banking and non-banking financial institutions.

Looking at the entry statistics and depository levels within the NBFIs in the early 1980s, one may observe that such a quick proliferation of more independent financial institutions may have sparked intense and vibrant competition enhancing financial efficiency by enabling financial development and providing the public with a wider choice of financial services. Despite this, a reversal of the government policy change from the mid-1980s and subsequent pressure from commercial banks discouraged successful establishment and further expansion of these infant institutions (NSE, 2001). This change in the government policy direction that favoured commercial banks in terms of depository access served as a backlash to NBFI development and became a turning point that finally led these institutions to play a peripheral role in the financial sector. Consequently, out of these challenges and financial difficulties emanated the 1987–1990 banking crisis in which many NBFIs were hit hard and collapsed as they became financially unsustainable. This triggered a loss of public confidence with NBFIs and the first phase of the private depository shift to established commercial banks began (see Fig. 4.6). It is observable that during this transformation, the interest rate spread had been going up while deposits in NBFIs were sharply declining.

Bad loans build up: Although the Kenyan Banking Act has been frequently reviewed for the purpose of enforcing effective banking procedures and providing prudential banking regulations, the banking sector continues to reel under

[25] Indeed, while NBFIs were allowed to undertake mortgage lending and charge higher lending rates, commercial banks were restricted from offering such facilities.

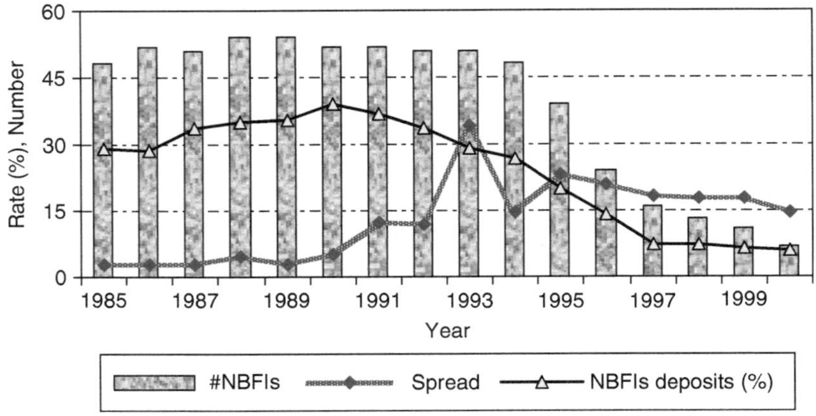

Fig. 4.6 Track of spread vs. other trends in NBFIs
Source: Central Bank, *Quarterly Economic Review*, various issues.

increasing levels of non-performing loans (NPLs) which, in addition to the above setbacks makes it fragile. While the central bank continues to play its role of supervising and strengthening the financial system, and particularly commercial banks,[26] the ratio of NPLs as a percentage of total loans steadily increased from 18% in 1995 (Kshs.59 billion) to 30% in 1997 (Kshs.97 billion) and further to 38% (Kshs.90 billion) in 2000 (see Table 4.9). Similarly in the period between 1995 and 2000 NPLs in NBFIs increased from 23 to 49%.

However, as the presence of huge NPLs might be a sensitive problem that surely jeopardize a conducive banking environment, the Bank Supervision department, in an attempt to figure out the source of the failure, have observed that the increasing trend in NPLs has mainly been caused by poor performance of the national economy, ineffective judicial procedures (where speedy recovery of matured loans through its security is delayed or restrained) and poor credit risk assessment and/or management through unrealistic and weak approval procedures of viable projects (CBK, 2001). On the other hand, the adoption of the financial liberalization program induced higher lending rates. The real lending rates increased from almost 3% in 1990 to 31% in 1995 (see Table 4.5). However, this also coincided with continuous deterioration in economic growth, from 2.8% in 1988 to 2.3% in 1993 and the GDP per capita growth remained negative except for 1995–1996 (see Table 4.9), typically reducing the net worth of the existing borrowers.

Presumably, these changes in the economic environment exacerbated adverse selection problems as the majority of the active borrowers could be classified as those who are largely big risk takers while the banking sector preferred bigger

[26]See, for example, the recent amendments to the Banking Act where the minimum capital requirement was raised from Kshs.150 million to 250 million during 1998–2000, and further to Kshs.400 million by December 2003 to enhance the quality of the banking sector.

rather than smaller loan sizes and business types, seriously crowding out smaller but 'may-be-worthy' borrowers. Accordingly, when borrowers were unable to repay such loans on maturity as a result of undertaking generally riskier projects, distress borrowing increased and institutions with a lower asset base such as smaller banks and NBFIs effectively became more susceptible to failure.[27] Hence, depositor trust towards such institutions declined as public scepticism about their survival deepened and that in turn made it much more likely they would collapse.[28] On the other hand, even though banking regulations were continuously amended to make the sector more efficient and independent, government presence through either total ownership or *de facto* control of many commercial banks and other financial institutions continued to hamper their lending procedures. Indeed, currently the government has effective control (through shareholding) of four out of the six leading banks in this sector and continues to hold large stake in many others (NSE, 2001). In this sense, political interference in banking activities has remained active even in the era of financial liberalization and thus lending to scrappy projects (under the umbrella of the patronage lending package) continued. However, as economic difficulties increased coupled with high real lending rates, servicing of such loans became more difficult. Ultimately, the impact of government-related borrowings started taking effect as the repayment rate declined. This led to the government owned banks become more vulnerable and accumulating large proportions of un-serviced loans, something which did not seriously show up in the pre-liberalization period (refer to Table 4.9).

In view of these predicaments, Table 4.10 gives a breakdown of NPLs in the top seven banking institutions in the country. It is observable that four of these leading seven banks which are government controlled have a significantly higher percentage of non-performing loans ranging from a minimum of 45–71% in 2000, compared to 2–9% in other types of banks respectively. This evidence strongly suggests that the

Table 4.10 Breakdown of NPLs within commercial banks (% of total loans)

Institution/year	2000	2001	2002	2003
National bank of Kenya[a]	71	56	52	53
Kenya commercial bank[a]	45	51	56	47
Co-operative bank of Kenya[a]	46	36	39	37
Consolidate bank of Kenya[a]	60	70	48	54
Barclays bank	9	12	15	15
Standard chartered bank	14	11	8	7
Citi bank N.A.	2	2	3	5

[a] indicates government owned (related) banks.
Source: Central Bank, Bank supervision department.

[27]This argument is supported by the level of NPLs in NBFIs as we observe an upward trend in general from 1994.

[28]Table 4.6 gives suggestive evidence indicating a shift of deposits in favour of bigger commercial banks.

government-related banks have other *idiosyncratic* factors, which further induced negative effects, in addition to the prevailing economic recession and other changes that increased adverse selection and distress borrowing which generally permeated all banking sectors. As illustrated by Table 4.9, a fundamental worry that requires examination is the consistent surging trend in NPLs. Here we review some factors which may have an influence on such a sustained pattern of non-performing loans.

Importantly, this may either be caused by a general market response phenomenon following reforms or by an externally influenced loan-effect which blossomed in the post-liberalization era. (1) The dramatic increase in lending rates following reforms will increase the servicing cost of outstanding loans. Additionally, if a high volume of outstanding loans were issued to favoured projects that 'jumped the ranking queue' in the pre-reform period, the non-payment risk may increase following liberalization because they were lower-return projects and particularly as banks were trying to rescue their earlier loans, (2) despite the establishment of market-oriented project evaluations, if there are chances of a continuation of influential lending mechanisms, non-performing loans are actually expected to increase. Accordingly, the intensifying trend of NPLs must be supported by either of these two factors individually or combined. Firstly, it is notable that lending rates have increased following reforms, although there has been a decline in recent years (refer to Table 4.9), making banks' lending activities too expensive and too risky. This may have reduced the repayment chances of outstanding loans. Secondly, there are strong indications of the existence of political influence in the lending activities of the public sector banks. It has been reported that lending rules and regulation of the state-owned banks have been bent in favour of a few politically sound and powerful individuals. Due to this, "institutions have found themselves with poorly secured debts".[29] Consequently, there has been intermingling of banking activities and political participation such that the restructuring and revival of the commercial banking business have become unachievable.[30] In this regard, the governor of the central bank once urged the state to get out of the banking business confirming that a significant quantity of NPLs was political. Indeed, some of the largest state-owned banks have for long been on the verge of collapse due to privileged but economically unviable borrowings where influential individuals accessed credit "even when they did not deserve to borrow the money".[31] Moreover, recent statistics suggest that the National Bank of Kenya is owed a total amount of Ksh.8.4 billion by top politicians, leading to a

[29]See the article "Government should get out of banking" in *Daily Nation*, Friday, April 23, 1999.

[30]Examples of bad government projects that banks had to invest in include a failed Soya bean project (Ksh.850m), Kenya National Trading Company (Ksh.303m) and the Cotton Board of Kenya (Ksh.52m).

[31]In fact there have been complaints that a sizeable ratio of non-performing loans was a result of some financial instruments issued to influential individuals on the advice of the Treasury department. See "National Bank needs Sh10b to save it from a shut down" in *Daily Nation*, Tuesday, July 10, 2001.

substantial liquidity problem.[32] Interestingly, this anecdotal evidence hints that although higher interest rates may have increased the cost of borrowing, inducing a higher non-payment risk, influential lending procedures seem to be the likely cause of the higher NPLs problem in Kenya. Undeniably, when these two factors are combined, the problem becomes even more acute.

4.2.3 Malawi

4.2.3.1 Policy Environment

After disappointing years of economic growth in the early 1990s, Malawi accepted the IMF-World Bank supported structural adjustment program that aimed to intensify growth potential through undertaking systematic reforms in both the public and private sectors. Thus, the financial reform programme that took place in Malawi in the late 1990s signalled a serious attempt towards removal of distortions in mobilizing and channelling of national resources, with the objectives of enhancing the efficiency of allocation of the limited funds and improving the intermediation process in the financial sector (UNDP, 1999). Following the implementation of the structural adjustment program, interest rates were gradually deregulated in Malawi. Initially banks were allowed to set their own lending rates in July 1987. This was followed by the deregulation of the deposit rates and consequent abolishment of preferential interest rates to the agricultural sector in 1988, before fully liberalizing all interest rates in 1990 (Malawi, 2000). The full deregulation of interest rates and moderation of entry and exit procedures in late 1990 were aimed at increasing competitive behaviour towards deposit mobilization, enhancing financial intermediation and reducing the intermediation margin.

As can be observed from Table 4.11, the real deposit rate remained negative in post-liberalization except for 2000, while real lending rates were similarly negative for a number of years. However, the spread has consistently been increasing throughout the period under liberalization, from as low as 5.5% in 1992 to almost 20% in 2000. From this simple observation, it is clear that the expected banking efficiency of greater competition, higher fund intermediation and lower profit margin have not been observed. In this sub-section, we revisit the predictions of financial liberalization theory and reflect on some of the possible reasons as to why the adjustments did not bring about the desired outcome in Malawi. Initially, focus is made on the allocation of capital to public and private post-reforms before conducting further investigation to identify important factors explaining these unexpected trends.

[32] Further details are given in the article "Obstacles Narc should remove" in *Daily Nation*, Sunday, January 5, 2003.

Table 4.11 Interest rates and intermediation margin in Malawi

Year	Nominal			Real		
	Lending	Deposit	Inflation	Lending	Deposit	Spread
1985	18	13	11	8	2	5.9
1986	19	13	14	5	−1	6.3
1987	20	14	25	−6	−11	5.3
1988	23	14	34	−12	−20	8.8
1989	23	13	12	11	0	10.3
1990	21	12	12	9	0	8.9
1991	20	13	13	7	0	7.5
1992	22	17	24	−2	−7	5.5
1993	30	22	23	7	−1	7.8
1994	31	25	35	−4	−10	6.0
1995	47	37	83	−36	−46	10.1
1996	45	26	38	8	−11	19.0
1997	28	10	9	19	1	18.0
1998	38	19	30	8	−11	18.6
1999	54	32	45	9	−12	20.4
2000	53	33	30	24	4	19.9

Source: IMF, International financial statistics (IFS).

4.2.3.2 Allocational Behaviour Post-Reforms

Prior to the structural adjustment programme, Malawi experienced various forms of credit ceiling and direction to priority areas, and in particular since the government maintained preferential lending incentives to agricultural and other ‘thought-to be important’ sectors. Right from independence, there was a strong belief that the agricultural sector could spearhead economic growth and provide substantial revenues for continuous investment (Chipeta & Mkandawire, 2002). On this basis, the commercial banking sector was instructed to support this cause. Nonetheless, as reforms proceeded, these preferential treatments were abandoned in December 1989 when credit ceiling policies were abolished (Malawi, 2000). In this regard, with the adoption of liberal financial policies, credit flows to the real economic sector are expected to improve. Table 4.12 gives the movement in both domestic credit (Doc) and credit to the private sector (Psc) by the commercial banks. It is observable that both these variables show an inverted U-shape trend with a turning point in 1994. Initially domestic credit flows, as well as the share of credit to the private sector, improved. However, with the suspension of foreign aid and continuous fiscal imbalances, Treasury bill rates increased abnormally to 46% as the government continued to heavily borrow from the domestic sector, crowding out the private sector demands (the share of the private sector credit was only 6% in 1995).

Evidently, following the significant increase in Treasury bill rates from 1993, commercial banks’ investment in government bonds and local registered stock increased proportionately. Recently, these holding were estimated to be more than 78% and 59% respectively (Chirwa, 2001), and were observably decreasing

Table 4.12 Macroeconomic indicators in Malawi

Year	TOT	EXR (K/USD)	C/A	Doc	Psc	T-bill rates
1983	175	1	−11	46	20	11
1984	180	1	−3	40	15	11
1985	158	2	−11	37	13	12
1986	136	2	−7	42	13	13
1987	131	2	−5	38	10	14
1988	121	3	−6	22	8	16
1989	131	3	−3	22	10	16
1990	141	3	−5	20	11	13
1991	149	3	−10	20	12	12
1992	122	4	−16	31	15	16
1993	108	4	−8	26	9	24
1994	85	9	−15	30	13	28
1995	100	15	−5	14	6	46
1996	106	15	−6	10	4	31
1997	111	16	−11	10	5	18
1998	98	31	0	9	7	33
1999	101	44	−9	11	7	43
2000	95	60	−4	11	8	40

Note: C/A, Doc and Psc are all in percentage of GDP; *TOT* terms of trade; *EXR* exchange rate; *C/A* current account including official transfers; *Doc* domestic credit; *Psc* credit to the private sector.
Source: Reserve Bank of Malawi, *Financial and Economic Review*, various issues.

their advances to the private sector. This phenomenon negatively influences the economy in two major aspects: (1) effectively, it merely reduces the biggest and most dominant financial institution in the country to act as an agent to intermediate the credit demands of the state rather than mapping out innovative financial strategies to seek new businesses,[33] (2) this further assists the overspending of the government sector – which is generally linked with a myriad of growth retarding problems, such as corruption and inefficiencies – while at the same time reducing the size of the corporate sector as it limits the attainment of the sector's expansion goals. This evidence suggests misallocation of resources, as the more productive and efficient sector of the economy is allowed to die out slowly. In a different dimension, liberalization policies induced compositional changes in commercial banks' advances to the private sector itself. The share of credit to the agricultural sector decreased from 53% in 1987 to barely 10% in 1999 (see Fig. 4.7). This is not surprising since the credit allocation through directed mechanisms to the less viable estate tobacco growers have now ceased with liberalization. Chipeta and Mkandawire (2002) observe that in the absence of directed credit "less viable/unviable borrowers in the priority subsectors of estate tobacco growing began to lose out"

[33]More precisely, this amounts to financial repression elements which obviate the need for intermediation.

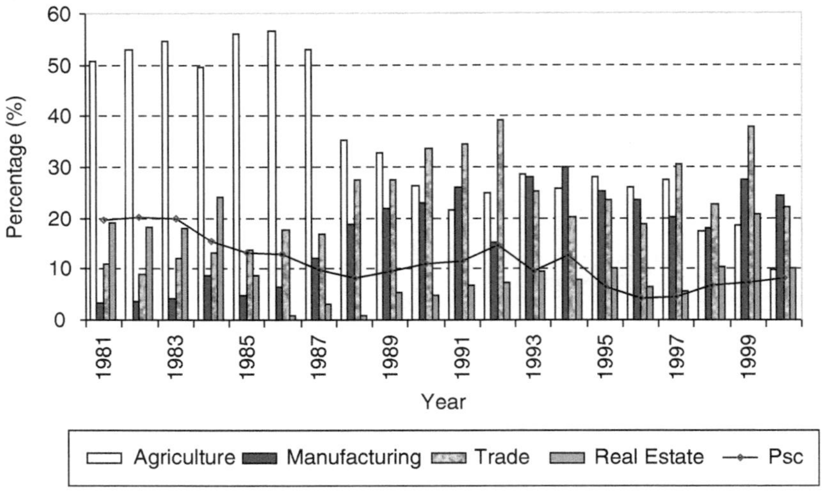

Fig. 4.7 Distribution of credit within the private sector in Malawi
Note: Psc is the share of commercial banks' credit to the private sector (% of GDP), all other variables are expressed as a ratio of total advances.
Source: Reserve bank of Malawi, *Financial and Economic Review*, various issues.

(p. 54). Although reforms were meant to change the product pricing policy and enhance efficiency, the performance of the agricultural sector had declined due to inadequate producer incentives[34] and unfavourable terms of trade (UNDP, 1999). This has adversely affected the sector's productivity. On the other hand, the proportion of advances to manufacturing, trade and real estate sectors increased much faster in the post-liberalization period, with manufacturing and trade showing particularly significant upward trends.[35] Most likely, having improved chances of adopting new technology in the post-reforms period, industrial application of such technologies in non-agricultural sectors have enabled them to raise their productivity (Chipeta & Mkandawire, 2002). Moreover, because banks favoured lending to corporate businesses where average return is higher, non-agricultural sectors were increasingly becoming large-scale enterprises relative to the mainly smallholder dominated agricultural sector. For these reasons it seems the non-agricultural sectors were able to attract more loan advances.

Despite this, in further assessing allocational changes in Malawi we make an important observation. Notably, reforms are expected to be growth-promoting by channelling funds to higher-yielding investments. While this may be true, it is observable from Fig. 4.7 that there has been a shift of investible resources to more

[34]Producer prices were still controlled and highly influenced by the Agricultural Development and Marketing Corporation (ADMARC), a body that existed even before reforms.

[35]This does not mean that the agricultural sector is now less productive as it contributed 37% of the GDP in 2000 compared to 17% from industry. However, it shows that the non-agricultural sectors are becoming more important and, hence over time, the gap between the two is closing.

secure but possibly less productive investments (i.e. real estate and trade sectors). In undertaking such allocative choice, this could be favoured due to the fact that such investments are less subjected to the effect of macroeconomic instabilities (since they are often shorter-term loans like trade credit), incur less inflation uncertainty and have more ability to repay at a high interest rate. Having spelled out the above market transformations, it is vital to point out first that loans are now allocated to much wider economic activities. Second, it seems reforms have brought about internal competitive consideration for loan allocation to various economic areas and activities, indicating improvements in efficiency, although within the declining private sector's share of total commercial banks' lending.

In the next sub-section, discussions will concentrate on explaining the performance after liberalization while also pointing out some striking factors which highlight reasons for failures to conform to the predicted outcome under the Mckinnon–Shaw hypothesis.

4.2.3.3 Level of Competition

Historically, the banking sector in Malawi has been dominated by two major banks, both in terms of total assets and size of deposits.[36] Chirwa (2001) estimates that the one-firm concentration ratio (proxy for one bank domination) was not less than 59% and the two-firm concentration ratio was 83% in the period before liberalization. Given this environment, it is usual that the few dominant banks have more influence in determining the level of interest rate since they have the monopoly power to do so. However with financial liberalization, entry of new banks is expected to dilute such powers, resulting in a lower interest rate spread while the real interest rate improves. For the case of Malawi, as licensing procedures were eased, the sector registered a number of new commercial banks benefiting from the lenient entry requirements (UNDP, 1999). Accordingly, the financial sector reforms have helped encourage new entrants in a number of ways: (a) the legal framework of the banking sector was revised to open up the financial sector. Specifically, these changes targeted to moderate the licensing requirements through making the approval process more systematic and transparent,[37] (b) it gave the Reserve Bank the full mandate of supervising the operations of the financial system and of formulating indirect instruments of monetary policy, hence reducing the government's direct control of banks' credit, (c) through abolishing preferential interest rates mechanisms,

[36]It has been shown that up until 1989, the National Bank of Malawi (NBM) alone held up to 76% of total deposits and over 60% of assets in the banking sector respectively, while in 1990 NBM and Commercial Bank of Malawi accounted for more than 80% total deposit liabilities of financial institutions (Nissanke & Aryeetey, 1998, pp. 69–70).

[37]As opposed to the pre-reforms era, the new amendments gave entry powers to the Central Bank with the Minister for Finance merely acting to endorse their recommendations or giving reasons for denial (Chirwa, 2001).

political interference in commercial banks' credit allocation was largely eliminated, handing banks the required freedom to allocate their funds effectively and with greater prudence.

By the year 2000, there were almost 12 banks compared to only two in 1989. Importantly, the entry of these new institutions was motivated by the fact that the old banks focused on a few core activities in which they were specialised. Besides, the two previously established banks were not forced to diversify in the post reform period, particularly in terms of innovating new financial products (UNDP, 1999), since this required extra facilities and training of extra manpower. Also, as commercial banks were free to price their non-lending services, this coupled with elimination of various restrictions on foreign borrowings, allocation of foreign exchange and import related activities gave the new banks additional opportunities to exploit. Despite this, the post-liberalization concentration ratio for two firms remains as high as 75%, indicating that the top two banks still control up to 75% of the market share (Chirwa, 2001). This evidence demonstrates that there have been little value-added benefits derived from the new entrants. The new entrants included one previously existing trade finance institution, two in leasing and three in the non-bank sector (Mlachila & Chirwa, 2002). Other later entries included the Malawi savings bank and the First merchant bank. In this aspect since the new entrants were either locally owned private or previously parastatal institutions, these banks may have just been established merely to invest in government securities, reap foreign exchange differentials, or simply invest in undervalued securities while providing few other banking facilities to local businesses. Thus, it is not surprising that the banking structure remains largely unchanged as the recent entrants contributed little to competitive pressure that would have influenced the functional efficiency and intermediation spread. In an ideal case, for spread to adjust downwards or efficiency to improve, we need either: (1) the entrance of big established banks that can withstand price competition and introduce new product innovations. Most likely, such established banks will be able to weather short-run losses in the hope of future establishment and profits, (2) entry of small local banks who, because of their market understanding and specialization, will have much lower operation costs while penetrating rural areas to enhance market share, improve efficiency and increase deposit mobilization.

Unfortunately, it is visible in the case of Malawi that firstly, the new commercial bank entrants did not improve the banking efficiency by introducing a differentiated banking service package that would enable them to compete aggressively with the old established banks. Secondly, in terms of geographical coverage, while the new banks only operate in the two major commercial cities, the two old established commercial banks still maintain their first-mover advantage as they retain their nationwide branch network (Mlachila and Chirwa, 2002) showing no effect of loss of market share caused by the increase in competition.[38] This does not necessarily

[38]Seemingly, under this structure, there appears to be no stronger platform for the newcomers to launch successful competition to break the existing uncompetitive oligopoly.

mean that there has been no room for more banks in other towns and semi-urban areas. However, since the majority of the new institutions were previously non-established small banks, their capital base was limited. Together these two factors show that the new banks did not induce sufficient competition for deposits and loans. Indeed, there has been a claim that the two old banks still collude and change their interest rates by an identical magnitude (Malawi, 2000). Evidently, although the number of banks increased in Malawi, from four in 1994 to 12 in 2000, banking structure still remains highly oligopolistic. Consequently, such structural rigidities have understandably allowed the deposit rate to be depressed relative to lending rates to permit a maximum profit margin.

4.2.3.4 Explaining the Spread: Other Reasons besides Competition

As revealed by Table 4.11 and as noted earlier, although the adoption of financial liberalization in Malawi encouraged competition to some extent through admission of new financial institutions, the evidence so far reveals a high and persistent spread. Here, we look at some of the reasons given for such limited success towards this direction.

Liquidity reserve requirements: With the adoption of the financial sector reforms programme, Malawi had somehow stopped the directed credit trend and eased entry conditions for both foreign and local banks. Despite this, there has been no indication of a reduction in liquidity reserve requirements. Liquidity and statutory reserve requirements are potentially one of the monetary policy tools to control private sector lending and/or finance the state's credit demands. In this regard, the monetary authorities set the proportion of commercial banks' total deposits that shall not be available for lending. This ratio increased from 10% in June 1989 to 35% in mid-1995 (Chirwa, 2001) and marginally reduced to 32% in 2000, showing little hope for it to drop significantly. This is a cause of concern since it seems the government is forcefully extracting heavy rents from the financial system and giving itself access to low-cost capital. Moreover, the liquidity reserve requirement ceased to earn interest in 1990. Therefore, this implicit financial taxation led to higher interest rates and intermediation spread through two interlinked channels. A high reserve ratio limits the income-generating process of the banks through reducing the lending side as commercial banks now have less excess reserve while they bear the opportunity cost of servicing and re-financing these liquidity requirements (Mlachila & Chirwa, 2002). Secondly, as opposed to lending in a competitive market system, such significant commercial banks' reserves with the central bank means inefficient allocation since they are given at a near-zero rate of return (non-optimal rate) instead of channelling them to high-yielding available investments (Ndungu & Ngugi, 2000). Systematically, this is an implicit taxing mechanism. Nevertheless, this also reduces the efficiency of the banking system as they have to charge a high intermediation margin to service the held reserves. In an attempt to maintain their profitability margin, given this additional banking-specific cost, banks are likely to raise the lending rates rather than decreasing the deposit rates to become effectively commensurate with the cost, further increasing the spread (Brock & Suarez, 2000). Recently, IMF urged the authorities to consider alternatives to reduce such high level reserve requirements that render the banking system less efficient (IMF, 2001).

Unstable macroeconomic environment: Coincidentally, financial reforms in Malawi took place in the presence of other macroeconomic instabilities, typically characterized by high inflation, frequent devaluations, and deteriorating terms of trade (refer to Table 4.12). Additionally, the country also experienced unsatisfactory GDP growth during the post-liberalization era. The attainment of a positive real interest rate in Malawi has frequently been constrained by such instabilities, particularly inflation. As observable, the rapid and frequent increase in the rate of inflation has rendered the achievement of a short-term real interest rate impossible. As inflation increased from 13% in 1991 to 45% in 1999 while recording an extreme peak of 83% in 1995, both real lending and deposit rates were negative (see Table 4.11). Additionally, deliberate actions by monetary authorities to halt rising inflation have failed to provide long-term stability due to consistent fiscal indiscipline and external macroeconomic factors (Chipeta & Mkandawire, 2002). Thus, continuous devaluations of the local currency (from 3 in 1991 to 60 per US dollar in 2000), which have led to higher import costs have instigated a considerable volatility pressure on inflation. Together, these factors tend to lower the capitalized value of firms in operation and increase default risk, ultimately affecting the cost of lending. Brock and Suarez (2000) have empirically tested relationships between a number of macroeconomic variables and spread. Their study shows that the inflation rate significantly influenced the spread in four Latin American countries. With high macroeconomic uncertainties through the above factors, the lending rate is sticky downwards while financial institutions regularly adjust their pricing and spread determination procedures to take these factors into account.

Government budget deficits and high operation costs: As the government implemented financial reforms under a number of internal and external uncertainties, fiscal deficit as a share of GDP was initially high recording 8.3% in 1987 and a current account deficit level of 5% (see Table 4.12). Some of the objectives of the stabilization and liberalization reforms were to restore economic imbalances by improving the allocation process to increase productivity and keep the macroeconomic environment stable through fighting inflation and reducing deficit gaps. Particularly this was achieved in the first 5 years of the liberalization, where fiscal deficit averaged 4.5% (Chirwa, 2001). But, while the commitment to a free market environment has been taking shape, terms of trade worsened to 85% leading to a current account deficit of the balance of payment of 15% in 1994 and likewise both inflation and the exchange rate deteriorated rapidly. Moreover, as donor aid was suspended in late 1992, all budgetary requirements were to be financed through domestic means. Thus, with limited access to foreign capital and a widening budget deficit, Treasury bill rates increased from 12% in 1991 to 46% in 1995. As a result, the non-competitive government securities market gave banks the opportunity to reorganize their portfolios accordingly accommodating higher risk-free assets. While the increase in the Treasury bill rate signalled an upward pressure on other interest rates, the lending rate increased much more than the deposit rate as the banks had little incentives to raise the deposit rate (Ndungu & Ngugi, 2000). This induced a higher interest rate margin while resulting in significant misallocation and a lower intermediation volume.

Another factor that had an influence on product pricing of the commercial banks is the general operation costs. Studies show that transport and insurance costs are almost double in Malawi relative to other countries in the region (Chipeta & Mkandawire, 2002). Since the early 1990s the business community has been faced with multi-dimensional inefficiencies including inadequate power supply, a sharp increase in crime rate, an endemic level of corruption and an unreliable telecommunication network.[39] Such unreliable infrastructural and supportive systems have led banks to invest privately in acquiring these necessary services. Given these circumstances, banks have invested in power supply, telecommunication and private security services. These factors have in particular induced surging overhead costs frequently causing the banks to push for higher intermediation margin.

4.2.4 Botswana

4.2.4.1 Policy Environment

It is observable from Table 4.2 that reforms towards financial liberalization in Botswana improved real interest rates, particularly the lending rate, although the intermediation spread increased marginally upwards. Unlike the cases of Kenya and Malawi, where reforms were an integral part of the structural adjustments program advocated by the World Bank and the IMF, Botswana's liberalization policy was ostensibly a move to improve efficiency and integrate the economy (Harvey, 1996). In this sense, although the move to liberalize the economy in Botswana was internally derived, the motivating factors were similar to that of other African countries in that they were guided by the McKinnon-Shaw hypothesis. Relative to other Sub-Saharan African countries, the financial environment of pre-liberalization in Botswana was untypical. First, as opposed to the other countries we have analysed so far, Botswana did not have locally owned commercial banks dominating the financial institutions. Since independence, only foreign owned banking institutions operated. These banks initially operated as foreign subsidiaries before they were locally incorporated in 1975 following the establishment of the Bank of Botswana. Comparatively, in most other African countries, having foreign-owned commercial banks dominating the banking system was seen as a direct continuation of the colonial legacy. Many local leaders thought such institutions may favour the expansion of foreign businesses while limiting trade involvement of local entrepreneurs (Central Bank, 2000). Additionally, newly independent states perceived

---

[39]Chipeta and Mkandawire (2002) provide a detailed coverage of these issues in Malawi.

foreign commercial banks as a threat to the national development needs since they may have conflicting commercial objectives which might undermine the country's development interest. Moreover, the existence of local commercial banks could ensure the government's direct control of the financial system. Consequently, many African states established local commercial banks to remedy the above problems. However, Botswana has been unique in this aspect as locally owned banks were not introduced. Even in the past decade, where entry and exit procedures in the banking sector were more liberal, the authorities pursued a more cautious attitude towards licensing local commercial banks relative to admitting foreign-owned commercial banks (Harvey, 1996). Second, since the state did not own or have *de facto* control over commercial banks' internal operation, it had little means of directing their funds to finance its 'ought to be essential' development projects. In the event, for this purpose the state established a number of financial parastatals with the objective of channelling funds to priority areas and providing lending for capital and long-term projects.

Third, as opposed to other countries where the state controlled commercial banks' activities directly or indirectly, the government intervention mechanism in Botswana was simply its effective ability to operate as the biggest lender in the economy. Moreover, unlike other Sub-Saharan African countries where availability of funds was a major obstacle, Botswana had a continuous accumulation of funds from both internal and external sources.[40] Thus, through directing its own funds to preferred sectors, the state suppressed the need for commercial banks to provide loans and quite often influenced the existing rates of interest when necessary. However, such a system, where the state acted as the single major lender, had a negative repercussion on the level of financial sector development (Motsomi, 1997, p. 77). Primarily, the private sector's role of innovating and introducing new financial instruments and products was seriously suppressed. This was because commercial banks and other private-run financial institutions were left with little incentive to develop sophisticated saving techniques and further diversify existing saving instruments. In this respect, this had quite obviously limited the supply side of the resources mobilization since savings from the private sector were not fully tapped or exploited.

On a regional comparative basis and as visible from Table 4.13, the impact of financial repression on Botswana did not appear to be the lack of funds for the required investment or a substantially lower rate of savings (Masalila, 2001). Liquidity reserve requirements have been lower in Botswana relative to other SSA countries. Up to 1993, reserve requirements were set at 8% and 3% for the current and saving deposits respectively, while from late 1993 the required reserve was a combined figure of only 3.25% of average daily balance deposits.[41] Relatively,

[40] In addition to having budget surpluses as indicated in Table 4.13, external sources such as foreign borrowing and aid were always available alternatives for the government.

[41] Arguably this reserve ratio is low. Practically, this could be (i) a government's belief that it has the necessary capital to bail out such institutions in the case of liquidity problems, (ii) a direct policy to encourage lending to the private sector.

Table 4.13 Macroeconomic indicators in Botswana

Year	C/A	Psc	GDS	OB	TRES
1985	7	9	38	20	11
1986	8	8	41	21	14
1987	32	8	42	15	17
1988	7	7	50	16	15
1989	16	7	49	9	18
1990	−1	9	43	11	16
1991	8	12	40	10	19
1992	5	15	37	10	19
1993	10	14	37	9	24
1994	5	14	37	2	25
1995	6	12	38	3	22
1996	10	10	41	9	24
1997	14	9	43	5	22
1998	3	12	40	−6	24
1999	12	15	38	6	24
2000	10	16	40	9	24

Note: C/A, Psc, GDS and OB are all in percentage of GDP. C/A is current account including official transfers, Psc is domestic credit to the private sector, GDS is gross domestic savings rate, OB is the overall budget and TRES is total reserves (months of imports).
Source: IMF, *International Financial Statistics*, various issues and IMF country reports.

such a ratio seems to be even lower than many countries in Europe. Instead, the country's major problem had been the lack of financial integration and excess liquidity traps, leading to inefficient management of the economy. Accordingly, liberalization policies were undertaken to create mechanisms to improve financial intermediation and introduce measures to integrate the economy. Thus, if achieved, these two changes together were expected to result in an economic environment in which financial surpluses are managed better.

Within this framework and following reforms towards financial liberalization, Table 4.14 shows the trend in both nominal and real interest rates. It is notable that real lending rates in Botswana were significantly positive in some years before reforms, while rates of deposit were insignificantly positive. Subsequently, following decontrol of interest rates, there had been little experience of large fluctuation in either real deposit or lending rates (see also Fig. 4.8). However, due to high inflation and other market imperfections, real lending rates have improved significantly relative to deposit rates. To elaborate this further, Fig. 4.8 presents the movement in real interest rates as well as the evolution of commercial banks in Botswana. Because of the gradual entry of new commercial banks following the financial reforms, nominal deposit and lending rates have improved reasonably from 1992 due to the competitive pressure for deposits and loans. Despite this, an upward surge in the intermediation margin is notable (see Table 4.15). The interest rate spread in Botswana increased from 2.1% in 1989 to 5.2% in 2000. Despite other

Table 4.14 Nominal and real interest rates in Botswana

Year	Nominal			Real	
	Deposit	Inflation	Lending	Deposit	Lending
1985	9.0	8.1	11.5	0.9	3.4
1986	8.7	10.0	11.0	−1.3	1.0
1987	7.5	9.8	10.0	−2.3	0.2
1988	5.0	8.4	7.8	−3.4	−0.5
1989	5.6	11.6	7.7	−6.0	−3.9
1990	6.1	11.4	7.9	−5.3	−3.5
1991	11.4	11.8	11.8	−0.4	0.1
1992	12.5	16.2	14.0	−3.7	−2.2
1993	13.5	14.3	14.9	−0.8	0.6
1994	10.4	10.5	13.9	−0.2	3.3
1995	10.0	10.5	14.3	−0.5	3.8
1996	10.4	10.1	14.5	0.3	4.4
1997	9.3	8.7	14.1	0.5	5.4
1998	8.7	6.7	13.5	2.1	6.9
1999	9.5	7.7	14.6	1.7	6.9
2000	10.1	8.6	15.3	1.5	6.7

Source: Bank of Botswana annual reports.

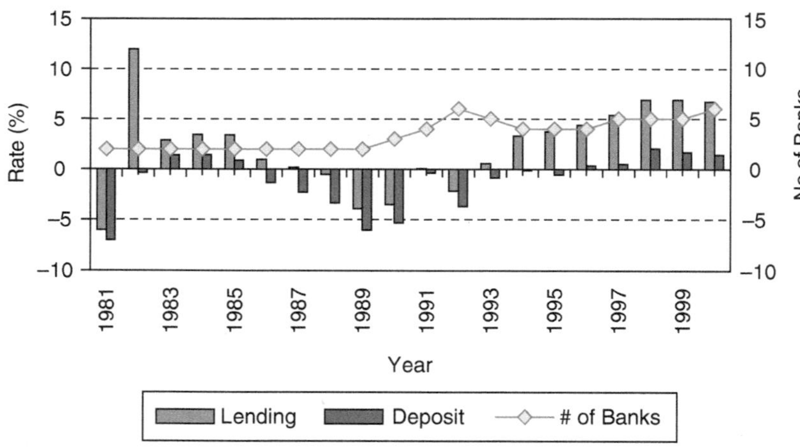

Fig. 4.8 Evolution of real interest rates and banks in Botswana
Source: Authors' calculation from IFS and various other sources.

factors, this was largely owing to movements in inflation. The growth in the share of credit to the private sector (see Table 4.13) and a general increase in prices of imported goods had induced inflation to increase from 11% in 1990 to 16% in 1992 and remained in double digits until recently. In the event, real lending rates adjusted upwardly much quicker compared to real deposit rates.

Table 4.15 Intermediation margins in selected countries

Year	Botswana	Chile	Malaysia	South Africa	UK
1985	2.5	7.9	2.7	4.5	0.5
1986	2.3	7.3	3.5	3.4	1.0
1987	2.5	7.4	5.2	3.8	1.1
1988	2.8	6.0	4.1	1.8	1.7
1989	2.1	8.2	2.4	1.7	2.4
1990	1.8	8.5	1.3	2.1	2.2
1991	0.4	6.2	0.9	3.0	1.3
1992	1.5	5.7	1.3	5.1	2.0
1993	1.4	6.1	2.0	4.7	1.9
1994	3.5	5.2	2.7	4.5	1.8
1995	4.3	4.4	1.7	4.4	2.6
1996	4.1	3.9	1.8	4.6	2.9
1997	4.8	3.7	1.8	4.6	3.0
1998	4.8	5.3	2.1	5.3	2.7
1999	5.2	4.1	3.2	5.8	1.3
2000	5.2	5.6	3.4	5.3	2.0
Average 1991–2000	3.5	5.0	2.1	4.7	2.1

Source: Calculated from Bank of Botswana reports and world development indicators.

Further, to examine the intermediation margin in Botswana relative to other developed and developing countries with similar economic characteristics in one way or the other, Table 4.15 provides interest rate spreads for a selected number of countries. With regard to this, it is important to recognize that on average (taking 1991–2000) the spread in Botswana is marginally higher than that of Malaysia and the UK and even lower than the levels in Chile and South Africa. This reveals that the interest rate margin is understandably realistic and looks justifiable to compensate for financial risk in Botswana. However, in the light of the financial liberalization thesis, we will look critically at the individual specific elements through which we expect financial liberalization and its impact to have a greater influence.

4.2.4.2 Allocational Behaviour Post-Reforms

Unlike other Sub-Saharan African counties, Botswana did not have the control or ownership of commercial banks, nor did it have local banks with which the state could forge close ties. In this aspect, the government did not have the ability to excessively intervene with the operations of commercial banks, in terms of directing their lending activities to its priority areas. As part of its financial repression policies, where funds could be offered at a concessional rate and under a longer repayment period, it established financial parastatals. The National development bank (NDB) and Botswana development corporation (BDC) were both founded for this purpose of channelling funds to preferred sectors such as agriculture, manufacturing and industrial development, which were largely neglected by the commercial banks as they concentrated on short-term loans and low-risk highly profitable foreign exchange transactions (Harvey & Lewis, 1990, p. 222). Under financial liberalization credit allocations are expected to be purely guided by economic visibility while the commercial banking sector is expected to resume fully the crucial role of financial intermediation. Therefore credits are to be allocated to the most competent economic sectors. In line with this, the trend in the share of commercial banks' advances to the private sector is shown in Table 4.13. Initially, the proportion of credit to the private sector (as a percentage of GDP) increased from 7% in 1988 to 15% in 1992. However, this did not last long as a declining trend is visible again, recording a lower level of 9% in 1997 before improving slightly upwards thereafter.

Surprisingly, despite having excess liquidity in the banking system, project and long-term financing did not improve in Botswana. It has been pointed out that the lack of profitable investment opportunities as well as the limited entrepreneurial expertise in the country have partly contributed to this (Maipose & Matsheka, 2002). Likewise, there have been no close ties between the industrialists and the bankers to reduce the cost of acquiring information about firms and assist in the identification of good investments. This would have also enabled the banks to transform short-term credit to long-term advances more easily by reconsidering the maturity terms (Levine, 1997). With these constraints, banks are biased towards short-term advances and mainly avoid unfamiliar projects and medium-scale financing even when adequate funds are available. In light of this, we look further at the sectoral distribution of private sector loans and advances. Between 1990 and 2000, credit to the manufacturing and trade sectors (which are mostly long-term in nature) declined continuously from 10% and 16% to 4% and 10% respectively (see Fig. 4.9). On the other hand agriculture, which received a good share of credit allocation in the pre-liberalization era, accounted for only 1% in 2000 compared to 4% in 1990. However, advances to the household sector untypically increased from 30 to 49% in the same period, seemingly indicating that households are more net borrowers than net savers in this economy.[42] This market behaviour can be explained by the fact that households' incomes have improved in recent years due to changes in the wage structure. Subsequently, they are now able to provide credit guarantees and other securities, enabling them to receive a larger share of commercial banks' advances.

In effect, this trend may have a number of macroeconomic implications for the future rates of saving, investment and growth. Primarily, the relaxation of borrowing constraints to the private households seems to have caused a structural change in the aggregate consumption. Specifically, when these changes lead to significant consumption growth, then the positive effect of financial liberalization on economic growth, through capital accumulation and improved efficiency, is partially offset (Chan & Hu, 1997). Therefore in the long-run this will induce future productivity loss as the level of productive investment (particularly in machinery, equipment

[42] In support of this Reinke (1997, p. 105) demonstrates that household advances in Botswana have continuously exceeded their share of deposits in the last decade.

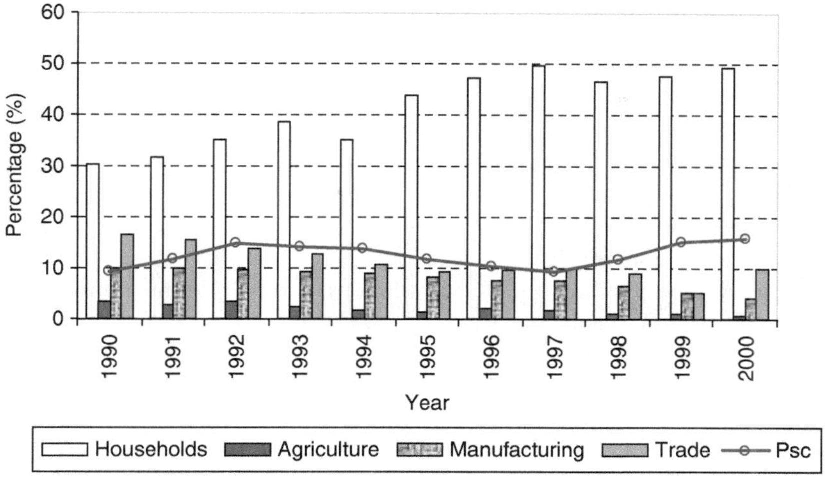

Fig. 4.9 Credit allocation within the private sector in Botswana
Note: Psc is the share of commercial banks' credit to the private sector (% of GDP); all other variables are expressed as a ratio of total advances.
Source: Authors' calculations from Bank of Botswana, Annual Reports, various issues.

and technology) declines. Alternatively, if the ability of households to borrow against their future income induces incentives for a higher human capital accumulation, this may translate into a faster rate of economic growth (De Gregorio, 1996). Importantly, easing borrowing constraints may lead to an optimum combination of physical and human capital which will have a positive effect on future productivity growth.[43] In light of the above possibilities a study of consumer credit in Botswana by Reinke (1997) supports the former argument rather than the latter. It is revealed that households have a stronger tradition of utilizing banks' credit facilities in the acquisition of durable consumer goods, especially cars. Taken together, these findings indicate that financial liberalization may have increased the growth in durable consumption in Botswana. This trend does not accord well with long-term productivity as it generates decreasing rates of saving and of capital investment.[44]

[43]Notably, De Gregorio (1996) comments that borrowing constraints may reduce the time devoted to formal education and acquiring of human capital. Thus, this enables individuals to have access to resources while in education.

[44]Contrastingly, the private savings rate has been increasing. Two reasons may explain this: (i) intertemporal substitution issue where individuals who borrowed in the past save more to honour their payments, (ii) the benefit of economic growth may be reaped more by those with a higher marginal propensity to save than otherwise. Increasing inequality in the country in question may be taken as evidence of this trend.

4.2.4.3 Level of Competition

From independence until 1990, Barclays and Standard Chartered were the only operating banks. Effectively, these two banks monopolized the sector with almost no competition between them while providing standard banking facilities with little innovative response to customers' new demands and changing needs over time (Harvey & Lewis, 1990, p. 222). With the adoption of liberalized financial policies, exit and entry procedures were made considerably easier to steer competition and enhance financial intermediation.[45]

In response to the easing of entry restrictions, a number of new foreign banks were attracted to the banking system. Between 1991 and 1993 four new foreign banks were licensed, increasing the number of operating commercial banks to five (see Fig. 4.8). More unusually, it is reported that within a short period of time, the entry of these new banks has actually exerted some much needed competition in this sector. Harvey (1996) remarks that there has been a significant structural change sparking aggressive competition as a result of the new entrants. Observably, (1) the admission of the new commercial banks has led to an increase in the availability of new and modern services in line with changing consumer needs. Previously, it was noted that the oligopolistic nature that had led to the accrual of large profits by the dominant banks have rendered them unresponsive to further innovation and market penetration (Harvey & Lewis, 1990, p. 227), (2) in addition to the improvement in the quality of services, the range of financial options and instruments has also increased. Consequently, Jefferis (1995) observes a significant shift in the maturity structure of the lending by the banks with almost 12.5% of advances having over 5 years' maturity period in 1992 relative to only 7.5% in 1990. At the end of 1995 close to 19% of commercial banks' loans had a similar long-term maturity period, (3) given such a relatively competitive market environment, margins of various operations that were previously highly profitable now showed a declining trend. Most importantly, margins on foreign exchange transactions – which enabled banks to make enormous profit in the pre-liberalization era – and other charges for banking services have now reduced (Harvey, 1996).

In effect, entry negatively affected the profitability of both the old established banks. As the ability of the old banks to increase and maintain a higher profit margin reduced under these new circumstances, it was reported that the operating profit of the previously existing banks declined significantly. Thus the profit levels of Barclays and Standard Chartered fell by 39% and 62% respectively between 1993 and 1994 (Harvey, 1996).[46] In contrast to Kenya and Malawi, the new commercial banks in Botswana have brought in a much needed value-added competition, offering quality services to both corporate and retail banking sectors. Moreover,

[45]Having a variety of different banks could also enable more product differentiation and specialization.

[46]Further, the return of assets of Barclays bank was almost 20% in 1994 compared to over 50% in 1987.

these new banks have quickly established themselves not only in large cities but also in rural areas.[47] In line with this, it is not surprising that the operating income of these new banks has been improving. For example, the return on capital of the First national bank of Botswana (FNBB) was 35%, while it reported a profit figure above that of Standard Chartered in 1995 (Harvey, 1996). This evidence shows that the entry of more players into the commercial banking sector in Botswana has helped reduce the market concentration and power of the previously existing institutions. Meanwhile, it appears that the entry of new foreign financial institutions also helped improve the speed and diversity of banking activities through transferring financial technology, obviously enhancing the access to modern banking services. This analysis suggests albiet within specified limits that the new entrants of commercial banks in Botswana have, in one way or the other, improved efficiency and laid down the foundation to enhance financial integration and development.

4.2.4.4 Explaining the Spread: Other Factors

Considering the financial repression hypothesis and given the above economic transformation, while both real lending and deposit rates are expected to adjust upwardly, the intermediation margin is expected to decline over time and converge to the international levels. However, contrary to this, as observable from Table 4.15, the interest rate spread has, in recent years, been increasing in Botswana. Hence, in the context of the new policy framework, we shed light on some of the factors that may have caused this phenomenon.

Macroeconomic environment: Relative to any other African country, Botswana had an impressive GDP growth recording an average of 8.5% for the last two decades despite showing a declining trend in recent years. As revealed by Table 4.13, the country had a well managed budget with continuous surpluses in both current account and overall balances. This led to accumulation of total reserves, measured in number of months available for import cover, from 6 in 1984 to 25 months in 1994 and consistently above 20 months until the year 2000. Clearly in one aspect, this is an indication of significant macroeconomic stability maintenance. With this strong foundation, a key intermediate target for the Bank of Botswana in the post-liberalization period had been the maintenance of positive real interest rates (Motsomi, 1997, p. 80). To achieve this and promote savings, the authorities had in the past been moderating the levels of inflation. However the inflation rate has been reasonably high in the last decade, recording above 10% in the most of the periods (see Table 4.14). Thus, it has been difficult to push interest rate levels above inflation to maintain positive and significant real rates of interest (refer to Fig. 4.8). In this

[47]On the other hand, statistics indicate that even though the old banks were closing down some of their unprofitable rural branches in response to shrinking market share, more unusually, the new banks were replacing them.

regard, to ensure price stability the authorities took actions to control government expenditure and domestic credit on numerous occasions to restrain domestic demand pressure. Additionally, Bank of Botswana certificates (BoBCs) were issued in 1997 to mob excess liquidity while nominal rates of interest were adjusted upwards (BoB, 2000). These adjustments resulted in an improvement in both the lending and deposit rates as depicted by Fig. 4.8. On the other hand, despite these corrective policies, it has been suggested that the domestic inflationary pressure in Botswana has an external influence, coming from changes in prices of tradeable goods of which more than two-thirds are sourced from South Africa (Kahauti & Wright, 1997, p. 63). Effectively, as banks' pricing behaviour takes this and the exchange rate fluctuations into account, this may have increased the costs faced by bank borrowers, and hence, raised the lending rate more frequently while deposit rates remained constant.

Lack of well functioning equity market: It has been argued that the stock market provides a different bundle of financial functions and offers additional vehicles to manage risk and boost liquidity (Levine, 1997). Generally, the stock market provides different instruments that attract both savers and investors in the form of providing new avenues for raising additional finance and improving earning capacity, thereby stimulating both saving and investment levels. Empirical evidence from Demirguc-Kunt and Huizinga (1997) demonstrates the possibility of substitution between equity-debt finance as the stock market grows. Precisely, this means that, *ceteris paribus*, as the equity market grows, competition for both savers and users of finance intensifies, forcing banks to improve their rates. Generally, one of the potential benefits of equity market development is to provide a new source of finance for the private corporate investors, primarily improving their gearing ratio, while reducing total reliance on commercial banks for long-term finances.

Despite the initial establishment of a stock market in Botswana, the evidence suggests little development in the securities segment particularly as the bond-market is non existent (Motsomi, 1997, p. 82). This absence of bond and equity markets does not only affect medium and long-term savings mobilization but also limits project financing. Ideally, even though financial reforms may have brought some benefits, the vital role of improved availability of long-term equity finance to the expanding economic sectors have not been achieved. Consequently, with limited channels of raising capital and apparent segmentation of the market for funds, where traditionally banks are biased towards short-term loans, commercial banks look to be in a stronger position to keep the lending rate higher.

High operation cost: Although recent financial reforms have led to the entry of new commercial banks, providing a greater competitive environment in terms of services and pricing, higher operation costs may have been one of the factors that had induced a widening intermediation spread. First, it has been recognized that unit labour cost (in real terms) in the financial sector rose on average by 1.2% annually from 1975 to 1993 (Mandlebe, 1997, pp. 442–443). This may have been caused by high real wages since the financial sector is skill-labour oriented. Second, to improve productivity and optimize performance in the public sector, in 1993 the government of Botswana launched a new incentive scheme named work improvement teams (WITs) to improve career prospects of skilled professionals (Adamolekun & Morgan, 1999). Under this new arrangement, professional grade salaries were increased by 45%, giving their fellow professionals in the private sector bargaining power for a favourable wage improvement to maintain their service. Third, since all commercial banks are foreign-owned, they are required to maintain a technological edge and keep up with global standards. In this dimension, new facilities and foreign expertise required to guarantee such technological competence and good management practices could only be supplied by foreign partners at a higher cost (Harvey, 1996). Fourth, in addition to being landlocked, where import and export are through neighbouring countries, other utility costs necessary for smooth operation of the business sector also remain high. Compared to South Africa and Zimbabwe, power and telecommunication costs are twice as high in Botswana, while water charges are estimated to be ten times higher compared to Zimbabwe (Maipose & Matsheka, 2002). Inevitably, due to the lack of diversification in the economy and given the above-mentioned factors, commercial banks have partly transferred these overhead and operating costs to their customers through charging higher prime lending rates.

4.3 Conclusion

In this chapter, we have outlined the important channels through which the impact of financial liberalization is expected to be observed. While deriving evidence from the countries of our sample, the chapter has given a detailed account of channels of transmission to evaluate the success and failure of the recent economic liberalization in these countries. More importantly, changes with regard to the levels of competition and allocational behaviour in the post reform period were considered. In the process, we have also examined various factors that may explain the behaviour of interest rate spread in these countries of interest.

From the analysis, an important finding of the study is that there are three major issues which may have limited the desired outcome of interest rate deregulations: government rapaciousness, macroeconomic instability and lack of competition in the banking sector. Especially for the cases of Kenya and Malawi, these factors seem to have limited the success of financial reforms. Indeed, it is strange that the competitive structure of the banking sector in Kenya and Malawi did not change following amendments in the legal framework that guide the financial sector. In the following chapter, investigation will focus on the issue of why competition in the banking sector did not increase. This is done firstly by looking at a brief theoretical treatment of the issue of imperfect competition and the resulting spread behaviour. The study will then provide some insight into the empirical question of whether there are barriers to entry, shrinking of demand for loans or increases in tax from the government.

Appendix

Table 4.16 Bank's market share by various indicators (percentages)

Year	Bank (Peer group 1 type only)	Asset	L/A	Deposits	C/R
1992	Barclays bank	22	18	21	n.a
	Kenya commercial bank	17	19	21	n.a
	Standard bank	14	17	17	n.a
	National bank of Kenya	13	16	10	n.a
	Co-operative bank	5	6	3	n.a
	Total	71	75	73	n.a
1994	Barclays bank	25	21	27	22
	Kenya commercial bank	20	19	20	17
	Standard bank	13	15	16	11
	National bank of Kenya	11	13	9	15
	Co-operative bank	5	5	3	2
	Total	74	73	75	67
1996	Barclays bank	19	17	21	22
	Kenya commercial bank	16	17	16	15
	Standard bank	10	10	10	9
	National bank of Kenya	9	11	8	9
	Co-operative bank	6	5	4	6
	Total	60	60	59	61
1997	Barclays bank	17	16	18	20
	Kenya commercial bank	16	15	16	15
	Standard bank	9	11	9	7
	National bank of Kenya	9	8	10	8
	Co-operative bank	6	5	4	5
	Total	57	55	57	55
1999	Barclays bank	18	15	19	19
	Kenya commercial bank	17	18	17	17
	Standard bank	10	9	12	11
	National bank of Kenya	8	10	7	−4
	Co-operative bank	6	5	5	5
	Total	59	57	60	48
2001	Barclays bank	17	23	18	22
	Kenya commercial bank	15	16	15	12
	Standard bank	12	7	14	9
	National bank of Kenya	10	9	6	5
	Co-operative bank	6	6	5	−1
	Total	60	61	58	48
2002	Barclays bank	18	24	20	20
	Kenya commercial bank	14	13	14	9
	Standard bank	12	8	15	9
	National bank of Kenya	10	9	5	4
	Co-operative bank	8	8	6	4
	Total	61	62	60	45

Note: L/A loans and advances; *C/R* capital and reserves.
Source: Central Bank, *Bank supervision department annual report*, various issues.

Chapter 5
An Analysis of the Economic Outcome of Financial Liberalization[1]

"A permissive environment is one where government seeks to reduce rather than increase the cost of doing business."

(Summers, 1992)

5.1 Introduction

In the last chapter, we have considered the impact of financial reforms program and the channels through which such outcomes were transmitted. Particularly, we have assessed the performance of various indicators expected to capture improvements in efficiency, competitiveness and allocational enhancements following the adoption of liberalized financial policies in our sample countries. From these results and assessments based on almost all conventionally used aggregates, it is observable that there has been modest contribution of financial liberalization in terms of promoting economic growth in Kenya and Malawi. Importantly, in both these two countries the monopolistic structure of the commercial banking system has limited the depth and breadth of the financial services offered even under liberalized financial regime. This chapter considers this issue further. Firstly, it provides a simple model within the framework of imperfectly competitive banking industry and looks at the behaviour of the interest rate spread. The strategy is to analyse the level of spread together with the impact of an entry by a new firm. In doing so, the model solution is initially given for liberalized market system and then extended for the case of repressed financial environment. Applying the solutions from these exercises, adverse effect of higher fixed (overhead) costs in terms of serving as a

[1]An earlier version of this paper has been presented at the PhD Conference in Economics and Business, held on 10–12 November 2004, in the Australian National University, Canberra. I have greatly benefited from comments by Professor Peter Dixon.

A.D. Ahmed and S.M.N. Islam, *Financial Liberalization in Developing Countries*, Contributions to Economics,
DOI: 10.1007/978-3-7908-2168-0_5, © Springer Physica-Verlag Berlin Heidelberg 2010

barrier to entry of new established financial institutions is considered. Secondly, with this theoretical treatment the chapter also provides empirical evidence on the issue of high fixed costs which explain the lack of entry by effective competitors in these economies.

This chapter is organized as follows. Section 2 discusses the model of imperfect competition and interest rate spread. In Section 3 the possible explanations for the lack of entry by well established financial institutions are exploited together with some supportive empirical evidence. Section 4 concludes.

5.2 A Simple Model of Imperfect Competition and Interest Rate Spread

A typically observable market structure in Kenya and Malawi is imperfectly competitive banking sector where few banks (two-to-four) have high concentration and control powers. The lack of effective competition and oligopolistic structure is highly visible. With respect to this development we will analyze here a simple model that looks at the intermediation margin with the objective of evaluating the direction of interest rate spread. Initially, taking financially liberalized economic environment, let us assume that there are two banks engaging in cournot-type oligopolistic competition for savings and investment. Within such market structure, although interest rates are market determined, banks have an influence over lending and deposit rates. Additionally, each bank chooses how much it wants to borrow and channel forward to investment sector taking the intermediation by the other banks as given. Here, Cournot strategy is applied where to derive the demand curve the firm faces the fixed or 'given' amount is subtracted from the market demand.[2] Let us specify that the supply of savings is given by:

$$D = \alpha d \tag{5.1}$$

where α indicates the interest rate sensitivity of savings and d is the interest rate on deposits. On the other hand, the loan demand curve is expressed as:

$$L = \bar{L} - \beta r \tag{5.2}$$

Where $\bar{L}$ is the autonomous level of loans, β is the sensitivity of investment to lending rates and r is the commercial banks' lending rate. Banks maximize their gain from the intermediation process and thus will prefer to increase the spread margin. Moreover, with the assumption that the amount banks borrowed (or rather accepted deposits) is the amount needed by investors, in equilibrium where the market clears we can show that:

---

[2]See for example, Dobbs (2000), McCloskey (1982) and Koutsoyiannis (1979) for further specifics and detail theoretical assessments of Cournot-type oligopolistic solutions.

$$L = L_1 + L_2$$
$$D = D_1 + D_2 \tag{5.3}$$

Here we assume two firms but extended to *n number* in the later part of the analysis. From equations (5.2) and (5.3) we can undertake a simple manipulation to derive an expression for the commercial bank rate of lending as:

$$r = \frac{\bar{L}}{\beta} - \left(\frac{L_1 + L_2}{\beta}\right) \tag{5.4}$$

Before we provide complete Cournot solutions in terms of the spread behaviour and loan size under both liberalized and repressed systems, let us highlight some expected behavioural patterns. Initially, let's ask beforehand the important question of what will be the oligopolist reactions under different repressed levels of lending rate so that consideration can be to the profit maximizing lending levels. Hence we trace the general relationship between level of loans (L) and $\bar{r}$ where such an imposed rate of interest may be above the market equilibrium. At this stage it should reasonably be understood that as $\bar{r}$ increases it reaches the market determined level of lending rate, r^*. Any repressed rate of interest beyond r^* is equivalent to no repression.

As demonstrated by Figure 5.1 below and given that the government imposes a ceiling on interest rates, there can be three regions in which the lender (oligopolist) will behave differently. When the repressed rate of interest is not binding, oligopolist banks can influence lending rates by manipulating the volume of loans made available to borrowers. In the zone above r^*, oligopolists are facing decreasing marginal revenue and therefore will be tempted to reduce loans volume to sustain higher prices. In the middle region (between A and B), the ceiling rate of interest

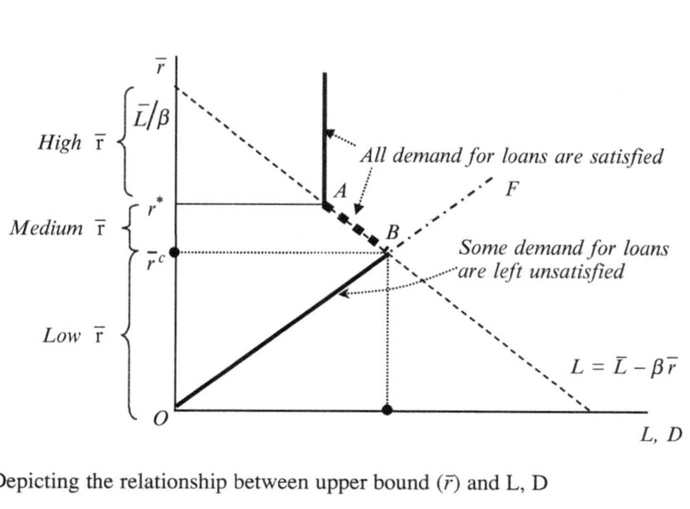

Fig. 5.1 Depicting the relationship between upper bound ($\bar{r}$) and L, D

becomes binding and the oligopolists face a constant marginal revenue curve. In this zone the lenders will behave as though the market is perfectly competitive since they cannot influence the lending rate by suppressing the volume of loans issued. To maximize their profits, oligopolist firms will be willing to supply to the fullest of their capacity but are only constrained by the loan demand curve ($L = \bar{L} - \beta\bar{r}$). At a lower $\bar{r}$, demand for loans increases as we move from A to B. In the flatter region along the OF curve, the oligopolists also face a binding capped rate of interest. At this lower rate of interest, the deposits base is small and loans are to be rationed. As $\bar{r}$ improves, loans that are not catered for by the banking system decline in demand until it is fully satisfied at point B.

Having mentioned this, Figure 5.1 depicts the relationship between L and $\bar{r}$ to show the behaviour of loans under different levels of capped rates of interest. Correspondingly, it is observable that L may remain unchanged, increase, or decrease following changes in the repressed rate of interest, $\bar{r}$, under the Cournot framework. With the exception of region A and B, the equilibrium solutions for L are well defined. However, even though the region between A and B corresponds to an area where marginal revenue is discontinuous, we can show that the solution is always at the 'kink' along the dotted portion of the demand curve. Thus, with a change in $\bar{r}$ we can conjecture that we will always be moving along this curve rather than any other point.[3] The behaviour of (L) and deposits (D) as we lower $\bar{r}$ can now be fully considered. It is shown that nothing happens to L and D until the upper bound ($\bar{r}$) on the lending rate is lowered to r^*. With a further fall in $\bar{r}$, both L and D increase since oligopolists are set to maximize their profits. Eventually a critical point is reached at which it becomes loss minimizing (or profit maximizing) for the oligopolistically behaving banks to reduce L and D, where part of the demand for loan will be left unsatisfied. Building on this outline, we further examine the detailed dynamics of spread and lending variables under each of the specified zones.

5.2.1 Liberalization: Market Determined Outcome

In a Cournot equilibrium, each firm maximizes its profits taking the volume of loans of the other banks as given. Commercial banks' revenue is the product of lending rate and the volume of loans issued ($R = rL$). Therefore the marginal revenue of, say, bank one can be expressed as:

$$\frac{\partial \mathrm{R}}{\partial L_1} = \frac{\bar{L}}{\beta} - \frac{2L_1}{\beta} - \frac{L_2}{\beta}$$

On the other hand, when banks' borrowing and lending activities are in equilibrium, while utilizing equation (5.1) we can also derive the marginal cost function as:

---

[3]To confirm this, an indicative proof is given in Appendix A5.1 where we examine whether the specified loan equation satisfy the conditions for a market equilibrium.

$$\frac{\partial Cost}{\partial L_1} = \frac{2L_1 + L_2}{\alpha}$$

Utilizing the above marginal revenue and marginal cost conditions we can compute the reaction curves of each firm in the market to be:

$$\begin{cases} L_1 = \dfrac{\alpha}{(\alpha+\beta)}\,\bar{L} - 2L_2 \\ L_2 = \dfrac{\alpha}{(\alpha+\beta)}\,\bar{L} - 2L_1 \end{cases}$$

Considering the profit maximization lending volume and using the reaction function of each firm in the market, the equilibrium amount of loan issued by the banking sector will be:

$$L = \frac{2\alpha\,\bar{L}}{3(\alpha+\beta)} \tag{5.5}$$

From this aggregate supply of loans and substituting it in equation (5.4) we can further simplify the lending rate expression to be:

$$r = \frac{1}{\beta}\left(1 - \frac{2\alpha}{3(\alpha+\beta)}\right)\bar{L} \tag{5.6}$$

Likewise from the supply curve of savings we can express the competitive equilibrium rate of deposits as:

$$d = \frac{2\,\bar{L}}{3(\alpha+\beta)}$$

From the commercial banks' point of view, the intermediation margin is determined from the difference between lending and deposit rates. Therefore the spread margin under this competitive market framework will be:

$$s = \left[\frac{1}{\beta} - \frac{2\alpha}{3(\alpha+\beta)\beta} - \frac{2}{3(\alpha+\beta)}\right]\bar{L} \equiv \frac{\bar{L}}{3\beta} \tag{5.7}$$

Initially increasing this into the case of three firms and generalizing it further, we can show that the more competitive the market gets through meaningful entry, the lower the spread will be. Representing n to be the number of identical firms we will have:

$$s = \frac{1}{\beta}\left[1 - \frac{n\alpha}{(n+1)(\alpha+\beta)} - \frac{n\beta}{(n+1)(\alpha+\beta)}\right]\bar{L} \equiv \frac{\bar{L}}{(n+1)\beta} \tag{5.8}$$

It is apparent from equations (5.5) to (5.8) that as the number of banks increases, most likely through pro-competitive financial policies and stronger and/or supportive legal framework, one would expect: the interest rate spread to narrow; quantities of loans and deposits to increase; the lending interest rate to decrease and the deposit interest rate to increase. Considering this and in accordance with the Cournot structure, these results are clear from Figure 5.2. The lower panel of Figure 5.2 shows that an increase in the number of banks decreases the price (spread) on the vertical axis thereby increasing L. With this and tracing through to the upper panel, the increase in L induces a decrease in lending rate and an increase in deposit rates.

5.2.2 *Financial Repression*

In this first part so far, we have looked at a liberalized market structure. To consider the intermediation spread under a non-competitive market mechanism, let us now work backwards by examining the intermediation margin under a financially repressed economic system. Thus, let us assume that the state imposes a lending rate of $\bar{r}_L$ instead of the market-determined rate of equilibrium.[4] We will consider the possible combinations where such an imposition of an upper bound is both not far below and also when it is significantly lower than the competitive market equilibrium rate r_L^*. Furthermore, as discussed earlier, such an imposition is irrelevant when it is above the market equilibrium. Accordingly, we will again provide model solutions and demonstrate diagrammatically the dynamics of lending activities and spread behaviour following the imposition of restrictions on the lending rate.

So what happens when we restrict the banking sector by imposing an upper bound, $\bar{r}$, that is above the market equilibrium rate, r^*? Without any difficulty and as apparent from Figure 5.1, it can be demonstrated that when we assume a level of ceiling rate that is above the liberalized value $(\bar{r} > r^*)$, the profit maximizing solution for the monopolistically behaving banks is left unchanged. Imposing an upper bound on the lending rate that is not far below the market equilibrium $(\bar{r} > r^*)$, we observe changes in the intermediation volume as well as in the interest rate spread solution. As illustrated by the lower panel of Figure 5.3 the imposition of an upper bound means that the banking sector now faces a kinked-demand curve, which is a kinked relationship between spread (s) and L. It is natural that the demand for loans will increase with the imposition of a ceiling on the lending rate below r^*. With this resulting increase in the demand for loans, oligopolist banks have the choice to either increase the lending volumes or maintain that of the pre-ceiling period. However, given that the price cannot be influenced by limiting

---

[4]For convenience we use $\bar{r}_L$ and $\bar{r}$ interchangeably.

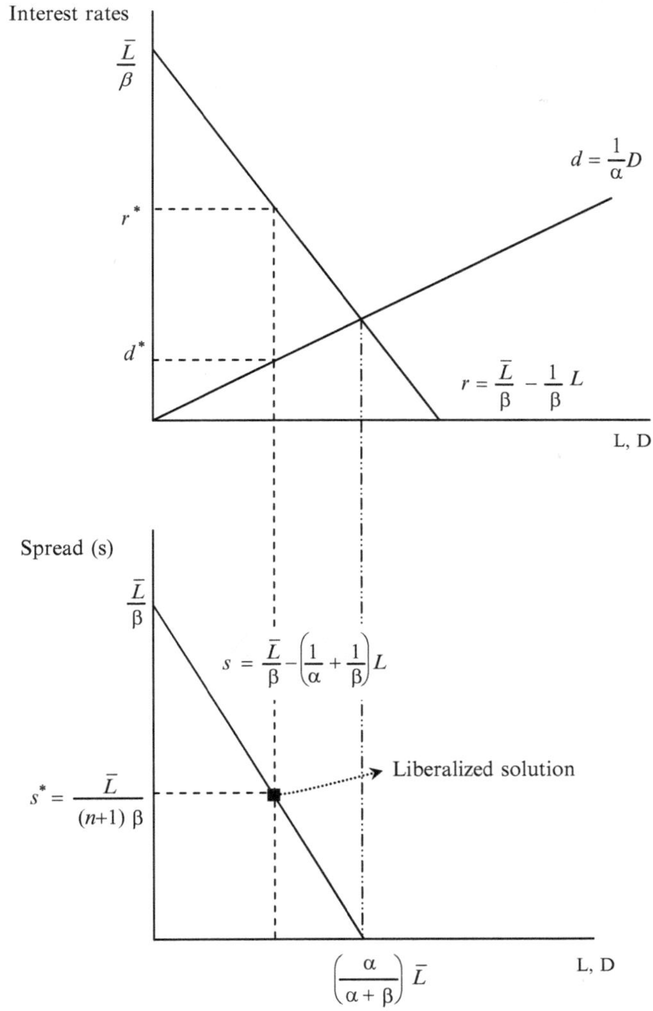

Fig. 5.2 Depicting the liberalized situation
Note: These diagrams and the underlying intuitions on the zones are directly taken from Professor Peter Dixon's comment at the PhD conference.

the supply in this case, these banks would rather adjust the lending volume upwards and receive 'normal' profits which could be earned if such resources were directed to an alternative investment. This induces such oligopolists to increase loans offered as long as the regulated rate is above or equal to the marginal cost (similar to lending under a competitive market). To calculate the commercial banks' spread under this specification (which corresponds also to the region A–B), we know that:

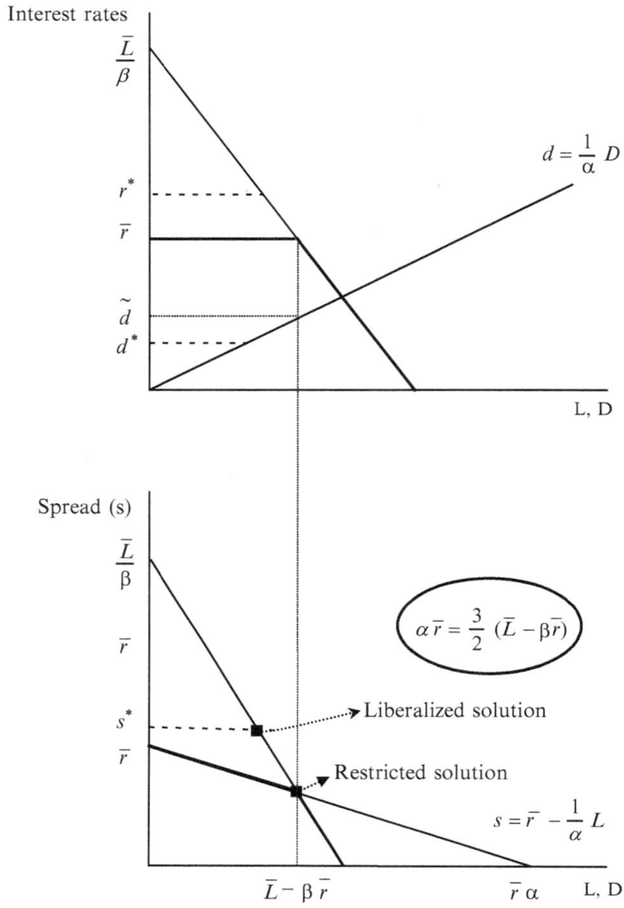

Fig. 5.3 Binding upper bound on lending rate and all demands satisfied

$$L = \bar{L} - \beta\bar{r}$$

The above equation holds since there is no rationing of loans in this zone. This is our loan demand curve that was specified earlier. On the other hand, from the supply of savings we can express the deposit rate as:

$$d = \frac{D}{\alpha}$$

Considering these two equations and taking into account that the spread equation is $\bar{r} - d$, the general spread function within this region can be specified as:

$$\bar{\bar{s}} = \bar{r}\left(1 + \frac{\beta}{\alpha}\right) - \frac{1}{\alpha}\bar{L} \tag{5.9}$$

Further from Figure 5.1, we can derive the value of $\bar{r}$ at the critical point of the 'kinked' curve beyond which the firms will find it beneficial to reduce the lending volume while leaving part of the market demand for loans unsatisfied. Taking a general profit equation for a representative firm while applying spread functions from liberalized and repressed markets, we specify that:

$$\pi_i = \left[\frac{\bar{L}}{\beta} - \left(\frac{1}{\alpha} + \frac{1}{\beta}\right)\left(L_i + \sum_{j \neq i} L_j\right)\right] L_i, \text{ if } L > \bar{L} - \beta\bar{r} \tag{5.10}$$

and

$$\pi_i = \left[\bar{r} - \frac{1}{\alpha}\left(L_i + \sum_{j \neq i} L_j\right)\right] L_i \text{ if } L < \bar{L} - \beta\bar{r} \tag{5.11}$$

A simple manipulation while collecting terms to derive corresponding levels of loan to these profit equations yields:

$$\begin{cases} L = \frac{\bar{L}}{\beta}\left(\frac{n}{n+1}\right)\frac{\alpha\beta}{\alpha+\beta} & \text{when (5.10) applies} \\ L = \bar{r}\left(\frac{n}{n+1}\right)\alpha & \text{when (5.11) applies} \end{cases} \tag{5.12}$$

Solving for $\bar{r}$ at the critical while taking the specific case of two firms, we derive:

$$\bar{r}^c = \frac{3\bar{L}}{(3\beta + 2\alpha)}$$

Substituting this term into equation (5.9) and simplifying further we obtain:

$$\bar{s}^c = \frac{\bar{L}}{2\alpha + 3\beta} \tag{5.13}$$

Considering Figure 5.1, let us identify the turning point, where continuous decrease in $\bar{r}$ would trigger a downward trend in the volume of loans. Specifically, this corresponds to the region where some demand for loans are left unsatisfied. From the behaviour of the lending sector in the critical region, it has been established that as $\bar{r}$ declines, L will continue increasing until the price (marginal revenue) is equal to the marginal cost. Beyond this point, further decline will induce commercial banks to decrease the lending volume since they earn sub-optimal profits. From this framework we can derive the implied condition as:

$$\bar{L} - \bar{r}\beta = \frac{2}{3}\alpha\bar{r} \equiv L \tag{5.14}$$

In this aspect, the shift in the profit maximizing solution of the commercial banks is depicted by Figure 5.3. We can show that, provided $\bar{r}\alpha \geq \frac{3}{2}(\bar{L} - \beta\bar{r})$, the later profit maximizing solution for the oligopolist bank is at the kinked point on the demand curve. Clearly, the spread, shown by the vertical axis of the lower panel, is now lower compared to the previous case.

In contrast, we take another case where the repressed lending rate, $\bar{r}$, is now sufficiently lowered. As before, while each firm takes the volume of deposits accepted by the other banks as given, we rewrite the *total profit* of a representative commercial bank as:

$$\pi_1 = \bar{r}_L L_1 - dD_1 \equiv \left(\bar{r}_L - \frac{D_1 + D_2}{\alpha}\right) D_1$$

From the market equilibrium, deposits are the combined total of D_1 and D_2 while $D = \alpha d$. The marginal profit function of this respective firm will be:

$$\frac{\partial\pi_1}{\partial D_1} = \bar{r}_L - \frac{(2D_1 + D_2)}{\alpha}$$

The above equation enables us derive the reaction curves of the two firms as:

$$\begin{cases} D_1 = (\alpha/2)\,\bar{r}_L - D_2/2 \\ D_2 = (\alpha/2)\,\bar{r}_L - D_1/2 \end{cases} \tag{5.15}$$

Using equation (5.15) to solve for the Cournot equilibrium, it can be shown that $D = \frac{2}{3}\alpha\bar{r}$ and $d = 2\bar{r}/3$. Utilizing this and the specified lending rate, one can simply derive an expression for the spread equation as:

$$\bar{s} = \frac{1}{3}\bar{r} \tag{5.16}$$

In Fig. 5.4 we have sufficiently lowered $\bar{r}$ and considered the banking environment with two or more commercial banks. It is observable that as $\bar{r}$ is significantly lowered, such that $\bar{r}\alpha < \frac{3}{2}(\bar{L} - \beta\bar{r})$, the kinked point moves downwards while the profit maximizing solution moves to the left away from the kink and along the flatter part of the demand curve.

Indeed, taking into consideration the dynamics illustrated under Figures 5.2–5.4 and the account provided by Figure 5.1, the behaviour of loans (L) and deposits (D), and the interest rate spread as the government imposes a binding capped rate of

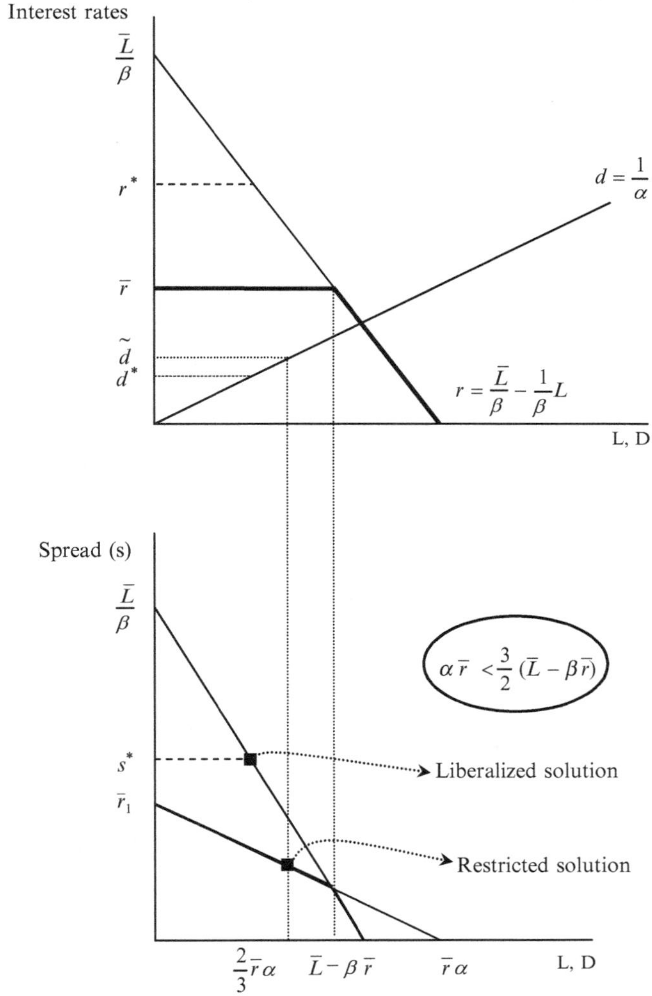

Fig. 5.4 Binding upper bound on lending rate, some unsatisfied demands

interest can be analyzed in the following way. We observe *first* that all demands are satisfied in the phase during which L and D are increasing, while in the later phase as L and D reduce, some demands for loans are left unsatisfied. *Second*, the imposition of a lending rate not far below the liberalized rate will: increase D and L; reduce spread; increase d and reduce r. However, the imposition of an upper bound on the lending rate that is well below the liberalized rate will: decrease D and L; reduce the spread severely and reduce both d and r.

Importantly, this theoretical coverage points out that mild financial repression may not be a bad option in a highly oligopolistic environment. In particular, this supports Stiglitz's (1994) advocacy for limited intervention in the financial market in which he argues 'there exist forms of government intervention that will not only make these [financial] markets function better but will also improve the performance of the economy' (p. 20). Accordingly, imposing a ceiling rate closer to the market-determined rate of interest increases capital allocation, while making it easier for firms to raise required capital with a lower level of spread margin. However, as it is apparent from Figure 5.1 the range within which this holds is narrow, and may be a difficult option to implement in practice.

Comparison of the two systems: Thus, to compare the spread under the two market systems, using equations (5.8) and (5.16) we know that with no change in the number of firms $s > \bar{s}$ when $\bar{r} < \frac{\bar{L}}{\beta}$ which always holds as:

$$\bar{r}_L < r_L = \left[1 - \frac{2\alpha}{3(\alpha + \beta)}\right] \frac{\bar{L}}{\beta} < \frac{\bar{L}}{\beta} \tag{5.17}$$

In this dimension, it is important to recognize that in a non-competitive banking structure there will always be an experience of widening interest rate spread following the liberalization of the financial system. Furthermore, since it is expected that the size of the spread would narrow as competition increases, with three firms in operation and hence for $\bar{r} > \frac{(\alpha+4\beta)}{4(\alpha+\beta)} \frac{\bar{L}}{\beta}$ the spread will decline. Consequently, we can show that for the range of $\bar{r}$ where $\frac{(\alpha+4\beta)}{4(\alpha+\beta)} \frac{\bar{L}}{\beta} < \bar{r} < r^*$ the entry of a third firm will reduce banks' intermediation spread to a lower level than that experienced under financial repression. However, if $\bar{r} < \frac{(\alpha+4\beta)}{4(\alpha+\beta)} \frac{\bar{L}}{\beta}$ even the entry of a third firm may not be sufficient to reduce spreads. With regard to the given dynamics, it also becomes quite clear that the imposition of any bidding upper bound on the lending rate will reduce profitability in the banking sector where in general this may open up the possibility of decreasing the number of operating banks.

5.2.3 The Level of Fixed Costs as a Barrier to Entry

In an oligopolistic banking environment where few firms' concentration ratio is high, it is expected that moderating entry requirements (restrictions) will open the banking system to new entries. However, it is apparent in Kenya and Malawi that there is a relatively significant stability of monopolistic power as reflected by a market share concentration of a few leading firms, even a decade and half after financial system liberalization. Presumably, a major reason to explain this phenomenon could be the existence of higher implicit entry costs which lowers the profitability of the banking industry.[5]

[5]This fact is further investigated in the next section while we have discussed some supporting anecdotal evidences in the previous chapter.

Suppose a bank incurs an amount of fixed costs F in a period, how many banks can the economy accommodate? With regard to this, let us assume that there are n number of firms before liberalization and m number of new firms following financial liberalization. A representative firm's profit is the intermediation spread times the volume of loans made (before taking F into account). Therefore, while utilizing the generalized approach of equation (5.8) the profitability under financially liberalized economic system will be:

$$\pi_n = \frac{\alpha\, \bar{L}^2}{(n+1)^2 \beta(\alpha+\beta)} - F$$

Following financial liberalization when profits increase, this signals the entry of new banking firms unless there are other implicit entry barriers. Therefore:

$$\pi_{n+m} = \frac{\alpha\, \bar{L}^2}{(n+m+1)^2 \beta(\alpha+\beta)} - F$$

The breakeven level of F can be calculated to be:[6]

$$F^{H2} = \frac{\alpha\, \bar{L}^2}{(n+m+1)^2 \beta(\alpha+\beta)} \tag{5.18}$$

where (n + m) is the number of profitable firms. More specifically, with two profitable firms in existence we can show that when the level of fixed costs is given by equation (5.19), three firms will operate in the market under financial liberalization, as they would earn positive profits.

$$F \leq \frac{\alpha\, \bar{L}^2}{16\beta(\alpha+\beta)} \tag{5.19}$$

However, if we have a level of fixed costs F such that:

$$\frac{\alpha\, \bar{L}^2}{16\beta(\alpha+\beta)} < F \leq \frac{\alpha\, \bar{L}^2}{9\beta(\alpha+\beta)} \tag{5.20}$$

it will only be viable to have two firms to stay in business and the entry of a third firm will stretch profitability to negative.

[6] Notice that each zone of high (H), medium (K) and low (L) $\bar{r}$ will have a fixed costs level corresponding to before and after the entry of new firms, marked 1 and 2 respectively, where the first is greater than the second.

Similarly, examination should be made of the case of financial repression. With the help of equation (5.9) and focusing on the medium region, the profitability of a representative firm in the industry can be calculated as:

$$\bar{\bar{\pi}}_n = \left[\left(1+\frac{\beta}{\alpha}\right)\bar{r} - \frac{\bar{L}}{\alpha}\right]\left(\frac{\bar{L}-\beta\bar{r}}{n}\right) - F \tag{5.21}$$

Accordingly, the breakeven level of the fixed cost without any entry of new firms can be calculated to be:

$$F^{K1} = \frac{\bar{L}}{n}\left[\frac{\alpha+n\beta}{\alpha}\right]\bar{r} - \frac{\beta}{n}\left(\frac{\alpha+\beta}{\alpha}\right)\bar{r}^2 - \frac{\bar{L}^2}{n\alpha} \tag{5.22}$$

However, when we have an additional entry of m new firms, the above level of fixed costs can be recomputed to represent:

$$F^{K2} = \frac{\bar{L}}{(n+m)}\left[\frac{\alpha+n\beta}{\alpha}\right]\bar{r} - \frac{\beta}{(n+m)}\left(\frac{\alpha+\beta}{\alpha}\right)\bar{r}^2 - \frac{\bar{L}^2}{(n+m)\alpha}$$

When the level of fixed costs is at a certain range such that $F^{K2} < F \le F^{K1}$ there will be two operating in the banking industry.

Finally, to illustrate these dynamics under the lower region of $\bar{r}$ while utilizing equation (5.16), the profitability under the second case of the repressed financial system is given by:

$$\bar{\pi}_n = \frac{\alpha\bar{r}^2}{(n+1)^2} - F \text{ and } \bar{\pi}_{\mathrm{n+m}} = \frac{\alpha\,\mathrm{r}^2}{(\mathrm{n}+1+\mathrm{m})^2} - \mathrm{F} \tag{5.23}$$

From these specifications one can express the breakeven level of fixed costs F as:

$$F^{Llow} = \frac{1}{(n+1+m)^2}\alpha\bar{r}^2 \tag{5.24}$$

Furthermore we can show that at a given range of fixed costs F such that:

$$\frac{1}{16}\alpha\bar{r}^2 < F \le \frac{1}{9}\alpha\bar{r}^2 \tag{5.25}$$

the market can only accommodate two firms rather than three.

To summarize the nature of the commercial banks' market structure and its reaction towards reforms, we can conclude that (1) the spread may go down if there were two firms before and three firms after liberalization. It will suffice to give a numerical example here. Let us assume that α = \$500, β = \$300 and $\bar{L}$ = \$600 while $\frac{(\alpha+4\beta)}{4(\alpha+\beta)}\frac{\bar{L}}{\beta} < \bar{r} < r^*(1 < \bar{r} < 1.2)$ say $\bar{r} = 1.1$, the spread for two firms under repression is 0.56 which goes down to 0.5 after liberalization with an entry of a third firm. At a fixed cost of say \$30 (which satisfies equation (5.19)), the level of profitability after the entry of a third firm goes down to \$16.8 from \$45.6 which is certainly positive. (2) The spread may first go up, if there is no further entry of new firms in the wake of reforms towards financial liberalization. Similarly, to give a numerical example, let's take that $r > \bar{r} = 1.15$ where r is derived under the numerical parameters of the values specified, the spread increases from 0.64 to 0.67 following a change from repression to liberalization. Further, while taking a level of fixed cost, say \$50 (which is within the range specified under equation (5.20)), the profitability increases, although marginally, from \$31.6 to \$33.5 respectively. Secondly, and probably the most interesting case, is where even with an entry of a new firm the spread may go up. Thus taking $\bar{r} < \frac{(\alpha+4\beta)}{4(\alpha+\beta)}\frac{\bar{L}}{\beta}$ say $\bar{r} = 0.9$, the spread, following a move from repression to liberalization, increases from 0.24 to 0.5 respectively. Indeed, taking a fixed cost say \$35 (as specified by equation (5.20)), the profitability declines from \$19.6 to \$11.8 under liberalization.

5.2.4 Graph of Fixed Costs and New Entry

Under financial liberalization, we can trace various combinations of fixed costs (F) and interest rate (r) where there may be room for a specific number of firms (see Fig. 5.5). Initially using equation (5.6) and equation (5.18), we can show the fixed cost and interest rate curves in relation to the number of profitable firms in the economy. It can be seen that when a fixed cost decreases, the number of profitable firms sufficient to exit in such an economy increases. On the other hand, as the interest rate charged increases and profitability improves, the economy can accommodate more firms enabling it to attract new banks. Therefore, when the fixed cost reduces (and r increases) the number of viable commercial institutions is expected to increase.

Similarly, assuming a repressed financial market and applying the profitability function specified under equation (5.21) and equation (5.23), the relationship between F, $\bar{r}$ and the number of firms the financial sector can accommodate is depicted by Figure 5.6. Curves O, A and B provide the combination of interest rate and fixed costs under which profitability margins are equal to zero. More specifically, they provide cut-off points under which further entry will drive profit levels to negative. Thus, it is observable that on the extreme left of curve O, there will be no bank under financial repression. In the area between O and A, it is viable to have only one operating bank while on the right of curve B the banking sector could accommodate three or more banks.

When the imposed rate of interest is not far below the liberalized rate, curves C and D exhibit these combinations. It is notable that curves C and D are quadratic functions in form, with the coefficient of $\bar{r}^2$ being negative (see equation (5.22)).

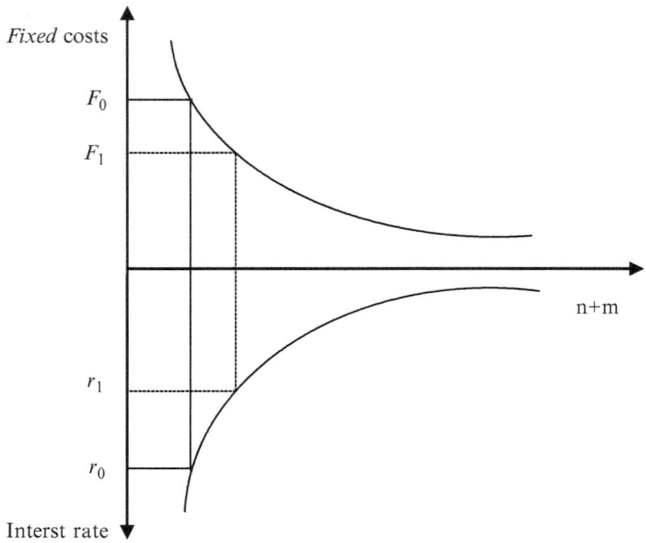

Fig. 5.5 Fixed costs, interest rate and competitive entry (liberalization)

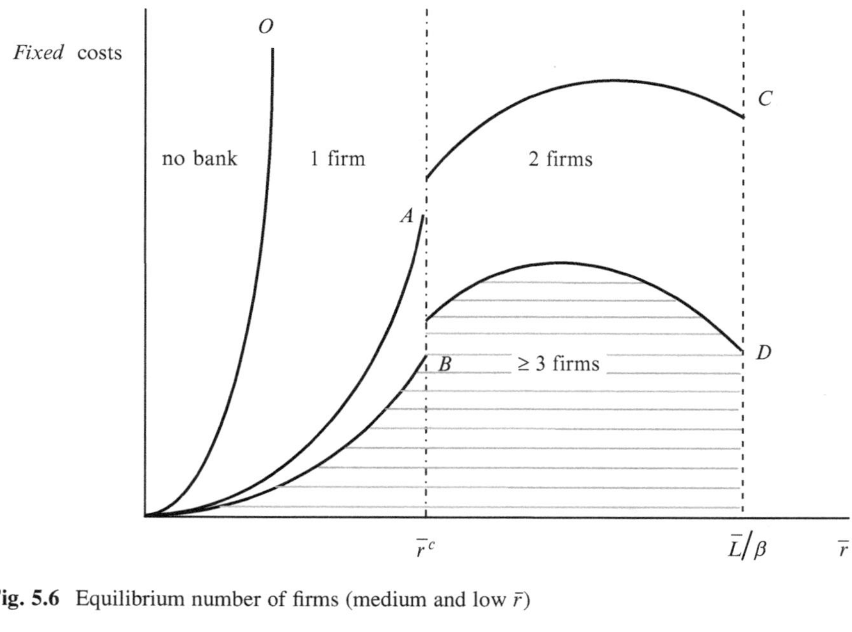

Fig. 5.6 Equilibrium number of firms (medium and low $\bar{r}$)

With these concave functions any turning point will be the maximum value. Additionally, from their dynamics it can be shown that when the number of firms increases, there will be a shift downwards while the horizontal intercept remains the same. On the horizontal axis it is indicated that the interest rate is bounded upwards by $\bar{L}/\beta$. Beyond this value, economic agents are not willing to borrow and hence reduce the lending activities to zero. At $\bar{r}^2$ the fixed cost in the medium region is higher than that of the lower region.[7] This is because in the 'kinked' region, the marginal cost is lower than marginal revenue, which means that firms can tolerate some extra fixed costs to bring their profitability to zero (as represented by the curves). In the region between the given curves it is only possible to have two firms whereas in the shaded area, there will be three or more firms operating under the financially repressive system. The entry of extra firm(s) is brought about by the decrease in the level of fixed costs.

Finally, after combining the dynamics of repression and liberalization (i.e. from high, medium and lower regions) along with the profitability and entry of additional firms, Figure 5.7 depicts the behaviour of these financial variables. It is shown that when interest rates are liberalized and fixed costs reduced, more firms are able to conduct commercial banking business. On the other hand, if fixed costs are substantial, there may only be room for one firm to operate in the banking sector even under financial liberalization, as depicted by the top part of Figure 5.7. At a lower fixed cost we may have more than three firms operating under the liberalized financial set-up, increasing the competitive pressure as required. In this regards, marks (i), (ii), and (iii) in the lower region of the figure represent areas where we will have changes in the number of operating banks from 1 to 2, 1 to 3 and 2 to 3 respectively. The shaded region in Figure 5.7 represents areas where the market can accommodate three or more firms under repressed and liberalized regimes.[8] It is observable from the behaviour of the market after liberalization that, taking into account the given level of fixed cost, the number of firms increases in the lower portion of the diagram.[9] On the other hand, every point on the vertical line r^* represents a different number of firms at different levels of fixed costs. Beyond r^* it is clear that $\bar{r}$ is irrelevant. Thus r^* puts an upper bound on $\bar{r}$. At this stage, an important question to ask is for what values of F and $\bar{r}$ does liberalization make the spread go down as a result of a competitive entry? From our previous analysis, the region within which the spread is expected to go down due to a resulting competitive pressure from the entry of new firms (and in particular, as the number firms increase from 2 to 3), was given to be $\frac{(\alpha+4\beta)}{4(\alpha+\beta)}\frac{\bar{L}}{\beta} < \bar{r} < r^*$.

---

[7]See Appendix A5.2 for the proof.

[8]In this combined version, we can show that maximal points of fixed cost curves under C and D are greater than the fixed cost lines specified under liberalization. See Appendix A5.3 for a formal proof.

[9]In the lower part of the figure, if the change in $\bar{r}^c$ was infinitesimal we would not have the gulf in between the two critical values as indicated. We can also show a small similar region on the top part.

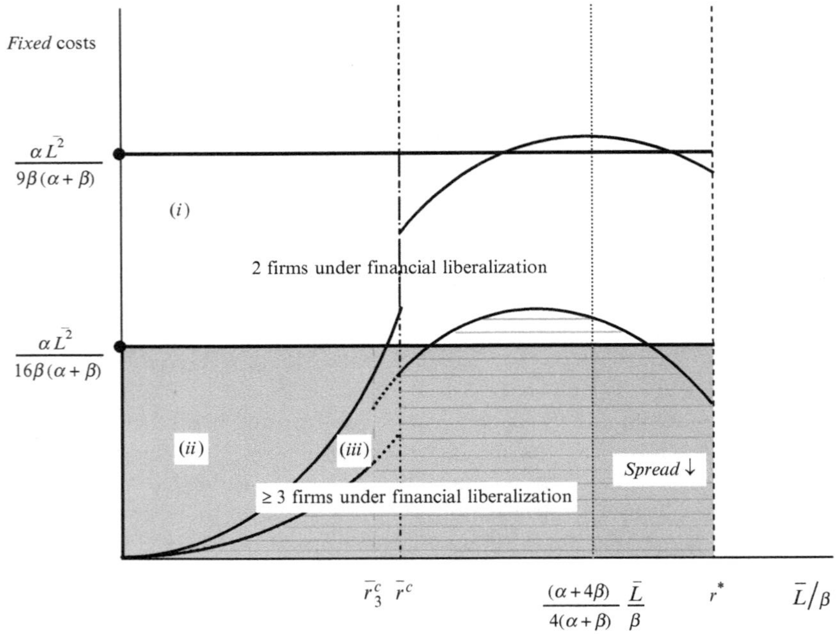

Fig. 5.7 Competitive entry under the three zones combined

This area is represented by the heavily shaded region on the right bottom corner of Figure 5.7. It is shown that, since $\bar{r}$ is less than its bound $\bar{L}/\beta$, the region shrinks even further to the left of the curve and only up to r^*. Therefore, although we may have an increase in the number of firms conducting commercial banking business, the chances remain small of such an entry resulting in the required decline in the spread to enhance efficiency, as claimed by McKinnon-Shaw hypothesis. In this sense, these graphs demonstrate the theoretical underpinning of the absence of the potential entry of new firms under the newly deregulated interest rate environment. It is observable that prospective entry, to a greater extent, will be limited by the magnitude of fixed costs to be borne by such institutions. Thus, this implies that as long as the fixed cost level is substantial, there will be little benefit of associated efficiency gain since this discourages a healthy competitive banking environment.

Further, Figure 5.8 indicates the change in deposit rates at various regions, assuming a given numerical value for the parameter specified under Figure 5.7. These changes in deposit rates (Δd) are relative to the liberalized solutions while considering the entry of an additional firm in the respective zones accordingly. Thus in the upper right region of the figure, the deposit rate initially increases by 1. 37 percentage points in that area. Similarly, in the left bottom area, it can be seen that the

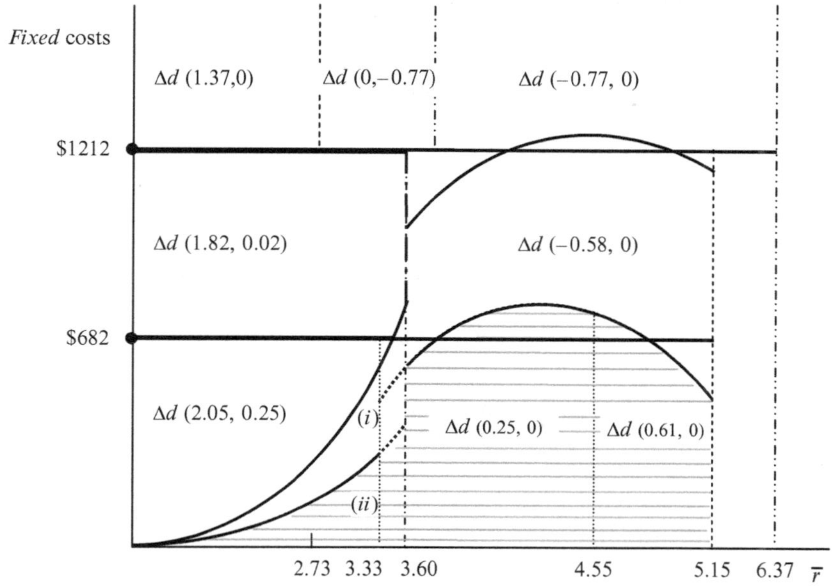

Fig. 5.8 Graphical representation of change in d in various regions

deposit rate is increasing at a decreasing rate ranging from 2.05 to 0.25 percentage points. It is observable that when fixed costs are lower and with a more competitive market (through entry), the change in deposit rates are positive. Thus, the areas in the lower zone of the figure depict regions that favour savings.

Meanwhile, Figure 5.9 illustrates the movement in deposit rates following liberalization, where depending on the initial point of the deposit rate, it may go up or down. In the region around A it is observable that it will actually go up following financial liberalization. However, in region B, where *d* had been around the critical zone before liberalization, there is a possibility that it may go down although interest rates go up (notice here that we are assuming there are the same number of firms in operation in pre-liberalization as in post-liberalization).[10] It is also worth mentioning that in the zones where *d* goes down in Figure 5.8, initial deposit rates seem to be around the critical region and thus it is not surprising that we observe a downward trend.

---

[10]We could also depict a different case where we observe a new entry following liberalization. However the institution about the change in *d* remains the same.

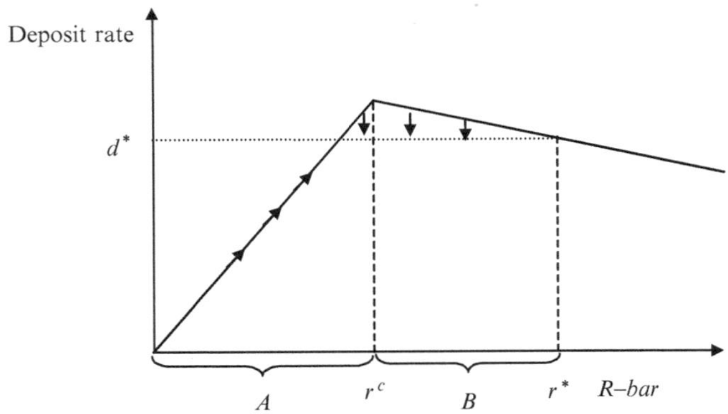

Fig. 5.9 Illustration of movements in deposit rate

5.2.5 *Dynamics of how much the Interest Rate goes up after Liberalization*

As a follow-up to our examination under Figure 5.7, in this section we will look at the savings behaviour given different levels of the interest rate ($\bar{r}$). In the previous section, it has been pointed out that the liberalization of the financial system will lead to a higher interest rate and further entry of a new financial institution may enable a better savings mobilization. While taking various ranges of $\bar{r}$ (similar to those used under Figure 5.7), we will look at the trends in deposit rates and savings level assuming the dynamics of both financial repression (Repressed) and that of financial liberalization (Liberalized). This exercise will enable us to focus on any adjustments and changes in the saving activities that are likely to take place. This will also help us point out the extent to which interest rate levels may have to improve before achieving savings volume that are higher than those attained under a financially repressive mechanism.

Figure 5.10a and b give movements in the deposit rates and saving levels realized if the dynamics were continuously dictated by the frameworks outlined under repressive (Repressed) or liberalized (Liberalized) financial set-ups. The vertical line in the middle of the figure represents $\bar{r}^c$ beyond which the repressive dynamic system changes. Thus the zone beyond this value corresponds to the area within which firms are willing to offer more loans at the existing capped rate of interest, but are only constrained by the loan demand curve. It can be noted that the trend in the deposit rates follows a similar pattern to that outlined by Figure 5.1. Under repressive financial mechanism, deposit rates initially increase as firms compete to serve the portion of the market left unsatisfied following an increase in interest rates. This continues until demands for loans are fully satisfied. On the other hand, deposit rate under a liberalized financial mechanism is positively related to $\bar{r}$. Notice that although we are interested in a specific solution under the

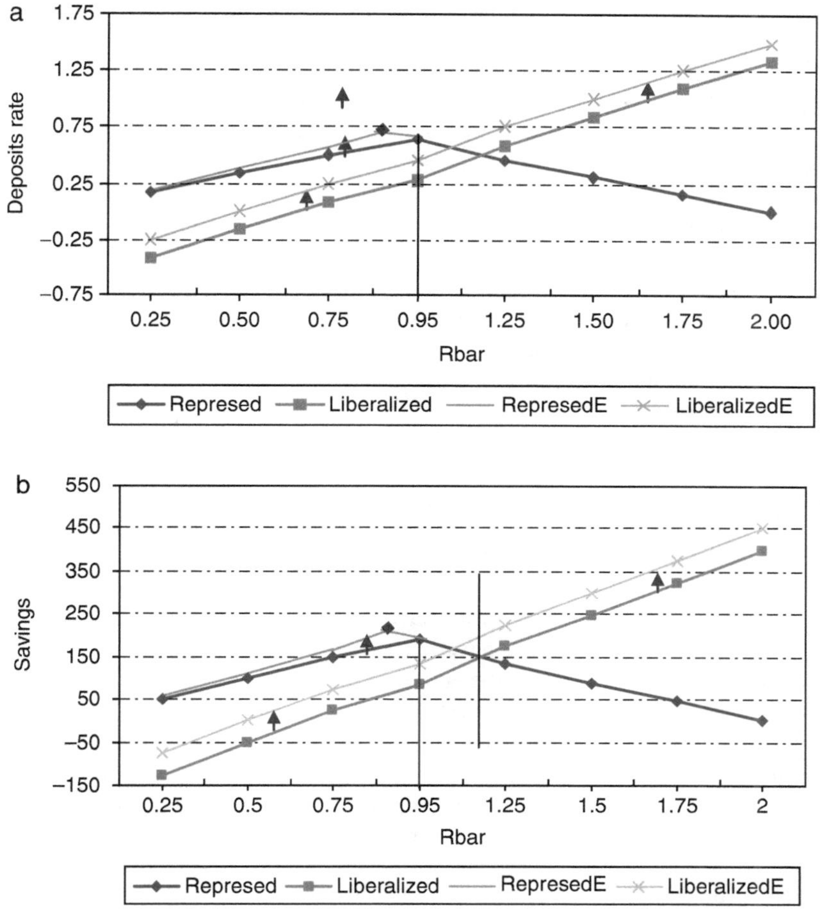

Fig. 5.10 Movements in deposits rate and savings volume; **(a)** trend in deposit rates. **(b)** trends in savings level
Note: E denotes entry of an additional firm.
Source: Authors own calculations.

liberalized dynamics, we have used a locus of liberalized solutions with respect to different α's and β's to help demonstrate the trend.

With the expectation that these changes in deposit rates generate similar changes in real financial savings, Figure 5.10b depicts savings volumes under the two market regimes. It is clear that the savings trends closely mimic the deposit rates path. From Figure 5.10a, the intersection of the two deposits rate curves (with the thick lines) represents the equilibrium rate interest, r^*. With the exception of a small region around the critical zone, liberalization of the interest rate market will generally ensure a higher savings level as deposit rates will be increasing. Considering the impact of an entry of a new financial institution (say a third firm), the liberalized solution shifts up to the left of the original curve, resulting in higher rates of deposit at every point. This is indicated by the arrows in Figure 5.10a and b. Allowing the entry of a new firm under the repressed market structure causes pivoting of the original curve to the left, while the point indicating the critical rate interest moves up to the central region of the figure with the same slope. Further, it can also be shown that considering the dynamics of both these market structures, there is a small region, (seemingly in between the interest rate levels of 0.85 and 0.975) where limited financial repression may lead to higher savings volume. Accordingly, with the exception of this, as the capped rate of interest increases, deposit rates under liberalized financial regime increase upwardly while the gap between repressive and liberalized solution decline. Under liberalization also, if interest rates are allowed to increase sufficiently, entry of an additional firm will lead to a higher savings volume that is greater than the level achieved under financial repression.

5.3 Financial Reforms and Absence of Entry by New Foreign Banks

From the policy and data analysis we have given so far, it is notable that in both Kenya and Malawi, where there have been changes in the banking legislations to moderate admission procedures, the entry of well-established foreign banks has not been forthcoming as opposed to the case of Botswana. Quite clearly, one of the key objectives of reforms towards financial liberalization was to attract new banks and particularly foreign-based institutions into the banking sector. Importantly, comment has been made that the attraction of foreign-based banking corporations into the financial system will enhance efficiency by improving the available quality of human capital and by bringing modern financial technology into the sector (Denizer, 1997). As illustrated by Figure 5.11, because the new institutions are more efficient[11] they have a lower average cost (AC_n) relative to incumbent banks (AC_o). Therefore, at a given number of customers (say N_o) such institutions can offer their services at a price P_n. However, before getting such a volume right, due to high switching costs since customers have had long relationships with incumbent banks and for the 'acceptance' effect to manifest, they face losses (SL) in the short-run requiring extra supportive capital before reaping profits in the long-run.

Given this mainstream view, the entry of foreign-banks may be an ideal since they have access to supporting capital from their foreign partners. Despite this, the new entries into the commercial banking system in Kenya and Malawi were small – mostly locally owned – institutions that did not have a strong supporting capital base to operate beyond a few big commercial cities. Indeed, in addition to limited capital capacity, the acquiring of experienced banking management expertise has been

[11]This may be because such institutions have a better technology, the required expertise and are able to get a better combination of physical and human capital.

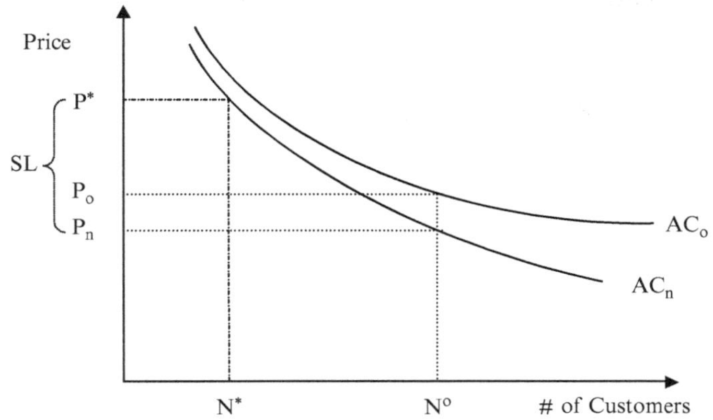

Fig. 5.11 Effect of entry by new banks

a problem for these new small institutions.[12] Together these factors have increased customers' switching costs, enabling the new entrants to only attract fewer clients.

On the basis of this, it is not surprising that the announcement of free entry under these circumstances may not promote strong competition as the incumbent banks have first mover advantage, while new entrants only concentrate on covering certain profitable niches rather than challenging dominant banks for a market share.[13] In both Kenya and Malawi, the entry of small scale firms to the market seems not to have altered the inter-firms rivalry. First, because of their size or capital base these institutions are largely either only active in or specialize in external trade and corporate wholesale banking. Moreover, their geographical distribution is such that they only operate in the capital city (Mlachila & Chirwa, 2002; Kinyua & Musau, 2004). Second, because such new entrants have no strategic plan to increase their customer base, they tend to work closely with large dominating firms, and therefore, are not a serious factor of competition or business diversion. With respect to this, even though the business targets of these small-scale entrants may be profitable, generally this is not the expected business plan for a well-established commercial bank that aims to effectively challenge for a market share and customer base in the retail banking business.

Researchers have remarked that to reduce monopoly power and foster healthy competition entry of foreign-based banking institutions is necessary (UNDP, 1999; Mlachila & Chirwa, 2002). However, following the announcement of free-entry, the successful attraction of well established foreign banks has not been seen. To our understanding, no one has addressed the question of why more competitive

[12]Relatively, as opposed to this well established foreign institutions are expected to bring in more human capital.

[13]Denizer (1997) has also observed similar behaviors by some new local bank entrants in the case of Turkey.

foreign-based institutions were not forthcoming. Perhaps, in this aspect, we highlight some possible factors that may explain such an unexpected trend. In general, there can be two hypotheses to explain the lack of meaningful entry in the commercial banking industry following the relaxation of entry restrictions. One is the existence of *implicit* barriers to entry and barriers to exit, and second is the unprofitable banking environment.

To consider the first issue, both Kenya and Malawi have revised their legal framework for the financial sector in order to ease new entries. In Malawi, following the move to liberalize the financial system, the central bank was given more powers to licence and regulate the sector (Mlachila & Chirwa, 2002). Similarly in Kenya, the recent amendment to the Banking Act has seen licensing and delicensing powers transferred to the central bank.[14] Such regulatory transformations were necessary to ensure a viable and healthy banking industry as such authorities have the required skills and information to vigorously 'vet' new entrants. Moreover, being in a position to efficiently and effectively assess applicants, the previously non-transparent and ad hoc evaluation mechanisms were now standardized. However, even though such a review of the banking sectors' operational mechanism seems to have sufficiently addressed entry policies, it is not clear whether new entrants informally pay bribes to get approved. Indeed, considering the high levels of corruption in these countries, it needs to be recognized that this may be a possibility. Additionally, reforms seem to have fallen short of covering strict and promptly-enforced exit procedures. An illustrative example is the case of Trust Bank, which was placed under statutory management in 1998 and allowed to reopen after some years after passing a solvency test before it was again suddenly liquidated. Together this process has taken 6 years and stakeholder have lost a combined total of Ksh. 13 billion.[15] This may affect both customers and banks in the sense that when businesses to which one is lending are failing, firms would like to be free to relocate. In this aspect and considering the unstable macroeconomic environment and sluggish economic growth, putting into place orderly, quick closure, and liquidation procedures are necessary. Thus without revised and friendly exit and repayments recovery systems, such imperfections may deter new entrants, acting as implicit entry barriers.[16]

Differently, an unprofitable banking environment could also restrain entrants of established foreign banks. In addition to the sluggish performance of the economy, if there are other institutional weaknesses and implicit operational costs, the sector's profitability may be further pushed down. In this respect, in places where corruption is endemic, contractual obligations may not be smoothly adhered to and property right enactment and establishment may be difficult. With regards to this,

[14]See Banking Supervision Report, 2001.

[15]See, for example, articles 'Taken for a ride by Central Bank' in *Daily Nation*, January 28th, 2004 and 'CBK liable to pay all Euro Bank depositors' in *Daily Nation*, April 8th, 2003.

[16]Brock and Suarez (2000) observe that lack of orderly exit procedures have resulted in a poorly managed banking environment in Latin America.

while Kenya and Malawi are plagued by systematic corruption, Botswana had been developing democratic accountability mechanisms to ensure property rights and response to economic needs.[17] It has been noted that property right systems not backed by a proper functioning court of law create moral hazard problems and seriously inhibit lending and borrowing mechanisms in financial institutions, leading to extreme inefficiencies (NSE, 2001). Quite conclusively, Botswana's judicial and legal systems have been termed as independent, efficient and transparent (Adamolekun & Morgan, 1999) having created a reputation for giving fair trials and predictable judgments.[18] Unlike Kenya and Malawi, such institutional soundness supports financial stability and encourages intermediation. Contrastingly, ambiguities in property rights definitions in Kenya have frustrated banks and individual creditors when such properties are used as a collateral security. Property ownership is indicated by the acquisition of '*title deeds*' and other legally acquired documents that prove adequate possession. However, due to corrupt deals, such documents can fraudulently be acquired or issued to multiple individuals under the same asset.[19] Additionally, even where such claims are valid, when debt-recovery complains are lodged on properties which were given as collateral security, other provisions in the Land Control Act require the approval of the Land Control Board. In this context, well-connected, corrupt and privileged executives and individual borrowers with political patronage might indeed block such boards' approvals (Kinyua & Musau, 2004). Due to this Kinyua and Musau observe that the liquidation of collateral became extremely difficult, leading to a long legal battle between banks and their borrowers. Alternatively, defaulters may also influence justice machinery by manipulating the legal process.[20] Observably, judicial systems in Kenya and Malawi have demonstrated serious underperformance in administering justice (Mulei & Mullei, 2001; IBA, 2002). It has been reported that quite commonly judges have pursued individual interests, and banks have complained of an increasing trend of defaulters rushing to courts to obtain last minute injunctions which they easily obtain, contrary to all reasonable expectations (Mulei & Mullei).[21] The predominance of corruption coupled with other inefficiencies, including lack of motivation and non-regard to commitment, rendered the judiciary sectors in both these countries incompetent and inefficient. Consequently, the

[17]Holm (2000, pp. 288-04) provides a classical discussion of institutional transformation in Botswana.

[18]In comparison, many judgments in Malawi and Kenya have been criticized as being peculiar and contrary to all reasonable expectations. See "All-Bank probe into $398M Bank Debts" in the East African Standard, October 20th, 2003.

[19]Likewise, such ownership documents may also be issued on lands that are non-existent. See also the article "Banks are warned on fake title deeds" in East African Standard, February 26th, 2004.

[20]Surprisingly, Kenya's Attorney General branded the legal sector as a failure, ineffective in administering justice and worst of all corrupt. See "Wako criticizes legal sector" in *Daily Nation*, June 8th, 1999.

[21]Similarly for a glaring lack of professionalism in Malawi see "Malawian Court Defeats Justice" in Society News, Wednesday, September 18th, 2002.

traditional judicial role of administering justice is compromised and the due process of law is abused regularly.

Different from other sectors, notably this affects the commercial banking sector in two closely related ways. Initially, well connected borrowers and corrupt individuals may intentionally default their loan payments as they know they can fight their way through to frustrate banks by acquiring injunctions to stop collateral security disposal through the court system. Similarly, since such litigation processes can drag for many years in favour of the corrupt defaulters, lending banks incur huge litigation costs through legal and administrative fees where ultimately such cases may prematurely come to an end (Mulei & Mullei, 2001). In view of such an increasing cost, banks are disadvantaged as this may drastically reduce their profitability margin and seriously jeopardize their liquidity position. Generally, these institutional deficiencies also prompt fraudulent activities and result in inefficiencies in the speed of loan repayments. Apparently, it is recognized that the problem of declining profitability in the banking sector may not be justified by sluggish economic factors alone.

Consequently, having looked at some of the issues that seem to be affecting the banking sectors' profitability, we now turn to some suggestive evidence to evaluate the relative performance of the banking sector. We first look at a synopsis of bank spread in Kenya to determine the driving factors behind such a level of spread. As indicated by Table 5.1 the overhead costs alone account for more than 37% of the interest rate spread of commercial banks in Kenya. Interestingly, this estimate is after considering provisions for loan losses and allowing some level of profit margin for these banks. In order to deconstruct such high levels of interest rate margin and overhead costs, the table also outlines major components that constitute these variables. This is for the purpose of exploring factors that explain why such indicators are significantly higher compared to the rest of the world. From the evidence, almost 42% and 28% of the deviations (differences) in interest margin and overhead cost respectively in Kenya relative to the world average are contributed to by ineffective legal and institutional systems (particularly regarding property right protection).[22] In an environment where judiciary and regulatory

Table 5.1 Factors driving interest rate spread and overhead cost (percentage)

Spread		Interest margin		Overhead cost
Total spread	14.9	Difference from world average	3.4	2.9
Contributed by:		Contributed by:		
Overhead cost	5.6	Failures in property right protection	1.4	0.8
Loan loss provision	2.5	Bank size	0.9	0.7
Profit margin	4.5	Country characteristics	0.1	0.0
Others	2.3	Others	1.0	1.4

Source: Statistics are based on Beck and Fuchs (2004) and cover year 2002 only.

[22]In addition to the corruption problem, these are other failures related to deficiencies in perfecting and registering securities/assets that can be used as collateral by bank borrowers.

institutions are weak, enforcing contractual obligations is difficult. Moreover, in the presence of high corruption regimes, settling disputes becomes difficult and banks may be forced to enormous legal costs. In such structures, it is likely that higher levels of interest rate spread will be observed (Demirguc-Kunt & Huizinga, 1997).

Additionally, from Table 5.1, another important factor which also seems to contribute to higher average interest margins and overhead costs in Kenya is the small size of banks. Of the 3.4 and 2.9 percentage point differences of these variables from the world average, 0.9 and 0.7 percentage points are accounted for by bank size-related factors. First, in a developing country environment with inadequate legal and supervisory frameworks governing the functions of the banking system, small banks may be more susceptible to banking crises and hence associated with failures. Thus, these small institutions may suffer from reputation bias. Second, entry of smaller banks may not change the competitive structure of the banking system. Because smaller size banks lack economies of scale advantage, these new entrants are active only in a few big commercial centres and cities both in Kenya and Malawi. In this regard customers, particularly of large and frequent depositors, have high switching costs enabling a few large banks to maintain their market share. Furthermore, small banks may only offer profitable services. In explaining the structure behind high monopoly power in Malawi, Chirwa (2001) remarks that almost all new entrants concentrated on wholesale type of banking but did not divert to clientele commercial banking. Third, smaller size banks may not pursue aggressive marketing strategies to increase competitive structure. To reap higher profits, such fringe firms may accept 'collusive price leadership' resulting in little change in the previously non-competitive market structure.[23] Thus, with little or none intense interbank competition, it is expected that larger banks will be able to charge higher interest rates on their loans. This evidence implies that what is important is not just 'the entry of new firms', but rather how an entry of a new firm(s) will influence the operation of the existing banking institutions, indicating that the size of the new entrants does matter.

To evaluate the profitability environment studies have mostly used return on assets (ROA) as an acceptable measure. Table 5.2 reports banking sector earning ratings in Kenya relative to other industries in the country and the banking sector abroad. First, return on assets of the banking sector has been significantly lower relative to other industries in Kenya. Thus, the sector's ROA has been 0.75% on average for the recent 5 years compared to 7.5% in the building (cement) industry. Second, compared to Botswana, the performance of Kenya's banking sector has continuously been far below. Third, the number of banking and non-banking financial institutions with earning performance rated either strong or satisfactory has declined from almost 50% (34 of 69) in 1998 to only 22% (13 of 58) in 2002.

Accordingly, even though financial sector reforms have reduced financial repression-related problems to some extent, potential banking sector costs have been increasing. This is because they operate in a cumbersome environment in

---

[23]Denizer (1997) has provided detailed discussion on this point.

Table 5.2 Bank earning statistics in Kenya compared to other sectors and countries

Year	Performance	SS	F	MU	Total	BPC Ltd	Botswana
2002	# of institutions	13	17	28	58		
	Net asset (Ksh bn)	93	155	208	457		
	Return on asset	n.a	n.a	n.a	1%	13.8%	3.9%
2001	# of institutions	23	10	18	51		
	Net asset	236	55	134	425		
	Return on asset	n.a	n.a	n.a	1.5%	8.9%	3.8%
2000	# of institutions	20	8	28	56		
	Net asset	214	27	194	435		
	Return on asset	n.a	n.a	n.a	0.5%	3.4%	3.8%
1999	# of institutions	26	10	27	63		
	Net asset	224	37	157	418		
	Return on asset	n.a	n.a	n.a	0.04%	6.5%	3.9%
1998	# of institutions	34	8	27	69		
	Net asset	168	61	205	434		
	Return on asset	n.a	n.a	n.a	0.8%	4.9%	3.4%

Note: SS stands for Strong/Satisfactory, F-Fair and MU-Marginal/Unsatisfactory. BPC is Bamburi Portland Cement of Kenya. Last column shows earnings in Botswana's banking sector.
Source: Respective Central Banks, Bank Supervision Department.

which they are significantly disadvantaged. Seemingly and based on the above assessment, our evidence reasonably points out the profitability problem as the major hindrance towards the entry of meaningful foreign-based banking institutions in Kenya and Malawi. Furthermore, due to the lack of accountability in the two countries there could be other invisible barriers to entry. To enhance the entry of established banks in order to break the monopolistic behaviour and serve as a catalyst for change, the state should reduce non-regulatory barriers. The provision of efficient legal and institutional frameworks should be regarded as a top priority. Likewise, states should invest in improving infra-structural support, such as security, which can only increase the cost burden of these commercial banks. In support of this argument, a recent study by Beck and Fuchs (2004) points out that an important explanation for high overhead costs in Kenya is as being directly related to deficiencies in the legal and institutional frameworks. Because overhead costs are almost twice as high in Kenya than in the rest of the world (Beck & Fuchs), entry of effective competitors (especially of a foreign type) may not be forthcoming. In this sense, the above-mentioned structural and institutional (and visibly non-market) impediments seem to explain quite well the absence of effective entry in Kenya and Malawi, which would have altered inter-firm market relationships in the banking sector.

5.4 Conclusion

From the assessments and results in Chapter 4, this chapter provides a theoretical modelling of imperfect competition in the commercial banking sector. The main question asked in this regard was, why didn't the level of competition increase following liberalization of the banking industry in Kenya and Malawi? While answering this question, the chapter also focuses on the behaviour of the spread and effective number of firms the financial industry can accommodate. To complement the findings of the theoretical treatment, the chapter provides some empirical evidence on the profitability of the commercial banking industry and whether high fixed costs had been a major factor behind lower profitability and hence acting as a barrier to entry.

The outcome of the theoretical treatment suggests that, given the oligopolistic structure of the commercial banking sector, the spread may decrease in the post-liberalization period if repressed rate interest was above a certain threshold level and the number of firms was allowed to increase resulting in effective competition. Secondly, the spread will increase if there is no further entry of new firms or even with entry if such a threshold level was not achieved. Thirdly, it is observed that there is a small range of imposed rate interest in which *mild* financial repression may be beneficial to the economy. Further, it is found that higher fixed cost, by reducing the profitability of the financial sector, deters new meaningful entrants. Thus, it will act as a barrier to the entry of new financial institutions through effectively limiting the number of firms the sector can accommodate. Finally, our empirical findings support this view, where, due to high fixed cost, the profitability in the Kenyan banking industry has been low. It follows that if such fixed costs were reduced through improving the prevailing institutional deficiencies, profitability would be enhanced, leading to a meaningful entry and competition in the future.

Appendix A 5.1: Deriving the Market Equilibrium Condition for Loan Equation

To define our market equilibrium level of loan in the region between A and B, let us consider $\bar{r}$ in the critical. Does $L = \bar{L} - \beta\bar{r}$ satisfy the condition for market equilibrium? For firm i:

$$\pi_i = \left[\bar{r} - \frac{1}{\alpha}(\bar{L} - \beta\bar{r})\right]L_i$$

What happens if L_i increases by one unit?

$$\Delta\pi_i = \bar{r} - \frac{1}{\alpha}(\bar{L} - \beta\bar{r}) - \left(\frac{1}{\alpha} + \frac{1}{\beta}\right)\frac{L}{n}$$

Substituting L in this equation we get:

$$\Delta\pi_i = \bar{r} - \frac{1}{\alpha}(\bar{L} - \beta\bar{r}) - \left(\frac{1}{\alpha} + \frac{1}{\beta}\right)\left(\frac{\bar{L} - \beta\bar{r}}{n}\right)$$

If this change has a non-increasing effect on the profit function then:

$$\bar{r}\left(1 + \frac{\beta}{n}\left(\frac{(n+1)}{\alpha} + \frac{1}{\beta}\right)\right) - \frac{1}{n}\left(\frac{(n+1)}{\alpha} + \frac{1}{\beta}\right)\bar{L} \leq 0$$

Without any difficulty and undertaking little manipulation we finally derive that:

$$\bar{r} \leq \left(\frac{(n+1)\beta + \alpha}{(n+1)(\alpha + \beta)}\right)\frac{\bar{L}}{\beta} \equiv r^*$$

Since this condition holds, this implies that as long as $\bar{r} \leq r^*$ we will be operating on our loan curve while the condition for market equilibrium is satisfied.

What happens if L_i decreases by one unit? This will imply that:

$$\Delta\pi_i = \left(\bar{r} - \frac{1}{\alpha}(\bar{L} - \beta\bar{r})\right)(-1) + \frac{1}{\alpha}\frac{L}{n} \leq 0$$

$$-\bar{r} + \left(\frac{1}{\alpha} + \frac{1}{\alpha n}\right)(\bar{L} - \beta\bar{r}) \leq 0$$

With little manipulation while further simplifying this equation and collecting terms we can derive:

$$-\bar{r}\left(\frac{n\alpha + \beta(n+1)}{n\alpha}\right) + \frac{(n+1)}{n\alpha}\bar{L} \leq 0$$

Through reformulation and simplification we observe a familiar equation such that:

$$\bar{r} \geq \left(\frac{(n+1)}{n\alpha + \beta(n+1)}\right)\bar{L} \equiv \bar{r}^c$$

Again since this condition holds, this indicates that as long as $\bar{r}$ is equal to or greater than the critical level of interest rate, $\bar{r}^c$, we will be operating on the curve. Combined together, we observe that the profit function is non-increasing in both directions within the region of $\bar{r}^c \leq \bar{r} \leq r^*$, thus we will be moving along the $L = \bar{L} - \beta\bar{r}$ curve.

Appendix A 5.2: Deriving the Fixed Cost Lines for Medium and Lower Regions at $\bar{r}^c$

In Figure 5.8, it is necessary to investigate whether $F^{M1} > F^{L1}$ along the $\bar{r}^c$ line. With the help of equation (5.21) and equation (5.22) while substituting the value of $\bar{r}$ at the critical, we can derive that:

$$F^{L1} = \frac{\alpha\, \bar{L}^2}{[n\alpha + (n+1)\beta]^2} \tag{A1}$$

$$F^{M1} = \frac{\bar{L}}{n}\left(\frac{\alpha + n\beta}{\alpha}\right)\frac{(n+1)\,\bar{L}}{n\alpha + (n+1)\beta} - \frac{\beta}{n}\left(\frac{\alpha+\beta}{\alpha}\right)\frac{(n+1)^2\,\bar{L}^2}{[n\alpha + (n+1)\beta]^2} - \frac{\bar{L}^2}{n\alpha} \tag{A2}$$

Simplifying equation (A2) while collecting terms, it can be expressed as:

$$F^{M1} = \frac{\bar{L}^2}{n\alpha}\left[\frac{(\alpha + n\beta)(n+1)}{n\alpha + (n+1)\beta}\right] - \frac{\bar{L}^2}{n\alpha}\left[\frac{\beta(\alpha+\beta)(n+1)^2}{[n\alpha + (n+1)\beta]^2} + 1\right]$$

With little manipulation and further substitution after collecting terms this equation is given as:

$$F^{M1} = \frac{\alpha\, \bar{L}^2}{[n\alpha + (n+1)\beta]^2}\left[\frac{(n\alpha+(n+1)\beta)(\alpha+n\beta)(n+1)}{n\alpha^2} - \frac{\beta(\alpha+\beta)(n+1)^2 + [(n\alpha+(n+1)\beta)]^2}{n\alpha^2}\right] \tag{A3}$$

Having derived this, since the first term in both equations is similar to that of equation (A1) it is understandable that if, in the second term the equation (A3) is greater than 1, that will imply that $F^{M1} > F^{L1}$. To investigate further whether this holds, let us propose that:

$$\frac{(n\alpha + (n+1)\beta)(\alpha + n\beta)(n+1)}{n\alpha^2} - \frac{\beta(\alpha+\beta)(n+1)^2 + [(n\alpha + (n+1)\beta)]^2}{n\alpha^2} < 1 \tag{A4}$$

Rearranging the above equation we can calculate that:

$$(n\alpha + (n+1)\beta)(\alpha + n\beta)(n+1) < n\alpha^2 + \beta(\alpha+\beta)(n+1)^2 - [(n\alpha + (n+1)\beta)]^2 \tag{A5}$$

Finally while taking the case of $n = 2$ for simplicity and convenience, we get:

$$6\alpha^2 - 21\alpha\beta + 18\beta^2 < -2\alpha^2 - 3\alpha\beta$$

This simplifies to:

$$4\alpha + 6\beta < 0 \tag{A6}$$

Since we know that this is not true, it implies that the last term in equation (A3) is greater than unity, which again means that $F^{M1} > F^{L1}$.

Appendix A 5.3: Maximal Points for C and D Curves

To investigate whether the maximal points of curves C and D are greater or lesser than the specified fixed costs under liberalization (F^{H1} and F^{H2}), let us take that:

$$F^{M2} = \frac{\bar{L}}{n+m}\left[1 + \frac{2\beta}{\alpha}\right]\bar{r} - \frac{\beta}{n+m}\left(1 + \frac{\beta}{\alpha}\right)\bar{r}^2 - \frac{\bar{L}^2}{(n+m)\alpha} \tag{A7}$$

$$F^{H2} = \frac{\alpha\,\bar{L}^2}{16\beta(\alpha+\beta)} \tag{A8}$$

For simplicity, equation (A7) can be re-written as:

$$F = a\,\bar{r} - b\,\bar{r}^2 - c$$

where a, b and c represent the given terms with respect to $\bar{r}$ in the original equation. Deriving the first order condition, we will get:

$$\frac{\partial F}{\partial \bar{r}} = a - 2b\bar{r} = 0 \tag{A9}$$

Therefore, solving for $\bar{r}$ and substituting this value into equation (A7), we will have:

$$\bar{r} = \frac{a}{2b} \quad \text{and} \quad F = \frac{a^2}{4b} \tag{A10}$$

Taking n to represent two firms initially and with the help of equation (A10), we can simplify equation (A7) to be:

$$F^{M2} = \left[\left(\frac{\alpha + 2\beta}{\alpha}\right)\frac{\bar{L}}{3}\right]^2 \frac{1}{4}\left(\frac{\alpha+\beta}{\alpha}\right)\frac{3}{\beta} - \frac{\bar{L}^2}{3\alpha} \tag{A11}$$

With little manipulation while collecting terms we derive:

$$F^{M2} = \frac{\alpha^2 \bar{L}^2}{12\alpha\beta(\alpha + \beta)} \quad \text{(A12)}$$

When equation (A12) is greater than equation (A8), it implies that $16\beta > 12\beta$ which actually holds. Thus the maximum point of curve C must be higher than F given under equation (A8).

Chapter 6
Testing the Potential Impact of Economic Changes on Savings in African Countries

"An honest man is one who knows that he can't consume more than he has produced".
(Rand, 1966)

6.1 Introduction

In the last chapter, our analysis has considered a theoretical model of imperfect competition in the commercial banking sector of the selected sub-Saharan African countries. Specifically, our discussions focused on determining the direction of interest rate spread following economic liberalization in the presence of a concentrated commercial banking environment. We also considered the issue of lack of entry by new 'meaningful' financial institutions, raising the possibility of high fixed (overhead) costs as a barrier to entry. The available anecdotal evidence also supported this theoretical claim.

This Chapter 6 considers a new dimension, where the potential impact(s) of the recent reforms on savings in the selected African countries is empirically tested. At least, theoretically, the market determination of interest rates together with improvements in the functioning of the financial system should increase real interest rates. Moreover, operational efficiency, modernization of banking services and other market efficiency measures should attract funds held outside the banking sector to the formal financial system. Consequently, these quantitative and qualitative enhancements should lead to a higher interest rate responsiveness of private savings, *ceteris paribus*.

The current chapter has the following objectives. Firstly, using facts from the three countries of our sample, the chapter aims to examine the trend in private savings mobilization. This is conducted for the purpose of assessing the effect of liberalization measures on savings and revealing the magnitude of savings response to reform programs. Secondly, it also aims to assess empirically the real interest rate responsiveness of private savings in the case of Botswana. Partly, this assessment is

A.D. Ahmed and S.M.N. Islam, *Financial Liberalization in Developing Countries*, Contributions to Economics,
DOI: 10.1007/978-3-7908-2168-0_6,

for the purpose of investigating the saving-interest rate relationship advocated by the Mackinnon–Shaw hypothesis. Thirdly, another objective is to develop a composite index of financial liberalization and investigate the relationship between this composite index of liberalization, private savings and wider range of other significant control variables such as income and macroeconomic policy variables in a regression model. As we have constricted such an index from wider reform measures, it is expected to reflect various aspects of liberalization which may not fully be represented by changes in interest rates. Finally, we will specify a model including some selected number of variables, which are closely related to competitiveness and improvements in efficiency of the financial sector, to examine the channels of transmission by allowing these variables to capture the effect of liberalization and impact of financial restructuring. In this later model financial liberalization index is excluded. The behaviour of these key variables then will allow us to understand whether improvements in the financial environment have led to higher private savings rates.

The chapter is organized as follows. Section 6.2 discusses reforms and savings mobilization with respect to the countries of interest. Section 6.3 discusses the model set-up to be used in the empirical investigation in Section 6.4. Major results and the empirical testing to highlight on the impact of structural factors of economic reform are analyzed in Sections 6.4 and 6.5. Section 6.6 concludes the discussion on the impact of savings in these selected African counties.

6.2 Econometric Research on the Effect of Various Financial Conditionings

Empirical research on the impact of various financial conditioning has been undertaken using specific country case studies, pooled time-series data from developing and industrialized economies and across-country investigations. In the early decades of the 1980s and 1990s, the focus was on evaluating the effect of financial conditions on savings behaviour, investment ratios and level of private credit, and partly also on investigating the link between such controlled interest rates, capital flight and misallocation of resources (Fry, 1995, pp. 156–161).

In the recent years, quantitative empirical evidence focuses on whether financial liberalization has an impact on the efficiency of allocating resources for investment, and on the efficiency with which markets can transform savings into investment and growth (Harmes & Lensink, 2005). Even though domestic financial markets have been reformed by many countries in the late 1980s and early 1990s, the role of these financial deregulation and liberalization policies, especially with respect to the finance-growth nexus, still remains inconclusive. So far, a handful of studies have empirically investigated the impact of financial liberalization from a quality and quantity perspective, while utilizing firm-level as well as cross-country datasets. Numerous papers which provided strong empirical supports for the hypothesis that financial liberalization reduces financial constraints and contributes positively are Nazmi (2005), Bekaert, Harvey, and Lundblad (2005), Koo and Shin (2004), Laeven (2003), Gelos and Werner (2002), Galindo, Schiantarelli, and Weiss (2001) and Guncavdi, Bleaney, and McKay (1998). In contrast to these, other studies' results are mixed. Demir (2005), Bonfiglioli (2005), Eichengreen and Leblang (2003), Bandiera, Caprio, Honohan, and Schiantarelli (2000), Hermes (1996), Schiantarelli, Weiss, Gultom, and Jaramillo (1994) and Capoglu (1991) find much less supportive evidence for the positive effect of financial liberalization particularly in terms of capital accumulation and allocative efficiency.[1]

By undertaking a case study of a developing country (Botswana), the Sections 6.3–6.5 aim to contribute to the empirical literature of financial liberalization and growth by using a more recent data and better measure financial liberalization. The studies of the similar issues of other African countries (Kenya and Malawi) are presented in Section 6.6.

6.3 Reforms and Savings Mobilization: Comparative Analysis

Following the adoption of stabilization and structural adjustment measures, where interest rates are deregulated and competition among different financial sectors improves, it is expected that savings mobilization will be encouraged and efficiency promoted. This part of the analysis will look at the changes in the savings behaviour, both in public and private sectors of post-liberalization in Kenya, Malawi and Botswana. Meanwhile, from our previous examination we have indicated that the competitiveness in the banking environment did not improve significantly in the post-reforms periods in Kenya and Malawi. Indeed, the strong monopolistic structures in the commercial banking sector and the effects of macroeconomic instability seemingly offset the expected benefits of financial liberalization in these two countries. Thus, the net effect of macroeconomic instability has translated into an escalating interest rate spread both in Kenya and Malawi. On the other hand, strong and stable macroeconomic foundations in Botswana, coupled with an improvement in the competitiveness of the commercial banking sector, have enabled a lower interest rate spread. In view of these effects, we first look at the changes in the trends of private and public savings in these two countries before considering the case of Botswana which has been quite different.

From the visible trends in the savings rate in Kenya and Malawi, it becomes quite apparent that savings have been on average higher in the period before liberalization compared to the period after. Disaggregating the aggregate savings levels into private and public, it is observable that private sector savings rates have been the driving force behind the trend in the gross levels of Kenya and Malawi

[1]For a comprehensive review of the discussion on financial liberalization-growth and differences in the empirical results, see Fry (1995) and Hermes and Lensink (2005).

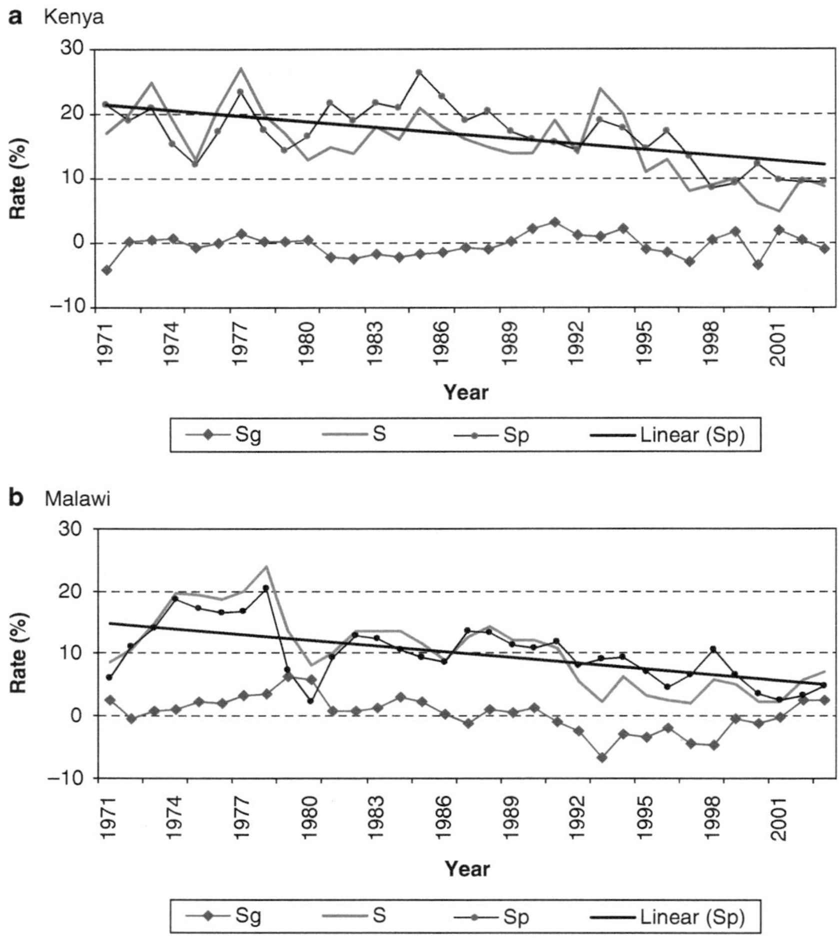

Fig. 6.1 Savings pattern in Kenya and Malawi
Note: In line with the empirical section, Sp is private savings, Sg is public savings and S is gross domestic savings. Adapted from World Bank: *World Savings Database*, respective central banks and IMF Country Report (various issues).

(Fig. 6.1). In the period between 1971 and 1990, Kenya's gross savings level has been fluctuating between the ranges of 15% and 25% reaching its peak in 1977 when it recorded 27%. Quite alike, the fluctuations in the gross domestic savings of Malawi have been the same – although slightly higher – ranging between 8% and 24% in the same period.

In both these two countries, the private savings rates have likewise moved within these ranges while the government sectors have continuously been dis-saving. In Kenya, after facing a sluggish decline from 1985 to 1990, both gross and private savings rates sharply recovered in 1991–1992, registering 24% and 19% levels respectively following liberalization.[2] However, this upward resurgence was short lived as gross savings levels started falling sharply again by 1994.

In Malawi, the private savings rate shows a little improvement in the post-reforms era as we observe a relatively declining trend demonstrated by the linear line included in Fig. 6.1b. Indeed, because private savings constitute a significant proportion of gross savings, it is not surprising that the gross domestic savings continued to decline even after liberalization reaching the lowest levels of 8% and 2.5% in Kenya and Malawi respectively in 1998. Relatively, these indicators point out that the structural adjustment efforts have failed to establish the expected upward trend in the savings rate. Domestic savings have been weakened by the public sector as governments in both countries continued to have negative or marginally low rate of savings. It is interesting to notice that the private savings rate (private agents) has failed to respond to the economic-wide implementation of liberalization and reform measures that began in 1991.

Similarly, even though financial reforms were expected to enlarge the size of the financial sector and introduce instruments that would promote savings mobilization, we observe a declining trend in the private savings rate. Indeed, because of unstable conditions, the decade-long economic rehabilitation was not enough to provide depositors with a reasonable rate of return. On average, private savings decreased from 22% to 12% and 12% to 6% in Kenya and Malawi between 1986–1990 and 1996–2000 respectively. From this evidence, it is clear that although the financial reforms resulted in the emergence of new forms and types of financial institutions, these did not boost savings mobilization in these countries. More generally, these changes did not exert a significant positive influence on the savings behaviour.

In Fig. 6.2, we provide patterns of various interest rates (in both nominal and real terms) between 1985 and 2005. In line with the literature, we compute the real rate of interest for both lending and deposit rates as the difference between the inflation rate (CPI) and nominal rates using the formula:

$$R_t = Nom_t - \left[\left(\frac{cpi_t - cpi_{t-1}}{cpi_{t-1}} \right) / \left(1 + \left(\frac{cpi_t - cpi_{t-1}}{cpi_{t-1}} \right) \right) \right]$$

where R and Nom represent real and nominal interest rates and t indicates time. In examining movements in interest rates in Kenya and Malawi, the evidence supports our previous findings on the countries savings ratios. With inflation rates averaging 20% and 25% during the period 1985–1995 in the two countries respectively, it has been difficult to achieve any positive real deposit rates (see Fig. 6.2). It is observable that real deposit rates were generally negative in the time period around 1985–1995, therefore had little significance on the financial impact to stimulate financial and overall domestic rates. Other economic factors such as

[2]For the period up to 1994 savings data is taken from the *World Savings Database* after extensive comparison with other records. From 1995 we rely on central banks and IMF country reports.

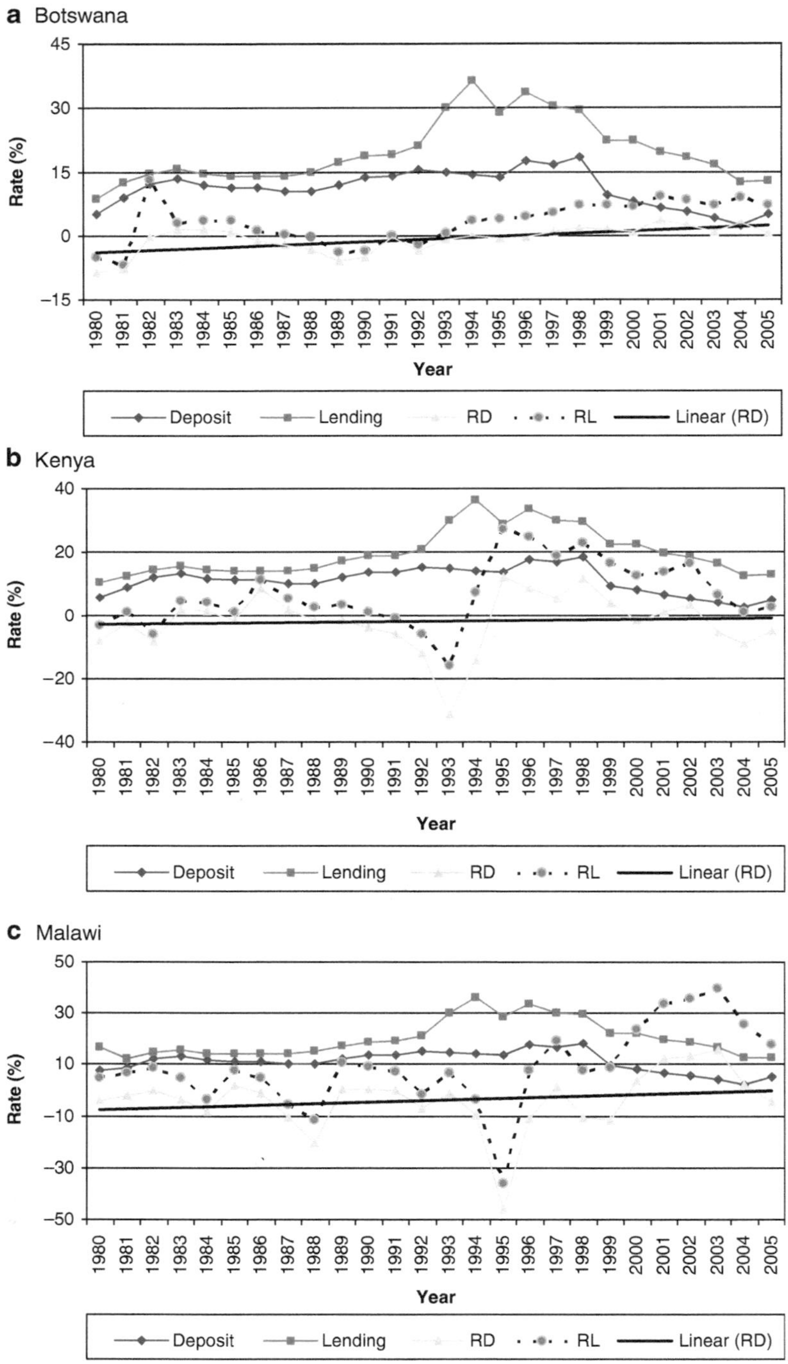

Fig. 6.2 Long-term interest rates trend
Note: RD and RL denote real interest rates in terms of deposit and lending respectively

local currency depreciation, higher interest rate spreads and consistent government budget deficits have led to lower savings and hence the observed investment patterns in both Kenya and Malawi.

In contrast, since the years after independence, Botswana's economic success was based on critical factors such as good institutions and policies, and a rigorous and strict budgetary process. As a result, the country has recorded continuous surpluses in both current account and overall balances together with significant reserve levels. Authorities in Botswana have continuously adopted measures to reinforce the stable economic environment and maintain positive real interest rates.[3] Based on this sound planning and proactive approach, the government has over the past been able to significantly influence the direction of interest rates and through channels of monetary transmission mechanism and open market operation attained a desired level of lending and deposit rates. Figure 6.3 elaborates the national savings trend in Botswana. Firstly, it is observable that there is no positive association between financial market liberalization and the public savings rate. Secondly, it is expected that such market reform measures (especially those geared towards liberalization of financial markets), will bring about significant changes in private saving rates. The evidence in Fig. 6.3 quantifies the improvements in private savings as we observe a moderate rise and steadily upward pattern probably due to changes in the behaviour of households following financial market deregulation in late 1990s. In support of the McKinnon–Shaw financial liberalization hypothesis, the positive effect of real interest rates on savings is evident, while other reforms including efforts to enhance privatization, fiscal consolidation, and developments in money and capital market may have positively influenced *private* corporate *savings*.[4] These changes in corporate and household savings have in turn led to a progressive rise in private savings and aided credit expansion.

Looking at the trend in saving levels of Botswana over the period of 1971–2005, gross *domestic savings* as a percentage of GDP increased from 16% in 1975 to about 40% in 1998, before slightly falling to around 36% in 2005. This compares quite favourably with the average gross domestic savings to GDP ratio for SSA countries which had declined from about 24% in 1975 to 17% in 2000 (World Bank, 1994, 2001). During the same period, the private savings rate continued to rise, from around 4.5 to 30%, indicating the strength of the formal financial system in mobilization and pooling savings in the post-reforms era. In 2005, the country's private savings rate declined marginally to about 28%. In line with macroeconomic theory, this observed trend must have substantially affected the evolution and composition of investment, which may in turn, have influenced Botswana's level of economic growth. Initially, real deposit rates were negative (especially in the early 1980s). This was the period during which the government imposed a ceiling on interest rates to encourage project lending and enhance the availability of credit

---

[3]See for example, Motsomi (1997, p. 80–83).

[4]In this regard, its worth noting that bond market development and new financial/money market instruments were particularly important (see Maipose and Matsheka, 2002).

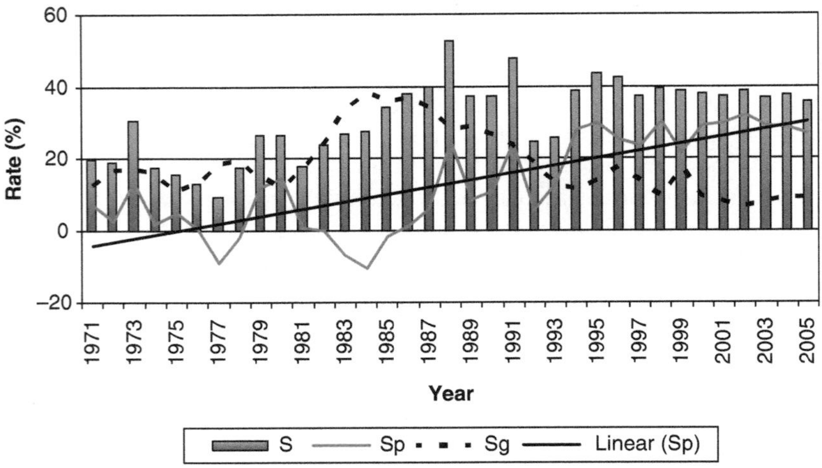

Fig. 6.3 Long-run trends in savings in Botswana. Adapted from *World Savings Database*, Banks of Botswana and IMF Country Report (various issues)

for citizen-owned companies (Harvey & Lewis, 1990). As interest rates were gradually allowed to increase following the adoption of a financial sector development strategy, real deposit rates increased steadily (see Fig. 6.2). Private savings rates show an upward rising trend, on average, from about 1 to 17.5% between 1985 and 2000 while gross savings increased steadily from 34 to 38.5%. While our data highlight that gross domestic savings in Botswana consisted almost entirely of private savings in the post liberalization period, evidence supports the view that households are changing their attitudes (BoB, 2000) and have adjusted their savings profile. More so, households are accepting to hold their savings in various financial assets and may even be in diversified type of savings since more stock of financial assets are becoming accessible to them.

In sum, it is clear that the economic reforms in Kenya and Malawi did not lead to a significant integration of the financial system and enhancement in income levels. The foregoing analysis of the process of economic change illustrates that the decade of economic reforms brought limited success in improving the process of fund mobilization and enhancing efficiency. In particular, the positive influence of liberalization in savings mobilization, investment appraisal and credit allocation has not clearly emerged. Understandably, the macroeconomic environment was troubled by increased uncertainties, frequent instabilities and unlimited economic shocks, making it hard to disentangle the contribution of financial liberalization from other influences. With regard to this, while concentrating on Botswana, we further empirically test the relationship between financial reforms, savings and economic performance. Moreover, it is important to also mention that there have been theoretical and empirical ambiguities on the overall effect of financial liberalization. From the theoretical perspective, although financial liberalization is expected to stimulate savings through higher interest rates, it has been shown that relaxation of the liquidity constraint may also lead to a consumption boom (Athukorala & Sen, 2004; Berube & Cote, 2000). On other hand, the move towards financial openness (FO) could also be associated with risks, including excessive risk-taking, higher inflation and rapid capital flows, making countries vulnerable to financial crisis (Kaminsky & Schmukler 2001; Bandiera et al., 2000). From the empirical perspective, there is little consensus on the issue of the effect of financial liberalization (Loayza, Schmidt-Hebbel, & Servén, 2000). This is particularly because financial and capital account liberalizations do not occur in isolation; therefore, 'difficult to tease out the connections between financial sector reform and the performance of key economic variables' (Nyawata & Bird, 2003). Studies are also different in their sample periods, estimation approaches, regional coverage and measurements of financial liberalization (or proxies of financial development), leading to a problem of comparability of results especially across regions.

While focusing on individual country impact, we sought to examine the effect of financial market liberalization and that of a more open capital account. In this attempt, the current empirical examination aims to provide further evidence on the current unsettled conclusions of the impact of financial reforms while taking into account an extensive list of key macroeconomic variables in addition to our variables of interest. In this process, we test a number of propositions that surfaced in the literature on economic liberalization and particularly intend to answer some of the following questions, to the extent possible:

1. Is financial liberalization a catalyst for higher savings in developing countries as proposed by the McKinnon and Shaw hypothesis?
2. Has financial liberalization been good for growth through an expansion of the supply of credit and hence enhanced economic performance from the Sub-Saharan African perspective?
3. Are gains from financial liberalization realized only under specific economic conditions?
4. What is the precise impact of interest rate liberalization on savings (measured by the private savings-GDP ratio)?
5. Are there any signs of crowding out effect in addition to the expected overall increased aggregate capital accummulation following economic liberalization?
6. Has the economic reform program undertaken in Botswana worked in a way that is different from the common evidence in the existing literature and from that of the early hypotheses of the McKinnon and Shaw?
7. What types of policies can be recommended in the post-reform era to strengthen domestic savings mobilization programs?

From the early works of research in income growth, the relationship between income, consumption and savings has been a major subject of discussion. A consumption puzzle arose from the Keynesian consumption function which predicted that as income rises, savings would constitute a greater share of it while average propensity to consume falls. However, early empirical evidence indicated that contrary to the Keynesian view, consumption grew and average propensity to consume is observed to be constant over time, independent of growth in the aggregate measure of income. In an attempt to explain this and come up with a better consumption function, both the Life-cycle hypothesis (LCH) and Permanent income hypothesis (PIH) were developed. Although they have slight differences in their structural foundations, these two theories arrived to a similar conclusion that temporary variation in income will not affect consumption behaviour but rather savings, whereas permanent variation in income will result in substantial change in consumption behaviour (Modigliani, 1970). Accordingly, with the assumption that consumption is not only determined by income but also wealth, LCH and PIH imply that across households, the higher income households will have a higher transitory income than the lower income group and hence lower average propensity to consume, while in aggregate average propensity to consume will be stable in the long run, in line with Keynesian consumption theory. Therefore in the short run, the unanticipated income or wealth that does not alter permanent income will change savings rather than consumption. In the recent years, it has been suggested that the aggregate consumption is not only affected by current income but other factors including financial market conditions and demographics (see, for example, Caroll & Summers, 1991).

Thus, to conduct our examinations we estimate a savings function of the form:[5]

$$Savings\ rate(Sp_t) = Sp(y_t, Z_t, F_t) \tag{6.1}$$

where y_t refers to logarithmic per capita real GDP, and Z_t represents a vector of conditioning information (set of explanatory variables) variables[6] that controls for other determinants observed to have significant influence in explaining variations in savings behaviour. F_t is an alternative measure of financial liberalization (financial openness[7] equals either the IMF's government restrictions index (IMF), Chinn-Ito index of financial openness (FO and our index of financial reforms (FL) (computed through weighted average method).[8] We employ these alternative indices in order to obtain a more robust and appropriate measure of financial reforms (financial liberalization). Full details of these indices are provided in the next section.

To explore the driving forces of domestic savings in developing countries, we have chosen an extensive list of controlling variables considering the economic

[5]The savings rate defined here is private savings rather than gross domestic because of our belief that private savings constitute a higher proportion of total savings in Sub-Saharan African countries. This has also been the case in Botswana in the recent years.

[6]With the exception of real per capita GDP (y) and number of commercial banks (*COM*) which are in log forms all other variables are in percentages or proportion of GDP.

[7]From here henceforth, financial liberalization and financial openness are used interchangeably. However, we accept that financial openness could be wider in scope than financial liberalization.

[8]Our approach is in line with papers such as MFE (2002) while other recent studies such as Bandiera et al. (2000) have constructed similar indices for various countries using the principal component approach. Further investigations while applying the latter method show that our alternative index to that of FL is very similar (see Figure 6.7 in the Appendix).

background of Botswana. In this regard, the explanatory variables of interest are per capita GDP (y), real deposit rate (*DRR*) and inflation (*CPI*); a variable that reflects changes in the macroeconomic policy environment. Others are short-term policy variables of changes in government budget balance (budget deficit) (BAD); and competition in the banking sector (COM) and interest rate spread (IRS – the last two variables capture functional characteristics of the financial system such as distribution of market power, intermediation efficiency and service delivery. Finally, we consider demographic changes (population growth *n*), a factor that could play an important role in influencing the household savings trend.

In this attempt, to explain the process of savings mobilization and capital accumulation, the given number of macroeconomic variables was considered in the savings model to account for the effect of monetary and fiscal policies, demographic developments and economic conditions. The theoretical support for the inclusion of these factors is particularly derived from consumption and saving behaviours under both the life-cycle model (LCM) and the permanent-income hypothesis (PIH. Under the much simpler life-cycle model, it is emphasized that individual consumption in each period depends on expectations about lifetime-income and savings, allowing individuals to move income from the phase in life when income is high to the period when income is low (Modigliani, 1986). Thus households' and economic agents, driven by motives for consumer's optimization and intertemporal consumption smoothing, will save during their working years and only to consume during the retirement period (Athukorala & Sen, 2002; Berube & Cote, 2000). Empirical evidence from various studies have shown that the level of real per capita income has a positive and significant influence on savings rates (Athukorala & Sen, 2002; Edwards, 1996). This relationship is based on the fact that high levels of income increase the per capita income of households enabling them to save more. Given this and looking at the characteristics of economic agents, richer households will be induced to save more for the future while poor households will consume at the minimal level. Examining evidence from developing countries, Loayza et al. (2000) find that a doubling of income per capita is estimated to raise long-run private savings by about 10 percentage points of households' disposable income, showing that a higher income enhances country's savings.[9]

Inflation which is an indicator of the macroeconomic policy environment could affect savings in various channels. Firstly, theoretical literature suggests that higher inflation raises uncertainty about future income growth and therefore risk-averse economic agents may be induced to increase their personal and precautionary savings (Berube & Cote, 2000). Secondly, through lowering real interest rates, higher inflation may also induce higher savings through portfolio readjustment toward real capital. However, this may not be the case in most developing countries given the under-developed nature of their financial and stock markets. Thus, inflation may have a negative impact on savings and investment. The exact direction

[9]Similar evidence is also provided by Schmidt-Hebbel and Servén (2002) for the case of developing countries.

of the effect of the interest rate on savings is ambiguous in the theoretical literature. Through the channel of substitution effect, a higher real interest rate may increase household savings, while under the income effect, it reduces savings. Generally, liberalizing interest rates will increase return on savings as the real deposit rate improves. Recent studies such as Athukorala and Sen (2004) suggest that the substitution effect may be greater in developing economy's set up, given that higher real interest rates provide incentives for savings in financial form.

According to the Ricardian equivalence hypothesis, the current pace of government expenditure is what is more important to the national savings pattern rather than the corresponding financing mechanism (i.e. through borrowing or increases in taxes). Under the simplifying assumption of rational actors, far-sighted economic agents and perfect capital markets, increases in government savings will be compensated fully by a decrease in private savings. Thus the national savings trend is unaffected by the government fiscal trend since the latter is a perfect substitute to private savings. However, this full offset is not supported by the literature, mostly reporting that the government budget deficit is estimated to increase private savings by about 0.55 dollars (Berube & Cote, 2000). Others have also reported that an increase in government spending (current expenditure) will lower resources available to the more productive private sector and therefore lower future private savings (Masson Bayoumi & Samiei, 1998). Our variables, competition in the banking sector (proxied by number of commercial banks) and interest rate spread, are used to represent the structure of the financial market which has undergone rapid transformation in the post-reform period. In an environment where the banking industry is not competitive, firms can easily include fees and commissions in the spread margin. This has the effect of reducing income to depositors. The distribution of market power and levels of competition are important indicators of the banking sector's maturity as well as institutional and intermediation efficiency. Mujeri and Islam (2008) observe that the 'competitive environment in the financial sector is critical to realizing a developed and matured financial market with diversified products'. A lower interest rate spread margin, from the perspective of lower lending rate, is also important in stimulating investment and productivity in the economy. In the wake of financial reforms, Botswana has seen increasing competition among local banks while market liberalization has enabled greater participation of foreign banks.

The view of the consumption and savings pattern under both the permanent-income hypothesis and life-cycle model make important assumptions about the structure of the population and therefore link demographic change and savings. Age distribution of the population in terms of the young, working class and pensioners has significant influences on household savings. Thus, variables such as dependency ratio, working population and proportion of population in retirement have been used as explanatory variables in some literature. First, from the LCM model, it can easily be understood that during working years individuals save more (since they produce more than they consume), at old age individuals produce less than they consume and therefore dissave, while during childhood they rely on their parents' income. On the other hand, with an increase in number of children, per capita household savings may go down since parents and children do not consume independently (Loayza et al., 2000; Berube & Cote, 2000). Parents with offspring may also intend to save less since they expect old-age support from their children in the future. Second, there could also be a positive association between age-structure and savings where under the assumption of a balanced population growth high population could mean an increase in the number of savers. Overall, we expect a negative association between age distribution and aggregate savings in a young nation such as Botswana.

6.3.1 Measures of Financial Liberalization

Authors of literature on financial openness and capital markets have used various measures in their attempts to capture the effectiveness of barriers and the complexity of real-world capital controls. Generally, two classes of measure are commonly used. The first group is called *de facto* or outcome based indicators which measure the actual financial and investment flows between sectors of the domestic economy and the rest of the world (also called cross-border financial flows). The advantage of these measures is that they are not subjective measures of capital control, and are also becoming widely available (Edison, Levine, Ricci & Slok, 2002). On the other hand, *de jure* measures of financial and capital openness reflect policy and regulatory restrictions on capital flows.

The IMF restriction indexes (IMF) are based on binary dummy variables. These indexes classify intensity of government restriction using four main components as: existence of multiple exchange rates, requirements for the surrender of export proceeds, openness of the current account transactions and openness of the capital account transactions.[10] The constructed index takes values between zero and four, where a value of zero indicates a country which has a closed current and capital account, has multiple exchange rate regimes, and places restrictions on exports receipts.[11] Compared to many other measures, the IMF-measured restriction is at times more reliable in the sense that records and information are classified in a systematic manner, both throughout the years and, more importantly, throughout the countries (Miniane, 2004, p. 282). Secondly, we also use the Chinn-Ito capital account openness index as an alternative. Although coming from the same source as the IMF index, Chinn-Ito's FO index captures restrictions on cross-border financial transactions. It is based on four binary dummy variables indicating: (1) presence of multiple exchange rates (*k1*), (2) restrictions on current account transactions (*k2*), (3) restrictions on capital account transactions (*k3*), and (4) requirement of the surrender of export proceeds (*k4*). The constructed index, which itself is the first

[10]We thank Professors Antu P. Murshid and Ashoka Mody for sharing with us their data and other updates on the Annual Report on Exchange Agreements and Exchange Restrictions (AREAER).

[11]Note that from 1996, IMF's AREAER has had changes in several aspects, enabling construction of a graded index of capital account restriction from this year henceforth. As indicated in Figure 6.4, there has been a drop in the index in 1995. For comparability, we have conducted a number of sensitivity analyses for this structural break, but our results did not change qualitatively.

standardized principal component, is then reversed to capture financial openness (Chinn & Ito, 2005, 2008). An important advantage of the FO measure is that it is available for more than 100 countries and covers long time periods 1970–2005.[12]

Our third measure of FO is the FL index of financial liberalization. This index is constructed from five reform indicators which represent a significant move towards a stronger liberal financial environment in Botswana. This typically comprises various aspects of interest rate regulation, exchange rate and capital account liberalization, reserve requirements, security markets-reforms, and bank ownership and pro-competition measures. We look at the historical evolution in each component from Botswana's perspective. While reflecting financial reforms in the perspective of a move towards government's gradual reduction in its direct intervention mechanisms, and in allowing outright deregulation, we follow the approaches used in earlier work such as MFE (2002) and Bandiera et al. (2000) in quantifying financial liberalization. Deregulation of interest rates, reduction in reserve requirements, and privatization and authorization of new commercial banks promote competition and encourage the market allocation of the available credits. Similarly, the liberalization of the exchange rate system allows the market reflection of changes in demand and supply of foreign exchange. Looking for a move towards this liberalized market system, we denote by a unit value in the year in which they were introduced. Thus, taking a value of 1 initially, an indicator will have a unit increase in its value when an additional new policy change is implemented (or rather specific controls relaxed). This is done for policy changes related to all the five selected measures. To compute our final liberalization index, we take the average of the five indicators.[13] As a possible alternative, we have also considered the principle component approach which is quite commonly used in the literature. The two indices show similar trends and are depicted in Figure 6.7.[14] In this regard, although constructing a summarized index may by itself have some limitations compared to using specific single dummy variables, the adoption of such procedure is inevitable to avoid losing substantial degrees of freedom. Likewise, difficulty in defining single date in which critical change takes place, renders it hard to use a specific dummy variable to counter for the effect of such changes.[15] In Figure 6.4, we plot these financial liberalization/openness indices for Botswana over the sample period of 1985–2005. The figure clearly shows that the three series move in the same direction despite FL index starting at a much lower point (3). Further we can see that financial liberalization has been a gradual process and measure to ease capital account restriction, which has been progressing in the last decade and half in Botswana.

---

[12]Some might say that the two indexes are similar. However due to computational differences and other changes, we will use both these indices separately.

[13]Full details of Botswana's reform era and chronology of the key events useful in constructing FL index was given in Ahmed (2007). Further information is provided in Table 6.10 in the Appendix.

[14]However, since it has been reported that the two methods, produce almost identical results (MFE, 2002), we have preferred the former.

[15]Understandably there may be differences in the practical and official timing of decontrols of various reform measures.

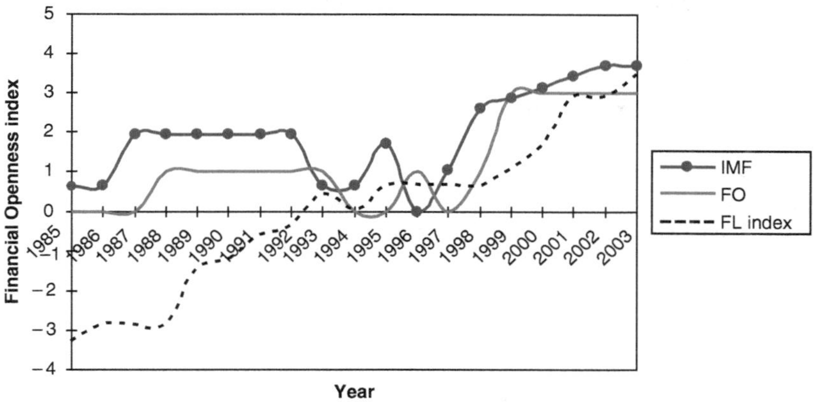

Fig. 6.4 Various measures of financial openness

6.3.2 *Basic Theory and other Specifications*

The literature on financial development and economic growth point out that among many ways that improvement in the standard of living can be achieved is through an increase in savings and therefore accumulation of capital. It is also important to note that the structure of the Botswana economy has changed radically in the last two decades in its attempt to boost savings mobilization. Most notably, the country has seen a wave of market liberalization and privatization that has led to greater market access and business confidence. In the recent years, these changes were associated with stock market development, financial deepening and improvements in financial innovation in the country. Having looked at the trends in financial development and other economic indicators, we attempt to go beyond visual inspection of the main economic variables and seek to provide an econometric relationship between savings, investment and economic growth. In this regard, we plan to closely look at the roles played by important variables such as financial liberalization, real interest rates and other indicators capturing financial depth and the competitive market environment. This leads us to a formal and empirically testable model. Using the standard Solow growth model, we can specify an aggregate Cobb-Douglas production function with three factor inputs as:

$$Y = f(K, L, H) = AK^{\alpha}H^{\beta}L^{1-\alpha-\beta} \quad \text{where } 0 < \alpha, \beta < 1 \tag{6.2}$$

In this production function the terms are defined as Y_t = real per capita output, A_t is a measure of technology known as total factor productivity, K_t = physical capital stock, L_t = labor input, and H_t = human capital stock, knowledge and skills acquired through education. Taking into account the economic factors outlined so far and considering the case of Botswana, we can provide an extended version of (6.2) to a more useful representation that also captures other key determinants of output, as:

$$Y_t = A_t \cdot f(K_t, L_t, H_t, NR_t) \tag{6.3}$$

In this set-up NR_t is natural resources while other inputs are as defined previously. In the outline above, the capital stock variable K_t is calculated on the basis of the permanent inventory method, $K_{t+1} = K_t + I_t - \delta K$. The last two terms are investment (I_t) and proportional capital depreciation where the depreciation rate δ is assumed. In this regard, initial capital stock can be computed using the formula $K_0 = I_0/\delta$.

Botswana is among the few good examples of developing countries where natural resource abundance has contributed to the improvement in living standards through enabling successful economic development. Thus, in the case of Botswana, because the major industry is diamond mining, we do take into account the harvested or utilized natural capital, NR_t. A_t is the stock of knowledge or technology – also known as the Solow residual – and captures the mongrel effects of all the others (including measurement and specification errors). From the Botswana perspective, we measure this heavy dependence on natural resources by mining as a share of GDP. Finally, it is generally believed that human capital plays an important role in economic development (Benhabib & Spiegel, 2005; Hoeffler, 2002; Islam, 1995; Mankiw, Romer, & Weil, 1992; Barro, 1991). Various measures have been used in the literature to capture the role of human capital as a determinant of economic growth including health and educational attainment. Following recent studies such as Dowrick and Rogers (2002) and Mankiw et al. (1992), we proxy investment in human capital (henceforth HC_t) using gross enrolment ratio at a secondary level.

6.4 The Macroeconometric Model

Generally, to examine a long-term relationship among macroeconomic variables, a suitable econometric model(s) is required. Quite commonly a standard formulation used is:

$$Y_t = \beta X_t + \mu_t \tag{6.4}$$

where μ_t is the residual error term, β is a row vector of β's and X is $n \times 1$ vector of exogenous variables. Under the assumption that μ_t is stationary, a long-term relationship of the model is obtained through estimating directly the above function. Alternatively, we could also estimate the above long-run relationship using an unrestricted autoregressive distributed lag (ADL) approach. As shown by Charemza and Deadman (1992, p. 157), (6.4) can be re-specified as an ADL model where the lag of the dependent variable is included as an explanatory variable together with other variables of interest. This can be depicted as:

$$y_t = c + \sum_{j=1}^{k} \sum_{i=0}^{p} \beta_{ji} x_{j,t-i} + \sum_{i=1}^{q} \alpha_i y_{t-i} + \mu_t \tag{6.5}$$

where the number of exogenous variables is indicated by k and number of lags by p and q. However, if the variables of interest are individually non-stationary, a major shortcoming of estimations by (6.4) and (6.5) is that the short-term dynamics are not captured. This leaves it impossible for one to infer short-run deviations that converge to long-run equilibrium. One way of getting out of this problem is by adopting a pure first-difference model. However, even though this may help us captures the short-run dynamics and achieve stationarity, it gives no direction over the long-run solution. Additionally, in this process, valuable level information may be lost (Hendry, 1996, pp. 287–289). Thus, to separate the short-run and long-run multipliers and take into account long-run information in the data, we can re-express (6.5) to represent an error correction framework as:[16]

$$\Delta y_t = \beta_1 \Delta x_t - (1-\alpha)\left[y_{t-1} - \frac{\beta_0}{1-\alpha} - \left(\frac{\beta_1+\beta_2}{1-\alpha}\right)x_{t-1}\right] + \varepsilon_t \tag{6.6}$$

where the term Δ denotes the difference operator. With little manipulation and simple reformulation, an equivalent equation of unrestricted ECM version while applying ADL set-up of (6.6) will be:

$$\Delta y_t = c + \sum_{j=1}^{k}\sum_{i=0}^{p-1} \beta_{ji}\Delta x_{j,t-i} + \sum_{i=1}^{q-1} \alpha_i \Delta y_{t-i} + \gamma ECM_{t-1} + \varepsilon_t \tag{6.7}$$

Equation (6.7) represents the error correction model (ECM) where the last term is known as the error correction term which contains:

$$ECM = y_{t-q} - \frac{1}{1-\sum_{i=1}^{q}\alpha_i}\sum_{j=1}^{k}\sum_{i=0}^{p}\beta_{ji}x_{j,t-p}\gamma = 1 - \sum_{i=1}^{q}\alpha_i$$

Under this formulation, the equilibrium error correction is given by the ECM where if this term is zero, the adjustment to changes takes place and is achieved in the same period. On the other hand, if it is non-zero, the model is not in equilibrium and this term works to restore this disequilibrium, where γ is the speed of adjustment in this process. Generally, the representation under (6.7) enables us to capture valuable long-run information given by the data, making it a preferred model to integrate a long-run relationship with short-run dynamics. Specifically, a *negative* γ provides evidence of cointegration under the Granger representation theorem, ensuring that the system converges to long-run equilibrium (Berube & Cote, 2000). Thus, through the necessary tests, a rejection of the non-cointegration hypothesis (i.e. $\gamma = 0$) against its alternative ($\gamma < 0$), should indicate the variables are cointegrated. Besides, under this structural presentation, since all variables in the system are stationary we can apply standard diagnostic tests to our results.

[16]Where the later equation includes intercept term c.

In general, when a common trend exists among variables, the causal relationship between two or more variables can be investigated using Granger causality methodology. For a bivariate VAR)(p) model:

$$\begin{pmatrix} X_{1t} \\ X_{2t} \end{pmatrix} = \begin{pmatrix} c1 \\ c2 \end{pmatrix} + \begin{pmatrix} \beta_{11}^{1} & 0 \\ \beta_{21}^{1} & \beta_{22}^{1} \end{pmatrix} \begin{pmatrix} X_{1t-1} \\ X_{2t-1} \end{pmatrix} + \ldots + \begin{pmatrix} \beta_{11}^{p} & 0 \\ \beta_{21}^{p} & \beta_{22}^{p} \end{pmatrix} \begin{pmatrix} X_{1t-p} \\ X_{2t-p} \end{pmatrix} + \begin{pmatrix} \mu_{1t} \\ \mu_{2t} \end{pmatrix} \tag{6.8}$$

where $\mu_t \sim$ white noise (0 Σ) and 'X_2 does not Granger-cause X_1' when $H_0 = \beta_{12}^{j} = 0$ for all j in the equation of X_1. Causality in this sense implies forecasting abilities where past changes in one variable (say X_2) help in the prediction of the actual changes in another variable (say X_1) and therefore β_{12}^{j}'s are jointly significantly different from zero (Granger, 1988).

6.4.1 VECM Set-up

Finally, with this structural formulation in mind and for the purpose of applying a model which uses economically interpretable restrictions while taking into account identification requirements, a vector equilibrium correction approach is taken. Given the specification under (6.7) and in the context of cointegration, the vector error-correction (VECM) representation is expressed as:

$$\Delta z_t = c + \sum_{i=1}^{p-1} \Gamma_i \Delta z_{t-i} + \Pi z_{t-k+1} + \mu_t \tag{6.9}$$

where z_t include all variables of the model, Γ is a matrix that contains information about the short-run adjustment of the system such that:

$$\Gamma = \sum_{i=1}^{p-1} \Pi_i - \mathrm{I}$$

and c is a vector of constants. On the other hand, the matrix Π, which expresses the long-run equilibrium relationships among the series, is also represented as:

$$\Pi = \sum_{i-1}^{p} \Pi_i - \mathrm{I}$$

with the existence of r cointegrating relationships and assuming that the matrix Π has a rank $r < n$, a dynamic representation of Π can be decomposed into α and β such that:

$$\Delta z_t = c + \sum_{i=1}^{p-1} \Gamma_i \Delta z_{t-i} + \alpha\beta' z_{t-k+1} + \mu_t \tag{6.10}$$

where α and β are $n \times r$ matrices and r is the cointegrating rank of the system.[17] Thus we can show that for the case of $r = 1$ and $n = 3$:

$$\alpha = \begin{pmatrix} \alpha_{11} \\ \alpha_{21} \\ \alpha_{31} \end{pmatrix} \text{ and } \beta' = (\beta_{11}\ \beta_{21}\ \beta_{31})$$

On the basis of the theories of savings discussed earlier and the potential possibility of endogeneity with respect to per capita income and investment rate, the following VAR system can be identified:[18]

$$\begin{aligned} Sp &= Sp(y, DRR, CPI, n, F) \\ y &= y(PIV, Sp, HC, DRR, CPI, n, F, NR) \\ PIV &= PIV(y, Sp, DRR, CPI, F) \end{aligned} \tag{6.11}$$

In the earlier section we have provided discussion on the theoretical determinants of savings as well as theoretical justifications for inclusion of various factors. In addition to this, in (6.11), it is proposed that per capita output is a function of private investment rate, ratio of private savings to GDP, investment in human capital (human capital formation rate),[19] interest rate (deposit rate), inflation rate, population growth rate and financial liberalization index.[20] This is in line with the standard and augmented version Solow-Swan growth model (such as that of Solow, 1956) and other recent neoclassical growth theory. Note that although terms of trade have been included as one of the determinants of private savings in the literature (Masson et al., 1998), we have excluded it in this study for two reasons: (1) when public savings and natural resource endowment are considered as controlling variables, the impact of trade is partly captured and its effect on economic growth via trade changes is also represented. Moreover, others have pointed out that changes in terms of trade may only be particularly significant for oil exporters (Ostry & Reinhart, 1992), (2) a permanent shock of terms of trade on private savings would be ambiguous and

---

[17]Under this reformulation we can show that the long-run equilibrium is in line with the Keynesian consumption function and also derive the average propensity to save equation.

[18]The identified equation in the VAR will be confirmed using multivariate cointegration analysis. This is also an initial outline which could be extended for robustness.

[19]Because we focus on the private savings rate in our empirical investigation, the investment rate taken here is that of private investment only.

[20]As observable in equation (6.11), both savings and investment variables are included in the output function. Since there is a big discrepancy between investment and private savings in Botswana (Ahmed, 2007), we can consider two alternative cases where either both or only investment is included in the per capita income equation.

small in magnitude (Masson et al., 1998). There is lack of conceptual clarity in the relationship between resource abundance and economic growth; however we take the view that natural resource abundance increases wealth and enhances investment rates and purchasing power over imports (Sachs & Warner, 1997; Gaitan & Roe, 2005). There is some consensus in the growth literature that higher inflation (a proxy of macroeconomic instability) is undesirable for economic growth. High inflation is associated with high price variability and lower levels of investment and productivity. On the other hand, it has been argued that control on interest rates encourages disintermediation (while under these circumstances bank allocations are not socially optimal) by the banking sector, discourages savings and hence lowers investment (Kwan, 2003).[21]

The third equation of the model specifies a simple neoclassical investment function in which the investment rate is a function of the private savings rate, per capita income, real interest rate (deposits rate), inflation and index of financial openness. In this growth framework, output is taken to be in labour intensive form. Thus first, our investment equation is a function of per capita output while also inspired by the multivariate nature of our estimation. Second, per capita output can be seen as a proxy for future earnings (Fedderke, 2000), where this enhances the demand for investment goods which generate higher profits. GDP per capita is the most often used indicator for future earnings capacity and, in general, a positive relationship between per-capita income and investment rate is expected (Athukorala & Sen, 2002). As is the case in most of developing country, higher inflation may reflect an uncertain macroeconomic environment in the country. This could lead to a major capital flight and further inefficient allocation of the available resources (Athukorala & Sen, 2002).

6.5 Data and an Analysis of Econometric Results

On the basis of the model formulations in the previous section, this study will use the multivariate cointegration (proposed by Johansen) and vector error correction (VECM) estimation techniques. This multi-equation modelling approach, which is part of the various Vector autoregressive (VAR) specifications, is now widely used in evaluating dynamic relationships in economic variables (see, for example, Charemza & Deadman, 1992, p. 157). Our empirical investigation uses annual data covering the period 1971–2005. All data used in this study (with the exception of IMF restriction and financial openness indices) were obtained from the IMF's *International Financial Statistics*, the World Bank's *World Savings Database* and Bank of Botswana annual reports (various issues). IMF restriction index was part of the dataset used in Mody and Murshid (2005) with recent updates from the

[21]Giving an alternative, some literature has suggested that an increase in interest rates may lower aggregate expenditure, thereby reducing the equilibrium level of income (Romer, 1986).

IMF's Exchange Arrangements and Agreements. Financial openness index is from Chinn-Ito (2005, 2008).

Prior to our empirical analysis, we start by testing for stationarity in the data used in the econometric estimations. Due to the fact that many macroeconomic variables appear to be non-stationary (graphs not shown), investigating the time series properties of our data is critical. This is also necessary for the purpose of ensuring consistency in subsequent econometric modelling. While Augmented Dickey–Fuller (ADF) test is the most commonly used methodology to establish the order of integration of a series in the literature, we provide both ADF and Phillip–Perron (PP) tests for unit root since ADF has been found to be sensitive to lag length selection. Our ADF test regression and test statistics with and without time trend are provided by Table 6.1. It is observable that, at least at 5% significance level, the null-hypothesis for a unit root cannot be rejected for all variables.[22] However, when we take the first differences of the variables and re-run the unit root tests, the null hypothesis of non-stationarity is rejected. Thus our examination concludes that all the series under study are integrated of order 1 (I(1)).

Having conducted extensive test to determine stationarity in our series, the next step is to set up a vector error correction representation to formally examine the determinants of savings and per capita GDP growth in Botswana. However, before considering an extended list of explanatory variables, we estimate an initial version of our savings equation where it is assumed to be a function of income, real interest rate, demographic variable of rate of growth of the population and index of financial openness. Following studies such as Bandiera et al. (2000), this will be used (a) as comparative indicative results; and (b) to investigate any major changes in the behaviour of the core variables to provide further insight into whether they fit the theoretical predictions given earlier.

As standard in the cointegration analysis literature, it is necessary to identify the cointegrating relationship before specifying various vector error correction models. Our next step is to apply the Johansen procedure to ascertain whether the series are cointegrated. From the cointegration literature (see, for example, Granger (1987)), if two variables, say X_{1t} and X_{2t}, are cointegrated, then first, there must exist a corresponding error correction model and a trend that adjusts to an equilibrium state. Second, causality to at least one direction must exist and third, spurious regression outcome is ruled out. Overall, this exercise is particularly important when we employ the VECM estimation framework since such modeling approach implies no specific endo–exogenous relationship among variables (Charemza & Deadman, 1992, p. 201).

As indicated by our results in Table 6.2, we applied the Johansen maximum likelihood procedure and provided results for both maximum eigenvalue and trace statistics tests to determine whether there exists a linear cointegrating relationship. In particular, the maximum likelihood procedure of testing for the number of

[22]Inflation reveals to be stationary at level form using constant only, however, the results do change with the inclusion of a trend term.

Table 6.1 Unit root (non-stationarity) tests

Variables	ADF		PP		Lags	ADF	
	Constant only	With trend and constant	Constant only	With trend and constant		First-differences	Order
Sp	−1.775	−3.095	−1.727	−3.157	1	−7.777*	I(1)
Y	−1.721	−0.554	−1.043	−2.108	2	−3.991**	I(1)
Piv	−1.954	−2.561	−2.146	−2.113	1	−4.281*	I(1)
HC	−1.868	−1.904	−0.872	−1.917	1	−6.267*	I(1)
N	−0.883	−0.385	−0.911	−1.311	2	−4.738*	I(1)
CPI	−2.994**	−3.013	−3.055**	−3.191	1	−7.239*	I(1)
BAD	−2.225	−1.975	−2.263	−1.785	1	−6.701*	I(1)
DRR	−1.691	−3.112	−1.571	−3.111	0	−6.776*	I(1)
IRS	−1.243	−1.377	−1.198	−1.389	0	−6.079*	I(1)
COM	−0.761	−2.589	0.215	−1.735	1	−3.855**	I(1)
NR	−1.496	−1.741	−1.373	−1.746	0	−4902*	I(1)
FL index	−1.978	−1.937	−1.888	−1.014	1	−6.029*	I(1)
IMF index	−1.313	−1.891	−1.406	−1.904	3	−6.081*	I(1)
FO index	−0.927	−1.644	−1.053	−1.654	2	−5.639*	I(1)

$$ADF: \ \Delta x_t = c + \beta x_{t-1} + \sum_{i=1}^{n} \lambda_i \Delta x_{t-i} + \alpha t + e_t$$

Note: ADF augumented Dickey–Fuller test, *PP* Phillips–Perron test;
** and * indicate the level of statistical significance at 5% and 1%, respectively. Our critical values for With Constant at the 5% and 1% significance levels are −2.96 and −3.65; and With Trend and Constant are −3.55 and −4.27. In the first differenced tests, lag length determination was based on AIC criteria. Figures in parenthesis in the last column indicate order of integration

Table 6.2 Determination of cointegration rank

Null hypothesis	Alternative hypothesis	λ-Trace	95% critical value	λ-Max	95% critical value
Cointegerating vector: Sp, Y, DRR, n, FL index					
$r = 0$	$r \geq 1$	89.22*	68.76	63.21*	41.18
$r \leq 1$	$r \geq 2$	38.10	49.42	18.67	31.51
$r \leq 2$	$r \geq 3$	22.41	31.39	10.80	21.37
$r \leq 3$	$r \geq 4$	10.15	16.12	8.98	15.85
Cointegarting vector: Sp, Y, DRR, n, IMF index					
$r = 0$	$r \geq 1$	119.91*	88.80	45.59*	38.33
$r \leq 1$	$r \geq 2$	61.33	63.88	30.97	32.12
$r \leq 2$	$r \geq 3$	38.36	42.92	22.54	25.82
$r \leq 3$	$r \geq 4$	15.82	25.87	9.26	19.39
Cointegarting vector: Sp, Y, DRR, n, FO index					
$r = 0$	$r \geq 1$	88.96*	69.82	42.79*	33.88
$r \leq 1$	$r \geq 2$	46.17	47.86	23.53	27.58
$r \leq 2$	$r \geq 3$	22.64	29.80	12.47	21.13
$r \leq 3$	$r \geq 4$	10.16	15.49	8.19	14.26

Note: Likelihood ratio (LR) tests and the Schwarz's Bayesian information criterion (BIC) were used in determining optimal lag order in the system.
*denotes rejection of the hypothesis at the 5% levels.

cointegrating vectors developed by Johansen (1995) presents a number of advantages over Engle and Granger's (1987) two-step estimation approach (Dolado et al., 2003, p. 646). Firstly, the assumption that the cointegrating vector is unique is relaxed, and, secondly, it considers the short-run dynamics of the system when testing for the existing set of cointegrating vectors in the system. In testing this system and the associated eigenvalues, the trace test statistics is:

$$\lambda_{\text{trace}}(r) = -T \sum_{i=r+1}^{k-2} \ln(1 - \hat{\lambda}_i) \tag{6.12}$$

where H_0 is the number of cointegrating vector equal to r and H_A: the number of cointegrating vectors are more than r, λ_i are the estimated values of ith characteristic roots and T is the number of usable observations. Similarly, the Johansen's maximal eigenvalue test statistics is calculated as:

$$\lambda_{\max}(r, r+1) = -T \ln(1 - \hat{\lambda}_{r+1}) \quad r = 0, 1, 2, \ldots, n-2, n-1 \tag{6.13}$$

where the null hypothesis of r cointegrating vectors is tested against an alternative hypothesis of at most r +1 cointegrating vectors. Table 6.2 shows that both maximum eigenvalue and trace test statistics. The results show one cointegrating equation and consistently so under a different index of financial liberalization. Therefore, in addition to concluding that there exists a long-run relationship among our series and with one just-identifying restriction, we estimate a private savings function.[23]

Using VECM methodology, where both the short-run dynamic and long-run stable equilibrium are modelled, Table 6.3 reports the result of our initial private savings model. For most of the variables, our results are consistent with a priori theoretical expectations. The speed of the adjustment coefficient estimate is negative and statistically significant using a 5% critical value in column (2) and (3). This confirms the error-correction argument that although cointegrating series may deviate from their relationship in the short run, there will be a gradual adjustment to the long run equilibrium (Enders, 2004, p. 328).

The results show that the real interest rate has a statistically significant positive effect on savings behaviour in Botswana. In the long run, the real deposit rate is significant at 5% and 10% level of significance under column (1) and (3), respectively. The results of the long-run private savings function imply, *ceteris paribus*, that 1 percentage point increase in the rate of interest (real deposit rate) enhances private savings rate by around 1.2 percentage points. On the other hand, the coefficient of per capita income level (y) is negative and significant at the 5% level in two out of the three equations in the long run. Although the positive impact of income variable in the short run confirms the Keynesian absolute income hypothesis reported by various empirical studies in developing countries (see, for example, Athukorala & Sen, 2002, 2004; Loayza et al., 2000; Hussein & Thirlwall, 1999), the negative long-run effect is contrary to *a priori* theoretical expectations. Masson et al. (1998) suggest that even though income may be an important factor of savings rates, higher per capita income may enhance capacity to save initially, but may decline as income increases and 'even become negative for rich countries'. This might be the case in Botswana where per capita income has been rising in recent decades.

Population growth rate has a negative effect on private saving, confirming Berube and Cote (2000). Thus, the Botswana's experience provides support that age composition is important. An increase in the proportion of young (0–15 years) and/or elderly (65 years over) groups in the population are expected to reduce the aggregate savings rate. The coefficients for financial liberalization indices have a positive and significant influence in our long-run savings function, suggesting that the financial reforms of the last two decades have had a positive impact on resource and savings mobilization.

Having looked at the long-run relationship which gives us the direction of association that maintains long-run stationarity in the system and the short-run behaviour, we now consider the dynamic interactions between variables. To capture these, we can either apply the impulse response method or alternatively use the variance decomposition approach. Here we take the second option and report the model's variance decomposition analysis. Basically, while the impulse response traces an effect of a shock to one endogenous variable on to the other variables in

[23] The t-statistics are in square brackets.

Table 6.3 Initial estimation: the identified long-run and short-run relationships

Cointegrating equations/financial liberalization index used	IMF (1)	FO (2)	FL (2)
Y	−0.920	−0.149*	−0.086*
	[−0.984]	[−3.135]	[−3.28]
DRR	1.177*	1.153	1.219**
	[4.926]	[1.378]	[1.704]
N	−8.196*	−11.836**	−3.820
	[−5.368]	[−1.737]	[−1.403]
F	4.387*	0.164*	1.026*
	[6.921]	[3.922]	[5.523]
Constant	1.982	0.787	0.213
Short-run relationship among variables	IMF	FO	FL
ECT	−0.430**	−0.404*	−0.077*
	[−1.944]	[−2.290]	[−2.247]
D(Sp(−1))	−0.796**	−0.964*	−0.321
	[−1.982]	[−3.351]	[−1.107]
D(Sp(−2))	−0.899*	−0.954*	−0.441
	[−2.908]	[−3.930]	[−1.569]
D(y(−1))	1.394*	1.398*	1.202*
	[2.262]	[2.579]	[2.241]
D(y(−2))	−1.556*	−1.211*	−1.322*
	[−3.234]	[−2.839]	[−2.875]
D(DRR(−1))	2.622**	2.643	1.283**
	[1.908]	[1.606]	[1.766]
D(DRR(−2))	2.666	−2.118*	2.276*
	[1.009]	[−2.868]	[2.844]
D(n(−1))	−12.691	−32.456*	−18.83
	[−0.834]	[−2.021]	[−0.829]
D(n(−2))	20.010	32.087*	1.130
	[1.372]	[2.365]	[0.081]
D(FL/IMF/FO(−1))	−0.010	0.056**	−0.051
	[−0.019]	[1.977]	[−1.029]
D(FL/IMF/FO (−2))	0.025	0.042	−0.058
	[0.369]	[1.541]	[−1.411]
Constant	0.066**	0.061**	0.033
	[1.841]	[1.961]	[0.875]
R-squared	0.601	0.674	0.615
Adj. R-squared	0.356	0.476	0.381

Note: Dependent variable is Sp. In the parenthesis are t-statistics, asterisks denote statistical significance at: *−5% level and **−10% level. We use IMF, FO and FL indices as measure of financial openness in columns (1) to (3), respectively. This will also be the case in later tables.

the system, the variance decomposition method separates the variance of the forecast error for each variable into components that can be attributed to each endogenous variable in the system (Enders, 1995, p. 311). Thus over the period, the variance decomposition gives us a relative change of a variable as a result of its own

Table 6.4 Variance decomposition of private savings in VECM

Time period (years)	Sp	y	DRR	n	FL Index
1	100	0	0	0	0
2	95.1	1.2	0.1	3.1	0.5
3	89.5	1.7	0.5	3.0	5.4
4	82.7	2.6	1.5	2.7	10.5
5	77.6	3.1	2.1	2.9	14.3
6	72.6	4.0	2.6	2.9	17.9
7	68.6	5.0	3.0	2.8	20.6
8	65.5	5.7	3.3	2.8	22.8
9	62.7	6.3	3.6	2.8	24.6
10	60.4	6.9	3.8	2.7	26.8

Note: Ordering: n, FL Index, y, DRR, Sp.
We have also conducted similar tests with IMF and FO financial indices and our results remain consistent.

random innovation and also a change due to random innovation of the other variables in the system.

To examine this, Table 6.4 outlines the variance decomposition analysis for private savings. From the results, it is observable that while the change in private savings account for about 60% in the variation in private savings, the financial liberalization index explains about 27% at the 10-years horizon. This suggests that the long-run variation in private savings which is accounted by the index is considerable. Importantly, it is also visible that together with our index, per capita income is another long-run relevant variable, contributing about 7% of variation in private savings.

To further analyse the complex direct and feedback effects between savings and income, and in the spirit of identifying the most economically meaningful relationship and interpretations, we consider a number of new variables in addition to the previously identified series used in the last section. This includes inflation (CPI), human capital (HC) and the investment rate (Pvi). As acknowledged by Harris (1995), when time series are non-stationary, applying conventional estimation methodology may not be able to overcome the problem of spurious regression. As usual, it is important to determine the existence of a cointegration relationship and the cointegration rank before estimating the VECM model specification. Again, to identify the cointegrating vectors, we use Johansen's maximum eigenvalue (λmax) and trace eigenvalue (λtrace) statistics. In the process of testing for a stable long-run movement of variables, the choice of lag orders of the vector autoregressive model (VAR), is important (Ibrahim, 2001) and has a significant bearing on the inference drawn from the system. Thus, it should not be too short, which causes an autocorrelation problems, or not too long, which may result in an inefficient estimation (Ahmed, 2007). Another econometric concern is that the trace test may be sensitive to lag selection and for choice of model specification. We have used the Akaike information criterion (AIC) to determine the optimal lag length and also to assess the most appropriate model specification in our cointegration test. Considering previous studies (Dutta & Ahmed, 2001) and taking into account the annual nature of our dataset – which to a reasonable extent becomes a natural constraint for the possible sample size –a lag order of 1 is chosen in this study.[24]

In Table 6.5, our findings from trace, λtrace, and maximal eigenvalue, λmax, test statistics are reported. As can be seen from Table 6.5, there are conflicting results from the maximum eigenvalue test and trace eigenvalue test as to the exact number of cointegarting vectors. Using 95% critical values, maximum likelihood based λmax statistics indicates two cointegrating vectors while the trace test (λtrace) rejects $r = 0$, $r = 1$ and $r = 2$, but fails to reject the null hypothesis $r \leq 3$, therefore indicating three long-run equilibrium relationships. Note that in comparing these two Johansen methods for determining cointegration rank, some studies have criticized the power of the trace test compared to the maximum eigenvalue test (Pentecost & Moore, 2004; Johansen & Juselius, 1990), suggesting that the critical values for the trace test are only indicative when there are deterministic variables. Given these considerations, our results from the maximum eigenvalue test forms the basis of our VECM model and further econometric analysis. In this case, we expect that the two-vector model (r = 2) identified represents the private savings and per capita GDP functions.

$$\Pi y_{t-k+1} = \begin{bmatrix} \alpha_{11} & \alpha_{12} \\ \alpha_{21} & \alpha_{22} \\ \alpha_{31} & \alpha_{32} \\ \alpha_{41} & \alpha_{42} \\ \alpha_{51} & \alpha_{52} \\ \alpha_{61} & \alpha_{62} \\ \alpha_{71} & \alpha_{72} \\ \alpha_{81} & \alpha_{82} \end{bmatrix} \begin{bmatrix} 1 - \beta_{12} & -\beta_{13} & \beta_{14} & \beta_{15} & 0 & 0 & -\beta_{18} \\ -\beta_{21} 1 & 0 & \beta_{24} & \beta_{25} & -\beta_{26} & -\beta_{27} & -\beta_{28} \end{bmatrix} \begin{bmatrix} Sp \\ y \\ DRR \\ CPI \\ n \\ Piv \\ HCF \end{bmatrix}_{t-k+1} \quad (6.14)$$

Having confirmed that there are two stable long-run equilibrium relationships – suggesting an inherent movement among variables that revert towards a long-run stable path despite having some short run shocks – we next present, in a multivariate context, the identified equations where per capita GDP (y) and ratio of private saving to GDP (Sp) are the dependent variables. Equation (6.14) presents the matrix representing the dynamics of the system and particularly elaborates on the long-run parameters. As we have discussed earlier, the β matrix represents the cointegrating vectors, while the matrix α gives the adjustment coefficients in the VECM model.

Despite confirming the number of cointegrating relationships amongst the variables, it is also important to investigate the relative importance of each variable in the system and hence the individual α values. Our discussion in the previous section

[24]We should acknowledge here that such a sample size is small. Sample size could not be increased due to difficulties in availability and accessibility of savings data, therefore this is taken to be an unavoidable shortcoming.

Table 6.5 Johansen tests for the number of cointegrating vectors

Null hypothesis	Alternative	Eigenvalue	λ_{trace}	λ_{trace} (95%)	Eigenvalue	λ_{max}	λ_{max} (95%)
Variables group: Sp, y, DRR, CPI, n, Piv, HC, FO							
$r = 0$	$R \geq 1$	0.900	71.373*	55.728	0.900	281.738*	175.172
$r \leq 1$	$R \geq 2$	0.888	67.759*	49.586	0.888	210.366*	139.275
$r \leq 2$	$R \geq 3$	0.752	47.244*	43.420	0.752	142.607	107.347
$r \leq 3$	$R \geq 4$	0.666	34.007	37.164	0.666	75.363	79.341
$r \leq 4$	$R \geq 5$	0.624	30.317	30.815	0.624	49.356	55.246
IMF replaces FO							
$r = 0$	$R \geq 1$	0.909	224.959*	143.669	0.909	74.221*	48.877
$r \leq 1$	$R \geq 2$	0.782	150.739*	111.781	0.782	47.157*	42.772
$r \leq 2$	$R \geq 3$	0.667	103.582*	83.937	0.667	34.092	36.630
$r \leq 3$	$R \geq 4$	0.631	69.490	60.061	0.631	28.918	30.440
$r \leq 4$	$R \geq 5$	0.518	38.572	40.175	0.518	22.647	24.159
FL replaces FO							
$r = 0$	$R \geq 1$	0.910	241.379*	143.669	0.910	74.573*	48.877
$r \leq 1$	$R \geq 2$	0.856	166.806*	111.781	0.856	60.135*	42.772
$r \leq 2$	$R \geq 3$	0.669	106.671*	83.937	0.669	34.291	36.630
$r \leq 3$	$R \geq 4$	0.647	60.380	62.061	0.647	27.273	30.440
$r \leq 4$	$R \geq 5$	0.443	36.108	40.175	0.443	18.152	24.159

Note: *Denotes statistical significance at 5% level.

and our *priori* economic theory indicate that six out of the eight variables are weakly exogenous: real deposit rate (DRR), inflation (CPI), population growth (n), investment rate (Pvi), human capital (HC) and financial liberalization index (F). Thus, we formally test for the required theoretical restrictions so that they can be incorporated into our VECM set-up. Weak exogeneity tests are linear restrictions on α while a variable is identified to be a long-run weakly exogenous with respect to long-run parameters 'if the cointegration vector does not have any influence on a particular variable, a case in which case, all the weights are zero' (Civcir, 2004). Hence, it is possible, without any loss of information, to condition the short-run model of that variable (Akbostanci & Tunc, 2002).[25] Thus, we tested the hypothesis $\alpha_{i1}, \alpha_{i2}, \alpha_{i3} \ldots \alpha_{in} = 0$ by placing restrictions on rows of the parameters where appropriate. We have the likelihood ratio (LR) test based on the Chi Square distribution in the process of checking for weak exogeneity. For each of the six variables mentioned above, we first estimate an unrestricted cointegrating vector and then restrict the parameters of α matrix to test whether the variable is weakly exogenous.

Following this exercise, our results of weak exogeneity tests are reported in Table 6.6. From column (1) of the table, we observe that inflation, human capital and our financial openness index are weakly exogenous at 5% significance level. Further, we cannot reject the weak exogeneity of the private investment rate at the 10% significance level. However, weak exogeneity is rejected for real deposit rate and population growth variables where the computed likelihood ratio statistics $\chi^2(2)$ were 6.648 (0.0136) and 9.835 (0.0092) respectively.[26] Studies such as Pentecost and Moore (2004) have proposed a small sample adjusted LR statistic since the small sample could present problems for testing.[27] In column (2) we provide small sample-adjusted likelihood ratio statistics. With the exception of the

Table 6.6 Test for weak exogeneity (linear restriction on)

Variables	LR test (1)	LR-adjusted (2)
DRR	6.648 [0.0136]**	5.146
CPI	1.048 [0.3173]	0.764
N	9.835 [0.0092]*	7.606**
HC	0.819 [0.7311]	0.605
Piv	5.863 [0.0919]	4.530
IMF	2.394 [0.2465]	1.742

Note: LR is the likelihood ratio statistics assuming rank = 2, LR adjusted is computed as (n−k)/n where k is the number of regressors and n is the number of observations.
* and ** denote significance at 99% and 95% respectively (critical values are 9.214 (1%) and 5.996 (5%)). Although not shown, weak exogeneity is also not rejected for FO and FL.

[25] Charemza and Deadman (1992, p. 256) elaborate that in the case where variables are exogenous, their marginal process contains no useful information and this can be tested through restricting the speed of the adjustment parameter.

[26] Note that given in brackets are the associated p-values.

[27] In their empirical testing, Pentecost and Moore (2004) have a sample size of 49 observations.

population growth variable, where a null hypothesis of weak exogeneity is rejected at the 10% significance level, the results show that the joint tests for weak exogeneity cannot be rejected with respect to the remaining variables of interest. The rejection of weak exogeneity in the population growth variable is contrary to our expectation for case of Botswanan economy and therefore our assumption of no loss of information from not modelling the determinants of the mentioned six variables is favoured.

We proceed to analyse the output and savings functions using the VECM framework where short-run dynamics can also be examined in the system. In estimating (6.14), we incorporate the appropriate over-identifying theoretical restriction on the basis of a priori economic theory and an empirical support for the case of Botswana (see Ahmed, 2007). In total, we have three exclusion restrictions and two normalization restrictions. In the savings equation, we zero restrict the investment rate and human capital indicator while in output function we impose a zero restriction on the real interest rate variable in the long-run identification matrix.[28] The validity of these over-identifying restrictions of (6.14) is tested using likelihood ratio (LR) tests. Our examination indicates that the corresponding statistics are smaller than the critical values (the computed LR statistic was 2.09 compared to the critical value of 3.84); the hypothesis of over-identified restriction is not rejected at 5% significance level.

Following this, the estimated results for the two models specified are presented in Table 6.7. The results summarized include β parameters and t-ratios for the cointegrating vectors. In literature, the consistency and asymptotic distribution of the long-run coefficients have been established (see, for example, Pesaran & Shin (2002); Ahn & Reinsel (1990)).[29] The table also provides various diagnostic tests to confirm the econometric and statistical adequacy of the model.

The estimated long-run cointegrating relationship for private savings using the three measures of financial liberalization indices is given as follows:[30]

$$\hat{Sp}_t = \underset{(0.992)}{0.028y_t} + \underset{(7.963)}{2.915DRR_t} + \underset{(5.278)}{1.989CPI_t} - \underset{(-6.485)}{23.513n_t} + \underset{(2.242)}{0.048IMF_t} + 0.816$$

$$\hat{Sp}_t = \underset{(1.150)}{0.032y_t} + \underset{(9.481)}{3.248DRR_t} + \underset{(5.797)}{2.243CPI_t} - \underset{(-6.270)}{24.068n_t} + \underset{(2.186)}{0.041FO_t} + 0.779$$

[28] The other variables employed in the per capita GDP equation are standard in the growth literature.

[29] In particular, the work of Pesaran and Shin (2002) is elaborative and derives the asymptotic distribution of the long-run coefficients supporting our econometric procedure.

[30] We have given the three corresponding error correction equations for income function in Table 6.11.

Table 6.7 Results from the vector error correction model (VECM)

	IMF (1)		FO (2)		FL (3)	
	ΔSp	Δy	ΔSp	Δy	ΔSp	Δy
ECT1	−0.669*	−0.028	−0.922*	−0.109	−0.094	−0.032
	[−4.262]	[−0.351]	[−6.154]	[−1.243]	[−0.464]	[−0.359]
ECT2	0.231*	0.028	0.129*	0.034**	−0.198*	−0.011
	[2.962]	[0.721]	[3.853]	[1.752]	[−2.574]	[−0.319]
ΔSp_{t-1}	0.523*	−0.084	0.599*	−0.085	0.404	−0.065
	[2.662]	[−0.844]	[3.749]	[−0.901]	[1.578]	[−0.568]
Δy_{t-1}	0.469	0.693*	0.889*	0.811*	−0.162	0.595*
	[1.142]	[3.330]	[2.267]	[3.520]	[−0.376]	[3.091]
ΔDRR_{t-1}	1.442**	0.078	2.117*	0.305	0.133	−0.034
	[1.944]	[0.206]	[3.151]	[0.772]	[0.172]	[−0.099]
ΔCPI_{t-1}	0.126	−0.419*	0.443	−0.710*	1.353*	0.267
	[0.204]	[1.749]	[0.735]	[2.008]	[2.308]	[1.018]
Δn_{t-1}	8.482	2.139	13.340	9.954	−17.579*	−1.143*
	[0.889]	[0.442]	[1.242]	[1.579]	[1.725]	[1.6721]
ΔHC_{t-1}	2.161*	−0.160	2.013*	−0.283	1.158*	−0.252
	[4.743]	[−0.691]	[5.877]	[−1.409]	[2.520]	[−1.228]
ΔPiv_{t-1}	0.518	0.018	1.688*	0.177	0.007	0.162
	[0.601]	[0.040]	[2.664]	[0.477]	[0.008]	[0.393]
ΔF_{t-1}	0.041**	0.014	−0.013	0.023*	−0.079	−0.021
	[1.837]	[1.231]	[−0.650]	[1.904]	[−1.087]	[−0.656]
C	−0.069*	0.016	−0.085*	0.015	−0.013	0.025*
	[−2.173]	[0.999]	[−3.211]	[0.967]	[−0.370]	[1.673]
R-squared	0.737	0.615	0.827	0.660	0.646	0.595
Adj. R-squared	0.606	0.423	0.741	0.490	0.468	0.393
F-statistic	5.614	7.196	9.572	7.883	5.983	5.944
Q-stat (*p* value)	0.072		0.131		0.096	
LM (2) (*p* value)	0.242		0.203		0.189	
LM (4) (*p* value)	0.348		0.215		0.371	
JB (2) (*p* value)	0.125		0.192		0.135	

Note: *, ** correspond to significance at 5% and 10% levels, t-ratios are in square brackets. Q-stat (Q-statistics lag of 4) is a multivariate Ljung–Box–Pierce test for Portmanteau autocorrelation. LM is multivariate test statistics for residual serial correlation and the JB is Jarque–Bera residual vector normality test.

$$\overset{\wedge}{Sp_t} = -0.326y_t + 2.054DRR_t + 2.213CPI_t - 12.282n_t + 0.281FL_t + 1.497$$
$$(-4.651)\quad (5.240)\qquad (6.421)\qquad (-0.766)\quad (6.298)$$

The long-run relations indicate that the real interest rate has a positive and significant influence on private savings. For example in the first estimation, a 1% rise in the real deposit rate would raise private savings by about 2.92% in Botswana. Moreover, financial liberalization is shown to have a positive and significant impact on private savings for the case of Botswana as indicated by the coefficient of financial liberalization indices. These findings suggest that post 1990s reforms may not only have a positive influence on economic growth through better resource allocation but also have improved domestic savings through better mobilization.

In all our estimations, most of the variables showed the expected signs. Among variables, inflation – our indicator of macroeconomic uncertainty – is an important determinant of the private savings rate. These are consistent with life cycle model prediction and findings of recent empirical studies on SSA (Nwachukwu & Egwaikhide, 2007) and other developing countries (Athukorala & Sen, 2004; Loeyza et al., 2000). During times of increased macroeconomic uncertainty, individuals increase their savings as a precautionary measure to support them in case of adverse changes in expected income. This may particularly be the case in developing countries where financial markets are not fully diversified. In support of these findings, some studies observe that this could explain why for the case of young consumers (or early career employees) who expects a future higher income, consumption is highly correlated with income (Carroll, 1991). As postulated by these models, an increase in inflation also induces households to increase their savings to maintain the real value of imperfectly indexed final assets (Berube & Cote, 2000). From the error correction specification, we find that higher per capita GDP growth and human capital endowment lead to higher savings rates in the Botswanan economy.

6.6 Impacts of Market Liberalization on the Macroeconomy and Growth

As was the cases in many other African countries, financial repression features were visible in Botswana prior to the early 1990s included control on interest rates and barriers to entry in the commercial banking sector. This had discouraged healthy competition in the formal financial system. An important goal and a major objective of the structural adjustment programme (which was adopted by many African countries) and of those financial reforms in particular were to establish more efficient, competitive and deeper financial markets. It is also a well known fact that formal financial markets in many SSA economies are dominated – both in terms of a capital-asset base and functional capacity – by commercial banking sectors (Ahmed, 2005, p. 99). It is therefore obvious that strengthening of the commercial banking system through enhancing the quality of banking supervision and establishing a well functioning legal system and regulatory environment, will improve the financial infrastructure in SSA countries. Since 1989, the government of Botswana has enacted a number of financial laws and regulations for the specific purpose of promoting competition and enhanced the financial intermediation and allocative efficiency (Kayawe & Amusa, 2003). As it has been elaborated in various sections of Chapter 4, these financial reforms, which target prime areas of decontrolling of interest rates and easing of financial sector entry restrictions in addition to strengthening regulatory and supervisory structures, will generate several benefits that would directly or indirectly improve domestic savings mobilization and increase credit availability. This type policy setting of financial deregulation – which will enable banks to have a greater autonomy in their financial activities – will encourage the development of new money market instruments and lead towards a more favourable investment climate. Further, as discussed by Brock and Suarez (2000), adoption of this market-oriented approach of continuous liberalization coupled with increased competition in the financial sector and better management and operation of commercial banks is expected, on average, to reduce the level of interest rate spread. In this section we further plan to investigate the impact of the above mentioned financial reform on savings mobilization and output growth. For this purpose, we consider three new variables (number of banks (COM)[31], government budget deficit (BAD) and interest rate spread (IRS)) in our next estimation.

In an environment where there are failures in the intermediation function of the commercial banking sector, efficient resource mobilization is discouraged. Previous studies indicate that in countries where banking market structure is characterized as monopolistic or oligopolistic (as in most of the African countries), interest rate spread (indicator of inefficient pricing) is usually high and deposit transformation rates are generally observed to be low (Nissanke & Aryeetey, 1998). However, in recent years, commercial banks in Botswana appear to have been modernized and matured on the grounds of a range of credit transactions and loans, security of banking transaction, and in utilization of new technologies. This has not only improved the banking service delivery and the real investment but also enhanced the effectiveness and the role of monetary policy in influencing macroeconomic aggregates. We introduce the above mentioned three variables in addition to those we have used earlier to capture the impact of these market liberalization policies in terms of entry, competition and impact of fiscal policy changes to asses any significant influence on savings behaviour.

Many studies have shown that the role of the financial system in resource mobilization and allocation is critical. To examine whether the impact of government policy changes has increased the overall propensity to save in post-reforms, we first introduce the variable *BAD* in Table 6.8, while maintaining all other variables that we utilized in our previous estimations. We use all three alternative measures of FO in Botswana. This is for the purpose of exploring the robustness of our results and testing the likely effect of financial liberalization using different indicators. More importantly, since these indices also partly capture other effects such as the announcement effect of the opening of the banking sector, and establishment of a prudent regulatory measure and financial supervision, we will consider them as separate regressors. Again, it is necessary to identify the cointegrating vectors before estimating VECM. We observe two significant equations that span the variables in the system. Once again our restrictions on the long-run identification matrix are on the basis of our earlier discussion and a priori theoretical grounds. We thus estimate savings and output functions.

[31] Although we could take the number of bank branches as an indicator of the banking competition, we favour opting for the number of banks of the industry considering the economic and financial evolution of Botswana.

Table 6.8 Estimated short-term relationship from the VECM model

Dep. Variable	IMF		FO		FL	
	ΔSpt	Δyt	ΔSpt	Δyt	ΔSpt	Δyt
ECT1	0.021	0.012	−0.060*	−0.013	0.873	0.282
	[0.331]	[0.589]	[−2.046]	[−1.216]	[1.004]	[0.882]
ECT2	−0.044*	0.011	0.107*	0.028**	−0.233*	−0.060
	[−2.298]	[0.231]	[2.594]	[1.970]	[−2.951]	[−1.088]
ΔSp_{t-1}	−0.106	−0.088	0.258	−0.041	−0.101	−0.067
	[−0.366]	[−0.973]	[0.952]	[−0.431]	[−0.395]	[−0.707]
Δy_{t-1}	0.027	0.645*	1.241**	0.905*	0.460	0.646*
	[0.038]	[2.957]	[1.900]	[3.991]	[0.872]	[3.327]
ΔDRR_{t-1}	−0.053	0.044	2.065**	0.450	1.951**	0.310
	[−0.043]	[0.114]	[1.701]	[1.066]	[1.831]	[0.531]
Δn_{t-1}	12.901	10.029	11.892**	10.207**	17.067	3.740
	[0.184]	[0.208]	[1.721]	[1.693]	[0.851]	[0.507]
ΔCPI_{t-1}	−1.722**	0.184	−0.228	−0.679**	2.637	−0.922
	[−1.943]	[0.524]	[−0.206]	[−1.770]	[1.216]	[1.156]
ΔBAD_{t-1}	−0.091	−0.046	−0.119**	−0.101	−0.783**	−0.223*
	[−0.227]	[−0.368]	[−1.991]	[−0.961]	[−1.744]	[−2.350]
ΔPiv_{t-1}	0.658	−0.073	−0.395	−0.016	−0.426	−0.133
	[0.440]	[−0.155]	[−0.377]	[−0.045]	[−0.366]	[−0.310]
ΔHC_{t-1}	0.354	−0.188	0.820**	−0.150	−0.867	−0.493
	[0.445]	[−0.755]	[1.729]	[−0.698]	[−1.032]	[−1.595]
ΔF_{t-1}	0.008	0.011**	0.016	0.019**	−0.030	−0.019
	[0.212]	[1.934]	[0.496]	[1.669]	[−0.355]	[−0.613]
C	−0.001	0.019	−0.072	0.007	0.012	0.030*
	[−0.018]	[1.117]	[−1.591]	[0.453]	[0.332]	[2.183]
R-squared	0.390	0.600	0.514	0.666	0.471	0.592
Adj. R-squared	0.122	0.369	0.233	0.473	0.165	
F-statistic	0.704		1.829		1.540	
Q-stat (*p* value)	0.134		0.078		0.089	
LM (2) (*p* value)	0.176		0.732		0.663	
LM (4) (*p* value)	0.085		0.100		0.570	
JB (2) (*p* value)	0.079		0.132		0.169	

Note: For details see note to Table 6.7.

Table 6.8 reports the short-run dynamics by the error correction model while the results for the cointegrating vector analysis are summarized in Table 6.12 in the Appendix.[32] From the two equilibrium relationships estimated, the signs of most of the coefficients conform to our theoretical expectations. However, inflation is found to have a negative impact on the saving rates as opposed to our previous finding. Importantly, we see that per capita income, real deposit rate and the financial liberalization index have positive effects on private savings. Government fiscal balance has a negative effect on the private savings rate, implying substitutability between public and private savings in Botswana. This is consistent with findings

[32] As usual we tested whether over-identifying restrictions in the system are valid. The test reveals that our restrictions are not rejected by our likelihood ratio test at the 5% level.

from various developing countries (such as Malaysia, Korea, and Mexico) where evidence supporting Ricardian Equivalence hypothesis is reported (Bandiera et al., 2000). On the other hand, variables of investment rate and human capital indicator have a positive and significant effect on per capita GDP. From the short-run results, it can be observed that there is a negative and significant association between government fiscal balance variables and the private savings to the GDP ratio and per capita output.

Following a wave of financial reforms that resulted in new type of banking operations and increased competition between banks, these economic reforms are expected to not only promote the creation of a sound financial system but also affect the speed at which capital accumulates.[33] In assessing the impact of these policy changes in terms of increasing efficiency and rising overall productivity, we now extend the analysis to competition in the banking sector (COM) and interest rate spread (IRS,[34] then employ a specification in which these reform variables are considered.[35] While leaving out our composite index of financial liberalization, we allow COM, IRS and other reforms variables to capture the effect of increased market liberalization and competition. Importantly, we will observe any changes in the overall explanatory power of the econometric model as well as other qualitative changes in the coefficients of independent variables.

Table 6.9 reports the two long-run VECM relations and short-run disequilibrium adjustment process including results from various diagnostic tests. The long-run equilibrium relationship indicates, *ceteris paribus*, that a percentage increase in competition (COM) (from say 2 to 3%) increases private savings rate by 0.91%. In the short-run dynamics, the coefficient of interest rate spread is negative and significant at the 10% level. A percentage point increase in the interest rate spread (an indicator of banking competitiveness) decreases the private savings rate by 1.42 percentage points. It is observable that the gain derived from a more competitive banking and financial sector cannot be underestimated. From this econometric evidence, if the entry of new established banking institutions in Botswana assisted in becoming more competitive in the banking industry, it is likely that this has contributed to the improved performance of the private savings rate in the recent years.

Finally, since Botswana is a resource dependent country, natural resource and diamond in particular have been an important factor for its economic growth. In this section, we include some new variable such as NR and further examine the relationship among NR, savings, per capita income and investment.[36] Cointegration

---

[33]In addition to promoting a competitive market environment, these market reforms will diversify the range of financial products.

[34]Alternatively, we could use the firm (market) concentration ratio to proxy market power. However lack of complete statistical data undermines the ability to use such index in our examination.

[35]An earlier discussion of these issues and further empirical evidence were also provided in Ahmed (2007).

[36]For consistency, we again allow the direct effect of financial and market reforms to be captured by the liberalization index rather than COM and IRS variables.

Table 6.9 Cointegrating vectors and error correction model (modified version)

Sp =	−3.74	+ 0.28y −	2.02DRR +	47.63n −	9.12CPI +	0.91COM −	6.45IRS
		(6.280)*	(−3.726)*	(7.475)*	(−8.231)*	(12.488)*	(−4.874)*
Y =	2.48	−1.58Sp +	2.68DRR +	12.36n −	12.65CPI +	4.83Piv +	5.76HC
		(−9.296)*	(0.836)	(7.774)*	(−9.661)*	(9.163)*	(10.213)*

Equation	ΔSp_t	Δy_t
ECT1	−0.262**	0.139*
	[−1.776]	[2.313]
ECT2	−0.020	−0.038
	[−0.24177]	[−1.112]
ΔSp_{t-1}	−0.323	−0.060
	[−1.32947]	[−0.613]
Δy_{t-1}	0.780*	0.630*
	[2.072]	[4.119]
ΔDRR_{t-1}	2.148**	−0.448
	[1.673]	[−0.687]
Δn_{t-1}	4.696	−0.417
	[0.353]	[−0.077]
ΔCPI_{t-1}	3.106	−0.623
	[1.367]	[−0.674]
ΔPiv_{t-1}	1.452	0.424
	[1.419]	[1.020]
ΔHC_{t-1}	0.427	−0.065
	[0.611]	[−0.229]
ΔCOM_{t-1}	−0.387*	0.042
	[−2.519]	[0.673]
ΔIRS_{t-1}	−1.423**	−0.051
	[1.952]	[0.043]
R-squared	0.578	0.602
Adj. R-squared	0.367	0.403
F-statistic	7.739	9.026
Q-sat (*p* value)	0.067	
LM (2) (*p* value)	0.132	
LM (4) (*p* value)	0.064	
JB (2) (*p* value)	0.718	

Note: For details see Note to Table 6.7.

tests from both trace statistics and maximal eigenvalue statistics indicate that the null hypothesis of $r = 2$ (two cointegrating vectors) against the specific alternative $r = 3$ is rejected at a 5% significance level. However, the null hypothesis of $r = 3$ against $r = 4$ cannot be rejected at the 95% confidence level and consequently we concludes that there are three cointegrating vectors present among the given variables. In this framework, we allow the indirect impact of policy reforms on per capita GDP through savings and/or investment, and having $r = 3$ requires r^2

restriction for just identification. Thus, taking into account these restrictions, the system represented by (6.11) can be given as:

$$\Pi y_{t-k+1}\begin{bmatrix}\alpha_{11} & \alpha_{12} & \alpha_{13}\\ \alpha_{21} & \alpha_{22} & \alpha_{23}\\ \alpha_{31} & \alpha_{32} & \alpha_{33}\\ \alpha_{41} & \alpha_{42} & \alpha_{43}\\ \alpha_{51} & \alpha_{52} & \alpha_{53}\\ \alpha_{61} & \alpha_{62} & \alpha_{63}\\ \alpha_{71} & \alpha_{72} & \alpha_{73}\\ \alpha_{81} & \alpha_{82} & \alpha_{83}\\ \alpha_{91} & \alpha_{92} & \alpha_{93}\end{bmatrix}\begin{bmatrix}1 & -\beta_{12} & 0 & -\beta_{14} & \beta_{15} & \beta_{16} & 0 & -\beta_{18} & 0\\ -\beta_{21} & 1 & -\beta_{23} & 0 & \beta_{25} & \beta_{26} & -\beta_{27} & -\beta_{28} & -\beta_{29}\\ -\beta_{31} & -\beta_{32} & 1 & \beta_{34} & \beta_{35} & 0 & 0 & -\beta_{38} & 0\end{bmatrix}\begin{bmatrix}Sp\\ y\\ Piv\\ DRR\\ CPI\\ n\\ HC\\ F\\ NR\end{bmatrix}_{t-k+1} \tag{6.15}$$

where private savings rate, per capita output and investment rate are taken to be the dependent variables respectively in each of the above cointegrating vectors. Normalizing the cointegrating relationships to Sp_t, y_t and Piv_t respectively, the long-run relationship observed in equation format is given as:[37]

$$\begin{aligned}Sp_t &= 1.912 - 0.245y_t + 0.691DRR_t - 1.818CPI_t + 2.156n_t + 0.145FO\\ y_t &= 12.351 + 0.299Piv_t + 0.521DRR_t - 2.788CPI_t - 8.167n_t\\ &\quad +0.267HC_t + 0.102FO + 1.816NR_t\\ \mathrm{Piv}_t &= 0.439Sp_t + 0.173y_t - 1.060DRR_t - 0.105CPI_t + 0.032FO - 0.499\end{aligned}$$

To test the validity of the imposed restriction, the likelihood ratio test for these imposed restrictions has a $\chi^2(2)$ of 3.052 (p-value = 0.112), which does not reject joint restrictions at any conventional significance level. The empirical finding also suggests that the explanatory variables explain almost 68%, 71% and 61% of variation in private savings rate, investment and per capita GDP respectively. Once again, we observe that most of our latest coefficients are consistent with theoretical predictions and findings discussed earlier. Financial liberalization is found to have a positive effect on private savings and per capita output in Botswana in line with other findings in the recent literature such as Bekaert, Harvey, and Lundblad (2001) where financial liberalization is observed, on average, to improve economic performance in the long term relative to the short run. Although number of studies have reported that financial liberalization has not resulted in higher economic growth in many SSA economies (Nissanke & Aryeetey, 1998, p. 86) and itself has a number of potential dangers, our empirical evidence seems to suggest that reforms have benefited the Botswana economy through enlarging the financial system, increasing its efficiency and improving fund collection and allocation. Moreover, this might have also been supported by well functioning legal and supervisory institutions, proper government planning and commitments. In support of this, Ang and McKibbin (2007), Fry (1995, 1997) and McKinnon (1993) argue

[37]We only report our result using the FO index of financial liberalization. However our results do not change qualitatively when we use IMF and FL measures. Further, the short-run dynamics equations obtained are presented under Table 6.13.

that for the benefits of financial liberalization to be realized, reforms should be carefully planned, timed and closely monitored. The negative effect of inflation on per capita GDP and investment supports Ogbokor (2004) and Hadjimichael and Ghura (1995) who find that, through creating uncertainty, higher inflation leads to an inefficient allocation of funds, and therefore discourages both savings and investment in developing countries. Overall, our empirical evidence shows that savings and per capita output have both direct and indirect links where the former also affects per capita GDP through the investment function. The positive and significant impact of the financial liberalization index on investment implies that the set of reforms may have stimulated investment through more efficient credit allocation and by allowing investors to enjoy greater financial flexibility.

6.6.1 Hypothetical scenario for Kenya and Malawi

A reasonable conclusion from our econometric investigation, which is also supported by the facts from the case studies, is that the presence of macroeconomic instability, continuous fiscal imbalances and lack of competition in the banking sector may not favour (or rather benefit) depositors and thereby provides less incentive to save. In the previous chapter, it has been indicated that lack of 'meaningful' entry in the commercial banking sector of Kenya and Malawi has enabled dominant banks to maintain a high interest rate spread. Essentially, it is believed that as financial liberalization impacts gain strength, the economic system in general benefits through efficiency improvement in the intermediation process where the interest rate differential (lending-deposits rate margin) narrows over time (Ndungu & Ngugi, 2000). Indeed, as the cost of financial intermediation reduces due to aggressive competitive pressure, interest rates paid to depositors would converge to international levels. Evidence suggests that when the gradual entry of new commercial banks following reforms triggers aggressive competition, firms tend to slim down their profits and offer higher rates to depositors with the view of gaining substantial market share.[38]

To capture the gain to the economy in terms of stimulating savings and investment, we will calculate the extent of pass-through from spread to savings using data from Kenya and Malawi. In the post-reform era, it has been observed that persistent and high interest rate spread in Sub-Saharan African and some Asian countries has been a major concern for policy makers in recent times (see, for example, Ndungu and Ngugi (2000) and Mlachila and Chirwa (2002)). In Kenya, Malawi and Botswana, the average intermediation spreads for 1991–2003 were 12.9%, 18.6% and 3.7% respectively. Applying the coefficient of spread variable from regression 2,

[38]See, for example, analysis by Montreevat (2000) about the impact of foreign entry on the Thai banking sector.

the quantitative effect of an improvement in the level of competitiveness on the savings rate can be calculated. Thus, if Kenya was able to reduce economic inefficiency through higher spread to the level of Botswana, this would have raised the private savings rate by more than 13 percentage points $[(12.9 - 3.7) \times 1.42]$. Similarly if Malawi was able to reduce the cost of financial intermediation through reduction in the spread level to that of Botswana, the private savings rate would increase by almost 22 percentage points $[(18.6 - 3.7) \times 1.42]$. It is noticeable that these figures represent a substantial improvement in the savings level in both the countries as a result of reduction in the cost of using the financial system. With a positive association between savings and investment, such enhancement in the capital accumulation will have a positive influence on income growth.

Next, we take a hypothetical case and look at the private savings behaviour in Kenya and Malawi and whether reforms have led to improvement in macroeconomic conditions and enhancement in the level of competitiveness. Initially, taking the actual values for the year 2000 as the starting values, we construct hypothetical data of ten observations for deposit rate (*DRR*), inflation (*CPI*), spread (*IRS*), and government budget deficit (*BAD*) variables. Using the respective estimated coefficients of these variables from our regression, we forecast private saving levels if the economic structures of Kenya and Malawi were similar to that of Botswana. Figures 6.5a and 6.6a depict the evolution of the hypothetical series chosen for these two countries, where a downward trend in the inflation and spread variables, and an upward improvement in the government deficit and real deposit rate, are observable. Figures 6.5b and 6.6b show individual contribution of each of these variables to the change in the private saving rates as well as the combined effect on private savings.

Considering its initial economic condition, Kenya seems to be closer to Botswana relative to Malawi as at 2000, and thus may have smoother transition in the process of catching up with Botswana. From Figures 6.5b and 6.6b, transitions are non-negative in all variables but government deficit. The spread variable (which is a measure of competitiveness of the banking sector) shows a stronger positive effect to the change in private savings in both countries. Deposit rate contribution is more significant in the case of Malawi (Fig. 6.6b) relative to Kenya (Fig. 6.5b). The variable *BAD* contributes negatively to the change in the private savings rate. This is expected since an increase in government savings (decrease in government deficit) will be met by a decline in private savings to some extent. However, in both countries the significant contributions of the *IRS* variable are visible and therefore appear to be important. It is understood that when the banking sector is imperfectly competitive, a considerable portion of the interest rate spread IRS will reflect the prevalence of market power. As the competitiveness in this sector improves, a higher proportion of increase in interest rates will be transferred to depositors. From this evidence generally, if macroeconomic stability is achieved, the banking sector is allowed to become more competitive, the government deficit is reduced and the real deposit rate is improved, private saving levels in Kenya will increase from the current level of 12.2% to more than 43% by the year 2009. Similarly, if the same changes are achieved and maintained in Malawi, the private

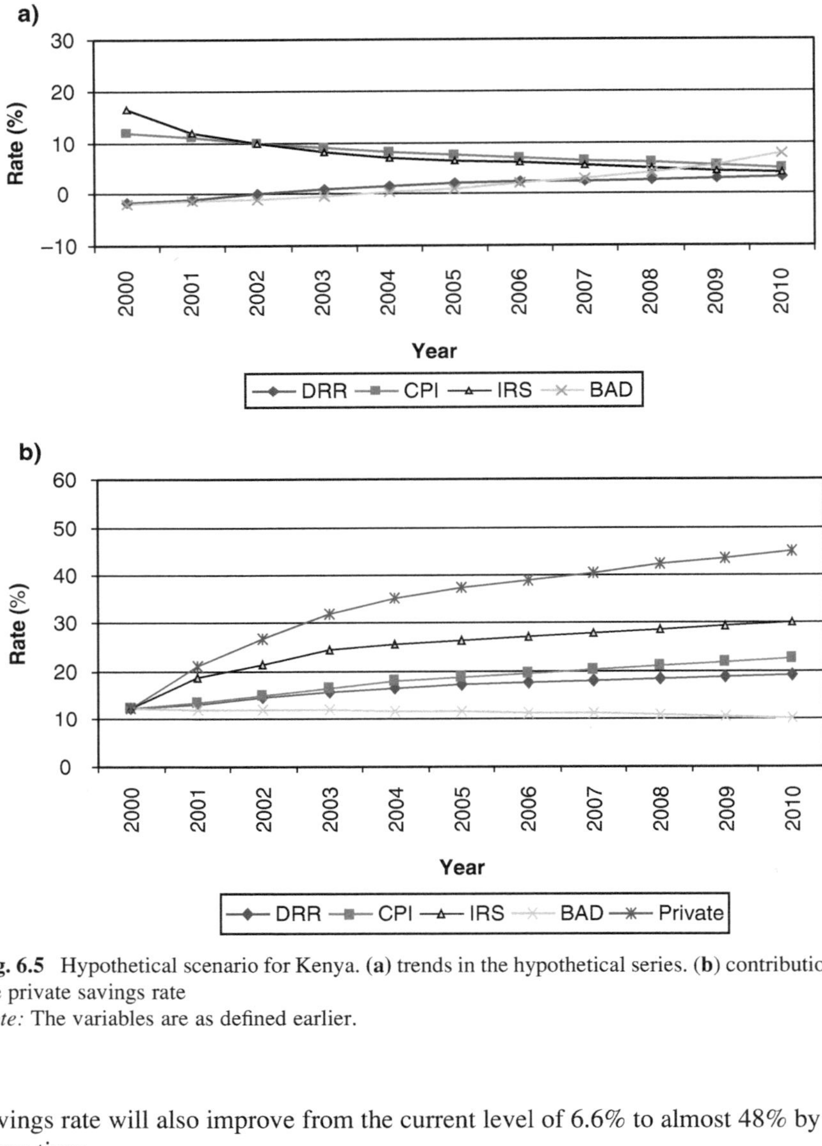

Fig. 6.5 Hypothetical scenario for Kenya. (**a**) trends in the hypothetical series. (**b**) contribution to the private savings rate
Note: The variables are as defined earlier.

savings rate will also improve from the current level of 6.6% to almost 48% by the same time.

This exercise supports our previous findings for the cases of Kenya and Malawi, where it is not surprising that we have observed a poor private savings response following financial liberalization. Given that the macroeconomic environment remained unstable and the entry of new banking institutions provided fringe competition, major banks were able to set the spread significantly above marginal cost, repressing deposit rates. However, if entry barriers are reduced to the level of Botswana to allow entry of well established banks, players will be forced to behave

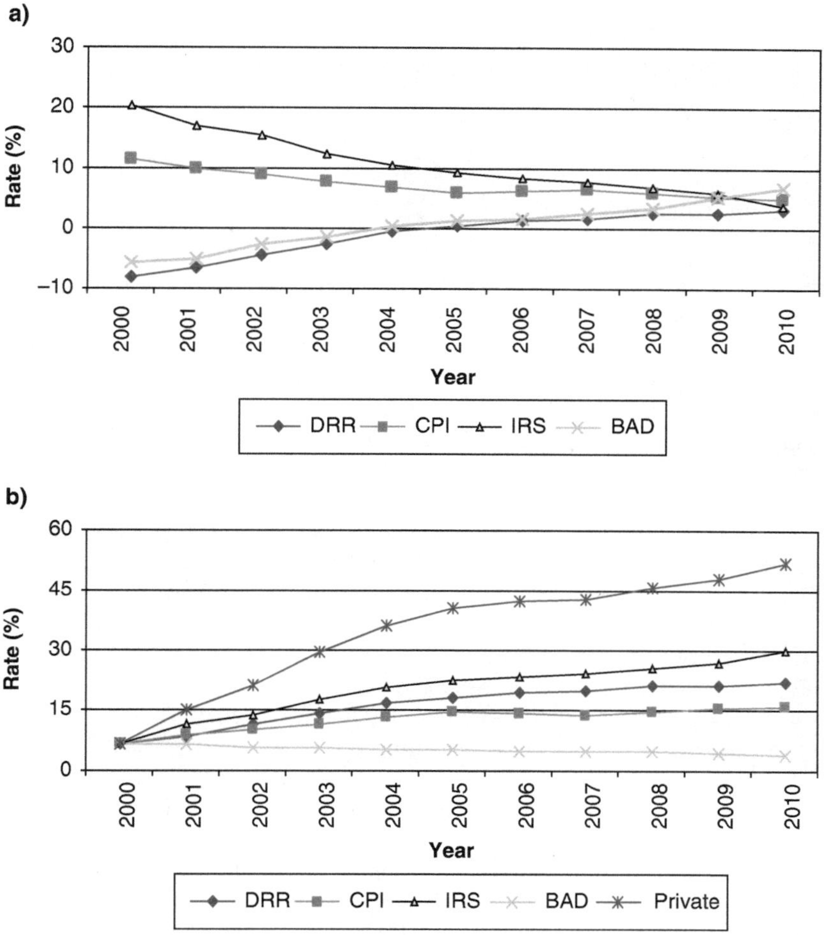

Fig. 6.6 Hypothetical scenario for Malawi. (**a**) trends in the hypothetical series, (**b**) contribution to the private savings rate
Note: The variables are as defined earlier.

more competitively, leading to an improvement in the private saving rates to much higher levels in the future. It has also been argued that large fiscal deficits and macroeconomic instability may be closely related and together influence savings negatively (UNDP, 1999). Higher fiscal imbalances cause higher inflation which may lower investment in productive activities. As it is apparent from Figures 6.5 and 6.6, if Kenya and Malawi were to pursue policies of better fiscal management and a stable macroeconomic environment – through reduction in the levels of inflation – a stronger response in the private savings rate will be observed.

Our hypothetical demonstrations show that, even when the improvement in deposit rate is low, the actions of the government and other macroeconomic conditioning will have significant bearing on the private savings trend.

6.7 Conclusion

In the light of the empirical results given above, our findings seem to be consistent with the theoretical expectations and other previous studies. Particularly since this investigation was at a country level rather than a cross-country level, it is important to highlight a number of issues. Savings in Botswana are sensitive to the real deposit rate. The empirical results indicate a positive and mostly significant relationship between private savings and real deposits rates. The impact of the financial liberalization on the steady state savings rate is consistently positive in Botswana. This result confirms the findings of previous literature which observed that liberalization will have stronger potential influence to boost economic performance in the long run since the feedback effects will only be realized over time. Furthermore, similar to other previous studies such as Bandiera et al. (2000) and MFE (2002), our composite index aimed to reflect several aspects of the recent financial reforms in Botswana which may not be fully represented by changes in interest rates. Additionally, in the later part of the investigation, the study considers the explanatory power of various reform-related variables which are expected to capture the impact of reform changes in the absence of our composite index. It is observed that firstly, a decrease in the government deficit will reduce private savings probably through relaxation in the domestic borrowing constraint. Secondly, the spread variable, which is a measure of banking competitiveness, negatively contributes to the private savings rates. In countries where banks have market power on deposits, such institutions may repress the deposit rate, widening the interest rate spread. This may effectively lower the level of acceptable deposits directly reducing the level of available savings. Third, the indicator of the number of banks is positively related to the savings rate in the steady state. Licensing more banks reduces the degree of market concentration (enhancing efficiency), modernization of banking services and speed of delivery of financial services. It is apparent from this analysis that in countries where the banking industry is concentrated with a few firms having dominating market power, private savings will be hampered.

Finally, by taking a hypothetical scenario, it is shown that if the economic structures of Kenya and Malawi were similar to or converged towards that of Botswana, their private savings rate would substantially increase within a reasonable period of time. This indicative evidence supports our previous argument in the case study analysis as to why savings are low and the interest rate spread is high in Kenya and Malawi unlike Botswana.

Appendix

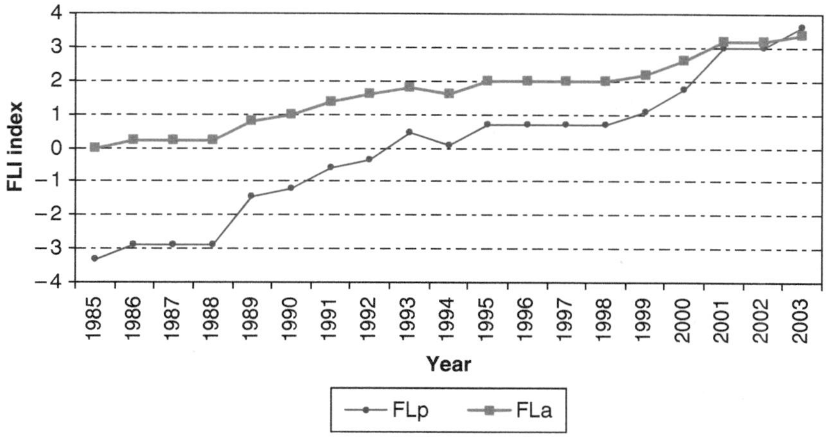

Fig. 6.7 FL index: average method vs. principle component approach
Note: FLa indicates the average method index while FLp index is derived through the principle component method.

Table 6.10 Market liberalization in Botswana, Kenya and Malawi

	Botswana
1986	Initial removal of controls of interest rates on minimum and maximum lending and deposit rates
Late 1989	Adoption of comprehensive reforms legislation to improve efficiency of operations and intermediary role of the country's financial institutions
	Commercial banks granted freedom to set fees and charges to facilitate market determination of interest rates
1991	Abolition of foreign exchange controls and gradual liberalization of the external sector
	Introduction of Bank of Botswana Certificate (BoBCs) as an instrument for the conduct of open market operations
	Kenya
1987	Introduction of cash requirement for commercial banks
1989	Beginning of significant institutional changes and introduction of legislation to reinforce sound banking system
1990	Establishment of capital market development authority to create conducive environment for investment
	Adoption of a market-based Treasury bill/bond auction mechanism
1991	Banking and Financial Institutions Act amended to strengthen regulation and supervision
	Interest rate liberalization was fully adopted

(continued)

Table 6.10 (Continued)

	Foreign/private banks and financial institutions were now free to enter the market to enhance healthy competition
1993	Suspension of Exchange Control Act and the beginning of market determined flexible exchange rate
1995	Restrictions of foreign ownership of local companies were further eased to encourage portfolio investment
	Malawi
1989	Abolition of interest rate controls and adoption of measures to enhance capital movement
1990	Introduction of a competitive monthly auction of reserve bank bills to enhance market determination of interest rates
	Gradual lowering of commercial banking sector entry barriers
1991	Removals of all credit ceiling and forced credit to specific sectors

Note: Authors' compilation from various sources.

Table 6.11 Identified cointegrating vectors (per capita income equation)

Index used	(1) IMF	(2) FO	(3) FL
Sp	0.656*	0.612	2.578*
	[4.656]	[1.507]	[4.861]
CPI	−0.404*	−7.602*	−2.237
	[−6.541]	[−4.557]	[−1.521]
n	4.219*	−10.606*	−3.687
	[5.713]	[−5.201]	[−0.719]
HC	2.230*	1.073*	1.143**
	[8.3447]	[2.086]	[1.913]
PIV	9.415*	13.373*	3.253*
	[7.865]	[5.6574]	[4.571]
F	0.057**	0.517*	0.398*
	[1.957]	[3.893]	[2.724]
C	4.889	2.679	5.050

Note: * and ** denote significance at 5% and 10% levels respectively.
F means financial reforms index used. Reported in [ ] brackets are t-statistics.

Table 6.12 Long-run cointegrating vectors

Index	IMF		FO		FL	
Dep. variable	Sp	Y	Sp	Y	Sp	y
Sp		0.307*		4.461*		4.689*
		[3.519]		[8.202]		[2.983]
Y	0.990*		−1.530*		−0.114*	
	[9.725]		[−9.814]		[− 7.699]	
DRR	1.464*	1.221*	3.213*	1.538*	1.776*	8.244**
	[3.844]	[3.783]	[2.151]	[0.733]	[3.155]	[1.807]
N	9.837*	6.197*	−7.332*	4.418*	5.225*	−6.655*
	[9.710]	[7.460]	[−4.272]	[5.526]	[6.810]	[−7.231]

(*continued*)

Table 6.12 (Continued)

Index	IMF		FO		FL	
Dep. variable	Sp	Y	Sp	Y	Sp	y
CPI	−5.624*	−5.612*	−3.592*	−1.897	−3.631**	−2.106*
	[−5.103]	[−9.314]	[−2.207]	[− 0.963]	[−1.924]	[−4.850]
BAD	−2.663*		−3.399**		−1.416*	
	[−3.195]		[−1.836]		[−2.456]	
PIV		7.536*		6.347*		2.252*
		[3.963]		[5.29]		[2.095]
HC		2.002*		0.079		2.746*
		[2.159]		[0.148]		[3.070]
F	0.052	0.023**	0.447*	0.688	0.168*	0.585
	[1.025]	[1.705]	[6.139]	[1.144]	[2.43]	[1.018]
C	4.380	5.960	−20.653	−0.033	0.665	−6.312

Note: * and ** denote significance at 5% and 10% levels respectively.
F means financial reforms index used. Reported in [ ] brackets are t-statistics.

Table 6.13 Short-run dynamics for the three vector model

Variable	ΔSp_t	Δy_t	ΔPvi_t
ECT1	0.007 (0.017)	0.155 (0.928)	0.040 (0.471)
ECT2	−0.483 (−1.834)***	−0.194 (−2.072)**	−0.103 (−1.850)***
ECT2	−0.560 (−0.583)	−0.259 (−0.649)	−0.497 (−2.437)**
ΔSp_{t-1}	0.222 (0.899)	−0.019 (−0.191)	−0.032 (−0.619)
Δy_{t-1}	0.275 (0.668)	0.542 (3.159)*	0.208 (2.375)**
ΔPiv_{t-1}	−0.044 (−0.047)	0.111 (0.288)	0.208 (1.055)
ΔDRR_{t-1}	1.663 (1.174)	0.457 (0.775)	0.305 (1.024)
ΔCPI_{t-1}	−0.017 (−0.010)	0.388 (0.544)	0.157 (0.430
ΔHC_{t-1}	0.824 (1.455)	−0.436 (−1.851)***	−0.204 (−1.699)***
ΔNR_{t-1}	−0.194 (−0.435)	−0.127 (−0.684)	0.051 (0.543)
Δn_{t-1}	−2.456 (−0.158)	0.043 (0.005)	1.667 (0.503)
ΔFO	−0.081 (−0.921)	−0.026 (−1.180)	−0.006 (−0.360)
Constant	−0.021 (−0.661)	0.034 (2.644)*	−0.006 (−1.010)

R-square 0.68 Q-stat = 438.22 [0.123] LM$-\chi^2$ (2) =81.56 [0.461] LM$-\chi^2$ (4) = 104.81 [0.039] JB$-\chi^2$ (4) = 49.72 [0.887]

Note: *, ** and *** denote significance at 1%, 5% and 10% levels respectively. Reported in brackets are t-statistics.

Chapter 7
Welfare Implications of Financial Liberalization in Thailand: A Cost–Benefit Analysis

By Mathew Clarke and Sardar M.N. Islam

7.1 Introduction

Over the past three decades, a smorgasbord of inter- and intra-dependent development issues, processes, innovations and public policies have intersected and accelerated social and economic change resulting in what is commonly referred to as globalization and (its by-product) financial liberalization (Bird & Rajan, 2001 - for a review of the welfare and political issues (see Sen (1999), Gilpin (2001)). It is possible to analyse financial liberalization from a social welfare perspective. Within development economics, two pertinent contemporary issues that impact on social welfare associated with globalization include the rise of the knowledge economy and financial liberalization.

Over the last three decades, most economies have moved towards financial liberalization - international economic deregulation. This deregulation has resulted in dismantling of trade barriers such as tariffs in both goods and services, relaxation of control over capital markets (including floating currencies and deregulation of financial markets and direct foreign investments), and the deregulation of internal markets for goods and services.

The desirability of globalization and financial liberalization is dependent upon who is being considered. A social welfare economic evaluation of financial liberalization can be preformed by adapting the framework of welfare economics (Sen, 1999). As a process it affects different sections of society in different ways. Financial liberalization results in both winners and losers and has both benefits and costs (Lindert & Williamson, 2001; Williams, 2002). As such, financial liberalization is an important issue for evaluating social welfare of a nation, especially for Thailand, for example, due to the experience within the 1997 Asian Financial Crisis which has been blamed on financial liberalization (Arunsmith, 1998; Julian, 2000; Ryan, 2000; Siamwalla, 2000).

A systematic consideration, quantification, and numerical estimations of the costs and benefits of globalization and financial liberalization have not yet been

A.D. Ahmed and S.M.N. Islam, *Financial Liberalization in Developing Countries*, Contributions to Economics,
DOI: 10.1007/978-3-7908-2168-0_7, © Springer Physica-Verlag Berlin Heidelberg 2010

undertaken within the current literature (with exception of Hansanti, Islam and Sheehan (2008)). Welfare economics is interested in whether people are becoming better or worse off over time (Kakwani, 1997b; McKenzie, 1983). The objective of this chapter is to develop a framework for considering and analysing social welfare issues arising from the process and implication of globalization (particularly financial liberalization) with an illustrative application to Thailand undertaken.

Actual or real estimates have not been undertaken, though the intuitively correct illustrative costs and benefits of financial liberalization and globalization allow these issues to be analysed within this social welfare framework.

The chapter is structured as follows: Section 7.1 introduced the chapter. Section 7.2 will present a brief review of the Thai experience of financial liberalization and financial crises before Sect. 7.3 which will introduce the welfare economics framework and illustrative cost benefit analysis as well as a welfare analysis of the results of this illustrative exercise. Section 7.4 reviews the policy implications of this exercise. Finally Sect. 7.5 concludes the chapter.

7.2 Financial Liberalization and its Implications in Thailand

A large set of controversial issues has emerged in regard to the process of financial liberalization, its causes, consequences and welfare impacts (see also Hansanti et al. (2008)). The set of issues relevant for social welfare analysis and measurement include:

1. Will globalization and financial liberalization increase social welfare via economic growth?
2. How can social welfare be measured and assessed within an open economy?
3. How much importance should be given to the influence of foreign factors relative to national factors especially to evaluate the importance of welfaristic and non-welfaristc elements of social welfare in a global economy?
4. Are financial liberalization and financial crisis beneficial for society given its consequences?

Financial liberalization has been a powerful force over the last two decades. Within Thailand though, the major effects of globalization have only been felt since the mid 1980s. Between 1975 and this time, the Thai economy was relatively closed and tightly controlled by government regulations. Regulations on foreign investment were tight and the value of the baht was fixed and later tied to the US dollar and later still a US dollar dominated basket of currencies. The Thai government sheltered the economy from the excesses of the volatility of the world economy (Dixon, 1996, 1999). However, from the late 1980s, the effects of financial liberalization, the rise of the knowledge economy and liberalization of finance and capital markets began to be implemented (Leightner, 1999; Warr & Nidhiprabha, 1996).

Foreign investment escalated, particularly into the export manufacturing sector, as a direct result of this process (Kittiprapas, 1999, 2000; Pilbeam, 2001).

Financial liberalization also directly impacted on rural communities at the village level. Rural villages produce agricultural and manufactured exports, supply labour to domestic market in cities and overseas, have access to telecommunication networks and most importantly have greater access to television (and satellite television). This globalization of the village is considered by many non-government organisation responsible for increased debt and its ensuing poverty and the inability to become self-reliant. However, less-globalised villages suffered more during the Financial Crisis of 1997, as they had fewer coping mechanisms and options available to them (Kaosa-ard, 2000).

The costs and benefits of financial liberalization can be divided into those arising from social integration of the rise of knowledge economy (Hansanti et al. 2008) and those arising from financial liberalization (Hallwood & McDonald, 2000).

7.3 Welfare Economics Framework: Social Choice and Cost Benefit Analysis of Globalization and Financial Liberalization

The process of financial liberalization can be effectively analysed from a welfare economic perspective. A global welfare economic perspective is the relevant paradigm for this analysis (Sen, 1999). As has been discussed, financial liberalization has both benefits and costs. By analysing these costs and benefits from such a perspective, new insights can be gained in whether social welfare has been enhanced or stunted by this process.

In the rest of the chapter, the above issues in welfare economics of financial liberalization and financial crisis are investigated by adopting a quantitative and empirical framework (assuming the aforementioned principles and features) of social choice theory based cost–benefit analysis.

There are several conceptual issues related to the analysis of society's welfare and economic performance which are central to all studies of welfare (see Clarke & Islam, 2003). They include:

- A definition of well-being and welfare.
- Criteria for evaluation of welfare and performance.
- The specification of an aggregate social welfare function such as possibility and impossibility theorems in social choice.
- The numeraire of welfare and performance such as utility, consumption, GDP, capabilities, entitlement, wealth, capital stock, clean environment, the level of

human development or a combination of non-economics factors such as rights, freedom, opportunity, equity etc.
- Tnits of measurement, i.e. money or physical units, market prices, shadow prices, contingent valuation or willingness to pay.
- The level of measurement at the aggregative (macro) or disaggregative (micro) levels; and
- Models for measurement and analysis such GDP or other aggregative performance indices, family budget analysis, economy wide macroeconometric models, econometric estimates of demand functions, game theory, constrained optimisation, cost-benefit analysis, micro and macro economic or growth models.

Social welfare here is defined as the sum of individual welfare adjusted for some non-welfaristic elements. It is assumed that social welfare can be estimated by adopting the cardinality perspective related to the possibility theorem. In this cardinality approach, a social welfare state is preferred by society if that state provides higher net social welfare (benefits) compared to other social states available related to a particular state or policy or outcome of economic activities. Social welfare is measured here in money metric and is represented by an aggregate measure of social welfare such as GDP (or adjusted GDP for non-wefaristic elements of welfare – see Clarke & Islam, 2003).

Cost–benefit analysis is a useful framework for this type of ranking of social states (or projects) especially when the forces of private profitability are unable to rank according to social orderings (Boadway & Bruce, 1984). It has several components or elements. The first component is to consider all the direct economic and non-economic inputs and outputs. Social states (or projects) considered within a cost–benefit analysis framework have economic inputs and outputs that would be considered in a financial analysis, but they also have non-economic inputs and outputs that also need to be fully captured. These may include time saved, risk taking or health improvements. The second component then is to consider all the indirect costs and benefits. These indirect effects are primarily externalities that are not captured elsewhere in the economy. The third component of cost–benefit analysis is to then assign monetary values to these effects. The monetary value of the direct, economic costs and benefits are found within the market. However, a variety of techniques have been developed (i.e. hedonic pricing, border prices, willingness to pay, etc.) to calculate the prices of indirect, non-economic costs and benefits. The final component of cost–benefit analysis is to sum all these impacts for each period over a certain pricing horizon but to also convert all these current values into a present value (Boadway & Bruce, 1984).

Social choice expands optimal outcomes beyond just that of an aggregation of individual preferences. Social choices are therefore very important in seeking optimal social outcomes that improve both present social welfare and sustainable social welfare as these outcomes are not assured through market based individual preferences (Islam & Clarke, 2002, 2003; Clarke & Islam, 2003).

Social choice theory focuses on the methodology of social or collective decisions concerning optimal levels of social welfare. The main concern within social choice theory is the process of aggregated individual choices to form a social choice that results in an optimal social welfare outcome for society.

An undertaking of a cost–benefit analysis largely depends on the underlying social preferences and value judgements which can be accomplished via social choice theory. In social choice theory, social choices can be estimated using expert opinion (or analyst), government formulated public policy, or specific interviews of individuals on social welfare outcomes. The methodology for each technique is well established. Using one, or a combination of the above, it is possible to determine the social choice perspectives on various social welfare issues (Clarke & Islam, 2003; Clarke, Islam & Sheehan, 2002; Islam & Clarke, 2003; Islam & Clarke, 2002). As the state maintains the functions of allocation, regulation and distribution (Musgrave, 1959), the state has a role to enforce these social choice preferences and 'incarnate the moral and political will of the people' (Stoleru, 1975, p. 1). This is done in two stages: (1) *quantification* of individual preferences; and (2) the *weighting* of these individual preferences by weights determined by some form of consensus (i.e. majority voting for particular social structures, etc.). Perhaps more importantly, with regards to certain concepts, such as sustainability, individual preferences will not achieve these outcomes and the state (or analyst) must interpret and then act upon these social preferences (Pezzey, 2001, 2002). That this emphasis be placed on achieving an optimal social outcome should not be considered unusual. 'Samuelson's (1956) consensus model of the household assumes that all members pool their resources and work in concert to maximise a common utility function' (Slesnick, 2001, p. 32). Social choice theory can be used to extend this consensus from the household to the society (Clarke & Islam, 2003; Sen, 1982).

Social choice theory has a long history (see Sen, 1999 for a survey). The difficulties in making a judgement on the state of social welfare have long been recognised (Borda, 1781 – reprinted 1953; de Condorcet, 1785). Bergson (1938) first suggested that social choices could be discussed within a social welfare function. Arrow (1951) formulated the difficulties and inconsistencies of doing so within his 'impossibility theorem'. Arrow showed through using axiomatic set theory that it was not possible to make a non-dictatorial social choice that satisfied a set of axioms of reasonableness. An alternative theorem arguing that Arrow's set of axioms of reasonableness were not so reasonable and it was possible to make non-dictatorial social choice decisions was developed by Sen (1966, 1970, 1973 and subsequently added to by others - see Hammond, 1976).

A social choice framework is normative and value judgements about the valuation of, and preferences for, social welfare maximisation must be considered. Social choice theory provides the normative framework for aggregating individual welfare and should be applied to social welfare measures as it highlights social preferences and value judgements (Bonner, 1986). It is concerned with economic and non-economic activities that are important in determining social welfare levels, quality and composition. Social choice theory can highlight changes within society and how these changes impact on sustainability (Clarke & Islam, 2003).

7.4 Costs and Benefits of Financial Liberalization (and Financial Crisis): Illustrative Numerical Estimation of the Costs and Benefits of Financial Liberalization

Financial liberalization is not new to Thailand. Following the sacking of its previous capital city, Ayutthaya in 1767 by the Burmeses, the strategically safer Bangkok was settled. By 1782 Bangkok had flourished and become an important regional trading centre. Bangkok become a regional centre for ship building and was soon building the largest ships outside of Europe. Trade brought Thailand into contact with Europe and various colonial powers, such as the Dutch, French and English, began to show political interest in Thailand. Thailand was able to avoid colonisation through establishing various trade treaties, such as the *Burney Treaty* in 1826 and the *Bowring Treaty* in 1855, with these colonial powers that both ensured independence but also incorporation into the then world economy.

The more recent experience of globalization has been financial liberalization and deregulation that has occurred through much of the world (including the developing countries) over the last two to three decades. This liberalization occurred within structural adjustment programs prepared for developing countries by the IMF and World Bank (Munasinghe, 1996). These packages of liberalization closely reflect the policies adopted by developed countries in removing trade barriers, reducing barrier to capital movements and investments, privatisation of state owned enterprises, reduction in government fiscal spending, deregulation of labour markets and a focus on global trade. The support for economic openness is now widespread (see Alesina, Spolaore & Wacziarg, 2000; Ben-David, 1993; Dollar, 1992; Edwards, 1992; Frankel & Romer, 1999; Sachs & Warner, 1995;). However, opposing views have recently resurfaced (see Rodrik, 1998; Harrison & Hanson, 1999; Rodrik & Rodriguez, 2000).

The costs and benefits of financial liberalization are not easy to estimate or quantify (McKibben, 1997, 1998) but are more readily identified.

7.4.1 Financial Benefits

The benefits of globalization, including financial liberalization (Wacziarg, 2001; Singh, 1999) include (but are not limited to):

1. Technological spillovers.
2. Transmission of knowledge.
3. Gains in efficient due to a wider scale of market interactions.
4. Improved government fiscl and monetary policies.
5. Productiveity increases.
6. Personal gains to currency traders which has grown to be valued at US$1.5 trillion per day.
7. Improved efficiency within the operation and regulation of financial markets.

7.4.2 Financial Costs

The major costs of globalization, including financial liberalization and crisis (Borland, Gregory & Sheehan, 2001b; Wacziarg, 2001; Arunsmithh, 1998; Siamwalla, 2000) have been identified as (but are not limited to):

1. An increase in divergence of earnings in various employment classifications.
2. An increase in polarisation of households between those with access to well-paid employment and those in poorly paid casual employment.
3. Pressure to decrease government size and market presence and government interference in resource allocation.
4. Loss of manufacturing jobs to cheaper overseas locations.
5. The floating of currencies and degradation of financial markets has left countries exposed to capital flight and unstable investments. The Asian financial crisis in 1997 was largely due to this financial deregulation and freedom from investment controls (Julian, 2000; Ryan, 2000).
6. Immediate increases in poverty levels and reduced incomes following the financial crisis.

Often though, these costs are not blamed on the process of financial liberalization but rather on insufficient liberalization and privatisation, too much corruption, etc. (Aziz, 1999).

Financial liberalization did not occur until the mid 1980s in Thailand (Dixon, 1996, 1999). Previously, there were strict controls over the value of the baht and capital movement. During the 1990s, foreign capital flooded Thailand's financial markets. The result was speculative spending, lending and borrowing creating macroeconomic imbalances aggravating the current account deficits and inflation. These poor outcomes occurred through poor management of both the domestic and the international financial systems (Kaosa-ard, 2000; APEC, 2000). However, despite these poor controls, the resultant financial crisis can be considered a consequence of financial liberalization. The Thai investment boom which occurred over the decade 1987–1996 was responsible for both the extraordinary growth rates experienced during that decade, and simultaneously responsible for the financial crisis in 1997 (Vines & Warr, 2000). Following the July 1997 crisis, a massive capital flight occurred leaving Thailand in debt to the value of US$89 billion (APEC, 2000).

7.5 Methodology, Numerical Estimates and Data Sources

The traditional method of welfare analysis in international issues is the use of consumer surplus theory involving either compensation valuation or equivalent valuation (Paavola & Bromley, 2002). However, this method will not be used in this instance. Three numerical estimates of the net benefits of financial liberalization will be made within this chapter using social choice theory. The social choice approach in this chapter is based on the requirements of measurability and comparability. *Measurability* refers to the social welfare possibility of putting real numbers to the object that provides meaningful information (about the state of social welfare). *Comparability* relates to the possibility of comparing the object (social welfare) at different times or in different states of the world.

The first measure of the net benefits of financial liberalization will be represented by movements within GDP. The second measure will be an adjusted measure of GDP. The final measure will incorporate non-welfaristic costs of financial liberalization previously not considered within previous estimates.

Whilst GDP was not designed to measure social welfare, it has assumed such a role (Hicks, 1940, 1946; Pigou, 1962, 1965). As an aggregate of economic activities it has assumed the authority as a proxy for social welfare:

$$SW = f(GDP) \tag{7.1}$$

where SW = social welfare and GDP = gross domestic product.

Within this grossly simplified illustrative cost–benefit analysis, the net benefits of globalization (financial liberalization) will be considered to be economic growth (measured in terms of GDP). As stated, this is an over simplification, but for the illustrative purposes of this paper, such a claim will be accepted (indeed, financial liberalization is considered to be the driving force of economic growth - see World Bank, 1999, 2001). No additional benefits will be attributed to financial liberalization as it is considered that all benefits are aggregated within this figure. The benefits that are captured within GDP include increased investment, technology, productivity, employment and higher incomes.

GDP (based on the Laspeyres method) has certain limitations as a measure of social welfare due to its construction and inherent limitations as a price index (see Clarke & Islam, 2000). However, some of these limitations can be overcome when it is adjusted to consider society as a system consisting of social, environmental and economic sub-systems (SEE) (Islam & Clarke, 2002; Dopfer, 1979; Clayton & Radcliffe, 1999).

Over the last 25 years, the Thai economy has experienced three distinct phases of economic growth. The first phase, 1975–1985, was steady growth. The second phase, 1986–1995, was accelerated growth, whilst the third phases, 1996–1999, is characterised by the financial crisis and apparent subsequent recovery (Clarke & Islam, 2003).

Achieving economic growth has been the major public policy priority for some time (NESDB, 1996, 2000) – often to the exclusion of other possible goals (Parnwell, 1996; Schmidt, 1996). All policies to plan or control the direction and outcome of economic growth in the early 1990s were abandoned (Phongpaichit ad Baker, 1995). In this regard, it has been very successful. Yet the cost of such success may have been that of environmental degradation, and growing inequality (see Figure 7.1).

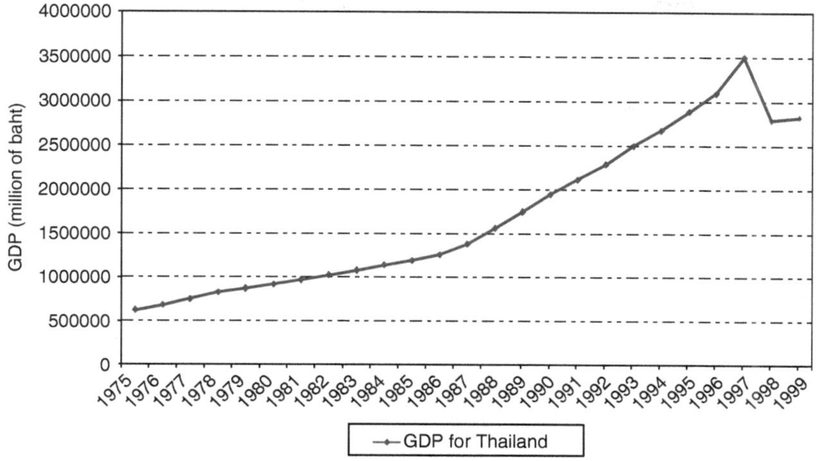

Fig. 7.1 GDP for Thailand, 1975–1999 (1988 prices – million of baht)

If these costs of economic growth are considered, the social welfare implications of financial liberalization can be reconsidered (Islam & Clarke, 2002; Clarke & Islam, 2003). Within this new illustration, eight adjustments are made to Thailand's GDP over a period of twenty five years, 1975–1999 (t) to estimate the costs of achieving economic growth. These SEE adjustments are income inequality (I), commuting (C), urbanisation (U) water pollution (W), air pollution (A), noise pollution (N), deforestation (D) and long-term environmental damage (L). The full calculation of these adjustments can be found in Clarke et al. (2002); Clarke & Islam (2004), where the relevant equation is:

$$\mathrm{NSW} = \mathrm{f}(\mathrm{B}\{\mathrm{GDP}\} - \mathrm{C}\{\mathrm{GDP}\}) \tag{7.2}$$

where NSW = net social welfare, B{GDP} = benefits of growth associated with a level of GDP and C{GDP} = costs of growth associated with a level of GDP

A noticeable difference between GDP and adjusted GDP exists (see Fig. 7.2). Not only are the absolute values different, there is a growing divergence between the two trend lines that suggests the net benefits of economic growth (globalization via financial liberalization) are reducing.

Having considered these additional costs of achieving economic growth, the most serious costs of the financial liberalization process experienced within Thailand were the absolute reduction in GDP following the financial crisis of July 1997. Sufficient evidence now exists that the crisis of July 1997 was caused by various factors attributed to financial deregulation (see Julian, 2000; Ryan, 2000). The most visible short-term cost of financial liberalization within Thailand (and the region) occurred in 1997. The impact of the 1997 financial crisis has been high. The costs of this crisis were obvious and not simply contained to multi-national corporations. Within southeast Asia, there was an immediate and large fall in the standard of

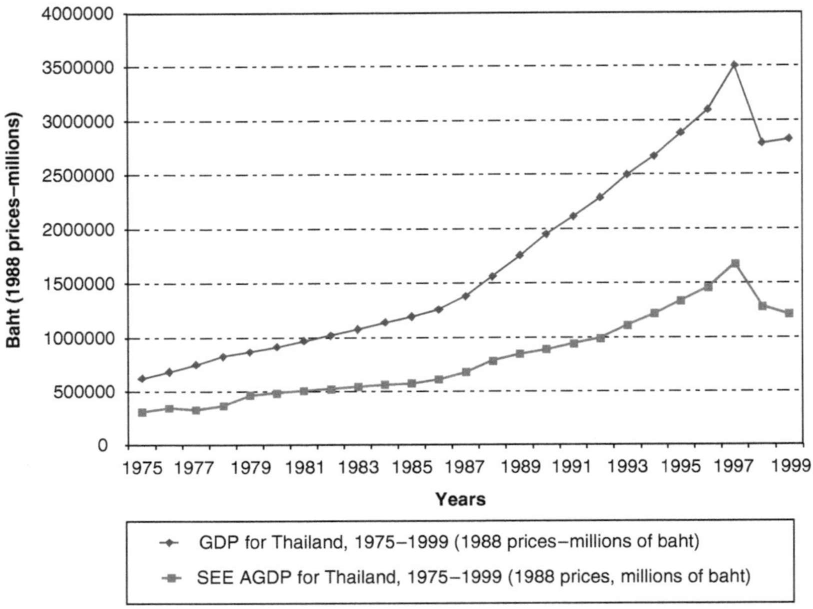

Fig. 7.2 Comparison of GDP and adjusted GDP for Thailand, 1975–1999 (1988 prices – millions of baht)

living of all sectors of society (Barro, 1997; McKibben, 1998; Aziz, Aziz, & Thorbecke, 2001; Kakwani and Pothong, 2000). The average reduction in real income across Thailand was over 21% in 1998 and up to 28% in rural Thailand (Kakwani & Pothong, 2000; also see Kaosa-ard, 2000). Those living under the poverty line increase by 1.5 million people, 7.9–9.4 million and nearly one million extra people were classified as ultra poor (Kakwani, 1999). The level of this full in real income is not dissimilar to those experienced in other countries (see Aziz et al., 2001). However, this initial full has not continued in the long-term and the levels of real income have begun to recover (Kakwani & Pothong, 2000).

Other costs of financial liberalization may also be considered. Often these short term costs result from the adjustment of capital movements (see, for example, Webber & Weller (2002) for a sectoral analysis of the textile industry of these adjustment costs in Australia). Further, these short term adjustment costs (such as factory closures and unemployment) can cause a loss in the political will for further trade liberalization required to for the benefits to become apparent (McKibben, 1997, 1998). These costs are not readily captured within GDP but it might be assumed that their social welfare impact might equal two percent of GDP (see Fig. 7.3):

$$\text{NSWG} = \text{f}[\text{B}\{\text{ADP(G\&FC)}\} - \text{C}\{\text{AGDP(G\&FC)}\}] \tag{7.3}$$

where NSWG is thenet benefits of economic growth adjusted for SEE adjustments and financial liberalization and financial crisis; B = benefits of growth associated with a level of GDP adjusted for SEE adjustments and financial liberalization and

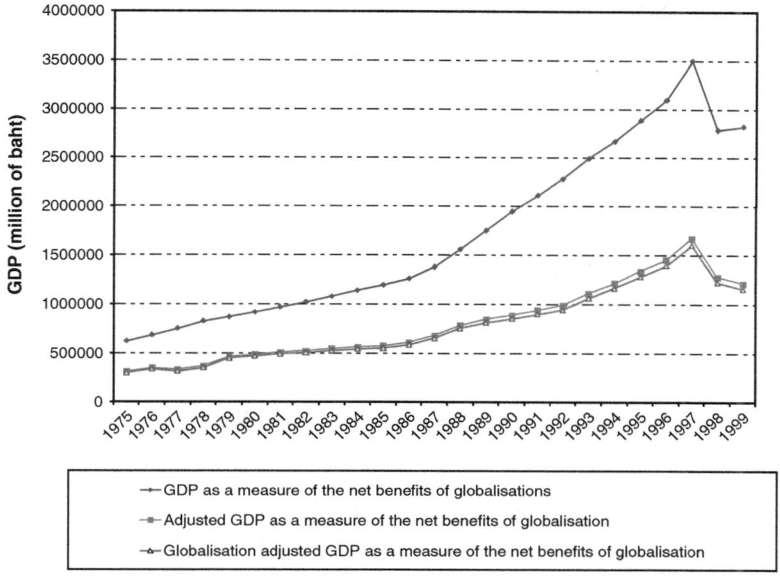

Fig. 7.3 Comparison of GDP, Adjusted GDP and Financial Liberalization adjusted GDP for Thailand, 1975–1999 (1988 prices – millions of baht)

financial crisis; C = costs of growth associated with a level of GDP adjusted for SEE adjustments and financial liberalization and financial crisis; and G&FC is the process of globalization and financial liberalization.

Following the financial crisis, GDP per capita fell by 2.1% in 1996, 9.6% in 1997 and only increased by 1% in 1998. If this fall in GDP reflects the direct costs of financial liberalization – or more general globalization process – such as the fall in incomes, increases in poverty, then the additional social welfare costs of the globalization of financial liberalziation must also be added to estimate the total costs. If we accept the above assumption that these indirect costs can be assumed to be 2% of GDP then the total costs of financial liberalization were 4.1% in 1996, 11.6% in 1999 and 1% in 1998. These are significant costs in terms of social welfare.

7.6 Welfare Implications of Economic Growth

Within this illustrative framework, an interesting outcome is observed. The benefits of financial liberalization all occurred in one specific time frame (1975–1995), whilst the costs occurred in a separate time frame (1996–1999). The analysis of social welfare within this illustration must consider intergeneration issues. Whilst the overall benefits outweigh the costs, are the benefits of the pass enough to outweigh the costs suffered in the recent short-term?. A social discount rate is generally applied to the future, yet the welfare analysis of economic growth also requires a social discount rate of the past, specifically 1975–1995 (see Sen, 1970, 1982; also see Atkinson, 1983; Kanbur, 1987). If a social discount rate of zero is selected (Islam & Clarke, 2002; Clarke & Islam, 2003), the analysis of these costs and benefits suggests that the previous benefits must be given equal value to current costs, suggesting then that social welfare increases caused by financial liberalization has been positive for Thailand.

To fully understand the welfare implication of economic growth, further issues of cost–benefits analysis, such as discounting, intergenerational equity, valuation of inputs and outputs (including shadow pricing), and incorporation of both tangible and intangible costs and benefits need to be included in future applied empirical work.

It is important to note that the welfare implication of the costs and benefits of financial liberalization in Thailand should include the intermporal nature of the experience of the costs and benefits. The costs are short-term but give way to longer term benefits. The needs of the present generation need to be considered in light of the needs of future generations. (This is an unusual example of the costs being borne in the present). How the separate costs and benefits are distributed must also be considered. Indeed, the financial crisis appeared to hurt the poorest in Thailand more so than other income groups (Kakwani & Pothong, 2000). Such an outcome raises issues of justice.

Developing countries will continue to further incorporate their domestic economies into the rise of the global economy as part of the process of financial liberalization. The welfare impact of the rise of financial liberalization must therefore be considered when discussing the desirability of economic growth.

The global market is both efficiency based and equity-neutral. Therefore efficient outcomes are considered to be Pareto optimal in an equity sense as well. There are, for example, arguments for the casualisation of labour and the divergence of labour rates between well-paid employment and poorly paid casual labour in developed countries (Borland, Gregory & Sheehan, 2001a). These new characteristics of the labour market in developed countries have increasingly come to more closely reflect the labour conditions (insecurity, high wage differentials, causal employment) typical of developing countries such as Thailand. Within developing countries, in which dualistic economies exist, these characteristics might be exacerbated by the increasing impact of financial liberalization. In this regard, the widening gap between high income and low income earners in Australia has increased (Borland, 1998), as is the case of the increase in wage income inequality in Thailand (Clarke, 2001a, 2001b).

Clearly, the rise of the global economy will affect the social welfare within Thailand. Thailand has recognised the importance of improving the performance, for example, of the knowledge economy in achieving "quality growth" in the future (Ministry of Finance, 2001). An illustrative estimation and quantification of some of the selected costs and benefits of financial liberalization allows greater insight, in terms of the above issues, into the social welfare impact of financial liberalization of Thailand.

The results of this illustrative cost–benefit analysis appear intuitively correct and plausible. It is reasonable to assume that the benefits of financial liberalization were significant in increasing the social welfare within Thailand. Likewise, the resultant financial crisis had serious negative implications for the Thai economy, particularly those on low incomes (Kakwani & Pothong, 2000; Kaosa-ard, 2000).

7.7 Conclusions

Comparably little work has been undertaken on exploring the social welfare implications of financial liberalization, in terms of its costs and benefits. This chapter has set out a conceptual framework in which the welfare processes, outcomes and implications of financial liberalization can be analysed. This chapter developed an illustrative application of this framework in which estimates of the costs and benefits of financial liberalization and financial crisis were made. The analytical framework and numerical calculation are based on the concepts and methods of welfare economics such as welfare criteria, cost–benefit analysis, welfare measurement and social choice theory. It was shown that whilst the financial crisis had a dramatic negative impact on average income levels, the processes of financial liberalization and globalization that preceded the crisis, also had negative impacts on the social welfare levels of Thailand. Conventional measures of social welfare, such as Gross Domestic Product or economic growth provide misleading information on social welfare movements. By adjusting this measure for the net benefits of financial liberalization, a more intuitively correct measure of social welfare was possible. This chapter developed a time series, 1975–1999, which estimated a new adjusted-GDP measure of social welfare. It showed stark differences exist between unadjusted GDP measures of social welfare and financial liberalization adjusted GDP measures of social welfare over this time period. It is expected that the results in this exercise would be replicated in other Asian countries.

Appendix 1 General Data[1]

See Tables 7.1–7.3

Table 7.1 Thai GDP (millions of baht)

Year	GDP
1975	621,555
1976	680,778
1977	750,054
1978	824,706
1979	867,797
1980	913,768

(continued)

[1]Data drawn from previous work of the authors (see Clarke, M. and Islam, S. (2004), *Economic Growth and Social Welfare: Operationalising Normative Social Choice Theory*, North Holland, Amsterdam.

Table 7.1 (continued)

Year	GDP
1981	967,374
1982	1,020,084
1983	1,075,922
1984	1,138,329
1985	1,191,089
1986	1,256,538
1987	1,377,026
1988	1,559,804
1989	1,750,228
1990	1,946,119
1991	2,111,740
1992	2,282,995
1993	2,494,748
1994	2,669,573
1995	2,884,495
1996	3,095,336
1997	3,502,012
1998	2,787,395
1999	2,823,416

Source: World Bank (2001).

Table 7.2 Adjusted GDP: adjustments are: income inequality (I), commuting (C), urbanisation (U) water pollution (W), air pollution (A), noise pollution (N), deforestation (D) and long-term environmental damage (L)

Year	GDP	Inequality	GDO x inequality	Air	Water	Noise	Deforestation
1975	621,555	0.3319	415,261	4,117	4,067	6,216	62,013
1976	680,778	0.3362	451,934	4,509	4,454	6,808	58,844
1977	750,054	0.3404	494,736	4,913	4,956	7,501	113,162
1978	824,706	0.3447	540,471	5,516	5,362	8,247	113,162
1979	867,797	0.3489	565,022	5,759	5,503	8,678	33,949
1980	913,768	0.3532	591,071	6,046	6,143	9,138	33,949
1981	967,374	0.3574	621,635	6,069	6,854	9,674	33,949
1982	1,020,084	0.3699	642,775	6,302	7,151	10,201	33,949
1983	1,075,922	0.3824	664,532	6,774	7,583	10,759	30,327
1984	1,138,329	0.3948	688,871	7,382	8,336	11,383	30,327
1985	1,191,089	0.4073	705,935	7,930	8,033	11,911	29,875
1986	1,256,538	0.4198	729,043	8,030	8,364	12,565	11,316
1987	1,377,026	0.4151	805,423	9,299	8,833	13,770	11,316
1988	1,559,804	0.4104	919,660	10,508	10,213	15,598	11,316
1989	1,750,228	0.4313	995,442	12,146	11,533	17,502	11,316
1990	1,946,119	0.4521	1,066,278	14,244	12,145	19,461	25,348
1991	2,111,740	0.4639	1,132,104	16,144	13,528	21,117	25,348
1992	2,282,995	0.4757	1,196,974	17,521	14,443	22,830	24,896
1993	2,494,748	0.4679	1,327,580	19,479	15,060	24,947	25,348
1994	2,669,573	0.4600	1,441,569	21,880	16,733	26,696	24,896
1995	2,884,495	0.4527	1,578,828	24,307	18,422	28,845	25,348
1996	3,095,336	0.4453	1,716,983	27,105	19,493	30,953	24,896
1997	3,502,012	0.4441	1,946,944	29,257	20,033	30,520	25,348
1998	2,787,395	0.4428	1,553,137	31,657	18,296	27,874	24,896
1999	2,823,416	0.4757	1,480,317	34,056	18,533	28,234	4,526

Year	Long term	Urbanisation	Commuting	Total of adjustments	GDP – Total adjustments
1975	4,960	18,084	3,066	102,523	312,738
1976	5,965	20,164	3,466	104,210	347,724
1977	6,932	22,255	3,829	163,548	331,187
1978	13,575	24,634	3,939	174,435	366,036
1979	16,893	25,712	3,787	100,281	464,742
1980	20,087	27,382	3,560	106,305	484,766
1981	23,175	29,172	4,704	113,597	508,037
1982	26,170	31,258	5,441	120,472	522,304
1983	28,255	30,869	6,171	120,738	543,795
1984	30,344	32,420	7,192	127,384	561,487
1985	32,428	33,843	9,141	133,161	572,773
1986	34,498	35,177	9,710	119,660	609,383
1987	35,653	37,963	10,012	126,846	678,576
1988	37,762	41,374	10,164	136,935	782,725
1989	38,981	48,611	9,133	149,222	846,220
1990	41,914	53,538	10,218	176,868	889,411
1991	44,848	62,459	9,947	193,391	938,713
1992	47,047	70,775	10,647	208,159	988,815
1993	49,194	70,927	11,497	216,452	1,111,128
1994	51,269	70,560	12,107	224,141	1,217,428
1995	53,460	81,507	12,406	244,295	1,334,533
1996	56,206	90,561	13,289	262,503	1,454,480
1997	58,210	93,200	17,099	273,667	1,673,277
1998	60,469	87,740	22,264	273,196	1,279,941
1999	62,727	98,231	22,495	268,802	1,211,515

Source: Authors' own calculation.

Table 7.3 GDP, adjusted GDP and adjusted GDP −2% of GDP

Year	GDP	Inequality	Adjusted	Air	Water	Noise	Deforestation
1975	621,555	0.332	415,261	4,117	4,067	6,216	62,013
1976	680,778	0.336	451,934	4,509	4,454	6,808	58,844
1977	750,054	0.340	494,736	4,913	4,956	7,501	113,162
1978	824,706	0.345	540,471	5,516	5,362	8,247	113,162
1979	867,797	0.349	565,022	5,759	5,503	8,678	33,949
1980	913,768	0.353	591,071	6,046	6,143	9,138	33,949
1981	967,374	0.357	621,635	6,069	6,854	9,674	33,949
1982	1,020,084	0.370	642,775	6,302	7,151	10,201	33,949
1983	1,075,922	0.382	664,532	6,774	7,583	10,759	30,327
1984	1,138,329	0.395	688,871	7,382	8,336	11,383	30,327
1985	1,191,089	0.407	705,935	7,930	8,033	11,911	29,875
1986	1,256,538	0.420	729,043	8,030	8,364	12,565	11,316
1987	1,377,026	0.415	805,423	9,299	8,833	13,770	11,316
1988	1,559,804	0.410	919,660	10,508	10,213	15,598	11,316
1989	1,750,228	0.431	995,442	12,146	11,533	17,502	11,316

(continued)

Table 7.3 (continued)

Year	GDP	Inequality	Adjusted	Air	Water	Noise	Deforestation
1990	1,946,119	0.452	1,066,278	14,244	12,145	19,461	25,348
1991	2,111,740	0.464	1,132,104	16,144	13,528	21,117	25,348
1992	2,282,995	0.476	1,196,974	17,521	14,443	22,830	24,896
1993	2,494,748	0.468	1,327,580	19,479	15,060	24,947	25,348
1994	2,669,573	0.460	1,441,569	21,880	16,733	26,696	24,896
1995	2,884,495	0.453	1,578,828	24,307	18,422	28,845	25,348
1996	3,095,336	0.445	1,716,983	27,105	19,493	30,953	24,896
1997	3,502,012	0.444	1,946,944	29,257	20,033	30,520	25,348
1998	2,787,395	0.443	1,553,137	31,657	18,296	27,874	24,896
1999	2,823,416	0.476	1,480,317	34,056	18,533	28,234	4,526

Year	Long term	Urbanisation	Commuting	Total	Adjusted GDP	2% of GDP	Adjusted GDP (2% of GDP)
1975	4,960	18,084	3,066	102,523	312,738	12,431	300,307
1976	5,965	20,164	3,466	104,210	347,724	13,616	334,109
1977	6,932	22,255	3,829	163,548	331,187	15,001	316,186
1978	13,575	24,634	3,939	174,435	366,036	16,494	349,542
1979	16,893	25,712	3,787	100,281	464,742	17,356	447,386
1980	20,087	27,382	3,560	106,305	484,766	18,275	466,490
1981	23175	29,172	4,704	113,597	508,037	19,347	488,690
1982	26170	31,258	5,441	120,472	522,304	20,402	501,902
1983	28,255	30,869	6,171	120,738	543,795	21,518	522,276
1984	30,344	32,420	7,192	127,384	561,487	22,767	538,721
1985	32,428	33,843	9,141	133,161	572,773	23,822	548,952
1986	34,498	35,177	9,710	119,660	609,383	25,131	584,252
1987	35,653	37,963	10,012	126,846	678,576	27,541	651,036
1988	37,762	41,374	10,164	136,935	782,725	31,196	751,529
1989	38,981	48,611	9,133	149,222	846,220	35,005	811,215
1990	41,914	53,538	10,218	176,868	889,411	38,922	850,488
1991	44,848	62,459	9,947	193,391	938,713	42,235	896,478
1992	47,047	70,775	10,647	208,159	988,815	45,660	943,155
1993	49194	70927	11497	216452	1111128	49895	1,061,233
1994	51,269	70,560	12,107	224,141	1,217,428	53,391	1,164,037
1995	53,460	81,507	12,406	244,295	1,334,533	57,690	1,276,843
1996	56,206	90,561	13,289	262,503	1,454,480	61,907	1,392,574
1997	58,210	93,200	17,099	273,667	1,673,277	70,040	1,603,236
1998	60,469	87,740	22,264	273,196	1,279,941	55,748	1,224,193
1999	62,727	98,231	22,495	268,802	1,211,515	56,468	1,155,047

Source: Authors'own calculation.

Appendix 2 Cost Benefit Data

See Tables 7.4–7.12

Table 7.4 Calculation of the net costs of commuting

Year	Number of cars registered in Bangkok	Cost per car (in 1988 US dollars prices)	Exchange Rate (baht per US$)	Deflator for 1988 prices	Costs of Commuting (1988 prices, millions of baht)
1975	334,804	219	20.4	48.8	−3,066
1976	394,804	219	20.4	50.9	−3,466
1977	461,205	219	20.4	53.8	−3,829
1978	522,316	219	20.39	59.2	−3,939
1979	545,249	219	20.425	64.4	−3,787
1980	571,267	219	20.63	72.5	−3,560
1981	733,920	219	23	78.6	−4,704
1982	891,241	219	23	82.5	−5,441
1983	1,048,562	219	23	85.6	−6,171
1984	1,205,883	219	23.64	86.8	−7,192
1985	1,363,204	219	27.16	88.7	−9,141
1986	1520526	219	26.3	90.2	−9,710
1987	1,677,847	219	25.72	94.4	−10,012
1988	1,835,169	219	25.29	100	−10,164
1989	1,721,586	219	25.7	106.1	−9,133
1990	2,045,814	219	25.59	112.2	−10,218
1991	2,112,518	219	25.52	118.7	−9,947
1992	2,373,288	219	25.4	124	−10,647
1993	2,656,107	219	25.32	128.1	−11,497
1994	2,963,043	219	25.15	134.8	−12,107
1995	3,241,681	219	24.92	142.6	−12,406
1996	3,549,082	219	25.34	148.2	−13,289
1997	3,849,082	219	31.36	154.6	−17,099
1998	4,149,082	219	41.36	168.8	−22,264
1999	4,449,082	219	37.84	163.9	−22,495

Source: NSO (various issues), Quarterly Bulletin of Statistics, Tanaborrboon (1990) and authors' own calculations.

CC = NRC(219.XR)

where CC = Cost of commuting; NRC = Number of registered cars in Bangkok and XR = Exchange rate

Table 7.5 Calculation of the net costs of urbanisation

Year	Average income for Bangkok Residents per capita (1988 prices)	Cost of Air Pollution for Bangkok Residents (8% of average income)	Cost of Water Pollution for Bangkok Residents (10% of average income)	Bangkok Population	Costs of Urbanisation (1988 prices, millions of baht)
1975	16,289	1,303	1,629	6,167,883	18,084
1976	17,502	1,400	1,750	6,400,483	20,164
1977	18,608	1,489	1,861	6,644,460	22,255
1978	20,042	1,603	2,004	6,828,375	24,634
1979	20,368	1,629	2,037	7,013,117	25,712
1980	21,047	1,684	2,105	7,227,779	27,382
1981	21,710	1,737	2,171	7465,007	29,172
1982	22,591	1,807	2,259	7,686,871	31,258
1983	23,368	1,869	2,337	7,338,883	30,869
1984	23,831	1,906	2,383	7,557,852	32,420
1985	23,982	1,919	2,398	7,839,816	33,843
1986	24,333	1,947	2,433	8,031,374	35,177
1987	25,435	2,035	2,544	8,292,009	37,963
1988	27,012	2,161	2,701	8,509,386	41,374
1989	30,941	2,475	3,094	8,728,335	48,611
1990	34,834	2,787	3,483	8,538,610	53,538
1991	39,878	3,190	3,988	87,01374	62,459
1992	45,397	3,632	4,540	8,661,228	70,775
1993	44,934	3,595	4,493	8,769,341	70,927
1994	44,288	3,543	4,429	8,851,180	70,560
1995	50,898	4,072	5,090	8,896,506	81,507
1996	55,846	4,468	5,585	9,009,004	90,561
1997	56,806	4,544	5,681	9,114,852	93,200
1998	52,742	4,219	5,274	9,242,038	87,740
1999	58,624	4,690	5,862	9,308,924	98,231

Source: NSO (various issues), Quarterly Bulletin of Statistics and authors' own calculations.
CU = BY(0.08) + BY(0.1)
where CU = cost of urbanization and BY = average income for Bangkok residents

Table 7.6 Calculation of the net costs of air pollution

Year	Total CO and CO_2 for Bangkok (in kilotons)	Cost for abatement (0.03335 baht per kg, 1988 prices)	Net Costs of Air Pollution caused by CO and CO_2 (1988 prices, millions of baht)	Total NO Bangkok (in kiloton)	Cost for abatement (2.84 baht per kg, 1988 prices)	Net Costs of Air Pollution caused by NOX (1988 prices, millions of baht)
1975	52,588.90	0.03335	1,753.84	220.34	2.84	625.78
1976	57,596.10	0.03335	1,920.83	241.32	2.84	685.37
1977	62,740.61	0.03335	2,092.40	263.61	2.84	750.52
1978	67,288.52	0.03335	2,244.07	282.74	2.84	804.98
1979	70,795.29	0.03335	2,361.02	289.62	2.84	824.56
1980	70,687.81	0.03335	2,357.44	290.99	2.84	828.45
1981	72,879.03	0.03335	2,430.52	300.89	2.84	856.65
1982	85,901.40	0.03335	2,531.31	311.59	2.84	887.11
1983	80,062.09	0.03335	2,670.07	336.40	2.84	957.76
1984	85,705.13	0.03335	2,858.27	370.01	2.84	1,053.44
1985	9,0031.02	0.03335	3,002.53	389.90	2.84	1,101.52
1986	92,631.53	0.03335	3,089.26	401.66	2.84	1,143.54
1987	103,813.57	0.03335	3,462.18	449.80	2.84	1,280.59
1988	115,374.01	0.03335	3,847.72	502.97	2.84	1,431.97
1989	133,749.06	0.03335	4,460.53	586.23	2.84	1,669.03
1990	151,441.91	0.03335	5,050.59	664.32	2.84	1,891.35
1991	165,832.16	0.03335	5,530.50	717.95	2.84	2,044.04
1992	180,329.54	0.03335	6,013.99	7,71.41	2.84	2,196.25
1993	201,600.08	0.03335	6,723.36	851.60	2.84	2,424.55
1994	225,034.04	0.03335	7,504.89	952.12	2.84	2,710.74
1995	249,357.61	0.03335	8,316.08	1,060.96	2.84	3,020.60
1996	274,150.06	0.03335	9,142.90	1,162.48	2.84	3,309.63
1997	373,717.54	0.03335	12,463.48	1,565.86	2.84	4,447.06
1998	404,374.21	0.03335	13,485.88	1,694.32	2.84	4,811.86
1999	435,018.29	0.03335	14,507.86	1,822.71	2.84	5,176.51

(*continued*)

Table 7.6 (continued)

Year	Total SOX for Bangkok (in kilotons)	Cost for abatement (7.4 baht per kg, 1988 prices)	Net Costs of Air Pollution caused by SOX (1988 prices, millions of baht)	Total SPM Bangkok (in kilotons)	Cost for abatement (4.15 baht per kg, 1988 prices)	Net Costs of Air Pollution caused by SPM (1988 prices, millions of baht))	Total Cost of Air Pollution (1988 prices, millions of baht)
1975	267.53	7.4	1,679.74	13.89	4.15	57.64	4,117.00
1976	248.60	7.4	1,839.67	15.21	4.15	63.13	4,509.00
1977	270.80	7.4	2,004.54	15.913	4.15	66.02	4,913.47
1978	321.65	7.4	2,380.95	20.649	4.15	85.67	5,515.67
1979	336.24	7.4	2,488.93	20.309	4.15	84.25	5,758.77
1980	371.99	7.4	2,753.63	25.761	4.15	106.87	6,046.39
1981	362.63	7.4	2,684.33	23.522	4.15	97.58	6,069.08
1982	376.12	7.4	2,784.16	23.846	4.15	98.93	6,301.50
1983	409.70	7.4	3,032.74	27.250	4.15	113.05	6,773.62
1984	451.99	7.4	3,345.80	30.033	4.15	124.60	7,382.10
1985	497.66	7.4	3,683.87	34.328	4.15	142.41	7,930.33
1986	494.36	7.4	3,659.41	33.223	4.15	137.83	8,030.04
1987	591.84	7.4	4,381.01	42.336	4.15	175.63	9,299.42
1988	678.52	7.4	5,022.66	49.658	4.15	206.01	10,508.37
1989	781.89	7.4	5,787.84	55.216	4.15	229.07	12,146.48
1990	946.97	7.4	7,009.82	70.335	4.15	291.79	14,243.55
1991	1,109.27	7.4	8,211.21	86.386	4.15	358.38	16,144.13
1992	1,205.13	7.4	8,920.78	93.994	4.15	389.94	17,520.97
1993	1,337.66	7.4	9901.81	103.563	4.15	429.64	19,479.37
1994	1,510.89	7.4	11,184.15	115.772	4.15	480.29	21880.07
1995	1,680.79	7.4	12,441.75	127.502	4.15	528.95	24,307.39
1996	1,897.28	7.4	14,055.29	146.490	4.15	607.73	27,104.56
1997	1,613.50	7.4	11,936.86	98.70	4.15	409.60	29,257.00
1998	1,745.41	7.4	12,916.06	106.80	4.15	443.20	31,657.00
1999	1,852.65	7.4	13,894.85	114.90	4.15	476.78	34,056.00

Source: Department of Energy Development and Promotion, Agotini and Col (1992 cited in Guenno and Tiezzo 1998) and authors' own calculations.
$AP = cCO_2 + cCO + cNOX + cSOX + cSPM$
where AP = Air Pollution
cCO2 = cost of carbon dioxide (0.03335 baht per kg)
cCO = cost of carbon monoxide (0.03335 baht per kg)
cNOX = cost of nitrogen monoxide (2.84 baht per kg)
cSOX = cost of ulphur monoxide (7.4 baht per kg)
cSPM = cost of suspended particulate matters (4.15 baht per kg)

Table 7.7 Calculation of the net costs of water pollution

Year	Total BOD for the Food Industry (in tons)	Total BOD for Beverage Industry (in tons)	Total BOD for the Textiles Industry (in tons)	Total BOD for Paper Industry (in tons)	Total BOD for the Chemical Industry (in tons)	Total BOD for All Industries (in tons)
1975	126,252	100,300	3,507	3,039	701	233,800
1976	141,084	112,083	3,919	3,396	784	261,266
1977	159,469	126,692	4,436	3,855	1,081	295,534
1978	171,874	138,440	5,133	4,741	1,340	321,427
1979	161,920	153,814	6,051	6,684	1,363	329,832
1980	169,518	185,059	5,826	9,671	1,371	371,445
1981	199,583	182,531	6,099	9,638	1,505	399,356
1982	229,250	188,745	6,284	9,567	1,498	435,343
1983	221,811	225,426	6,720	10,067	1,609	465,633
1984	249,194	246,130	7,090	10,539	1,842	514,795
1985	260,482	212,677	7,401	10,593	1,924	493,076
1986	288,786	203,468	8,408	11,463	2,138	514,263
1987	282,309	226,943	9,814	13,064	2,436	544,566
1988	336,041	270,772	11,466	13,902	2,739	634,920
1989	379,852	311,294	12,840	15,013	2,909	721,909
1990	37,7931	350,981	13,645	18,104	3,262	763,923
1991	421,510	395,014	15,003	20,705	3,423	855,655
1992	453,417	419,004	16,504	23,165	3,715	915,806
1993	446,363	462,804	16,516	26,989	4,013	956,685
1994	486,078	525,849	17,000	32,877	4,4,12	1,066,215
1995	511,264	607,720	17,702	36,280	5,233	1,178,198
1996	539,619	644,207	17,263	41,868	5,707	1,248,663
1997	547,601.9	676,146.9	16,710.86	39,848.96	5,141.802	1,285450
1998	500,121.2	617,520.5	15,261.91	36,393.79	4,695.973	1,173,973
1999	506,919.3	625,914.4	15,469.37	36,888.49	4,759.805	1,189,951

(*continued*)

Table 7.7 (continued)

Year	Cost for abatement (7.5 baht per kg, 1988 prices)	Net Costs of Water Pollution caused All Industries (1988 prices, millions of baht)	Total BOD for Municipal Population (in tons)	Cost for abatement (7.5 baht per kg, 1988 prices)	Net Costs of Water Pollution by Municipal Population (1988 prices, millions of baht)	Total Costs caused by Water Pollution (1988 prices, millions of baht)
1975	7.5	1,753,502	37,333	7.5	279,998	4,067
1976	7.5	1,959,498	35,667	7.5	267,502	4,454
1977	7.5	2,216,505	34,897	7.5	261,728	4,956
1978	7.5	2,410,703	36,019	7.5	270,143	5,362
1979	7.5	2,473,740	37,012	7.5	277,590	5,503
1980	7.5	2,785,838	38,088	7.5	285,660	6,143
1981	7.5	2,995,170	39,593	7.5	296,948	6,854
1982	7.5	3,265,073	41,390	7.5	310,425	7,151
1983	7.5	3,492,248	39,919	7.5	299,393	7,583
1984	7.5	3,860,963	40,918	7.5	306,885	8,336
1985	7.5	3,698,070	42,462	7.5	318,465	8,033
1986	7.5	3,856,973	43,390	7.5	325,425	8,364
1987	7.5	4,084,245	44,316	7.5	332,370	8,833
1988	7.5	4,761,900	45,966	7.5	344,745	10,213
1989	7.5	5,414,318	46,933	7.5	351,998	11,533
1990	7.5	5,729,423	45,740	7.5	343,050	12,145
1991	7.5	6,417,413	46,204	7.5	346,530	13,528
1992	7.5	6,868,545	47,057	7.5	352,928	14,443
1993	7.5	7,175,138	47,325	7.5	354,938	15,060
1994	7.5	7,996,613	49,317	7.5	369,878	16,733
1995	7.5	8,836,485	49,947	7.5	374,603	18,422
1996	7.5	9,364,973	50,858	7.5	381,435	19,493
1997	7.5	9,640,878	50,083	7.5	375,622	20,033
1998	7.5	8,804,950	45,740	7.5	343,050	18,296
1999	7.5	8,924,635	45,582	7.5	341,865	18,533

Source: Phansawas et al. (1987), TESCO (1993), Department of Industrial Works (1986) and authors' own calculations.

$WP = (7.5 \times IP) + (7.5 \times 4.6 \times MP)$

where WP = Cost of water pollution

IP = Industrial pollution = (FI + DI + PI + CI + TI)

FI = Food industry BOD

DI = Drink industry BOD

PI = Paper industry BOD

CI = Chemical industry BOD

TI = Textile industry BOD

MP = Municipal population BOD × 4.6 kg per years

Table 7.8 Calculation of the net costs of noise pollution

Year	Gross Domestic Product (1988 prices, millions of baht)	Ratio of Benefits (10%)	Costs of Noise Pollution (1988 prices, millions of baht)
1975	621,555.33	0.10	6,216
1976	680,778	0.10	6,808
1977	750,053.9	0.10	7,501
1978	824,706.08	0.10	8,247
1979	867,796.58	0.10	8,678
1980	913,768.28	0.10	9,138
1981	967,374.05	0.10	9,674
1982	1,020,083.64	0.10	10,201
1983	1,075,921.73	0.10	10,759
1984	1,138,329.49	0.10	11,383
1985	1,191,089.06	0.10	11,911
1986	1,256,537.69	0.10	12,565
1987	1,377,026.48	0.10	13,770
1988	1,559,804	0.10	15,598
1989	1,750,228.09	0.10	17,502
1990	1,946,118.54	0.10	19,461
1991	2,111,739.68	0.10	21,117
1992	2,282,995.16	0.10	22,830
1993	2,494,747.85	0.10	24,947
1994	2,669,572.7	0.10	26,696
1995	2,884,495.09	0.10	28,845
1996	3,095,336.03	0.10	30,953
1997	3,502,012.29	0.10	30,520
1998	2,787,395.14	0.10	27,874
1999	2,823,416.11	0.10	28,234

Source: NSO (various issues), Quarterly Bulletin of Statistics and authors' own calculations.
NP = GDP(0.01)
where NP = Cost of noise pollution and GDP = Gross domestic product

Table 7.9 Calculation of the net costs of deforestation

Year	Amount of Thai forests as a percentage of Total Land	Amount of Thai forests in Hectares	Amount of Deforestation from previous period	Cost of Deforestation per hectare (1988 prices)	Total Cost of Deforestation (1988 prices, millions of baht)
1975	40.3	2,128,878,630	69,991,930	886	62,013
1976	39	2,058,886,700	66,415,700	886	58,844
1977	36.5	1,992,471,000	127,722,500	886	113,162
1978	34	1,864,748,500	127,722,500	886	113,162
1979	33.25	1,737,026,000	38,316,750	886	33,949
1980	32.5	1,698,709,250	38,316,750	886	33,949
1981	31.75	1,660,392,500	38,316,750	886	33,949
1982	31	1,622,075,750	38,316,750	886	33,949
1983	30.33	1,583,759,000	34,229,630	886	30,327
1984	29.66	1,549,529,370	34,229,630	886	30,327
1985	29	1,515,299,740	33,718,740	886	29,875
1986	28.75	1,481,581,000	12,772,250	886	11,316
1987	28.5	1,468,808,750	12,772,250	886	11,316
1988	28.25	1,456,036,500	12,772,250	886	11,316
1989	28	1,443,264,250	12,772,250	886	11,316
1990	27.44	1,430,492,000	28,609,840	886	25,348
1991	26.88	1,401,882,160	28,609,840	886	25,348
1992	26.33	1,373,272,320	28,098,950	886	24,896
1993	25.77	1,345,173,370	28,609,840	886	25,348
1994	25.22	1,316,563,530	28,098,950	886	24,896
1995	24.66	1,288,464,580	28,609,840	886	25,348
1996	24.11	1,259,854,740	28,098,950	886	24,896
1997	23.55	1,231,755,790	28,609,840	886	25,348
1998	23	1,203,145,950	28,098,950	886	24,896
1999	22.9	1,175,047,000	5,108,900	886	4,526

Source: Phongpaichit and Baker (1995), Trebuil (1993), Bello (1997), Dixon (1999), Panayotou and Parasuk (1990) and authors' own calculations.

$D = DF(886)$

Where D = Cost of deforestation and DF = Hectares of deforestation

Table 7.10 Calculation of the net costs of long-term environmental damage

Year	Forest Area Loss (in rai)	Carbon released due to Forest Loss (in tons)	Wet Rice Paddy Farming (in rai)	Methane Emissions due to Wet Rice Paddy Farming (in tons)	Carbon equivalents released due to Wet Rice Paddy Farming (in tons)
1975	5,311,477	209,059,750	53,254,959	490,797	9,189,440
1976	1,076,217	42,359,888	10,790,475	99,445	1,861,973
1977	7,436,600	292,704,576	71,497,303	658,919	12,336,750
1978	7,059,025	277,843,224	73,270,474	675,261	12,642,708
1979	3,122,018	122,882,628	72,957,034	671,450	12,571,370
1980	2,974,247	117,066,362	73,562,985	677,956	12,693,181
1981	2,836,310	111,637,162	73,523,312	677,591	12,686,335
1982	2,707,425	106,564,248	73,222,199	674,816	12,634,379
1983	1,607,634	63,276,474	73,634,692	678,617	12,705,554
1984	1,571,903	61,870,102	73,909,386	681,149	12,752,952
1985	1,537,189	60,503,759	73,902,435	681,085	12,751,752
1986	1,503,439	59,175,359	74,233,442	684,135	12,808,867
1987	360,683	14,196,483	72,169,171	665,111	12,452,680
1988	1,413,970	55,653,859	70,827,661	652,748	12,221,205
1989	244,557	9,625,764	70,189,879	646,870	1,211,156
1990	2,147,089	84,509,423	69,436,107	639,923	11,981,094
1991	2,052,252	80,776,639	69,253,120	638,237	11,949,520
1992	1,092,115	72,985,646	68,835,616	634,389	11,877,480
1993	893,546	35,169,971	68,336,567	629,790	11,791,370
1994	649,068	25,549,316	68,320,651	629,643	11,788,624
1995	623,394	24,536,788	68,292,753	629,386	11,783,810
1996	1,101,733	43,364,211	68,292,753	629,386	11,783,810
1997	805,908	31,720,553	49,955,622	460,391	8,619,758
1998	908,457	35,756,851	56,312,176	518,973	9,716,583
1999	908,054	35,741,023	59,287,219	518,743	9,712,281

(continued)

Table 7.10 (continued)

Year	CO_2 Emissions by Fuel Consumption (in tons)	Carbon equivalents released due to Fue Consumption (in tons)	Total Carbon (or equivalents released (in tons)	Cost of Damage due to Carbon (or equivalents) emissions (per tons)	Total Cost of Long-term Damage (1988 prices, millions of baht)
1975	42,087,630	11,486,799	229,735,989	21.59	4,960
1976	8,527,835	2,327,466	46,549,328	21.59	5,965
1977	58,678,206	16,014,794	321,056,121	21.59	6,932
1978	63,170,668	17,240,903	307,726,835	21.59	13,575
1979	66,678,868	18,198,381	153,652,379	21.59	16,893
1980	66,589,310	18,173,938	147,933,481	21.59	20,087
1981	68,622,964	18,278,975	143,052,472	21.59	23,175
1982	71,551,834	19,528,339	138,726,966	21.59	26,170
1983	75,452,850	20,593,027	96,575,054	21.59	28,255
1984	81,013,157	22,110,578	96,733,631	21.59	30,344
1985	85,245,021	23,265,563	96,521,074	21.59	32,428
1986	87,586,900	23,904,722	95,888,948	21.59	34,498
1987	98,295,429	26,827,355	53,476,518	21.59	35,653
1988	109,356,238	29,846,135	97,721,199	21.59	37,762
1989	127,103,326	34,689,772	56,426,692	21.59	38,981
1990	144,239,628	39,366,711	135,857,228	21.59	41,914
1991	158,280,507	43,198,858	135,924,987	21.59	44,848
1992	172,069,327	46,962,153	101,825,279	21.59	47,047
1993	192,372,921	52,503,527	99,464,867	21.59	49,194
1994	215,246,696	58,746,369	96,082,309	21.59	51,269
1995	238,875,088	65,195,166	101,515,764	21.59	53,460
1996	262,871,574	71,744,425	126,892,446	21.59	56,206
1997	19,228,833	52,480,440	92,820,750	21.59	58,210
1998	216,756,158	59,158,340	104,631,774	21.59	60,469
1999	216,660,206	59,132,152	104,585,456	21.59	62,727

Source: Royal Forestry Department (various issues), Ministry of Agriculture (1992), Office of Agricultural Economics (1986), Department of Energy Development and Promotion (1990), Nordhaus (1991).

ED = cCD + cCWR + cCF

where ED = long-term environmental damage

cCD = cost of carbon emissions of deforestation (i.e. 21.59 × tonne of carbon emission); cCWR = cost of carbon emissions of wet rice (i.e. 21.59 × tonne of carbon emission; and cCF = cost of carbon emissions of fuel consumption (i.e. 21.59 × tonne of carbon emission)

Table 7.11 Selected income distribution and Atkinson's measure of inequality for Thailand

	1975	1981	1986	1990	1992	1994	1996	1998	1999
Quintile 1	6	5.4	4.6	4.2	3.9	4.0	4.2	4.2	3.8
Quintile 2	9.3	9.1	739	7.4	7.0	7.3	7.5	7.6	7.1
Quintile 3	13.3	13.4	12.1	11.5	11.1	11.6	11.8	11.9	11.3
Quintile 4	21.4	20.6	19.9	19.2	19.0	19.6	19.9	19.8	19.3
Quintile 5	50.1	51.5	55.6	57.7	59.0	57.5	56.7	56.5	58.5
μ	12,143	16,184	18,417	26,481	29,943	34,470	38,227	31,952	32,828
I	0.3319	0.3574	0.4198	0.4521	0.4757	0.4600	0.4453	0.4428	0.4757

Source: Clarke (2001b).

Table 7.12 National Income per capita adjusted for Income Inequality for Thailand, 1975–1999 (1988 prices – millions of baht)

Year	Aggregate National Income	Atkinson's Measure of Inequality (I)	Net Benefits of Economic Growth on Economic Sub-system for Thailand	Net Benefits of Economic Growth on Economic Sub-system for Thailand per capita (in baht)
1975	514,777	0.3319	343,934	8,113
1976	563,800	0.33615	374,279	8,661
1977	614,143	0.3404	405,089	9,150
1978	675,676	0.34465	442,804	9,792
1979	700,213	0.3489	455,909	9,887
1980	736,822	0.35315	476,613	10,149
1981	774,824	0.3574	497,902	10,400
1982	822,023	0.36988	517,973	10,604
1983	861,383	0.38236	532,025	10,745
1984	896,725	0.39484	542,662	10,728
1985	937,965	0.40732	555,913	10,733
1986	975,516	0.4198	565,994	10,685
1987	1,071,338	0.4151	626,626	11,631
1988	1,198,771	0.4104	706,795	12,860
1989	1,357,294	0.43125	771,961	13,813
1990	1,490,961	0.4521	816,898	14,509
1991	1,609,476	0.4639	862,840	15,148
1992	1,730,397	0.4757	907,247	15,699
1993	1,868,278	0.46785	994,204	17,043
1994	2,037,046	0.46	1,100,005	18,614
1995	2,213,825	0.45265	1,211,737	20,379
1996	2,298,050	0.4453	1,274,728	21,204
1997	2,230,072	0.44405	1,239,809	20,386
1998	1,963,940	0.4428	1,094,307	17,803
1999	2,024,239	0.4757	1,061,309	17,212

Source: Authors' own calculations.

Chapter 8
Summary, Findings and Conclusion

8.1 Background and Motivation

The desirability of financial reforms and liberalization has been a controversial issue on the public agenda in developing countries. In the initial post-independence period and up until the late 1980s, extensive financial repression has been the norm in almost all developing countries in Asia and Africa. Major objectives of these excessive controls and high level government interventions were not only to correct market failures, but also to channel funds to high priority areas with a view to increasing productivity and maximizing social returns. However, there has been a strong claim that these suppressive financial policies have retarded the mechanisms that lead to economic development (World Bank, 1994). In response to this, many developing African countries have accepted the need to liberalize their financial systems in the early 1990s in order to promote growth and revive the process of successful economic performance. Some Asian countries including Thailand have also adopted financial liberalization to support economic development, financial efficiency and stability and global integration.

A number of studies have attempted to explain econometrically the economic impact of these reforms (Olomola, 1994; Hoeffler, 1999). Nevertheless, due to inherent limitations regarding the credibility of the available data and constraints on the number of observations, results from such studies are generally open to question and may not be comprehensive enough. To investigate the impact of the structural adjustment and financial reform program, this study took a case study approach while using a sample of three representative countries of the region. This approach has a number of advantages. First, while deriving supportive evidence from various countries, one can critically evaluate the outcome of the liberalization exercise. It is understood that despite the theoretical support for financial liberalization, the success of the reform program may vary from country to country and it can be considered as a pragmatic empirical issue. A comprehensive and thorough examination of the workings of each financial system is undertaken in this book to arrive at a more realistic conclusion about the effect of liberalization and the conditions

A.D. Ahmed and S.M.N. Islam, *Financial Liberalization in Developing Countries*, Contributions to Economics,
DOI: 10.1007/978-3-7908-2168-0_8, © Springer Physica-Verlag Berlin Heidelberg 2010

which may cause it to succeed of fail. Second, by evaluating individual countries separately, the study identifies the key causes of the failure of reforms, and the policies that are needed to create a successful environment for financial liberalization. Third, having derived rich country information, this study has provided a framework for such analyses in the future which can easily be undertaken for the relevant empirical examination of the issues discussed in this book by other researchers when and if a sufficient number of observations can be obtained. In this manner, the study also highlights why a comparative (Africa and Asia – Thailand) case study is useful. Typically, outcomes that are easily subsumed into one aspect of market failure at a cross-country level can now be disentangled into country-specific structural imperfections.

In a more general sense, the purpose of this book was to evaluate the financial sector reform measures undertaken and to examine the factors that had limited growth potential despite the move towards a more integrated financial market. With these broad objectives, the specific goals of the study were to:

1. Examine how financial liberalization was undertaken in each of the countries in the sample.
2. Investigate the effect of reform towards a liberalized financial environment in terms of improving efficiency of allocation, enhancing growth performance and net social welfare.
3. Analyse theoretically and empirically the outcome of the economic reforms in these countries and attempt to infer some policy lessons that emerge from this experience.

8.2 The Summary and Empirical Results

Whereas broadly the book remains focused on evaluating the extent to which financial reforms can contribute to improvement in economic development, the outline is closely structured to meet the above research objectives. Chapter 2 gives the economic background of each individual country of our sample. It provides a broad picture of the major economic structures that existed before economic reforms and in the immediate years after liberalization. It also highlights some of the existing market failures stemming from various repressive government policies. It turns out that Kenya and Malawi have taken similar development strategies in post-independence. Unlike Botswana, these countries had pervasive economic interventions and imposed controls that skewed resource allocation and discouraged financial and institutional development in the pre-liberalization period. From the growth trends, the findings of this chapter support the view that such policies have retarded economic growth and negated the traditional economic role played by the private financial sector.

Chapter 3 presents a literature review which looks at some of the important theoretical and empirical works that have been done in the areas of financial liberalization and financial development, and outlines mechanisms under which such developments may be linked with economic growth. Through the identified interaction mechanisms, it is revealed that there is a fairly strong theoretical argument in support of a move towards an environment of a financially liberalized market relative to a repressed one. However, it also identifies that in places where institutional development is not well advanced, liberalizing the financial sector may have some destabilizing effects. Finally, the chapter surveys the status of financial sector development in Sub-Saharan African, preluding a deeper investigation of how market liberalization and depth contributes to economic development.

In Chapter 4, the study began with a systematic analysis of the theoretical underpinning of the financial liberalization hypothesis. Thus, it outlines the routes via which liberalizing financial markets are expected to influence economic development. Based on this channel of transmission and deriving evidence from the three countries of our interest, the impact of financial liberalization is examined. Quite different from Botswana, it is observed that the financial sectors in Kenya and Malawi show similar behaviour in the post-reforms period where interest rate spreads significantly increase. Typically, because the new entrants were mostly either locally owned private or previously-parastatal institutions, they were not able to induce a competitive pressure in the lending markets of both the countries. On the other hand, by attracting well-established foreign commercial banks, Botswana was able to develop a competitive financial market. From these examinations, it is found that government rapaciousness, macroeconomic instability, and the lack of competition in the banking sector are the major factors that may have limited the desired outcome. Further, through assessing the indicators of allocational efficiency, the results show that there has been some improvement in allocational enhancement in these economies.

Based on the results and implied findings from the previous chapter, the book provides a theoretical treatment of the issue of imperfect competition and spread behaviour in Chapter 5. The focus on this issue is vital since competitiveness in the financial sector influences both allocational efficiency and savings mobilization that in turn affects investment and productivity. In this respect, some of the important findings out of this examination are that firstly, given the oligopolistic structure of the banking industry in these countries, the spread may decrease in the post-liberalization period if, and only if, the repressed rate of interest was above a certain threshold level and the number of firms was allowed to increase to create effective competition. On the other hand, the spread will increase in the post-reforms period if there is no further entry of new firms or, even with entry, if the threshold level was not achieved. It has been shown that given the significant stability of the monopoly power indicated by the market share concentration in the banking sector of these countries, the chances of the spread declining to enhance efficiency in line with the McKinnon-Shaw hypothesis remain small. Secondly, the finding also suggests that government intervention is essential, as is strongly stressed by the Stiglitz school (Fry, 1995). This evidence shows that some financial regulation is beneficial to the economy in terms of promoting the level of investment and economic growth. Thirdly, the indicative results suggest that higher fixed costs (which are mainly caused by prevailing institutional deficiencies), reduce the profitability of the financial sector, deterring new meaningful entrants. Thus, it will act as a barrier to the entry of new financial institutions through effectively limiting the number of firms the sector can accommodate.

Chapter 6 makes an empirical assessment of the potential impact(s) on savings in line with the theoretical expectation of the financial liberalization hypothesis. Initially, the chapter examines the trends in private savings mobilization in each of the three countries of our sample. Overall, it is observed that private savings in Botswana show a significant change in the post-liberalization period. Thus, by taking time series data from Botswana and selecting a considerable list of a controlling variables and carefully constructing an index of financial liberalization, the chapter further investigates the factors affecting private savings. It is found that saving rates are positively related to real deposit rates and the financial liberalization index in Botswana. Another finding is that in the absence of financial liberalization, the size of the coefficients of the deposit rate (*Drt*) and the number of banks (*Nb*) increase. The interest rate spread (quite often taken as an indicator of efficiency) has a negative effect on private savings in the long-run relationship. Although these results cannot be considered conclusive or definitive, they indicate the explanatory power of these variables in terms of explaining private savings behaviour.

A cost benefit analysis of the financial reform experience in Thailand given in Chapter 7 shows the costs of financial liberalization in Thailand have been higher than their benefits during the sample period, a finding which has probably profound significance for other developing countries in the world. Our finding here complements the findings from the African countries in providing some more empirical facts in resolving the liberalization controversy.

8.3 Policy and Institutional Implications

A major objective of this study, similar to some other previous studies (such as Nissanke, 1998), was to assess the developmental effect of the recent reforms in many countries of Sub-Saharan Africa and Asia (Thailand). Moreover, this work also aimed at addressing the dismal contribution of the financial reforms towards reigniting the growth process. With respect to this, the book looks at some of the policy challenges which should be undertaken for a positive contribution of a liberalized financial system to be realized.

Firstly, financial liberalization should be calculated, controlled and supplemented by proper public policies for regulation and institutional development and welfare enhancement, as advocated by Stiglitz (1994). This process of financial liberalization should follow a sequential process. Without proper sequencing of liberalization program and monetary policy coordination, reforms may expose greater risks of financial instability and crisis (Hansanti, Islam and Sheehan, 2008).

Secondly, it was observed that the unstable macroeconomic environment has affected the allocational efficiency and reduced the productivity of investment. Lack of fiscal discipline, high inflation and volatile exchange rates have all reduced the capitalized value of firms and business enterprises in operation. These have encouraged banks to increase lending to the government sector at the expense of the private sector while encouraging high interest rate spread. Hence, it will be necessary to adopt policies that will ensure fiscal balances and keep the economy stable prior to liberalization. Nevertheless, with histories of large budget deficits, this will be a challenge for policy makers. Secondly, it has been demonstrated that structural deficiencies and inadequate institutional developments have also discouraged a more competitive financial environment. Specifically, the lack of a sound legal system, shortcomings in contractual enforcements and ineffective loan repayment systems have exorbitantly increased transaction and administrative costs of commercial banks. These increases in costs have reduced the profitability of the banking industry, discouraged potential and/or new entrants and, thereby, undermined competition. Accordingly, future policies should concentrate on eliminating or significantly reducing these institutional constraints for an ultimately positive impact of the liberalization measures to be seen. Such corrections will not only encourage entry of "meaningful" firms but will also reduce spread, improve savings mobilization and enhance efficiency of allocation in these economies. Further details of the required policies and regulation to deal with the current and emerging issues, and problems in international and development finance may be seen in Fry (1995, pp. 109–131).

Finally, there are a few limitations in this study that could be considered in future research. Firstly, although the observed behaviour of the financial variables from the countries of our study is largely consistent with the theoretical analysis we have focused on, many of the deviations from the expected outcome can be attributed to market imperfections, moral hazard, incomplete or poor contract enforcement, the non-existence of some markets, and the lack of institutional development and policy formulations. In addition, factors such as macroeconomic uncertainties and high government borrowings were probably other significant contributors. This abstraction in the modelling is taken as a limitation that may be considered in future research. Secondly, future analysis may be also required to explore how Botswana was able to create a more competitive environment which encouraged entry and competition in the banking and financial sector over time. The Thai case study needs to be extended to incorporate a wider range of costs and benefits of financial liberalization and more appropriate measures of social welfare.

Finally, given the above-mentioned empirical results and other observations, the findings of this book support the current mainstream consensus that financial liberalization by itself cannot be considered as a panacea for sustained economic growth and better management.

Appendix

1 Movement from Repression to Liberalization

Figure A.1 depicts this process where for simplicity it is assumed that the real interest rate is positive even with presence of financial repression. Under financial repression system, government fixes the level of interest at i_0 which is below the equilibrium rate of interest. At this rate $S(Y_0)$ represents the savings function derived from the income level. Because of the prevailing controls, the existing financial institution will be forced to consider not only returns, but other non-price fund rationing criteria to allocate the limited amount of savings. Hence in the most likely scenario, the funds will be channelled into investment projects that have highest incentives or those backed by some political pressure even though they are classified as low yielding project types.

Under such considerations, when the level of financial repression is reduced, the rate of interest moves from i_o to i_1. As this takes place some low-yielding investment projects will be forced out and replaced by more efficient investment projects with higher yield. This increases the level of income in the process and shifts the savings function to the right (i.e. to $S(Y_1)$) and the investment level improves to I_1. Following this, the ultimate policy preference should be that of financial liberalization where the real interest rate will be determined by market forces only and hence in equilibrium, this level is at i_e. This process will result increase in financial intermediation as well as efficient allocation of resources. Savings and investment levels will both increase further to $S(Y_e)$ and I_e respectively. Assuming that investment is an important determinant of the rate of growth, the effect of controlled interest rate works to restrict the rate of growth. Indeed, as recognized by Kitchen (1986, p. 81) and visible from the above figure, an important assumption of financial repression hypothesis is that the level of savings is largely, if not wholly, determined by interest rates. Precisely, it is expected outcome that where the market is fully liberalized – through its empowerment and complete interest control elimination – savings mobilization and investment allocation are both at an optimally desirable level. This will accelerate economic growth (see Figure A.2).

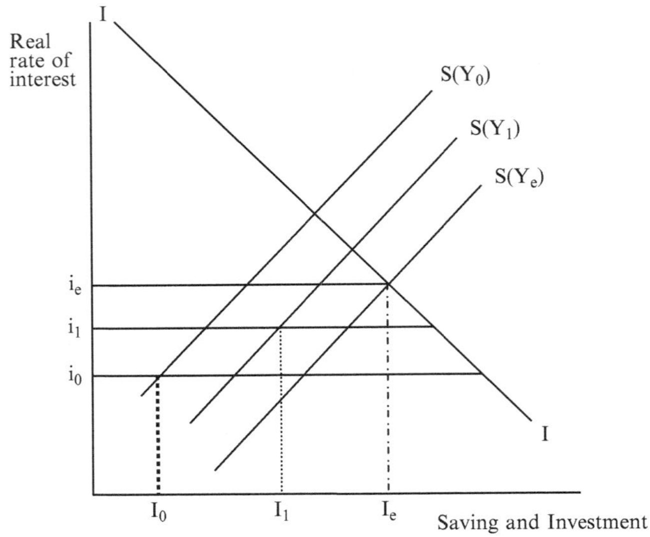

Fig. A.1 Saving and Investment behaviour in liberalization process

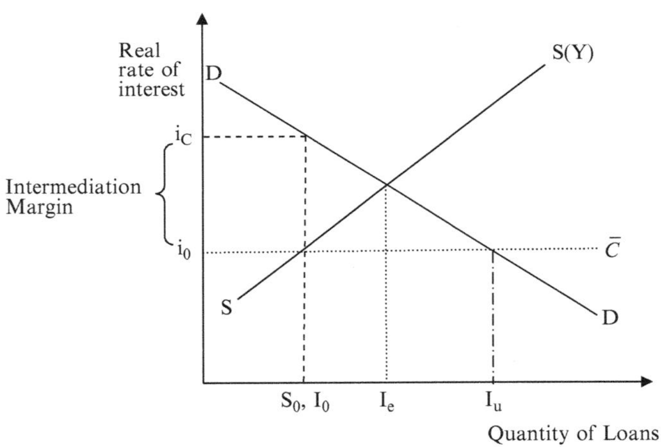

Fig. A.2 Financial repression regime

Table A.1 Financial Deepening (M2 to GDP ratio)

Country	1992	1993	1994	1995	1996	1997	1998	1999	2000	2001	2002	2003	% Growth	Annualized Growth (%)
Algeria	0.49	0.55	0.49	0.4	0.36	0.39	0.46	0.45	0.41	0.49		0.65	32.46	2.59
Botswana	0.3	0.23	0.22	0.22	0.22	0.23	0.29	0.34	0.29	0.34	0.3	0.3	1.97	0.16
Cote d'Ivoire	0.28	0.28	0.28	0.29	0.27	0.24	0.23	0.22	0.22	0.23	0.29	–	3.24	0.29
Egypt	0.85	0.85	0.85	0.8	0.79	0.78	0.77	0.76	0.77	0.82	0.88	0.97	15.05	1.18
Ghana	0.21	0.2	0.23	0.22	0.21	0.24	–	–	–	–	–	–	16.16	2.53
Kenya	0.37	0.37	0.41	0.44	0.48	0.48	0.45	0.44	0.43	0.4	0.41	0.4	10.23	0.82
Malawi	0.21	0.22	0.26	0.19	0.16	0.14	0.17	0.16	0.19	–	–	–	−11.11	−1.3
Mauritius	0.69	0.7	0.71	0.77	0.74	0.77	0.76	0.81	0.79	0.8	0.83	0.84	21.07	1.61
Morocco	0.6	0.63	0.62	0.66	0.62	0.73	0.71	0.78	0.83	0.87	0.89	0.92	53	3.61
Namibia	0.28	0.32	0.33	0.37	0.4	0.38	0.38	0.41	0.41	0.37	–	–	31.77	2.8
Nigeria	0.23	0.28	0.29	0.16	0.13	0.15	0.18	0.21	0.21	0.23	2.68	0.32	35.23	2.55
South Africa	0.5	0.47	0.49	0.5	0.51	0.54	0.57	0.58	0.56	0.59	0.62	0.64	27.41	2.04
Swaziland	0.34	0.32	0.29	0.25	0.25	0.26	0.26	0.26	0.22	0.21	0.21	–	−36.83	−4.09
Tanzania	0.22	0.24	0.19	0.2	0.17	0.17	0.16	0.17	0.17	0.18	0.22	–	−0.92	−0.08
Tunisia	0.47	0.46	0.46	0.46	0.46	0.49	0.48	0.52	0.55	0.57	0.57	0.56	20.65	1.58
Uganda	0.07	0.1	0.11	0.11	0.12	0.13	0.14	0.14	0.16	0.16	0.19	0.19	165.87	8.49
Zambia		0.14	0.15	0.17	0.18	0.17	–	–	–	–	–	–	20.1	3.73
Zimbabwe	0.17	0.23	0.23	0.27	0.25	0.29	0.24	0.21	0.25	–	–	–	54.06	4.92

Source: Senbet and Otchere (2005) and World Bank, World Development Indicators.

Table A.2 Gross interest rate margin

Country	1992	1993	1994	1995	1996	1997	1998	1999	2000	2001	2002	2003	Growth (%)	Annualized Growth (%)
Algeria	–	–	4	3	4.5	2.75	2.5	2.5	2.5	3.25	3.25	2.75	−31.25	−3.68
Botswana	1.5	1.43	3.49	4.31	4.07	4.83	4.81	5.17	5.24	5.6	5.66	6.1	306.67	12.4
Egypt	8.3	6.3	4.7	5.6	5.1	4	3.6	3.8	3.7	3.8	4.5	5.3	−36.14	−3.67
Kenya				15.2	16.2	13.53	11.09	12.83	14.24	13.03	12.96	12.44	−18.16	−2.2
Malawi	5.5	7.75	7	10.06	19	18.04	18.61	20.37	19.88	21.21			285.64	14.45
Mauritius	7.06	8.18	7.88	8.58	10.04	9.84	10.64	10.71	11.16	11.32	11.12	11.47	62.46	4.13
Morocco	–	–	–	–	–	–	6.2	7.1	8.1	8.3	8.6	8.8	41.94	6.01
Mozambique–	–	–	–	–	–	–	16.13	11.77	9.34	7.63	8.72	12.54	−22.26	−4.11
Namibia	8.85	8.41	7.87	7.67	6.6	7.48	7.78	7.66	7.89	7.74	6.03	5.94	−32.88	−3.27
Nigeria	6.72	8.41	7.39	6.7	6.78	10.63	8.07	7.48	9.58	8.18	8.1	6.49	−3.42	−0.29
South Africa	5.13	4.66	4.47	4.36	4.61	4.62	5.29	5.76	5.3	4.4	4.98	5.2	1.36	0.11
Swaziland	5.43	6.46	6.71	7.61	7.59	7.5	7.58	7.56	7.47	7.1	7.23	7.04	29.65	2.19
Tanzania	–	–	–	18.2	20.38	18.44	15.41	14.14	14.19	15.45	13.14	11.43	−37.2	−5.04
Tunisia	–	–	–	–	–	–	–	–	–	–	–	–	–	–
Uganda	–	–	–	12	9	9.53	9.5	12.82	13.08	14.19	13.54	9.09	−24.25	−3.04
Zambia	6.07	–	24.42	15.29	11.65	12.21	18.72	20.25	18.56	22.82	21.87	18.62	206.75	9.79
Zimbabwe		6.88	8.11	8.81	12.65	13.95	13	16.88	18.04	24.07	18.1	61.37	792.01	22.01

Source: Senbet and Otchere (2005) and World Bank, World Development Indicators.

Table A.3 Credit to the private sector (percentage of GDP)

Country	1995	1996	1997	1998	1999	2000	2001	2002	% Growth	Annualized Growth (%)
Algeria	5.2	5.5	4	4.6	5.5	6.1	8	6.8	30.77	3.41
Botswana	13.2	11.1	9.9	11.9	15.2	16.1	16.2	18.4	39.39	4.24
Cote d'Ivoire	20.2	19.7	19.4	18.6	16	17.2	15.9	14.8	−26.73	−3.81
Egypt	47.1	41.5	46.6	54	59.7	59.3	61.6	60.6	28.66	3.2
Ghana	5.2	6.6	8.2	9.4	12	14.1	14.1	12	130.77	11.02
Kenya	33.8	34.6	34.9	30.3	30.5	30.1	24.6	23.4	−30.77	−4.49
Malawi	7.8	4.2	3.9	6.1	5.6	6.2	6.8	4.1	−47.44	−7.72
Mauritius	48.3	44.7	50.5	59.2	58.5	26.7	62.7	61.3	26.92	3.02
Morocco	48.9	45.8	33.5	50.4	54.6	58.6	54	54.4	11.25	1.34
Namibia	56.9	50.5	52.6	51.2	49.2	44.7	47.3	48.4	−14.94	−2
Nigeria	7.8	10.6	8.2	9.1	13.8	13.9	17.8	17.8	128.21	10.86
South Africa	130.6	137.1	135.7	118.9	136.3	141.9	148.5	131.7	0.84	0.1
Swaziland	–	–	–	–	–	14.2	13.1	14.3	0.7	0.23
Tanzania	8.9	3.4	3.9	4.7	4.6	4.6	4.9	6.3	−29.21	−4.23
Tunisia	68.4	63.5	64.5	50.8	65.1	66.2	67.9	68.6	0.29	0.04
Uganda	4.1	4.7	4.3	5.2	5.9	6.3	5.9	6.7	63.41	6.33
Zambia	7.2	9.3	8	6.8	7.4	9.5	7.2	6.2	−13.89	−1.85
Zimbabwe	35.3	35.4	37.6	38.8	27.2	25.2	25.8	37	4.82	0.59
Sub-Saharan Africa	–	68.1	65.1	57.9	66.2	66	65.2	53.5	−21.44	−3.39
Developing nations	–	18.7	47.2	50.2	52.7	55.3	52.1	55.9	198.93	16.93
World	–	107.7	109.7	103.1	109	119.5	120.7	118.1	9.66	1.33

Source: Senbet and Otchere (2005) and World Bank, World Development Indicators.

Table A.4 Gross and private Savings (percentage of GDP)

Countries	Savings (Gross)					Private Savings				
	1971–1975 (%)	1976–1980 (%)	1981–1985 (%)	1986–1990 (%)	1991–1994 (%)	1971–1975 (%)	1976–1980 (%)	1981–1985 (%)	1986–1990 (%)	1991–1994 (%)
Benin	7	8	3	0	0	3	2	4	12	12
Botswana	15	15	25	33	20	6	1	−1	8	13
Burkina Faso	2	1	3	6	4	22	12	9	11	12
Burundi	0	0	9	7	7	0	0	1	3	3
Cameroon	3	6	10	5	1	8	10	9	12	13
Central African Republic	0	−1	5	6	1	0	5	0	1	8
Chad	1	1	3	12	3	11	15	−16	−8	−5
Congo	1	0	13	−5	−13	11	11	21	18	21
Cote d'ivoire	6	14	3	−8	−9	14	6	7	14	7
Ethiopia	0	0	−4	0	1	0	0	8	9	9
Gabon	14	24	27	3	2	39	30	23	21	27
Gambia, The	2	6	2	4	7	2	−2	7	9	9
Ghana	−2	−2	0	3	2	14	9	5	6	7
Guinea	0	0	0	6	6	0	0	0	6	6
Guinea-Bissau	0	0	6	13	10	0	0	7	4	4
Kenya	1	0	−2	0	2	17	18	22	19	17
Lesotho	5	6	3	5	9	3	14	19	25	33
Liberia	7	6	0	−3	0	29	21	13	16	0
Madagascar	2	−1	1	4	0	3	5	−1	1	3
Malawi	1	4	2	0	−3	13	13	11	4	10
Mali	1	2	9	9	7	10	8	−3	1	10
Mauritania	3	1	5	6	5	12	12	2	2	6
Mauritius	2	−2	−2	5	4	22	21	18	8	22

(*continued*)

Table A.4 (Continued)

Countries	Savings (Gross)					Private Savings				
	1971–1975 (%)	1976–1980 (%)	1981–1985 (%)	1986–1990 (%)	1991–1994 (%)	1971–1975 (%)	1976–1980 (%)	1981–1985 (%)	1986–1990 (%)	1991–1994 (%)
Mozambique, Rep. of	0	5	0	5	18	0	−2	−3	1	6
Namibia	0	0	6	7	2	0	0	16	5	19
Niger	0	4	4	3	0	0	12	5	3	9
Nigeria	4	4	2	1	−2	15	22	6	4	24
Rwanda	0	3	5	3	0	11	13	7	2	6
Senegal	1	2	0	2	3	12	6	0	2	7
Sierra Leone	4	−1	−3	−2	−1	3	3	9	1	−1
South Africa	3	2	1	−2	−5	25	26	26	8	22
Sudan	1	1	0	0	0	9	7	0	0	0
Swaziland	8	17	8	11	4	21	3	14	6	17
Tanzania	*	*	−2	2	0	0	0	17	6	18
Togo	0	10	6	5	−7	0	21	16	5	13
Uganda	0	−1	0	1	4	0	4	−14	2	8
Zaire	1	−2	1	−3	0	12	12	6	11	0
Zambia	−2	−4	−6	−2	3	30	20	10	8	7
Zimbabwe	–	−6	−3	−2	1	0	21	16	23	18

Source: World Bank, World Savings Database.

Table A.5 GDP per capita growth (annual percentage)

Country	1970–1975	1976–1980	1981–1985	1986–1990	1991–1995	1996	1997	1998	1999	2000	2001	2002	2003
Benin	–0.99	0.78	1.11	–1.79	0.16	2.28	3.05	1.58	1.70	2.66	1.77	1.21	0.59
Botswana	14.20	9.42	6.95	8.39	2.68	3.37	8.05	8.69	5.71	7.11	4.53	5.31	6.14
Burkina Faso	0.38	1.31	1.74	0.06	0.79	4.23	2.42	–1.70	3.75	–1.34	2.69	1.12	3.11
Burundi	3.04	2.06	1.91	0.88	–3.20	–8.82	–2.30	3.94	–2.11	–2.49	–0.21	1.62	–4.29
Cameroon	3.37	3.71	5.94	–3.21	–4.22	2.53	2.73	2.76	2.20	2.07	2.44	2.01	2.09
Central African Republic	0.06	–1.44	–0.67	–1.96	–1.57	–6.20	3.02	2.59	1.68	0.58	–0.03	–2.14	–8.76
Chad	–1.10	–5.57	4.58	–0.12	–0.51	–0.81	2.53	3.74	–3.78	–4.10	7.86	4.68	10.72
Congo, Dem. Rep.	–1.02	–3.93	–1.52	–2.78	–9.05	–3.44	–7.57	–3.48	–6.14	–8.93	–4.50	0.72	2.82
Congo, Rep.	4.50	2.36	6.32	–1.80	–2.53	0.90	–3.87	0.30	–5.75	4.21	0.60	1.64	–1.30
Cote d'Ivoire	2.57	0.19	–3.46	–2.68	–1.74	4.76	2.89	2.08	–0.79	–5.38	–1.75	–3.25	–3.16
Ethiopia	1.58	1.85	0.96	–1.26	4.50	8.80	0.92	–6.42	3.48	3.43	5.28	–0.93	–5.47
Gabon	13.74	0.21	–0.45	–1.35	–0.25	0.70	2.86	0.81	–11.11	–4.01	0.16	–1.99	0.84
Gambia, The	2.20	1.27	0.04	0.17	–1.15	–1.22	1.40	0.11	3.00	2.23	2.62	–6.06	3.95
Ghana	–0.91	–0.93	–3.15	1.00	1.41	2.10	1.81	2.37	2.12	1.43	1.74	2.24	2.95
Guinea-Bissau	0.96	–3.57	2.72	1.37	0.20	8.44	3.62	–30.00	4.91	4.52	–2.69	–9.85	–2.41
Kenya	3.77	2.67	–0.62	1.57	–0.90	1.48	–1.98	0.87	–0.03	–1.62	1.57	–1.57	0.80
Lesotho	2.98	6.87	1.54	3.73	2.91	8.45	6.79	–5.66	–0.83	1.79	1.30	2.64	2.67
Liberia	–0.49	–0.81	–4.12	–14.28	–20.59	5.19	89.83	18.98	14.23	19.29	–0.20	2.23	–31.65

(*continued*)

Table A.5 (Continued)

Country	1970–1975	1976–1980	1981–1985	1986–1990	1991–1995	1996	1997	1998	1999	2000	2001	2002	2003
Madagascar	−1.21	−1.26	−3.80	−0.74	−2.76	−0.88	0.61	0.85	1.59	1.74	3.02	−15.10	6.79
Malawi	3.34	1.80	−0.57	−2.56	1.35	5.12	1.16	0.97	0.15	−1.08	−7.26	0.52	3.76
Mali	1.13	2.28	−3.45	0.57	0.35	0.48	3.91	3.17	3.80	0.29	8.86	1.08	4.25
Mauritania	0.16	0.34	−1.16	−0.05	0.59	3.02	−6.63	−0.05	3.67	−1.07	−0.11	−1.89	2.46
Mauritius	Na	na	4.35	4.51	4.16	4.12	4.54	4.89	4.49	3.01	4.41	1.83	2.13
Niger	−4.15	1.14	−4.23	−1.18	−2.15	0.01	−0.69	6.68	−3.95	−4.75	3.50	−0.46	0.92
Nigeria	6.24	1.86	−4.20	1.28	−0.12	1.44	−0.08	−0.84	−1.56	2.67	0.47	−1.00	7.96
Rwanda	−1.45	5.37	0.54	−1.30	0.55	8.08	4.52	−1.71	−1.82	−0.95	2.16	6.45	−0.71
Senegal	0.63	−0.97	0.11	0.17	−0.93	2.47	0.74	1.86	3.55	0.49	2.06	−1.74	4.14
Seychelles	5.13	6.59	1.11	4.16	1.87	3.39	10.66	6.30	−0.11	3.90	−2.30	−1.72	−4.88
Sierra Leone	1.59	0.57	−0.86	−1.39	−4.66	4.24	−18.48	−2.35	−10.15	0.74	13.82	21.94	4.36
South Africa	1.62	1.01	−0.78	−0.69	−1.13	2.01	0.32	−1.82	−0.08	1.61	0.87	2.52	1.82
Sudan	2.11	−0.06	−1.93	1.60	2.49	3.43	3.85	4.00	3.99	4.26	4.00	4.39	3.65
Swaziland	6.54	1.03	−0.25	5.69	0.72	0.69	0.50	0.05	0.57	−0.45	−0.57	0.99	1.31
Tanzania	Na	na	0.86	0.93	1.78	1.78	0.97	1.26	1.09	2.56	3.60	4.52	2.96
Togo	0.59	2.08	−2.90	−1.18	−1.85	5.31	10.38	−5.80	−1.07	−3.98	−3.13	1.27	0.02
Uganda	Na	1.52	0.75	2.15	3.16	5.83	2.02	1.83	4.82	2.38	1.59	2.84	1.20
Zambia	−0.75	−2.43	−2.69	−1.73	−3.50	4.38	0.88	−4.08	0.03	1.50	2.93	1.49	3.36
Zimbabwe	4.15	−0.59	0.20	0.91	−0.56	8.59	1.22	1.60	−4.65	−8.77	−3.49	−5.06	−10.94

Source: World Bank; World Development Indicators, various years.

Table A.6 Inflation, consumer prices (annual)

Country	1970–1975	1976–1980	1981–1985	1986–1990	1991–1995	1996	1997	1998	1999	2000	2001	2002	2003
Botswana	11.97	11.88	11.10	10.37	12.28	10.08	8.72	6.66	7.75	8.60	6.56	8.03	9.19
Burkina Faso	6.00	10.51	8.34	1.00	5.77	6.17	2.31	5.05	−1.07	−0.30	5.01	2.18	2.03
Burundi	7.49	14.02	9.72	6.94	10.26	26.44	31.11	12.50	3.40	24.31	9.24	−1.32	10.68
Cameroon	9.86	10.51	11.84	5.64	7.77	3.92	4.79	3.17	1.87	1.23	4.42	2.83	0.62
Chad	8.52	19.15	11.85	9.56	10.52	11.33	5.57	4.26	−8.03	3.82	12.43	5.19	−1.75
Congo, Dem. Rep.	17.23	60.50	47.53	71.18	5442.79	492.44	198.52	29.15	284.89	550.01	313.72	38.09	12.87
Cote d'Ivoire	8.00	15.30	7.24	5.17	8.94	2.48	4.02	4.69	0.79	2.46	4.28	3.11	3.35
Ethiopia	4.77	14.13	8.83	2.77	11.70	−5.07	2.40	2.58	7.94	0.66	−8.24	1.65	17.76
Gabon	9.65	12.46	10.29	3.55	4.77	0.69	3.97	1.45	−1.94	0.50	2.14	0.04	2.24
Gambia, The	8.64	9.98	12.97	20.87	9.02	1.10	2.78	3.49	2.16	0.19	4.42	8.61	17.03
Ghana	14.72	60.81	62.08	36.72	29.02	46.56	27.89	14.62	12.41	25.19	32.91	14.82	26.67
Kenya	9.67	12.45	13.23	11.37	22.52	8.86	11.36	6.72	5.74	9.98	5.74	1.96	9.82
Lesotho	13.82	14.61	13.49	13.51	13.17	9.33	7.15	6.11	5.95	6.13	−9.62	33.81	6.67
Madagascar	8.38	9.21	18.55	15.95	22.85	19.77	4.49	6.21	9.93	12.03	6.94	15.93	−1.22
Malawi	10.05	12.95	13.85	15.65	10.50	37.60	9.14	29.75	44.80	29.58	22.70	14.74	9.58
Mali	n.a	9.85	7.25	11.05	6.50	6.81	−0.36	4.04	−1.20	−0.68	5.19	5.03	−1.35
Mauritania	n.a	n.a	6.85	5.25	4.45	4.68	4.63	8.03	4.07	3.25	4.71	3.90	5.15
Mauritius	10.76	16.32	10.31	7.96	7.25	6.55	6.83	6.81	6.91	4.20	5.39	6.46	3.92

(continued)

Table A.6 (Continued)

Country	1970–1975	1976–1980	1981–1985	1986–1990	1991–1995	1996	1997	1998	1999	2000	2001	2002	2003
Niger	6.56	13.50	8.83	−1.02	5.35	5.29	2.93	4.55	−2.30	2.90	4.01	2.63	−1.61
Nigeria	14.21	16.16	15.52	24.15	44.78	29.27	8.53	10.00	6.62	6.93	18.87	12.88	14.03
Rwanda	12.46	11.58	7.39	3.10	11.16	7.41	12.02	6.21	−2.41	4.29	2.98	2.25	7.15
Senegal	12.06	7.71	11.23	2.04	6.62	2.75	1.58	1.16	0.83	0.73	3.07	2.23	−0.03
Seychelles	19.36	14.50	5.86	2.67	1.80	−1.10	0.62	2.58	6.35	6.27	5.97	0.20	3.29
Sierra Leone	8.44	13.17	45.85	85.24	54.31	23.14	14.95	35.53	34.09	−0.84	2.09	−3.29	7.60
South Africa	8.33	11.43	13.57	15.04	11.93	7.35	8.60	6.88	5.18	5.34	5.70	9.16	5.86
Sudan	14.05	18.09	29.75	45.22	95.26	132.82	46.65	17.11	15.99	5.69	5.85	8.30	7.70
Swaziland	8.24	13.20	14.84	13.83	11.40	6.43	7.13	8.11	6.09	12.21	5.94	12.02	7.29
Tanzania	11.99	13.36	27.40	30.44	27.96	20.98	16.09	12.80	7.89	5.92	5.13	0.98	3.54
Togo	8.86	10.54	7.57	1.96	9.72	4.69	8.25	0.97	−0.07	1.89	3.91	3.07	−0.96
Uganda	10.25	9.28	10.68	9.25	7.15	7.22	6.93	−0.02	6.60	2.83	2.00	−0.32	7.84
Zambia	n.a	19.56	13.85	21.29	28.63	43.07	24.42	24.46	26.79	26.03	21.39	22.23	21.40
Zimbabwe	4.61	9.18	14.12	13.10	25.16	21.43	18.74	31.82	58.52	55.86	76.71	140.08	..

Source: World Bank; World Development Indicators, various years.

Table A.7 Export of goods and services (percentage of GDP)

Country	1970–1975	1976–1980	1981–1985	1986–1990	1991–1995	1996	1997	1998	1999	2000	2001	2002	2003
Benin	15.31	15.72	17.74	15.21	16.63	15.79	16.08	17.09	16.14	15.18	15.18	13.54	13.68
Botswana	36.42	49.49	57.16	64.24	52.13	54.19	56.25	48.88	48.79	52.58	48.61	47.38	45.16
Burkina Faso	6.56	7.90	8.97	9.52	10.68	9.96	10.26	12.94	10.21	9.11	9.24	8.49	8.53
Burundi	9.98	12.66	10.60	10.38	10.27	5.82	9.84	8.00	7.58	7.75	6.85	6.16	9.26
Cameroon	23.07	23.90	29.38	21.05	20.41	23.38	21.43	21.43	21.50	23.25	21.92	19.93	20.24
Central African Republic	27.36	24.30	23.16	17.14	16.59	17.32	19.52	17.01	11.15	13.18	12.51	12.07	..
Chad	15.88	16.41	14.07	14.20	14.77	17.54	18.54	18.49	18.32	16.89	14.67	12.69	24.76
Congo, Dem. Rep.	13.07	12.84	18.15	24.89	20.73	30.00	18.75	29.79	23.54	22.38	18.65	21.16	26.13
Congo, Rep.	36.06	45.53	55.86	46.71	50.35	68.72	75.60	76.28	72.29	80.30	77.42	81.51	79.27
Cote d'Ivoire	36.61	37.85	39.75	34.48	34.69	41.10	41.42	39.41	40.35	40.40	41.29	49.60	45.73
Equatorial Guinea	40.10	44.71	37.40	36.52	33.32	77.58	100.82	101.75	na	98.55	101.28	98.74	96.39
Ethiopia	4.52	5.18	5.28	7.42	8.56	9.26	11.83	13.39	12.02	12.45	12.43	13.23	14.19
Gabon	59.17	56.89	60.81	44.54	51.29	62.66	61.30	47.41	59.61	69.03	59.03	53.56	55.34
Gambia, The	37.12	37.71	45.25	51.10	54.72	47.23	44.99	51.05	46.02	47.99	35.89	42.47	43.09
Ghana	19.49	12.29	7.44	15.91	20.02	32.11	32.41	33.87	32.27	49.08	45.15	42.44	40.31
Guinea-Bissau	4.80	7.84	9.34	9.54	10.24	10.52	21.02	14.44	24.86	31.78	28.61	30.25	32.92
Kenya	29.32	30.16	27.55	24.30	31.01	25.20	22.69	20.17	20.83	21.59	22.86	25.40	24.52
Lesotho	13.91	17.35	15.84	16.79	19.19	24.09	26.97	27.07	23.94	29.99	42.42	56.77	50.02

(continued)

Table A.7 (Continued)

Country	1970–1975	1976–1980	1981–1985	1986–1990	1991–1995	1996	1997	1998	1999	2000	2001	2002	2003
Liberia	71.20	65.28	56.38	53.23	53.23	n.a	8.79	10.79	14.55	21.47	23.18	19.86	32.35
Madagascar	15.58	15.38	12.37	15.41	18.56	20.49	21.87	21.52	24.47	30.68	29.08	16.01	23.09
Malawi	25.96	26.27	24.62	23.15	24.29	22.83	21.36	32.77	28.02	25.60	27.99	24.34	27.22
Mali	11.41	12.24	15.12	16.19	18.30	20.03	26.12	24.79	26.45	26.78	33.30	31.88	26.42
Mauritania	43.80	36.32	45.45	49.41	36.49	35.09	30.68	44.39	41.56	46.24	33.82	33.26	27.70
Mauritius	na	35.91	38.56	43.21	48.32	62.05	62.49	63.99	63.78	62.68	65.61	60.60	59.05
Niger	14.06	21.94	21.91	18.77	16.48	16.95	16.39	17.77	15.89	17.80	16.92	15.20	16.03
Nigeria	14.94	21.96	17.57	27.09	39.95	48.14	44.95	33.53	36.90	54.27	43.28	40.87	49.74
Rwanda	10.49	14.93	11.88	8.38	6.32	6.03	7.80	5.59	5.92	8.35	9.23	7.66	8.28
Senegal	30.99	32.58	32.23	26.12	27.62	29.48	29.18	30.33	30.81	29.87	30.72	30.56	28.49
Sierra Leone	27.32	21.86	16.19	22.53	22.89	17.83	13.95	16.23	12.61	18.14	16.02	16.36	19.93
South Africa	25.01	30.99	27.90	28.13	23.10	24.73	24.60	25.65	25.33	27.87	29.96	32.71	27.83
Sudan	14.61	10.61	9.16	6.47	6.47	7.08	5.09	5.26	7.75	15.30	12.81	13.33	14.70
Swaziland	71.60	68.85	64.12	75.05	75.15	71.94	73.39	78.72	73.07	81.59	91.78	94.93	82.88
Tanzania	7.98	12.18	13.41	13.27	14.67	19.94	16.22	14.53	14.88	16.82	15.94	16.72	19.66
Togo	46.38	50.03	48.59	41.79	31.59	33.28	28.98	29.69	28.87	30.74	31.67	33.77	33.81
Uganda	17.08	15.02	12.43	9.38	8.87	11.96	13.36	9.64	12.25	11.18	12.15	11.94	12.44
Zambia	46.00	41.50	33.71	35.22	35.30	31.33	30.12	26.71	22.39	21.06	26.93	23.68	20.60
Zimbabwe	22.76	22.22	19.63	22.94	29.60	36.13	37.60	43.39	46.39	35.95	23.10	9.22	25.06

Source: World Bank; World Development Indicators, various years.

Table A.8 Gross fixed capital formation (percentage of GDP)

Country	1970–1975	1976–1980	1981–1985	1986–1990	1991–1995	1996	1997	1998	1999	2000	2001	2002	2003
Botswana	38.12	30.56	29.15	28.80	27.94	24.78	24.97	26.06	25.03	21.65	20.77	21.94	21.47
Burundi	5.97	11.52	15.24	16.28	10.98	8.37	5.30	5.97	5.88	6.14	6.22	6.09	11.31
Cameroon	16.38	29.83	22.11	21.29	15.29	13.58	14.34	14.90	14.66	16.00	20.26	19.82	18.07
Congo, Dem. Rep.	14.39	11.69	10.41	12.99	7.61	27.10	2.50	2.10	3.09	3.45	5.20	8.96	12.23
Congo, Rep.	35.49	29.39	39.40	23.16	26.06	25.85	21.60	24.34	26.59	20.91	26.27	22.54	25.12
Cote d'Ivoire	20.85	25.00	18.92	12.13	10.63	14.81	14.34	10.69	14.41	10.37	12.42	9.26	10.52
Ethiopia	9.25	9.78	10.12	11.05	10.15	16.60	12.70	14.40	14.41	19.17	19.55	22.45	21.61
Gabon	39.81	41.51	35.90	32.51	24.55	23.46	30.15	38.41	26.17	21.90	25.71	24.51	23.96
Gambia, The	14.12	13.65	17.42	18.65	20.81	21.57	17.20	18.40	17.80	17.40	17.40	21.20	19.16
Ghana	10.72	7.97	6.06	10.75	17.80	20.30	23.84	22.36	20.66	24.00	26.58	19.73	23.24
Guinea-Bissau	15.40	21.81	28.55	33.53	31.31	23.05	24.00	11.34	16.80	11.30	15.00	9.60	12.60
Kenya	20.65	20.70	18.48	18.99	18.63	16.01	15.39	15.68	15.59	16.71	18.16	17.48	16.12
Lesotho	12.93	26.91	35.89	43.20	58.06	58.87	55.46	49.41	47.99	44.88	43.40	43.50	40.53
Madagascar	8.41	10.53	9.54	11.70	11.14	11.64	12.81	14.78	14.92	15.04	18.50	14.26	17.89
Malawi	21.40	24.27	15.69	16.97	17.62	9.75	9.32	11.10	12.61	12.32	13.80	10.41	10.85
Mali	14.02	14.60	14.51	20.33	22.83	22.90	20.60	20.90	21.20	24.56	31.01	18.61	24.23
Mauritania	n.a	7.52	10.65	12.03	10.15	−23.76	15.14	19.02	12.53	19.37	21.99	21.05	25.91
Mauritius	n.a	18.65	17.64	18.32	21.63	25.03	26.07	24.85	24.96	25.32	23.11	22.30	22.23
Nigeria	21.34	25.48	18.14	16.86	20.19	14.16	17.43	24.11	23.38	20.26	24.09	26.23	23.86
Rwanda	9.80	12.75	14.30	14.61	14.07	14.37	13.81	14.81	17.23	17.53	18.41	16.92	18.42
Senegal	11.32	11.52	12.21	12.60	14.04	16.32	15.74	17.59	19.37	16.96	18.82	16.39	20.38
South Africa	25.84	26.79	25.76	20.34	16.48	16.28	16.51	17.09	15.45	15.14	15.05	15.02	15.78
Sudan	na	6.84	6.34	7.56	5.69	3.23	8.97	10.23	10.34	12.08	11.11	13.15	14.07
Swaziland	18.33	31.73	28.80	20.78	21.05	19.79	19.78	22.39	18.75	18.61	18.41	19.80	17.96
Tanzania	10.37	11.26	12.89	12.86	14.65	16.47	14.72	16.02	15.38	17.43	16.81	18.98	18.49
Uganda	11.16	8.05	8.52	10.22	14.59	16.97	16.89	15.92	19.27	19.64	18.17	18.95	20.11
Zambia	31.14	23.54	15.97	10.57	11.29	11.25	13.07	14.82	16.00	17.24	18.69	21.63	24.81
Zimbabwe	18.28	15.41	16.72	15.95	21.41	18.04	18.05	20.60	13.25	11.80	12.12	10.17	13.81

Source: World Bank; World Development Indicators, various years.

Table A.9 Thailand's key economic indicators

	1979	1985	1990	1993	1995	1996	1997	1998	1999	2000 P	2001 P	2002
1. Population (millions) (Average)	46.11	51.79	55.84	58.44	59.28	59.90	60.50	61.20	61.80	61.88	62.31	62.58
2. GDP												
2.1 GDP at constant 1988 price	5.3	4.6	11.2	8.3	9.2	5.9	−1.4	−10.5	4.4	4.6	1.8	....
(% change)												
Agriculture	−1.8	4.5	−4.7	−2.4	3.5	4.1	−0.9	−1.5	2.0	4.9	1.5	....
Non-agriculture	7.4	4.7	14.1	9.8	10.0	6.1	−1.4	−11.6	4.7	4.6	1.8	....
2.2 GDP at current price(billion baht)	558.9	1,056.5	2,183.5	3,165.2	4,186.2	4,611.0	4,732.6	4,626.4	4,632.1	4,904.7	5,099.6	....
(% change)		(6.9)	(17.6)	(11.8)	(15.3)	(10.1)	(2.6)	(−2.2)	(0.1)	(5.9)	(4.0)	....
2.3 GNP per capita (baht)	12,098	20,141	38,613	53,772	69,326	75,146	76,057	72,979	72,901	77,362	80,083	....
3. Inflation												
3.1 Headline Inflation (% change)	9.9	2.4	5.9	3.3	5.8	5.9	5.6	8.1	0.3	1.6	1.6	0.6
3.2 Core Inflation (% change)			6.1	4.8	5.3	5.2	4.7	7.2	1.8	0.7	1.3	0.9
4. External account (billions of US$)												
4.1 Export	5.2	7.1	22.9	36.6	55.7	54.7	56.7	52.9	56.8	67.9	63.2	15.0
(% change)	(30.0)	(−2.7)	(15.1)	(13.7)	(24.6)	(−1.8)	(3.7)	(−6.8)	(7.4)	(19.6)	(−6.9)	(−6.3)
4.2 Import	7.5	9.3	32.7	45.1	70.4	70.8	61.3	40.6	47.5	62.4	60.7	14.3
(% change)	(38.9)	(−8.8)	(29.8)	(12.5)	(31.8)	(0.6)	(−13.4)	(−33.8)	(16.9)	(31.3)	(−2.8)	(−10.2)
4.3 Trade balance	−2.3	−2.2	−9.8	−8.5	−14.7	−16.1	−4.6	12.2	9.3	5.5	2.5	0.7
4.4 Current account balance	−2.1	−1.5	−7.1	−6.1	−13.2	−14.4	−3.1	14.3	12.5	9.3	6.2	1.8

(*continued*)

Table A.9 (Continued)

	1979	1985	1990	1993	1995	1996	1997	1998	1999	2000 P	2001 P	2002
(% of GDP)	(−7.6)	(−3.9)	(−8.3)	(−4.9)	(−7.9)	(−7.9)	(−2.0)	(12.7)	(10.2)	(7.6)	(5.4)	....
4.5 Net capital movement	1.6	1.9	9.7	10.5	21.9	19.5	−4.3	−9.8	−7.9	−10.0	−5.5	−0.8
– Private/	0.6	0.7	11.0	10.3	20.8	18.2	−7.6	−15.5	−13.8	−9.5	−4.5	−1.8
– Public	1.0	1.2	−1.2	0.2	1.1	1.3	1.6	1.8	1.9	−0.3	−0.6	0.0
– BOT			–	–	–	–	1.7	3.9	4.0	−0.2	−0.4	1.0
4.6 Balance of payments	−0.4	0.5	3.8	3.9	7.2	2.2	−10.6	1.7	4.6	−1.6	1.3	0.9
4.7 International reserves (billions of US$)	3.1	3.0	14.3	25.4	37.0	38.7	27.0	29.5	34.8	32.7	33.0	33.6
4.8 Swap Obligation (billions of US$)							18.0	6.6	4.8	2.1	2.1	1.6
4.9 Total debt outstanding (billions of US$)	6.8	17.5	29.3	52.1	100.8	108.7	109.3	105.0	95.2	79.7	67.3	65.3
(of which: public debt)	(3.1)	(10.6)	(11.5)	(14.2)	(16.4)	(16.8)	(24.1)	(31.6)	(36.2)	(33.9)	(28.3)	(27.8)
4.10 Total debt service ratio (%)	18.1	27.4	10.8	11.3	11.4	12.3	15.7	21.4	19.4	15.4	20.4	....
of which: public (included BOT since 1997)	(4.7)	(14.3)	(6.0)	(3.7)	(2.8)	(2.5)	(2.7)	(3.3)	(4.0)	(4.0)	(8.0)	....
5. Government finance (fiscal year) (billions of baht)												
5.1 Cash balance	−12.3	−34.4	+103.3	68.9	112.5	104.3	−87.1	−115.3	−134.4	−116.6	−107.9	−137.9
(as % of GDP)	(−2.2)	(−3.3)	(4.7)	(2.2)	(2.8)	(2.3)	(−0.7)	(−2.5)	(−2.9)	(−2.4)	(−2.1)	....
5.2 Total public debt outstanding						735.1	936.2	1,242.3	1,956.7	2,180.8	2,316.0	2,310.7
– domestic debt						(310.3)	(316.6)	(524.9)	(1012.6)	(1200.0)	(1337.2)	(1408.2)

(continued)

Table A.9 (Continued)

	1979	1985	1990	1993	1995	1996	1997	1998	1999	2000 P	2001 P	2002
6. Monetary statistics												
6.1 M2 (billions of baht)	205.5	593.5	1,529.1	2,507.1	3,310.6	3,726.6	4,339.3	4,753.4	4,854.7	5,032.7	5,243.6	5,369.1
(% change)	(14.7)	(−10.3)	(26.7)	(18.4)	(17.0)	(12.6)	(16.4)	(9.5)	(2.1)	(3.7)	(4.2)	(5.0)
6.2 M2a (billions of baht)	205.5	593.5	n.a	3,024.6	4,193.4	4,725.2	4,821.8	5,118.1	5,182.5	5,297.0	5,538.0	5,528.3
(% change)	(14.7)	(−10.3)	(0.0)	(0.0)	(18.1)	(12.7)	(2.0)	(6.1)	(1.3)	(2.2)	(4.6)	(5.4)
6.3 Domestic credit (% change)	20.7	8.4	26.9	22.7	22.9	13.9	34.5	−1.2	−4.2	−7.4	−6.1	−4.6
Private (% change)	22.9	10.7	33.2	23.3	24.1	14.4	30.5	−7.9	−5.7	−8.5	−7.5	−5.9
6.4 Deposit (% change)	12.7	12.2	27.5	19.2	18.2	13.7	16.0	8.8	−0.5	5.3	4.0	5.3
6.5 Interest rate (year end)												
Prime rate	14.50	15.50	16.25	10.50	13.75	13.00–13.25	15.25	11.50–12.00	8.25–8.5	7.50–8.25	7.00–7.50	7.00–7.25
Fixed deposits (1 yr.)	9.00	11.00	13.00–15.50	7.00	10.25–11.00	8.50–9.25	10.00–13.00	6.00	4.00–4.25	3.50	2.75–3.00	2.50–3.00
Exchange rate												
Baht: US$ (reference rate) average	20.42	27.16	25.59	25.32	24.92	25.34	31.37	41.37	37.84	40.16	44.48	43.74

Source: Bank of Thailand (BOT), various issues.

Table A.10 Thailand's total quantity and value of exports

Line		Unit	1993	1994	1995	1996	1997	1998	1999
1	*1. Manufactured products*	Millions of Baht	752,557	922,791	1,151,370	1,151,365	1,489,055	1,849,753	1,865,705
2	Textile products:	Millions of Baht	116,669	133,469	142,440	118,521	147,402	183,025	166,108
3	a. Garments	Millions of Baht	89,529	100,580	101,904	79,601	96,702	122,709	109,890
4	b. Spinning	Millions of Baht	8,542	13,384	16,624	15,983	20,960	23,185	22,562
5	c. Fabrics	Millions of Baht	18,601	19,508	23,912	22,938	29,741	37,135	33,654
6	Other textile products:	Millions of Baht	12,899	16,140	18,119	19,488	22,274	25,997	26,976
7	a. Home textile	Millions of Baht	2,962	3,066	3,208	3,107	4,419	4,736	4,962
8	b. Socks and stocking	Millions of Baht	1,071	1,159	1,482	1,413	1,463	1,883	1,951
9	c. Brassieres	Millions of Baht	2,155	3,121	2,984	2,692	2,823	4,060	4,299
10	d. Silk fabrics	Millions of Baht	793	807	753	864	913	945	1,010
11	e. Others	Millions of Baht	5,918	7,987	9,692	11,412	12,656	14,373	14,754
12	Machinery and mechanical appliance:	Millions of Baht	90,802	118,020	160,938	196,343	264,028	364,622	346,649
13	a. Computer and parts	Millions of Baht	62,744	92,059	128,432	165,240	227,783	316,102	299,780
14	of which: Parts	Millions of Baht	38,758	38,847	56,997	75,344	141,768	241,488	226,449
15	b. Others	Millions of Baht	28,058	25,961	32,506	31,103	36,245	48,520	46,869
16	Precious stones and jewellery	Millions of Baht	41,030	44,684	49,946	51,494	52,847	54,130	56,659
17	Electrical apparatus for making and breaking electrical circuits	Millions of Baht	75,622	102,438	130,246	137,451	178,792	234,829	257,182
18	a. Integrated circuits and parts	Millions of Baht	35,550	45,308	58,150	58,483	75,741	92,906	111,645
19	of which: Parts	Millions of Baht	8,977	8,686	9,850	7,727	14,493	20,299	20,779
20	b. Telecommunication equipment	Millions of Baht	9,646	9,897	10,745	12,814	15,888	21,956	25,379
21	c. Others	Millions of Baht	30,426	47,233	61,351	66,154	87,163	119,967	120,158

(*continued*)

Table A.10 (Continued)

Line		Unit	1993	1994	1995	1996	1997	1998	1999
22	Footwear	Millions of Baht	27,936	39,258	53,752	33,508	35,243	38,348	32,359
23	Electrical appliance:	Millions of Baht	62,634	88,124	102,849	106,569	134,865	161,821	153,768
24	a. Air conditioning	Millions of Baht	8,320	13,492	20,177	24,072	27,412	32,413	33,656
25	b. Refrigerators and equipment	Millions of Baht	4,363	5,298	7,755	7,290	8,391	9,934	10,961
26	c. Microwave ovens	Millions of Baht	3,378	3,949	4,359	5,065	5,436	7,564	6,681
27	d. Television	Millions of Baht	18,226	22,195	23,774	26,062	32,463	37,319	27,594
28	e. Radio	Millions of Baht	262	177	395	1,339	3,340	12,395	9,727
29	f. Fan	Millions of Baht	1,918	2,530	1,552	2,172	2,439	3,099	3,561
30	g. Others	Millions of Baht	26,167	40,483	44,837	40,569	55,384	59,097	61,588
31	Base metal products:	Millions of Baht	19,261	24,718	34,324	35,962	46,913	64,416	61,723
32	a. Tube and pipe	Millions of Baht	4,706	5,205	6,247	6,108	6,853	7,461	6,922
33	b. Aluminium structures	Millions of Baht	1,782	1,907	2,005	2,482	2,675	2,941	2,956
34	c. Others	Millions of Baht	12,773	17,606	26,072	27,372	37,385	54,014	51,845
35	Furniture and parts	Millions of Baht	16,738	19,530	20,562	20,731	23,977	28,170	32,131
36	Plastic products	Millions of Baht	39,453	30,351	62,156	31,591	49,643	70,574	75,712
37	Canned food	Millions of Baht	42,984	50,308	53,292	57,125	73,659	93,890	100,283
38a	a. Canned fish	Metric tons	317,938	392,780	332,745	286,562	306,569	328,103	373,777
b		Millions of Baht	16,658	19,810	18,841	17,539	23,878	32,303	29,648
39a	b. Canned crustaceans	Metric tons	61,424	70,822	79,368	87,562	91,941	104,182	123,450
b		Millions of Baht	11,436	15,558	18,652	21,158	30,816	40,839	42,808
40a	c. Canned pineapple	Metric tons	502,835	527,491	383,990	346,926	279,514	226,319	439,382
b		Millions of Baht	7,190	6,607	5,762	6,511	5,903	6,925	11,434
41a	d. Canned fruits	Metric tons	38,901	46,862	50,217	66,684	59,297	37,562	51,065
b		Millions of Baht	1,165	1,321	1,544	2,186	2,326	1,657	1,971
42a	e. Canned pet food	Metric tons	149,681	136,440	144,899	146,724	135,120	120,731	138,040
b		Millions of Baht	4,306	4,315	5,011	5,621	6,814	7,911	7,914
43	f. Others	Millions of Baht	2,229	2,697	3,482	4,110	3,922	4,255	6,508

(continued)

Table A.10 (Continued)

Line		Unit	1993	1994	1995	1996	1997	1998	1999
44a	Sugar	Metric tons	2,218,986	2,610,824	3,757,028	4,464,920	4,032,240	2,290,447	3,269,099
b		Millions of Baht	12,185	17,201	28,752	32,080	31,494	26,609	20,902
45a	Molasses	Metric tons	569,181	838,191	1,194,209	1,043,700	877,283	636,054	617,431
b		Millions of Baht	557	1,108	1,714	1,977	1,429	1,444	780
46	Cements	Metric tons	2,205,961	2,934,213	3,621,697	3,945,595	6,415,961	9,583,347	15,541,915
		Millions of Baht	2,154	2,831	3,753	4,385	7,622	8,854	12,652
47	Petroleum products	Millions of Baht	7,818	5,904	7,142	18,346	35,805	28,876	35,551
48	Rubber products	Millions of Baht	11,373	12,802	20,472	18,831	24,789	35,342	31,999
49	Travel goods	Millions of Baht	8,974	10,546	11,275	10,092	12,262	17,138	16,958
50	Ceramic products	Millions of Baht	6,712	7,718	7,826	7,459	9,293	12,306	13,170
51	Clocks, watches and parts	Millions of Baht	7,266	9,828	11,533	11,100	12,387	14,074	9,686
52	Transformers, generator, and motors	Millions of Baht	10,381	16,163	24,676	30,117	45,001	50,806	58,155
53	Insulated electric wire cable	Millions of Baht	10,365	11,372	11,922	12,592	15,567	19,208	19,998
54	Vehicle parts and accessories:	Millions of Baht	13,227	19,979	16,342	18,848	33,581	53,561	74,899
55	a. Passenger cars and parts	Millions of Baht	5,335	9,961	3,808	3,366	6,077	12,016	17,445
56	b. Motor cycle parts	Millions of Baht	4,411	6,353	9,138	9,331	9,918	12,287	12,358
57	c. Bicycle parts	Millions of Baht	784	933	685	474	540	579	443
58	d. Others	Millions of Baht	2,697	2,732	2,711	5,677	17,046	28,679	44,653
59	Optical appliance and instruments	Millions of Baht	7,838	11,054	12,428	14,521	18,303	26,272	8,079
60	Glass and glassware	Millions of Baht	3,912	4,365	4,988	5,301	5,748	7,522	7,848
61	Wood products	Millions of Baht	7,226	8,257	9,550	9,140	11,097	15,477	17,086
62	Paper products	Millions of Baht	1,933	4,041	8,318	4,750	11,393	20,526	21,016
63	Medicical and surgical instruments	Millions of Baht	394	354	363	253	380	426	6,783

(continued)

Table A.10 (Continued)

Line		Unit	1993	1994	1995	1996	1997	1998	1999
64	Photographics & cinematographic instrument & apparatus	Millions of Baht	2,213	2,619	3,983	5,270	6,470	8,007	16,278
65	Chemical products	Millions of Baht	5,089	5,827	9,630	13,598	20,739	22,371	28,929
66	Leather products	Millions of Baht	4,257	5,738	6,712	7,214	9,660	9,213	7,046
67	Toys, games	Millions of Baht	7,928	8,468	8,880	7,852	8,285	8,975	8,678
68	Sport requisities	Millions of Baht	6,801	7,508	8,796	8,665	8,921	9,394	10,150
69	Ball bearing	Millions of Baht	5,585	5,421	6,521	6,880	7,747	6,962	7,449
70a	Artificial flower,foliage	Metric tons	7,959	13,499	7,011	5,334	4,629	5,377	5,346
b	or fruit and parts	Millions of Baht	2,598	2,517	2,200	1,668	1,706	2,220	1,808
71	Container	Millions of Baht	3,307	2,167	2,208	1,607	399	736	488
72	Others	Millions of Baht	56,436	71,963	92,762	90,036	119,334	123,612	119,768
73	2. *Agricultural products*	Millions of Baht	110,695	129,559	160,312	167,131	183,962	211,092	184,947
74a	Rice	Metric tons	5,012,262	4,858,639	6,197,992	5,460,220	5,567,308	6,540,360	6,838,794
b		Millions of Baht	32,947	39,188	48,629	50,737	65,088	86,801	73,811
75a	Rubber	Metric tons	1,492,795	1,711,648	1,747,269	1,922,042	1,919,429	1,998,232	2,031,167
b		Millions of Baht	29,180	41,820	61,262	63,370	57,447	55,411	43,936
76a	Tapioca products	Metric tons	7,342,150	5,667,963	4,080,860	4,632,814	5,435,658	4,122,381	5,315,751
b		Millions of Baht	21,736	18,774	18,254	20,649	22,457	22,092	23,000
77a	Frozen fowl	Metric tons	163,274	158,255	154,657	140,886	154,491	217,439	220,432
b		Millions of Baht	9,294	10,223	10,047	9,398	11,272	17,040	15,450
78a	Fresh fruits	Metric tons	93,186	115,832	136,602	189,069	219,826	141,711	224,721
b		Millions of Baht	1,420	2,065	2,791	3,555	4,737	3,265	4,734
79a	Coffee	Metric tons	58,484	68,150	76,143	61,005	71,297	53,514	28,337
b		Millions of Baht	1,249	2,153	4,615	2,450	2,083	3,500	1,293
80a	Tobacco leaves	Metric tons	45,907	38,645	21,987	33,413	30,828	30,309	25,024
b		Millions of Baht	2,640	2,206	1,403	2,276	2,525	2,993	1,803
81a	Maize	Metric tons	213,035	145,048	108,188	56,656	61,248	136,860	80,730

(*continued*)

Table A.10 (Continued)

Line		Unit	1993	1994	1995	1996	1997	1998	1999
b		Millions of Baht	720	589	549	430	536	855	528
82	Others	Millions of Baht	11,509	12,541	12,762	14,266	17,817	19,135	20,392
83	*3. Fishery products*	Millions of Baht	55,689	67,903	71,190	63,511	72,227	89,268	78,851
84a	Shrimp, fresh and frozen	Metric tons	148,886	174,175	175,091	161,463	137,079	142,477	138,092
b		Millions of Baht	37,843	49,155	50,302	43,400	47,184	58,342	48,348
85a	Dried shrimps	Metric tons	1,647	1,429	1,531	1,296	1,124	1,246	1,067
b		Millions of Baht	311	288	350	323	301	382	331
86a	Fish, fresh and frozen	Metric tons	281,584	286,390	309,742	306,834	326,858	382,209	363,700
b		Millions of Baht	8,195	8,452	9,851	9,575	12,192	14,704	14,420
87a	Fish, salted, dried or smoked	Metric tons	18,347	15,572	16,544	17,461	21,123	19,260	18,914
b		Millions of Baht	524	556	615	641	772	823	776
88a	Cuttle fish, salted	Metric tons	2,429	1,442	1,077	815	408	438	467
b		Millions of Baht	879	497	410	340	181	186	188
89a	Cuttle fish, fresh and frozen	Metric tons	58,541	60,565	55,455	56,998	67,143	78,455	86,891
b		Millions of Baht	5,886	7,082	7,203	6,982	9,345	11,669	11,413
90	Others	Millions of Baht	2,051	1,873	2,459	2,250	2,252	3,162	3,375
91	*4.Mineral products*	Millions of Baht	5,750	6,816	7,656	10,404	16,561	17,869	13,886
92a	Gypsum	Metric tons	6,442,534	6,492,564	6,511,789	6,425,567	6,772,085	3,973,203	4,260,735
b		Millions of Baht	1,881	2,102	2,341	2,778	3,523	2,445	1,881
93a	Condensate	Metric tons	490,770	745,003	747,444	1,081,771	595,976	343,100	0
b		Millions of Baht	2,108	2,857	2,869	4,426	3,032	1,961	0
94a	Tin	Metric tons	3,496	2,750	2,675	4,919	8,078	11,319	12,536
b		Millions of Baht	452	379	406	766	1,427	2,536	2,493
95	Others	Millions of Baht	1,309	1,478	2,040	2,434	8,579	10,927	9,512
96	*5. Others*	Millions of Baht	11,171	10,531	15,783	19,700	44,894	79,472	70,576
97	*6. Total exports*	Millions of Baht	935,862	1,137,600	1,406,311	1,412,111	1,806,699	2,247,454	2,213,965

Source: Bank of Thailand (BOT), various issues.

Bibliography

Acemoglu, D., Johnson, S., & Robinson, J. A. (2001). *An African success story: Botswana* (Working Paper WP01–37), Working Paper Series. Department of Economics, M.I.T.

Adamolekun, L., & Morgan, P. (1999). Pragmatic institutional design in Botswana: Salient features and an assessment. *International Journal of Public Sector Management, 2*(7), 584–603.

Aghion, P., & Howitt, P. (1998). *Endogenous growth theory*. Cambridge, MA: MIT.

Aglietta, M. (2000). *Financial globalisation*. Texas: University of Texas Press.

Ahmed, A. D. (2005). 'Financial liberalization and economic development: The case of Sub-Saharan Africa' (PhD thesis, University of Melbourne, Melbourne).

Ahmed, A. (2006). The impact of financial liberalization policies: The case of Botswana. *Journal of African Development, formerly Journal of African Finance and Economic Development, 8*(1), 13–38.

Ahmed, A. (2007). Potential impact of financial reforms on savings in Botswana: An empirical analysis using a VECM approach. *Journal of Developing Areas, 41*(1), 203–220.

Ahn, S. K., & Reinsel, G. C. (1990). Estimation for partially nonstationary multivariate autoregressive models. *Journal of the American Statistical Association, 85*(411), 813–823.

Aizenman, & Joshua. (2005). *Financial liberalizations in Latin-America in the 1990s: A reassessment* (Working Paper 11145). Cambridge: National Bureau of Economic Research.

Akbostanci, E., & Tunc, G. (2002). *Turkish twin deficits: An error correction model of trade balance', No 106*. (ERC Working Papers from ERC – Economic Research Center). Ankara: Middle East Technical University.

Akerlof, G. (1970). The market for lemons: Quality uncertainly and the market mechanism. *Quarterly Journal of Economics, 84*(3), 488–500.

Alba, P., Hernandez, L., & Klingebiel, D. (1999). *Financial liberalisation and the capital account: Thailand 1988–1997*. Washington, DC: World Bank.

Alesina, A., Grilli, V., & Milesi-Ferretti, G. M. (1994). The political economy of capital controls. In L. Leiderman & A. Razin (Eds.), *Capital mobility: The impact on consumption, investment, and growth* (pp. 289–321). Cambridge: Cambridge University Press.

Alesina, A., Spolaore, E., & Wacziarg, R. (2000). Economic integration and political disintegration. *American Economic Review, 90*(5), 1276–1296.

Allen, D. S., & Ndikumana, L. (1998). *Financial intermediation and economic growth in Southern Africa*. (Working Paper 1998-004B). Federal Reserve, Bank of St. Louis.

Andrews, D. M., & Daniel, M. (1994). Capital mobility and state autonomy – Toward a structural theory of international monetary relations. *International Studies Quarterly, 38*(2), 193–218.

Ang, J. B., & McKibbin, W. J. (2007). Financial liberalization, financial sector development and growth: Evidence from Malaysia. *Journal of Development Economics, 84*, 215–233.

APEC. (2000). *Towards knowledge-based economies in APEC*. Singapore: APEC Secretariat.

Arestis, P., & Demetriades, P. (1999). Financial liberalization: The experience of developing countries. *Eastern Economic Journal, 25*(4), 441–457.

Arrow, K. (1951). *Social choice and individual value*. New York: Wiley.

Arunsmith, K. (1998). Thailand in economic crisis: A multisectoral forecasting simulation (1997–1999) derived from a CGE model (CAMGEM). *Chulalongkorn Journal of Economics, 10*(1), 15–41.

Aryeetey, E., & Senbet, L. M. (2004). Essential financial market reforms in Africa. (Technical publication No.63). ISSER Technical Publication Series, University of Ghana, Ghana.

Aryeetey, E., & Udry, C. (2000). *Savings in Sub-Saharan Africa*. (CID Working Paper No. 38). Centre for International Development at Harvard University.

Aryeetey, E., Hettige, H., Nissanke, M., & Steel, W. (1996). *Financial market fragmentation and reforms in Sub-Saharan Africa*. (Working Paper). Private Sector Development and Economic Division, World Bank.

Athukorala, P. C., & Sen, K. (2002). *Saving, investment and growth in India*. New Delhi: Oxford University Press.

Athukorala, P. C., & Sen, K. (2004). The determinants of private saving in India. *World Development, 32*(3), 491–503.

Atieno, R. (2001). Formal and informal institutions. Lending policies and access to credit by small-scale enterprises in Kenya: An empirical assessment. (AERC Research Paper 111).

Atkinson, A. (1983). *The economics of inequality*. Oxford: Clarendon Press.

Azam, J. P., & Daubree, C. (1997). *Bypassing the state: Economic growth in Kenya 1964–1990*. OECD.

Aziakpono, M., & Babatope-Obasa, S. (2003). *Financial Liberalization, Currency Substitution and Savings in Nigeria: Evidence from Cointegration and Error Correction Modelling*. Paper presented in 8th Annual Conference on Econometric Modelling for Africa of the African Econometric Society. July, 1–4.

Aziz, I. (1999). Challenges for International Development Cooperation: Reforming the Global Financial Architecture? Paper prepared for comments in a session on Reforming the Global Financial Architecture at Responding to Financial Crisis: Challenges for Domestic Policy and International Cooperation conference. Taiwan Institute of Economic Research, Taipei, March, 22–23.

Aziz, I., Aziz, E., & Thorbecke, E. (2001). *Modeling the socio-economic impact of the financial crisis: The case of Indonesia*. mimeo, IFPRI, World Bank, Washington, DC.

Bagehot, W. (Eds.) (1873). *Lombard street: A description of the money market*. New York: Scribner.

Bandiera, O., Caprio, G., Honohan, P., & Schiantarelli, F. (2000). Does financial reform raise or reduce saving? *Review of Economics and Statistics, 82*(2), 182–211.

Bank of Thailand (BOT). (1996). *Analysing Thailand's short-term debt. Bank of Thailand Economic Focus, 1*(3), 23–39. July, Bangkok: Bank of Thailand.

Bank of Thailand (BOT). (1998). *Financial institutions and markets in Thailand*. Economic Research Department, Bangkok: Bank of Thailand.

Barajas, A., Steiner, R., & Salazar, N. (2000). The impact of liberalization and foreign investment in Colombia's financial sector. *Journal of Development Economics, 63*(1), 157–196.

Barkan, J. D. (1994). *Beyond capitalism vs. socialism in Kenya and Tanzania*. Boulder: Lynne Rienner.

Barro, R. (1997). *Determinants of economic growth*. Cambridge, MA: MIT.

Barro, R. J. (1991). Economic growth in a cross-section of countries. *Quarterly Journal of Economics, 106*(2), 407–443.

Beck, T., & Fuchs, M. (2004). *Structural issues in the Kenyan financial system: Improving competition and access*. (Working Paper 3363). World Bank Policy Research.

Bekaert, G., Harvey, C. R., & Lundblad, C. (2005). Does financial liberalization spur growth? *Journal of Financial Economics, 77*(1), 3–55.

Bekaert, G., Harvey, C., & Lundblad, C. (2001). *Does financial liberalization spur growth?* (NBER Working Paper w8245). Cambridge, MA: National Bureau of Economic Research.

Bencivenga, V. R., & Smith, B. D. (1991). Financial intermediation and endogenous growth. *Review of Economic Studies, 58*(2), 195–209.

Bencivenga, V. R., Smith, B. D., & Star, R. M. (1995). Transactions costs. Technological choice and endogenous growth. *Journal of Economic Theory, 67*(1), 53–177.

Ben-David, D. (1993). Equalizing exchange: Trade liberalization and income convergence. *Quarterly Journal of Economics, 108*, 653–679.

Benhabib, J., & Spiegel, M. (2005). Human capital and technology diffusion. In P. Aghion & S. N. Durlauf, (Eds.), *Handbook of economic growth, 1A* (pp. 935–966). Handbooks in economics, (p. 22). Amsterdam/San Diego: Elsevier/North-Holland.

Bergson, A. (1938). *A reformulation of certain aspects of welfare economics. Quarterly Journal of Economics, 52*: 310–334.

Berthelemy, J. C., & Varoudakis, A. (1996a). *Financial development policy and growth.* Development Centre Studies, Long-term growth series. OECD.

Berthelemy, J. C., & Varoudakis, A. (1996b). Economic growth, convergence clubs, and the role of financial development. *Oxford Economic Papers, 48*(2), 300–328.

Berube, G., & Cote, D. (2000). *Long-term determination of personal savings rate: Literature review and some empirical result for Canada.* (Working Paper 2000–2003). Bank of Canada.

Bevan, D., Collier, P., & Gunning, J. W. (1999). Anatomy of a temporary trade shock: The Kenya coffee boom of 1976–79. In J. W. Paul Collier, Gunning and associates (Eds.), *Trade shocks in developing countries* (vol. 1). Oxford: Oxford University Press.

Bhatt, V. V. (1986). Improving the financial structure in developing countries. *Finance and Development, 33*(2), 20–24.

Bigsten, A., & Ndungu, N. S. (1991). *Structural adjustment and African farmers: Kenya case study.* In A. Duncan & J. Howell (Eds.), *Structural adjustment and the African farmer.* London: ODI.

Bird, G., & Rajan, R. (2001). *Economic globalisation: How far and how much further.* Mimeo: School of Economics, Adelaide University, Adelaide.

Boadway, R., & Bruce, N. (1984). *Welfare economics.* Oxford: Basil Blackwell.

BoB. (2000). Recent developments in Botswana economy. Annual Report, Bank of Botswana.

Bonner, J. (1986). *The introduction to the theory of social choice.* Baltimore: The Johns Hopkins University Press.

Bonfiglioli, A. (2005). *How does financial liberalization affect economic growth?* (Seminar Paper 736). Stockholm: Institute for International Economic Studies, Stockholm University.

Borda, J. (1781 – reprinted in 1953). Memoire sur les elections au scrutin. Histoire de L'Academic Royale des Sciences. In A. de Grazia [Mathematical derivation of an election system]. *Isis, 44*(1–2), 42–51.

Bordo, M. D., & Schwartz, A. J. (1996). *Why clashes between internal and external stability goals end in currency crises.* (NBER, Working Paper 5710). Cambridge, MA: National Bureau of Economic Research.

Borland, J. (1998). *Earnings inequality in Australia: Changes, causes and consequences.* Centre for Economic and Policy Research. (Discussion Papers 390). Canberra: Australian National University.

Borland, J., Gregory, B., & Sheehan, P. (2001a). *Work rich, work poor: Inequality and economic change in Australia.* Melbourne: Centre for Strategic Economic Studies.

Borland, J., Gregory, B., & Sheehan, P. (2001b). Inequality and economic change. In J. Borland, B. Gregory, & P. Sheehan (Eds.), *Work rich and work poor.* Melbourne: Centre for Strategic Economic Studies.

Borota, T., & Kutan, A. (2008). Regional integration and economic growth: The case of the European Union. *Journal of International Trade and Diplomacy, 2*(1), 93–113.

Brock, P. L., & Suarez, L. R. (2000). Understanding the behaviour of bank spreads in Latin America. *Journal of Development Economics, 63*(1), 113–134.

BOT (Bank of Thailand) (1996). "Analysing Thailand's Short-Term Debt", *Bank of Thailand Economic Focus*, *1*(3), 23–39, July, Bangkok: Bank of Thailand.

BOT (Bank of Thailand) (1998). "Financial Institutions and Markets in Thailand", Economic Research Department, November, Bangkok: Bank of Thailand.

Campbell, J., & Mankiw, G. (1991). The response of consumption to income: A cross-country investigation. *European Economic Review*, *35*, 723–767.

Capiro, G., & Summers, L. (1993). Finance and its reforms: Beyond Laissez-faire. (Policy Research Working Paper 1171). The World Bank.

Capoglu, G. (1991). *The Effect of Financial Liberalization on the Efficiency of the Turkish Financial System: 1980–88*. Paper presented at the EEA annual conference, Lisbon.

Carroll, C. (1991). *Buffer stock saving and the permanent income hypothesis. Board of governors of the federal reserve system. Economic activity section.* (Working Paper Series 114). Washington, DC.

Caroll, C., & Summers, L. (1991). Consumption growth parallels income growth. In D. Bernheim & J. Shoven (Eds.), *National saving and economic performance*. Chicago: NBER/University of Chicago Press.

Cavoli, T., Rajan, R., & Siregar, R. (2003). A survey of financial integration in East Asia: Trends, issues and implications. Report prepared for the Asian Development Bank.

CBK. (2001). Bank supervision annual report. Central bank of Kenya.

Central Bank. (2000). *The practice of monetary policy in Kenya*. Nairobi: The Central Bank of Kenya.

Chaisrisawatsuk, W. & Chaisrisawatsuk, S. (2006). "The Role of Financial Liberalization in Growth: A Case of 4-ASEAN Economies", *NIDA Economic Review*, Volume 1 no.1, June.

Chan, V. L., & Hu, S. C. (1997). Financial liberalization and aggregate consumption: The evidence from Taiwan. *Applied Economics*, *29*(11), 1525–1535.

Channock, M. (1972). The political economy of independent agriculture in colonial Malawi: The great war to the great depression. *Journal of Social Science*, *1*(1), 36–49.

Charemza, W., & Deadman, D. (1992). *New directions in econometric practice: General to specific modelling, cointegration and vector autoregression*. Hants: Edwards Elgar Publishing.

Chichilnisky, G. (1997). *Markets with privately produced public goods; the knowledge revolution*. Mimeo: Program on Information and Resources, Columbia University.

Chinn, M., & Ito, H. (2005). What matters for financial development? Capital controls, institutions, and interactions. (NBER Working Paper 11370). Cambridge, MA: National Bureau of Economic Research.

Chinn, M. D., & Ito, H. (2008). A new measure of financial openness. *Journal of Comparative Policy Analysis*, *10*(3), 309–322.

Chipeta, C. (1993). "Malawi". In A. Aderanti (Ed.), *The impact of structural adjustment on population of Africa*. UNFPA.

Chipeta, C. (1994). The links between the informal and the formal/semi-formal financial sectors in Malawi. *African Journal of Economic Policy*, *1*(1), 159–184.

Chipeta, C., & Mkandawire, M. (1992). Interest rate, financial savings and macroeconomic adjustment in Malawi. In Frimpong-Ansah & Ingham (Eds.), *Savings for economic recovery in Africa*. London: James Currey.

Chipeta, C., & Mkandawire, M. (2002). Explaining African economic growth performance: Case study of Malawi. AERC collaborative research project on explaining African economic growth performance.

Chirwa, E. W. (2001). *Market structure, liberalization and performance in the Malawian banking sector*. (ERC Research Paper 108).

Cho, Y. J. (1986). Inefficiencies from financial liberalization in the absence of well-functioning equity market. *Journal of Money, Credit and Banking*, *18*(2), 191–199.

Civcir, I. (2004). The long-run validity of the monetary exchange rate model for a high inflation country and misalignment: The case of Turkey. Emerging markets finance and trade. New York: M.E. Sharpe, Inc., *40*(4), 84–100.

Claessens, S., & Forbes, K. J. (2001). International financial contagion. Boston: Kluwer.

Claessens, S., & Glaessner, T. (1998). *Internationalization of financial services in Asia.* (Policy Research Working Paper 1911). Washington, DC: World Bank.

Clarke, M. (2001a). *Does economic growth reduce poverty? A case study of Thailand.* Poster prepared for UNU/WIDER development conference. *Growth and Poverty*, Helsinki, 25–26 May.

Clarke, M. (2001b). *An alternative view on economic growth and poverty reduction: An empirical application to Thailand.* mimeo: Centre for Strategic Economic Studies, Victoria University, Melbourne.

Clarke, M., & Islam, S. (2000). *Social Welfare and GDP: Can We Still Use GDP for Welfare Measurement?* Seminar paper presented at the centre for strategic economic studies. Victoria University, 7 September.

Clarke, M., & Islam, S. (2003). Measuring social welfare: Application of social choice theory. *Journal of Socio-economics, 32*, 1–15.

Clarke, M., & Islam, S. (2004). *Economic growth and social welfare: Operationalising normative social choice theory*. In *Contribution to economic analysis series*. Amsterdam: North Holland.

Clarke, M., Islam, S., & Sheehan, P. (2002). *Achieving Simultaneous Economic Growth and Sustainability – The New Impossibility Theorem for Development Economics.* Paper presented at regional symposium on environment and natural resources, Kuala Lumpur, 10–11 April, 2002.

Clayton, A., & Radcliffe, N. (1996). *Sustainability: A systems approach.* London: Earthscan Publications.

de Condorcet, M. (1785). *Essai sur l' application de l'analyse a la probabilitie des decisions rendues a la plualite des voix.* Paris: L'Imprimerie Royal.

Cromwell, E. (1992). "Malawi". In A. Duncan & J. Howell (Eds.), *Structural adjustment and African farmers.* London: Heinemann.

Dahl, H. -E. (1981). Economic and social development in Botswana. In H. Charles (Ed.), *Papers on the economy of Botswana.* London: Heinemann.

De Gregorio, J. (1996). Borrowing constraint, human capital and growth. *Journal of Monetary Economics, 37*(1), 49–71.

De Gregorio, J., & Guidotti, P. E. (1995). Financial development and economic growth. *World Development, 23*(3), 433–448.

Demetriades, P. O., & Luintel, K. B. (2001). Financial restraints in the South Korean miracle. *Journal of Development Economics, 64*(2), 459–479.

Demir, F. (2005). *Financial liberalization, private investment and low growth traps in Argentina, Mexico and Turkey: Limits of growth without investment.* Notre Dame, IN: University of Notre Dame. Mimeo.

Demirguc-Kunt, A., & Detragiache, E. (1998). *Financial liberalization and financial fragility.* (IMF Working Paper wp/98/83).

Demirguc-Kunt, A., & Huizinga, H. (1997). *Determinants of commercial bank interest margins and profitability: Some international evidence.* (Policy Research Working Paper No.1900). The World Bank.

Demirguc-Kunt, A., & Maksimovic, V. (1996). *Financial constraints, uses of funds, and firm growth: An international comparison.* (Working Paper 1671). The World Bank.

Denizer, C. (1997). *The effect of financial liberalization and new bank entry on market structure and competition in Turkey.* (Working Paper WPS 1839). The World Bank.

Dixon, C. (1996). Thailand's rapid economic growth: Causes, sustainability and lessons. In M. Parnwell (Ed.), *Uneven development in Thailand.* Aldershot: Avebury.

Dixon, C. (1999). *The Thai economy: Uneven development and internationalism.* London: Routledge.

Dobbs, I. M. (2000). *Managerial economics: firms, markets, and business decisions.* Oxford: Oxford University Press.

Dolado, J., Gonzalo, J., & Marmol, F. (2003). Cointegration. In B. Baltagi (Ed.), *Companion in econometric theory* (pp. 634–654). New York: Basil Blackwell.

Dollar, D. (1992). Outward orientated developing economies really do grow more rapidly: Evidence from 95 LDCs, 1976–1985. *Economic Development and Cultural Change, 40*, 523–544.

Dopfer, K. (1979). *The new political economy of development: Integrated theory and Asian experiment*. Melbourne: Macmillian.

Dowrick, S., & Rogers, M. (2002). Classical and technological convergence: Beyond the Solow-Swan growth model. *Oxford Economic Papers, 54*(3), 369–385.

Dutta, D., & Ahmed, N. (2001). *An aggregate import demand function for India: A cointegration analysis*. (Working Paper 2001–2003). Department of Economics, University of Sydney.

Edison, H., Levine, R., Ricci, L. A., & Slok, T. (2002). International financial integration and economic growth. *Journal of International Money and Finance, 21*, 749–776.

Edwards, S. (1992). Trade orientation, distortion and growth in developing countries. *Journal of Development Economics, 39*(1), 31–57.

Edwards, S. (1996). Why are latin America's savings rates so low? An international comparative analysis. *Journal of Development Economics, 51*(1), 5–44.

Eichengreen, B., & Leblang, D. (2003). Capital account liberalization and growth: Was Mr. Mahathir right? *International Journal of Finance and Economics, 8*(3), 205–224.

Enders, W. (1995). *Applied econometric time series*. New York: Wiley.

Enders, W. (2004). *Applied econometric time series* (2nd ed). USA: Wiley.

Engle, R. F., & Granger, C. W. J. (1987). Co-integration and error correction: Representation, estimation and testing. *Econometrica, 55*, 251–276.

Fedderke, J. (2000). *Investment on fixed capital stock: The South African manufacturing industry, 1970–1997*. (ERSA Working paper16).

Flood, R., & Garber, B. (1984a). Collapsing exchange rate regimes: Some linear examples. *Journal of International Economics, 17*(1), 1–13.

Flood, R., & Garber, B. (1984b). Gold monetization and gold discipline. *Journal of Political Economy, 92*(1), 90–107.

Frankel, J., & Romer, D. (1999). Does trade cause growth? *American Economic Review, 89*(3), 379–399.

Frimpong-Ansah, J. H., & Ingham, B. (1992). *Saving for economic recovery in Africa*. London: James Curry.

Fry, M. J. (1982). Models of financially repressed developing countries. *World Development, 10*(9), 731–750.

Fry, M. J. (1988). *Money, interest and banking in economic development*. Baltimore: The Johns Hopkins University Press.

Fry, M. J. (1995). *Money, interest, and banking in economic development*. Baltimore: The Johns Hopkins University Press.

Fry, M. J. (1997). In favour of financial liberalization. *Economic Journal, 107*(1), 754–770.

Gab, J. J. (2000). The role of international capital flows and financial contagion in the Asian financial crises (Phd thesis, The Claremont Graduate University, California).

Gaitan, B., & Roe, T. (2005). *Natural Resources Abundance and Economic Growth in a Two Country Model. Presented at the* Dynamic, Economic Growth and International Trade Conference, Mexico City, Mexico, June 3–4.

Galbis, V. (1977). Financial intermediation and economic growth in less-developed countries: A theoretical approach. *Journal of Development Studies, 13*(2), 58–72.

Galindo, A., Micco, A., & Ordonez, G. (2002). *Financial liberalization and growth: Empirical evidence*. IDB: Mimeo.

Galindo, A., Schiantarelli, F., & Weiss, A. (2001). *Does financial liberalization improve the allocation of investment?* (Working Paper 503). Boston College.

Gelbard, E. A., & Leite, S. P. (1999). Measuring financial development in Sub-Saharan Africa. (IMF Working Paper wp/99/105).

Gelos, R. G., & Werner, A. M. (2002). Financial liberalization, credit constraints and collateral: Investment in the Mexican manufacturing sector. *Journal of Development Economics*, *67*, 1–27.

Ghosh, J. (2005). *The economic and social effects of financial liberalization: A primer for developing countries*. (Working Paper No.4, United Nations). New York: Department of Economics and Social Affairs.

Ghura, D., & Hadjimachael, M. T. (1996). *Growth in Sub-Saharan Africa: International Monetary Fund*. (Staff Paper, 605–633).

Gibson, H. D., & Tsakalotos, E. (1994). The scope and limits of financial liberalisation in developing countries: A critical survey. *The Journal of Development Studies*, *30*(3), 578–628.

Gilpin, R. (2001). *Global political economy: Understanding the international economic order*. Princeton: Princeton University Press.

GoK. (1983). Budget speech 1983/1984. Ministry of Finance, Government of Kenya.

GoK. (2000). Survey of the financial service sector. Ministry of Labour and Human Resource Development, Government of Kenya.

Goldsmith, R. W. (1969). *Financial structure and development*. New Haven: Yale University Press.

Good, K. (1992). Interpreting the exceptionality in Botswana. *Journal of Modern African Studies*, *30*(1), 69–95.

Granger, C. W. J. (1988). Some recent developments in a concept of causality. *Journal of Econometrics*, *39*, 199–211.

Greenwood, J., & Jovanovic, B. (1990). Financial development, growth, and the distribution of income. *Journal of Political Economy*, *98*(5), 1076–1107.

Grosh, B. (1990). Parastatal-led development: The financial sector in Kenya, 1971–1987. *African Development Review*, *2*(2), 27–36.

Guncavdi, O., Bleaney, M., & McKay, A. (1998). Financial liberalization and private investment: Evidence from Turkey. *Journal of Development Economics*, *57*(2), 443–455.

Gurley, J., & Shaw, E. S. (1967). Financial structure and economic development. *Economic Development and Cultural Change*, *15*(3), 257–268.

Gurley, J. G., & Edwards, S. (1955). Financial aspects of economic development. *The American Economic Review*, *45*(3), 515–538.

Hadjimichael, M., & Ghura, D. (1995). *Public policies and private savings and investment in Sub-Saharan Africa: An empirical investigation*. (IMF Working Paper, WP/95/19).

Hallwood, C., & MacDonald, R. (2000). *International money and finance* (3rd ed). MA: Blackwell.

Hammond, P. (1976). Equity, arrow's conditions and Rawls' difference principles. *Econometrica*, *44*(4), 793–804.

Hansanti, S., Islam, S. M. & Sheehan, P. (2008). *International finance in developing countries: Emerging issues, m*odels and welfare economics analyses. Heidelberg: Physica-Verlag.

Harland-Thunberg, P. (1978). *Botswana: An African growth economy*. Boulder, CO: Westview.

Harrigan, J. (1999). Malawi's positive 1977–79 trade shock. In J. W. Paul Collier, Gunning and associates (Eds.), *Trade shocks in developing countries* (vol. 1). Oxford: Oxford University Press.

Harris, R. (1995). *Cointegration analysis in econometric modelling*. London: Harvester Wheatsheaf.

Harrison, A., & Hanson, G. (1999). Who gains from trade reform? Some remaining puzzles. *Journal of Developing Economics*, *59*(1), 125–154.

Harvey, C. (1985). Successful adjustment in Botswana. *IDS Bulletin*, *16*(3), 47–53.

Harvey, C. (1992). Botswana: Is the economic miracle over? *Journal of African Economies*, *1*(3), 335–368.

Harvey, C. (1996). Banking policy in Botswana: Orthodox but untypical. (IDS Discussion Paper no.39). Institute of Development. Sussex.

Harvey, C. (1997). "Monetary independence: The contrasting strategies of Botswana and Swaziland". In Salkin, J. S., et al. (Eds.). *Aspects of the Botswana economy: Selected paper.* Gaborone: Lentswe la Lesedi, Oxford: James Curry Ltd.

Harvey, C., & Lewis, S. R. (1990). *Policy choice and development performance in Botswana.* Bristol: Macmillian and OECD Development Centre.

Hazelwood, A. (1979). *The economy of Kenya.* London: Oxford University Press.

Henderson, H. (1999). *Beyond globalisation.* West Hartford: Kumarian Press.

Hendry, D. F. (1996). *Dynamic econometrics.* London: Oxford University Press.

Hermes, N. (1996). Financial reform and financial intermediation in Chile, 1983–1992. In N. Hermes & R. Lensink (Eds.), *Financial development and economic growth: Theory and experiences from developing countries* (pp. 310–335). London: Routledge.

Hermes, N., & Robert Lensink, R. (2005). *Does financial liberalization influence saving, investment and economic growth?* (Research Paper No. 2005/69,UNU-Wider).

Hicks, J. (1940). The valuation of social income. *Economica, 7*, 104–124.

Hicks, J. (1946). *Value and capital.* Oxford: Oxford University Press.

Hill, C., & Knight, J. (1999). The diamond boom, expectations and economic management in Botswana. In J. W. Paul Collier, Gunning and associates (Eds.), *Trade shocks in developing countries* (vol. 1). Oxford: Oxford University Press.

Himbara, D. (1994). *Kenyan capitalists, the state and development.* Boulder: Lynne Rienner.

Ho, Y. K. (1991). *The Hong Kong financial system.* New York: Oxford University Press.

Hoeffler, A. E. (1999). "The Augmented Solow Model and the African Growth Debate", CSAE, University of Oxford, Mimeo.

Hoeffler, A. E. (2002). The augmented Solow model and the African growth debate. *Oxford Bulletin of Economics and Statistics, 64*(2), 135–158.

Holm, J. D. (2000). Curbing corruption through democratic accountability: Lessons from Botswana. In K. R. Hope & B. C. Chikulo (Eds.), *Corruption and development in Africa: Lessons from country case-studies.* London: Macmillan.

Hope, K. R. (1997). *African political economy: Contemporary issues in development.* New York: M.E. Sharpe.

Hope, K. R. (1999). Development prospects and policy for Africa: Structural adjustment and beyond. *The Review of Black Political Economy, 26*(4), 75–92.

Hubbard, M. (1981). Botswana's beef export subsidy: The issue of the proposed northern Abattoir. In H. Charles (Ed.), *Papers on the economy of Botswana.* London: Heinemann.

Hussein, K., & Thirlwall, A. (1999). Explaining differences in the domestic savings ratioacross countries: A panel data study. *Journal of Development Studies, 36*, 31–52.

IBA. (2002). *Report of a mission to Malawi by international bar association.* International Bar Association.

Ibrahim, M. H. (2001). Financial factors and the empirical behaviour of money demand: A case study of Malaysia. *International Economic Journal, 15*(3), 55–72.

IBRD. (1963). *The economic development of Kenya.* The International Bank of Reconstruction and Development (IBRD). Baltimore: The Johns Hopkins University Press.

IEA. (2000). Moderating the interest rate spread. "The point". *Bulletin of the Institute of Economic Affairs*, 42. Nairobi.

Ikhide, S. I. (1996). Commercial bank offices and the mobilization of private savings in selected sub-Saharan African countries. *Journal of Development Studies, 33*(1), 117–132.

IMF. (2001). Malawi: 2000 article IV consultation. MF Country Report No. 01/38, Washington, DC: International Monetary Fund.

Islam, S. M., & Watanapalachaikul, S. (2005). *Empirical finance: Modelling and analysis of emerging financial and stock market.* New York: Physica-Verlag.

Islam, N. (1995). "Growth Empirics: a panel data approach", *Quarterly Journal of Economics*, 110, 1127–1170.

Islam, S. M. N. and Mak, C. (2006). Normative Health Economics: *A New Pragmatic Approach to Cost Benefit Analysis, Mathematical Models and Applications*, UK, Palgrave Macmillan.

Islam, S., & Clarke, M. (2002). The relationship between economic development and social welfare. *Social Indicators Research, 57*(2), 201–228.

Islam, S., & Clarke, M. (2003). Indicators for social, ethical and environmental performance: Using systems analysis based social choice theory for social welfare measurement. In J. Batten & T. Fetherston (Eds.), *Governance and social responsibility*. Amsterdam: North Holland.

Jackson, R. (1977). *Plural societies and new states: A conceptual analysis*. Berkeley: Institute of International Studies, University of California.

Jappelli, T., & Pagano, M. (1989). Consumption and capital market imperfections: An international comparison. *The American Economic Review, 79*(5), 1088–1105.

Jaramillo, F., Schiantarelli, F. & Weiss, A. (1992). *The effect of financial liberalization on allocation of credit: Panel data from Ecuador*. (Policy Research Working Paper 1092). The World Bank.

Jefferis, K. (1995). Botswana stock market and its role in financial and economic development. *World Development, 23*(4), 663–678.

Johansen, S. (1995). *Likelihood-based inference in cointegrated vector autoregressive models*. Oxford: Oxford University Press.

Johansen, S., & Juselius, K. (1990). Maximum-likelihood estimation and inference on cointegration with applications to the demand for money. *Oxford Bulletin of Economics and Statistics, 52*(1), 169–210.

Jones, D. (1981). "Arable agriculture in Botswana: The case for subsidies". In Harvey Charles (Eds.), *Papers on the economy of Botswana*. London: Heinemann.

Julian, C. (2000). The impact of the Asian economic crisis in Thailand. *Managerial Finance, 26* (4), 39–48.

Kabubo-Mariara, J., & Kariti, T. W. (2002). *Structural adjustment, poverty and economic growth: An analysis for Kenya*. (AERC Research Paper 124). African Economic Research Consortium.

Kahauti, A., & Wright, M. (1997). The real cost of inflation in Botswana. In J. S. Salkin, et al. (Eds.), *Aspects of the Botswana economy: Selected paper*. Gaborone: Lentswe la Lesedi; Oxford: James Curry Ltd.

Kakwani, N. (1999). Poverty and inequality during the economic crisis in Thailand. In *Indicators of well-being and policy analysis* (vol. 3). Bangkok: NESDB, January.

Kakwani, N., & Pothong, J. (2000). *Impact of economic crisis on the standard of living in Thailand*. NESDB, Bangkok: Mimeo.

Kaminsky, G. L., & Schmukler, S. L. (2001). On booms and crashes: Financial liberalization and stock market cycles. The World Bank: *Mimeo*.

Kaminsky, G. L., & Schmukler, S. L. (2002). *Short-run pain long-run gain: The effect of financial liberalization*. (Woking Paper 2912). The World Bank.

Kanbur, E. (1987). The standard of living: Uncertainty, inequality and opportunity. In G. Hawthorn (Ed.), *The standard of living*. Cambridge: Cambridge University Press.

Kaosa-ard, M. (2000). *Social impact assessment: Synthesis report*. Bangkok: TDRI.

Kapur, B. K. (1976). Two approaches to ending inflation. In Ronald, I. M. (Ed.). *Money and finance in economic growth and development, essay in honor of Edward S. Shaw*. New York: Marcel Dekker.

Kakwani, N. (1997). *Welfare based approaches to measuring real economic growth with application to Thailand*. (Discussion Paper 14). School of Economics, The University of New South Wales, Sydney.

Kayanula, D., & Quartey, P. (2000). *The policy environment for promotion of small and medium-size enterprises in Ghana and Malawi. Finance and Development Research Programme*. (Working Paper Series, No. 15). IDPM University of Manchester.

Kayawe, T., & Amusa, A. (2003). Concentration in Botswana's banking sector. *South African Journal of Economic and Management Sciences, 6*(4), 823–847.

Kenya, (1965). The sessional Paper No.1 on African socialism and its application to planning in Kenya. Government of Kenya.

Killick, T., & Mwega, F. M. (1990). *Monetary policy in Kenya 1967–1988*. (ODI Working Paper 39). London: Overseas Development Institution.

King, R., & Levine, R. (1993). Finance and growth: Schumpeter might be right. *Quarterly Journal of Economics*, *108*(3), 717–738.

Kinyua, W., & Musau, B. (2004). *Reforms for enhanced performance of Kenya's financial sector*. Nairobi: Kenya Bankers Association Report.

Kitchen, R. L. (1986). *Finance for the developing countries*. New York: Wiley.

Kittiprapas, S. (1999). *The Asian financial crisis and social changes in Thailand*. Bangkok: TDRI.

Kittiprapas, S. (2000). *Causes of the recent Asian economic crisis: The case of Thailand*. Bangkok: TDRI.

Koo, J., & Shin, S. (2004). Financial liberalization and corporate investments: Evidence from Korean firm data. *Asian Economic Journal*, *18*(3), 277–292.

Kose, M. A., Prasad, E. S., & Terrones, M. E. (2003). *Financial integration and macroeconomic volatility*. (IMF Working Paper WP/03/50). Washington, DC: International Monetary Fund.

Kose, M. A., Prasad, E., Rogoff, K., & Wei, S. (2006). *Financial globalization: A reappraisal*. (IMF Working Paper WP/06/189). Washington, DC: International Monetary Fund.

Koutsoyiannis, A. (1979). *Modern microeconomics*. London: Macmillan.

Krugman, P. (1979). A model of balance-of-payments crises. *Journal of Money, Credit and Banking*, *11*(3), 311–325.

Kwan, S. H. (2003). Impact of deposit rate deregulation in Hong Kong on the market value of commercial banks. *Journal of Banking and Finance*, *27*(12), 2231–2248.

Laeven, L. (2003). Does financial liberalization reduce financing constraints? *Financial Management*, *32*(1), 5–34.

Lau, L. (1996). The sources of long-term economic growth: Observations from the experiences of developed and developing countries. In R. Landau, T. Taylor, & G. Wright (Eds.). The mosaic of economic growth. Stanford, CA: Stanford University Press.

Leightner, J. (1999). Globalisation and Thailand's financial crisis. *Journal of Economic Issues*, *333*(2), 367–373.

Leith, J. C. (1997). Growth and structural transformation in Botswana. In J. S. Salkin, et al. (Eds.), *Aspects of the Botswana economy: Selected paper*. Gaborone: Lentswe la Lesedi, Oxford: James Curry Ltd.

Lensink, R., Hermes, N., & Murinde, V. (1998). The effect of financial liberalization on capital flight in African economies. *World Development*, *26*(7), 1349–1368.

Levine, R. (1991). Stock markets, growth, and tax policy. *Journal of Finance*, *46*(4), 1445–1465.

Levine, R. (1992). Financial intermediary services and growth. *Journal of the Japanese and International Economy*, *6*(3), 383–405.

Levine, R. (1996). Foreign banks, financial development and economic growth. In C. E. Barfield (Ed.), *International financial markets: Harmonization versus competitions* (pp. 131–142). Washington, DC: The American Enterprise Institute Press.

Levine, R. (1997). Financial development and economic growth: Views and agenda. *Journal of Economic Literature*, *35*(2), 688–726.

Levine, R., & Zervos, S. (1998). Stock markets, banks, and economic growth. *American Economic Review*, *88*(3), 537–558.

Levy-Livermore, A. (1998). *Handbook on the globalization of the world economy*. London: Edward Elgar.

Limskul, K. (2000). The Financial and Economic Crisis in Thailand: Dynamic of the Crisis-Root and Process, *Chulalongkorn Journal of Economics*, *12*(1), 1–30.

Lindert, P. H., & Jeffrey, G. W (2001). *Does globalization make the world more unequal?* (National Bureau of Economic Research Working Paper no. 8228). Cambridge, MA: National Bureau of Economic Research.

Loayza, N., Schmidt-Hebbel, K., & Servén, L. (2000). What drives savings across the world? *Review of Economics and Statistics*, *82*(2), 165–181.

Maipose, G. S., & Matsheka, T. C. (2002). Explaining African growth performance: The Botswana case study. AERC Collaborative Project Papers on Explaining African Economic Performance.

Maje, E. H. (1996). Financial sector reforms in Tanzania: Nature and prospects. *African Journal of Economic Policy, 3*(2), 49–62.

Makgetla, N. S. (1982). Finance and development: The case of Botswana. *Journal of Modern African Studies, 20*(1), 69–86.

Malawi, X. (1971). *Statement of development policies 1971–1980*. Zomba: Government Printer.

Malawi, X. (1986). *Economic report*. Zomba: Government Printer.

Malawi, X. (2000). *Exchange and interest rate determination in Malawi: Past and present.* (Research Paper). Lilongwe: Reserve Bank of Malawi.

Manda, D. K. (2002). *Globalization and the labour market in Kenya*. (Discussion Paper 6). KIPPRA.

Mankiw, G., Romer, D., & Weil, D. (1992). A contribution to the empirics of economic growth. *Quarterly Journal of Economics, 107*, 407–437.

Mandlebe, W. (1997). Trends in real wages and labour productivity in Botswana. In J. S. Salkin, et al. (Eds.), *Aspects of the Botswana economy: Selected paper*. Gaborone: Lentswe la Lesedi, Oxford: James Curry Ltd.

Masalila, K. (2001). Financial liberalization and monetary policy effectiveness: A comparison of Botswana, Malawi and Zimbabwe. *The Research Bulletin, Bank of Botswana, 19*(1), 9–26.

Masson, P. R., Bayoumi, T., & Samiei, H. (1998). International evidence on the determinants of private saving. *The World Bank Economic Review, 12*(3), 483–501.

Mathieson, D. J. (1980). Financial reform and stabilization policy in a developing economy. *Journal of Development Economics, 7*(3), 359–395.

Mauro, P. (1997). The effect of corruption on growth, investment, and government expenditure: A cross-country analysis. In K. Elliott (Eds.), *Corruption and the global economy*. Washington, DC: Institute for International Economics.

McCloskey, D. N. (1982). *The applied theory of price*. New York: Macmillan.

McKenzies, G. (1983). *Measuring economic welfare*. Cambridge: Cambridge University Press.

McKibben, W. (1997). *Regional and Multilateral Trade Liberalization: The Effects on Trade, Investment and Welfare*. Paper presented at the *US International Trade Commission APEC Symposium*, Washington, DC, 11–12 September.

McKibben, W. (1998). *The crisis in Asia: An empirical assessment*. Brookings Discussion Papers in International Economics No. 136. Washington, DC: The Brookings Institution.

McKinnon, R. I. (1973). *Money and capital in economic development*. Washington, DC: The Brookings Institution.

McKinnon, Ronald. (1993). *The order of economic liberalization: Financial control in the transition to a market economy* (2nd ed). Maryland: The Johns Hopkins University Press.

McNutt, P. (2002). *The economics of public choice* (2nd ed). Cheltenham: Edward Elgar.

MFE. (2002). Financial liberalization and domestic savings in Korea. Ministry of Finance and Economy, 9th APEC Finance Minister's Process, Los Carbos, Mexico. September, 3–6.

Miniane, J. (2004). *A new set of measures on capital account restrictions*. (IMF Staff Papers, *51*(2), 276–308). International Monetary Fund.

Ministry of Finance. (2001). *Strategy plan framework toward quality and sustainability of Thailand economic development*. Bangkok: NESDB.

Mishkin, F. (2001). Financial policies and prevention of financial crisis in emerging market countries, NBER Working Paper 8087. Cambridge, Mass.: National Bureau of Economic Research.

Modigliani, F. (1986). Life cycle, individual thrift, and the wealth of nations. *American Economic Review, 76*, 297–313.

Mlachila, M., & Chirwa, E. W. (2002). *Financial reforms and interest rate spread in the commercial banking system in Malawi*. (IMF Working Paper WP/02/6). International Monetary Fund.

Modigliani, F. (1970). The life cycle hypothesis of saving and intercountry differences in savings ratio. In W. A. Eltis (Ed.), *Induction, growth and trade: Essay in the honour of Sir Roy Harrod*. Oxford: Clarendon.

Mody, A, & Murshid, A. P. (2005). Growing up with capital flows. *Journal of International Economics*, *65*(1), 249–266.

Montreevat, S. (2000). Impact of foreign entry on the Thai banking sector: Initial stage of bank restructuring. *Economics and Finance*, *5*(1), 1–27.

Motsomi, A. (1997). Policy options for savings mobilization in Botswana. In J. S. Salkin, et al. (Eds.), *Aspects of the Botswana economy: Selected papers*. Gaborone: Lentswe la Lesedi, Oxford: James Curry Ltd.

Mouna, C., & Reza, J. (2002). *Trade Liberalization, Real Exchange Rate, and Export Diversification in Selected North African Economies*. Presented at the ERF's 8th annual conference in Cairo, Egypt.

Mujeri, M. K., & Islam, M. E. (2008). "Rationalizing interest rate spread in the banking sector: Some policy suggestions" policy analysis unit policy paper 0804. Central Bank of Bangladesh.

Mulei, C., & Mullei, A. (2001). Corruption in the court system. In A. Mullei (Ed.), *The link between corruption and poverty: Lessons from Kenya case studies*. Nairobi: African Center for Economic Growth.

Munasinghe, M. (Eds.), (1996). *Environmental impacts of macroeconomic and sectoral policies*. Washington, DC: The World Bank.

Musgrave, T. (1959). *The theory of public finance*. New York: MacGraw-Hill.

Mwega, F. M., & Ndungu, N. S. (2002). Explaining African economic growth performance: The case of Kenya. AERC Collaborative Project on Explaining African Economic Performance.

National Economic and Social Development Board (NESDB). (1996). *Eighth five year plan*. Bangkok: NESDB.

National Economic and Social Development Board (NESDB). (2000). *Ninth five year plan*. Bangkok: NESDB.

Naude, W. (1995). Financial liberalization and interest rate risk management in Sub-Saharan Africa. Centre for the Study of African Economics, WPS/96–12.

Nazmi, N. (2005). Deregulation, financial deepening and economic growth: The case of Latin America. *Quarterly Journal of Economics and Finance*, *45*(4–5), 447–459.

Ndungu, N. S. (1999, March). *Monetary and exchange rate policy in Kenya*. (AERC Research Paper No. 94). African Economic Research Consortium.

Ndungu, N. S., & Ngugi, R. W. (2000). *Banking sector interest rate spread in Kenya*. (Discussion Paper Series DP 05/2000). KIPPRA.

Newlyn, W. T., & Avramides, U. (1977). *The financing of economic development*. Oxford: Clarendon Press.

Ngugi, R. W., & Kabubo, J. W. (1998). *Financial sector reforms and interest rate liberalization: The Kenyan experience*. (AERC Research Paper No.72). African Economic Research Consortium.

Nissanke, M., & Aryeetey, E. (1998). Financial integration and development in Sub-Saharan Africa. London: Routledge.

NSE. (2001). *Reforming Kenya's financial sector for economic recovery*. Nairobi Stock Exchange (NSE): Financial Institution Committee.

Nwachukwu, T., & Egwaikhide, F. (2007). An error-correction model of the determinants of private saving in Nigeria. In *Conference Proceedings of the 12th African Econometric Society (AES) Annual Conference*, Cape Town, South Africa, July, 4th–6th.

Nyawata, O., & Bird, G. (2003). *Financial liberalization in Southern Africa: An assessment*. (Working Paper). Department of Economic, University of Surrey.

Obstfeld, M. (1986). Rational and self-fulfilling balance of payments crises. *American Economic Review*, *76*(1), 72–81.

Obstfeld, M. (1998). The global capital market: benefactor or menace? *Journal of Economic Perspectives*, *12*(4), 9–30.

Oden, B. (1981). *The macroeconomic position of Botswana*. Uppsala: The Scandinavian Institute of African Studies.

Ogbokor, C. A. (2004). Impacts of inflation on Namibian growth: An empirical study. *Journal of Applied Sciences*, *4*(4), 644–648.

Olomola, A. S. (1994). Financial liberalization and economic growth under structural adjustment in Nigeria. *African Journal of Economic Policy*, *1*(1), 141–157.

Ostry, J., & Reinhart, C. (1992). Private saving and terms of trade shocks: Evidence from developing countries. *International Monetary Fund*, *39*, 495–517.

Oyejide, A. (2000). Markets and economic growth in Africa. Framework Paper for AERC Collaborative Research Project, Explaining Africa's Growth Performance.

Paavola, J., & Bromley, D. (2002). Contested choices. In D. Bromley & J. Paavola (Eds.), *Economics, ethics and environmental policy*. Oxford: Blackwell.

Park, D. (1998). Southeast Asia's economic crisis. *Contemporary Review*, *272*(1584), 6–14.

Parnwell, M. (1996). Conclusion: Future paths toward development in Thailand. In M. Parnwell (Ed.), *Uneven development in Thailand*. Aldershot: Avebury.

Pentecost, E. J., & Moore, T. (2004). Financial liberalisation in India and a new test of McKinnon's complementarity hypothesis. Conference Paper, European Economics and Finance Society, May, 13–16.

Pesaran, M. H., & Shin, Y. (2002). Long-run structural modelling. *Econometric Reviews*, *21*(1), 49–87.

Pezzey, J. (2001). Sustainability policy and environmental policy. Mimeo: Centre for Resource and Environmental Studies, Australian National University, Canberra.

Pezzey, J. (2002). Concern for sustainable development in a sexual world. Mimeo: Centre for Resource and Environment Studies, Australian National University, Canberra.

Phongpaichit, P., & Baker, C. (1995). *Thailand: Economy and politics*. Kuala Lumpur: Oxford University Press.

Phongpaichit, P., & Baker, C. (1998a). *Thailand's boom and bust*. Chiang Mai: Silkworm Books.

Phongpaichit, P., & Baker, C. (1998b). Thailand's crisis: Neo-liberal agenda and local reaction. *Thammasat Economic Journal*, *16*(3), 26–50.

Phongpaichit, P., & Baker, C. (2000). *Thailand's crisis*. Chiang Mai: Silkworm Books.

Pigou, A. (1962). *The economics of welfare* (4th ed). London: Macmillian.

Pigou, A. (1965). *Essays in applied economics*. London: Frank Cass and Company.

Pilbeam, K. (2001). The East Asian financial crisis: Getting to the heart of the issues. *Managerial Finance*, *27*(1/2), 111–133.

Pill, H., & Pradhan, M. (1997). Financial liberalization in Africa and Asia. *Finance and Development*, *34*(2), 7–10.

Prasad, E. S., Rogoff, K., Wei, S. -J., & Kose, M. A. (2004). *Financial globalization, growth and volatility in developing countries*. (NBER Working Paper No. W10942). Cambridge, MA.

Pryor, F. L. (1988). *Income distribution and economic development in Malawi: Some historical statistics*. (World Bank Discussion Paper, No.36). The World Bank.

Pryor, F. L. (1990). *The political economy of poverty, equity and growth: Malawi and Madagascar*. Oxford: Oxford University Press.

Rajan, R. G., & Zingales, L. (1998). Financial dependence and growth. *American Economic Review*, *88*(3), 559–586.

Ratanakomut, S. (1999). Thailand's economic crisis: Some unexpected experiences. *Chulalongkorn Journal of Economics*, *11*(1), 43–55.

Reinhart, C. M., & Tokatlidis, I. (2003). Financial liberalization: The African experience. *Journal of African Economies*, *12*(3), 53–88.

Reinke, J. (1997). Savings mobilization in the household sector: The case of Botswana. In Salkin, J. S., et al., (Eds.), *Aspects of the Botswana economy: Selected papers*. Gaborone: Lentswe la Lesedi; Oxford: James Curry Ltd.

Robinson, J. (1952). *The generalization of the general theory: The rate of interest and other essays* (pp. 67–142). London: Macmillan.

Rodrik, D. (1998). Globalisation, social conflict and economic growth. *World Economy, 21*(2), 143–158.

Rodrik, D., & Rodriguez, F. (2000). Trade policy and economic growth: A skeptic's guide to the cross-national evidence. In B. Bernanke & K. Rogoff (Eds.), *NBER macroeconomics annual 2000*. Cambridge, MA: MIT.

Romer, P. (1986). Increasing returns and long-run growth. *Journal of Political Economy, 94*(5), 1002–1037.

Rousseau, P. L. (2002). *Historical perspectives on financial development and economic growth*. (Working Paper 9333, NBER). Cambridge, MA.

Rousseau, P. L., & Wachtel, P. (2000). Equity markets and growth: Cross-country evidence on timing and outcomes, 1980–1995. *Journal of Banking and Finance, 24*(2), 1933–1958.

Ryan, L. (2000). The "Asian economic miracle" unmasked. *International Journal of Social Economics, 27*(7), 802–815.

Sachs, J., & Warner, A. (1995). *Economic reform and the process of global integration*. (Brookings Papers on Economic Activity). Washington, DC: The Brookings Institution.

Sachs, J., & Warner, A. M. (1997). *Natural resource abundance and economic growth*. (NBER Working Paper No.5398). Cambridge, MA: National Bureau of Economic Research.

Saint Paul, G. (1992). Technological choice, financial markets and economic development. *European Economic Review, 36*(4), 763–781.

Samatar, A. I. (1999). *An African miracle: State and class leadership and colonial legacy in Botswana development*. Portsmouth: Heinemann.

Samuelson, P. (1956). Social indifference curves. *Quarterly Journal of Economics, 70*(1), 1–22.

Sauve, P. (1999). The benefits of trade and investment liberalisation: Financial services. In D. H. Brooks & M. Queisser (Eds.), *Financial liberalisation in Asia: Analysis and prospects* (pp. 173–188). Paris: OECD.

Savvides, A. (1995). Economic growth in Africa. *World Development, 23*(3), 449–458.

Schiantarelli, F., Weiss, A., Gultom, M., & Jaramillo, F. (1994). *Financial liberalization and the efficiency of investment allocation*. (Working Paper 266). Boston: Boston College.

Schmidt, J. (1996). Paternalism and planning in Thailand: Facilitating growth without social benefits. In M. Parnwell (Ed.), *Uneven development in Thailand*. Aldershot: Avebury.

Schmidt-Hebbel, K., & Servén, L. (2002). *Financial Liberalization, Savings and Growth*. Presented at the Banco de Mexico conference on Macroeconomic Stability, Financial markets, and Economic Development. Mexico DF, November, 12–13.

Schumpeter, J. A. (1911). *A theory of economic development*. Cambridge, MA: Harvard University Press.

Seck, D., & ElNil, Y. H. (1993). Financial liberalization in Africa. *World Development, 21*(11), 1867–1881.

Sen, A. (1966). A possibility theorem on majority decisions. *Econometrica, 34*, 491–499.

Sen, A. (1970). *Collective choice and social welfare*. Amsterdam: North Holland.

Sen, A. (1973). Behaviour and the concept of preference. *Economica, 40*, 241–289.

Sen, A. (1982). *Choice, welfare and measurement*. Oxford: Basil Blackwell.

Sen, A. (1999). *Development as freedom*. Oxford: Oxford University Press.

Senbet, L. W., & Otchere, I. (2005). *Financial Sector Reforms in Africa: Perspectives on Issues and Policies*. Presented at the Annual World Bank Conference on Development Economics (ABCDE), Dakar, Senegal, January.

Sharma, K. C., & Mhlauli, E. G. (1994). Botswana: Confronting the realities of capacity building. In L. A. Picard & M. Garrity (Eds.), *Policy reforms for sustainable development in Africa*. London: Lynne Rienner.

Shaw, E. S. (1973). *Financial deepening in economic development*. New York: Oxford University Press.

Sheehan, P. (1998a). "International overview". In 'Crisis in East Asia: Global Watershed or Passing Storm?', Conference Report presented by Centre for Strategic Economic Studies, Victoria University and Australian Centre for Innovation and International Competitiveness, The University of Sydney, March, 99–110.

Sheehan, P. (1998b). "The Global Context". In 'Crisis in East Asia: Global Watershed or Passing Storm?', conference Report presented by Centre for Strategic Economic Studies, Victoria University and Australian Centre for Innovation and International Competitiveness, The University of Sydney, March, 3–20.

Sheehan, P., & Tikhomirova. (1998). "The Rise of the global knowledge economy". In P. Sheehan & G. Tegart (Eds.), *Working for the Future*. Melbourne: CSES.

Siamwalla, A. (2000). *Anatomy of the Thai economic crisis*. Bangkok: Thailand Development Research Institute.

Siamwalla, A. (2000). *Anatomy of the Thai economic crisis*. Bangkok: TDRI.

Sikorski, T. M. (1996). *Financial liberalization in developing countries*. Cheltenham: Edward Elgar.

Siksamat, S. (1998). A multi-regional computable general equilibrium model of the Thai economy (Phd thesis, Centre of Policy Studies and the Department of Economics, Monash University, Melbourne).

Singh, K. (1999). *The globalisation of finance*. New York: Zed Books.

Slesnick, D. (2001). *Consumption and social welfare*. Cambridge: Cambridge University Press.

Solow, R. M. (1956). A contribution to the theory of economic growth. *Quarterly Journal of Economics*, *70*(1), 65–94.

Stiglitz, J. E. (1994). The role of state in financial market. In M. Bruno & B. Pleskoric (Eds.), *Proceedings of the World Bank Annual Conference on Development Economics, World Bank, Washington, DC*.

Stoleru, L. (1975). *Economic equilibrium and growth*. Amsterdam: North-Holland.

Stulz, R. M. (1999). Globalization, corporate finance, and the cost of capital. *Journal of Applied Corporate Finance*, *12*(3), 8–25.

Summers, L. (1992). The challenges of development: Some lessons of history for Sub-Saharan Africa. *Finance and Development*, *29*(1), 6–12.

Tseng, W., & Corker, R. (1991). *Financial liberalisation, money demand, and monetary policy in Asian countries*. (Occasional Paper no. 84). Washington, DC: International Monetary Fund.

UNDP. (1999). *Malawi globalization, liberalization and sustainable human development*. Country Assessment Report, UNDP/UNCTAD, December.

Van Wijnebergen, S. (1983). Interest rate management in LDCs. *Journal of Monetary Economics*, *12*(3), 433–452.

Vines, D., & Warr, P. (2000). *Thailand's investment-driven boom and crisis*. (Working Paper No. 00/11) Canberra: Asia Pacific School of Economics and Management, Australian National University.

Wacziarg, R. (2001). Measuring the dynamic gain from trade. *The World Bank Economic Review*, *15*(3), 393–429.

Warr, P., & Nidhiprabha, B. (1996). *Thailand's macroeconomic miracle: Stable adjustment and sustained growth*. Kuala Lumpur: Oxford University Press.

Warr, P. (2001). *Poverty Reduction and Sectoral Growth: Evidence from Southeast Asia*. Paper presented for the WIDER development conference *growth and development*, Helsinki, 25–26 May 2001.

Webber, M., & Weller, S. (2002). *Refashioning the rag trade: Internationalizing Australia's textile*. Clothing and Footwear Industries, Sydney: UNSW Press.

Williamson, J. (1983). *The open economy and the world economy*. New York: Basic Books.

Williamson, J. (2002). *Winners and Losers in Two Centuries of Globalization*. Paper presented at *Wider Annual Lecture*, Copenhagen, September 5.

World Bank. (1993). *The East Asian miracle: Economic growth and public policy*. New York: Basil Blackwell.

World Bank. (1984). *Agricultural credit sector policy paper*. The World Bank: Second.

World Bank. (1985). *Malawi economic recovery: Resources and policy needs – An economic memorandum*. Washington, DC.

World Bank. (1988). *World development report*. New York: Oxford University Press.

World Bank. (1989). *Sub-Saharan Africa: From crisis to sustainable growth*. Washington, DC.

World Bank. (1994). *Adjustment in Africa: Reforms, results and the road ahead*. Oxford: Oxford University Press.

World Bank. (1999). *Thailand social monitor: Challenge for social reform*. Bangkok: World Bank.

World Bank. (2001). *World development report 2000/2001: Attacking poverty*. New York: Oxford University Press.

Index

FSC
www.fsc.org
MIX
Papier | Fördert
gute Waldnutzung
FSC® C083411

Kolibri 360 GmbH
Ferdinand-Jühlke-Straße 7
99095 Erfurt, Deutschland
produktsicherheit@kolibri360.de